SAGE was founded in 1965 by Sara Miller McCune to support the dissemination of usable knowledge by publishing innovative and high-quality research and teaching content. Today, we publish over 900 journals, including those of more than 400 learned societies, more than 800 new books per year, and a growing range of library products including archives, data, case studies, reports, and video. SAGE remains majority-owned by our founder, and after Sara's lifetime will become owned by a charitable trust that secures our continued independence.

Los Angeles | London | New Delhi | Singapore | Washington DC | Melbourne

Sociopolitical Thought of
RABINDRANATH
TAGORE

Sociopolitical Thought of
RABINDRANATH
TAGORE

Bidyut
CHAKRABARTY

Los Angeles | London | New Delhi
Singapore | Washington DC | Melbourne

First published in 2021 by

SAGE Publications India Pvt Ltd
B1/I-1 Mohan Cooperative Industrial Area
Mathura Road, New Delhi 110 044, India
www.sagepub.in

SAGE Publications Inc
2455 Teller Road
Thousand Oaks, California 91320, USA

SAGE Publications Ltd
1 Oliver's Yard, 55 City Road
London EC1Y 1SP, United Kingdom

SAGE Publications Asia-Pacific Pte Ltd
18 Cross Street #10-10/11/12
China Square Central
Singapore 048423

Published by Vivek Mehra for SAGE Publications India Pvt Ltd. Typeset in 10.5/13 pt Berkeley by Zaza Eunice, Hosur, Tamil Nadu, India.

Library of Congress Cataloging-in-Publication Data

Name: Chakrabarty, Bidyut, author.
Title: Sociopolitical thought of Rabindranath Tagore/Bidyut Chakrabarty.
Description: New Delhi; Thousand Oaks, California: SAGE Publishing, 2020.
| Includes bibliographical references and index.
Identifiers: LCCN 2020032719 | ISBN 9789353884987 (hardback) | ISBN
9789353885007 (ebook) | ISBN 9789353884994 (epub)
Subjects: LCSH: Tagore, Rabindranath, 1861–1941—Political and social
views. | Tagore, Rabindranath, 1861–1941—Criticism and interpretation.
| Authors, Bengalee—20th century—Political and social views.
Classification: LCC PK1727.P66 C43 2020 | DDC 891.4/414—dc23
LC record available at https://lccn.loc.gov/2020032719

ISBN: 978-93-5388-498-7 (HB)

SAGE Team: Rajesh Dey, Shipra Pant and Rajinder Kaur

*Dedicated to my ideologically non-pretentious colleagues
and compatriots for regularly attending
Wednesday prayers (upasana)
in the Mandir of Visva-Bharati*

Thank you for choosing a SAGE product!
If you have any comment, observation or feedback,
I would like to personally hear from you.

Please write to me at **contactceo@sagepub.in**

Vivek Mehra, Managing Director and CEO, SAGE India.

Bulk Sales

SAGE India offers special discounts
for purchase of books in bulk.
We also make available special imprints
and excerpts from our books on demand.

For orders and enquiries, write to us at

Marketing Department
SAGE Publications India Pvt Ltd
B1/I-1, Mohan Cooperative Industrial Area
Mathura Road, Post Bag 7
New Delhi 110044, India

E-mail us at **marketing@sagepub.in**

Subscribe to our mailing list

Write to **marketing@sagepub.in**

This book is also available as an e-book.

CONTENTS

PREFACE

Being an academic administrator, a Vice Chancellor has to discharge the twin roles of being both an academic and an administrator. In reality, however, he/she is accused of being neither; his/her role as an academic is vitiated by his/her being an administrator, and vice versa. I don't have empirical data to conclusively prove my claim, but an informal interaction with my Vice Chancellor colleagues makes me believe that in view of the responsibilities, especially in Indian universities, it is difficult, if not impossible, to be true to these two integrally connected tasks. The role becomes terribly multifaceted, because it is expected of a Vice Chancellor in an Indian university to deal with many stakeholders, both within the university and outside. With my limited knowledge of how universities function elsewhere, especially in the English-speaking countries, I am persuaded to believe that presidents or Vice Chancellors in these places seem to have more time at their disposal to pursue what they prefer to do besides performing their assigned duties. Here in India, the Vice Chancellors do not have the luxury of spending time in accordance with their priority, given the multifarious nature of the responsibility. My purpose here is not to ponder over why it is so but to explicate the complexities that usually go with the assignment.

This book is a historical document in the sense that it was written at a critical time in India's recent history when the entire nation voluntarily accepted home quarantine to defeat the invisible enemy in the form of the COVID-19 virus that led to a pandemic in 2020. This was a testing time for humanity as a whole, and the exemplary steadfastness shown by everybody cutting across spatial boundaries once again proved that we win if we are united and fail when divided.

With the above prefacing remarks, let me salute those of my colleagues who continue to remain academically vibrant and also true to the responsibilities of being an administrator. It is easier said than done. Nonetheless, there are many of them who, being at the helm of the university administration in various parts of the country, remain productive by adding new academic titles to their already very impressive curriculum vitae. While being engaged in academic works along with the assigned task of managing Visva-Bharati—the university that the Nobel laureate Rabindranath Tagore founded in 1921. I have realized how difficult it is to be truthful to the job given by the Government of India and at the same time realize the joy of putting creative texts in the public domain. It is, in other words, an endeavour to execute a successful marriage between two different kinds of responsibilities and enjoyments. This book on Tagore's sociopolitical ideas is just a baby step towards seeking to fulfil the twin roles as successfully as is humanly possible.

For the Bengalees, Tagore is omnipresent in their lives. I haven't come across any Bengalee, here in India and abroad, who is not politico-ideologically baptized in the ideas that Tagore articulated in his songs, poems, novels, plays, dance-dramas, critical essays and speeches. We are all, generally speaking, instinctively 'Rabindra Sangeet' singers. We all are introduced to the complexities of human life by Tagore's texts. Whether the scenario has changed now, I am not sure, though it cannot be disputed that the poet, by dwelling on various aspects of our worldly existence, put before us a tapestry to easily negotiate the difficulties of human life.

As a Bengalee who has spent more than half of his life away from Bengal, I have been nurturing a desire to write a book on Tagore's politico-ideological and socio-economic ideas. What inspired me were his critical essays that he compiled in a 1937 publication entitled *Kalantor*, though the first interpretative text that created a deep fascination for Rabindranath's views on contemporary socio-economic and political issues was Edward Thompson's *Rabindranath Tagore:*

Poet and Dramatist (1926), which I read as early as in 1971. Later, I enriched myself with many other books that were both informative and thought-provoking. My desire reached the peak by leaps and bounds once I joined Visva-Bharati as its vice chancellor in the late 2018. The reasons are simple: this was Tagore's *karmabhumi* (the place of work), which was also a witness to the unfolding of his creative self. My joy knew no bounds when I had a chance to be the *Acharya* in the important prayers that take place in the prayer hall (or Mandir, in Visva-Bharati's parlance) or *Chhatimtola* (the place where Tagore's father, Maharshi Debendranath Tagore, used to sit for prayer) during every calendar year. The opportunity to visit endlessly the five houses where Tagore lived was a godsend to me. The regularly held cultural festivals, including the Poush Utsab and Vasanta Utsab, provide me with joy and self-gratification in many ways. The regular Wednesday prayers that begin in the early part of the morning is what I look forward to every week, since it gives me sustenance for the entire week. I am also fortunate to have had access to the archives, which is a gold mine for researchers. There are many colleagues in Visva-Bharati who extend all kinds of help to understand the contextual relevance of Tagore's creative interventions. As far as I am concerned, this book is just the beginning of an endeavour that I have undertaken to fathom the complexities of Tagore's writings on various aspects of equally complex human life.

For an author, what is required is a hassle-free environment, which is made available by those who are located in the vice chancellor's residence, Purbita. By being truly attentive to their assigned duties, Bijoy and his team made my stay here in Santiniketan most worthwhile. Gopal, by offering tea whenever I wanted to sustain my energy, was of great help to me during the time of the day when I worked in the office. Dr Tanmoy Nag, my confidential secretary, helped me tread through cobwebs of administration as smoothly as possible. For any academic work, library access is of utmost importance. I am grateful to the Visva-Bharati librarian, Dr Nimai Saha, who put before me any text I wanted as quickly as possible. I am impressed by the speed with which he procured what I asked for, which made my task easier; perhaps, he understood my psychology—that I remain stuck unless

I get the stuff that I requisite for my work. For having appreciated this aspect of my creative self, I know that our readers in the campus are in safe hands. I remember my colleagues in the department of Bengalee at Visva-Bharati, Professor Amal Pal, Professor Manabendra Mukhopadhyay, Dr Biswajit Ray and Sri Nilanjan Bandyopadhyay of Rabindra-Bhavana, Visva-Bharati who were always liberal in sharing their thoughts on Tagore's sociopolitical ideas that they evolved out of their in-depth study of the poet's creative texts. I am thankful to Professor Amrit Sen of the department of English, Visva-Bharati for being meticulous in reading the entire text to avoid any typos and other mistakes. It was of great help to me in locating appropriate texts while being engaged in putting my views on Tagore's sociopolitical discourses in black and white. Toofan and Amit made my journey to and from Kolkata very smooth and also less tiring by taking extra care while driving.

My sisters, Mini and Tinku, and their daughters, Sreeja and Debiporna, were always of great help to me. By making my stay the most comfortable in Kolkata whenever I visit the city of joy, they provide an important ingredient for my emotional gratification. Sanchita, my wife, and our kids, Mamma and Pablo, despite being away from me, sustain my zeal for creativity by being extremely critical of what they don't like; this is a boon in disguise, because the critique help me deal with life differently, which is an important aid for my being aware of the aspects that may not have attracted my attention earlier. I am grateful to them. Finally, I express my heartfelt gratitude to Rajesh Dey of SAGE and his team for having inspired me to embark on this project and complete the manuscript within the stipulated time.

INTRODUCTION

Reinventing Rabindranath Tagore: A Universal Voice in the Nationalist Context

I

An icon of humanism and universalism who always privileged India's argumentative traditions, Rabindranath Tagore, popularly known as Gurudev, remains a source of inspiration for humanity as a whole. Born in a wealthy family with serious concerns for India's cultural heritage, Gurudev designed, through his creative writings, a uniquely textured tapestry for India and the globe. Based on his own understanding of India's cultural past, Tagore revived the lost socio-cultural traditions and ideological inclinations of the past just to develop a repertoire of knowledge that, he thought, was one of the effective means of rejuvenating a moribund nation reeling under colonialism. He was a fighter, but of a different kind. Unlike his colleagues in the national campaign for freedom, he was engaged in creating a mindset championing freedom, fairness and justice, which were denied to the colonized for obvious reasons. He can be said to have, in other words, contributed immensely to the germination and also the consolidation of the idea of freedom among the Indians who appeared to have undermined the distinctive Indian cultural heritage to please their colonial masters. It is true that Gurudev was not a street fighter like the conventional nationalists who battled for freedom; his role was most critical in bringing back those empowering ideas for which India had stood out in the past. For Tagore, the ancient Indian texts, such as the

Vedas, Upanishads and Puranas, not just were famous for their literary flavour but also provided humanity with powerful designs of change and improvement in collective existence, despite humans being polar opposites in socio-cultural terms. The idea is a persuasive articulation of India's multicultural existence in which the socio-cultural differences were not divisive but a means of bringing people together for a cause shared by humanity as a whole. This was not a new idea but a reiteration of views and thoughts which are reflective of a concern, a transcendental concern perhaps, that also led to a collective search cutting across social, cultural and also geographical borders. This was a global concern that in Tagore's writings was graphically illustrated. So, at one level, Gurudev's creative literary texts were endeavoured towards recapitulating the ancient, but inspiring, ideas which had their origin in India. They appeared to have received inadequate attention, presumably because of the hegemonic influence of the derivative Western ideas and thoughts. At a far more perceptive level, his texts resonate and also establish the collective human concerns that completely seem to have become seamless. These ideas needed to be revived for (a) awakening the nation and also (b) providing the desire for freedom a voice, a powerful voice indeed, which, by being emotionally connected with the multitude, became effective in fulfilling the goal for which the nationalists were fighting. The basic here was the articulation and consolidation of a voice that was emotion-driven and socio-culturally meaningful to those who plunged into the nationalist campaign regardless of the consequences. The voice that Gurudev sought to generate was not meant for a section of the population but for all who held the nation (though loosely defined) as prior to anything else. The purpose here is to put across two major arguments: on the hand, given the immense importance of Tagore's ideas and views in revitalizing a nation that almost lost its distinctive identity, the aim here is to draw attention to those aspects in his writings which are imbued with values supportive of building a collectivity regardless of socio-cultural diversities and schisms; there is, on the other hand, the effort on the part of Tagore to put in practice the ideas that he held so dear, also to demonstrate that he was hardly just an idealist like many of his nationalist colleagues. Being a *zamindar* who had close contact with his *praja* (subjects) and was aware of the sufferings among the villagers, Gurudev can be said to have articulated his experience-based feelings in his literary texts.

There is a misconception that Gurudev Tagore was merely a poet, which is clearly misleading because behind the garb of a poet there also existed a social reformer who, while challenging the lackadaisical attitude of his brethren, strove to galvanize the people who, blindly following the Western mode of thinking as the only organizing tool for freedom, happily forgot the repository of knowledge left behind by India's ancient texts. It is fair to argue that Tagore can be conceptualized in two complementary ways: on the one hand, he was a poet *par excellence*; on the other, he expressed in clear terms his ideas of freedom, justice and fairness, which he brought out in his novels, short stories, songs and poems, besides those critical essays that he wrote on various occasions to highlight his viewpoints on socially meaningful issues and concerns. The point being made here relates to the need for taking into account both his literary texts and the contemporary essays in which he responded to the sociopolitical and ideological issues that were bothersome. Being an organic thinker who also played the role of a public intellectual, Rabindranath carved a space in the Bengalee psyche in numerous ways that were both inspired by his poetic innovations and driven by his socio-cultural concerns.

One should also add a disclaimer: Tagore, unlike his colleagues in the nationalist movement, did not codify his views bluntly while being critical of the colonial rule and supportive of the campaign for freedom. Implicit here was his fantastic capability of couching his views in such a way as not to attract the British wrath nor to antagonize his colleagues fighting for liberation from colonial rule. That he tempered his views on many occasions was illustrative of his twin concerns. On the one hand, he sincerely believed that without being economically self-dependent, political independence was futile. Hence, he insisted on evolving a *swadeshi samaj* to take care of the needs of those living in the *samaj*. Similar to Gandhi's village republic, or *gram swaraj* in Gandhi's parlance, which he formulated first in the context of his South Africa sojourn and later in India, Gurudev developed his model in a small booklet, entitled *Swadeshi Samaj*, published in 1904. This was the model that was made public in 1904; it was clearly articulated in his novel of 1916, *Ghare Baire* (Home and the World), where he defended the idea of a *swadeshi samaj* through the character Nikhilesh. A local zamindar, Nikhilesh, asper the storyline of *Ghare Baire* (which reached the global stage once the famous film-maker Satyajit Ray picturized the novel), devoted his energy intomaking the local people self-dependent by being involved in producing household goods by themselves. In contrast, Sandip, the protagonist of the *swadeshi* philosophy, contradicted his ideological commitment to *swadeshi* products by being appreciative of foreign goods, as they were purportedly better in quality. In other words, Sandip represented a mindset which was full of contradictions in terms of what he preached and what he practised. This was the characteristic of the historical phase that Tagore had confronted. In public life and utterances, people raised the voice for *swadeshi* (indigenous) goods and products, though, in their private existences, they were found, in large numbers, to have abdicated what they had stated regarding public consumption.

The above discussion highlights a critical point, namely, most of Tagore's novels were powerful examples of the equally powerful sociopolitical messages which he put forward through his essays. This was possible because he, being involved in the mission for awakening the Indians socio-economically, took up the cudgels against the social ills that he strongly believed crippled the Indian masses. Being ruled by a foreign power, Indians, as Gurudev stated mincing no words, lost not only their vitality but also the humanness to realize what they should do having been born as human beings. For Tagore, it was a calamity that needed to be mitigated first before one embarked on a campaign for political freedom. It was an unpleasant truth, and most of his colleagues who were part of the nationalist campaign did not find his argument persuasive, since there was hardly a dispute on the view that India was ready for a political independence. Given the differences of opinion between Tagore and his compatriots, the battle that he had waged against the mainstream nationalist campaign continued unabated. Besides the negative outcomes of such incessant fighting, the chasm that the debate between Tagore and his colleagues had revealed also had a positive aspect, because the exchange of opinions had enriched the nationalist understanding of the freedom struggle that was meant to attain not merely political emancipation but also human emancipation, which Gurudev had always insisted on. Fundamental here is the premise that a thorough study of Tagore will help us understand the complexities of the long-drawn nationalist movement that was conformist at one level since the mainstream nationalist movement privileged the philosophy of the Enlightenment; at another level, as Tagore emphasized, it was both innovative and non-conformist because it drew on the ancient texts which were dismissed as archaic by those who believed in the Enlightenment values.

II

Metaphorically speaking, with the acceptance of Brahmoism as his creed in 1888 and his stiff opposition to Hindu idolatry, in opposition to his father, Dwarkanath, Debendranath Tagore, also known as Maharshi, planted a sapling that grew into one of the most challenging social movements with sustenance from his illustrious son, Rabindranath Tagore. Born in a wealthy family of Bengal, Tagore had a different childhood, for obvious reasons. What is striking was his devotion to theism, which he inherited from his father. While admitting his father being a critical source of the ideas that he held so dear throughout his life, Tagore thus stated:

> I am proud to say that my father was one of the leaders of that great movement, a movement for whose sake he suffered ostracism and braved social indignities. I was born in this atmosphere of the advent of new ideals, which at the same were old, older than things of which that age was proud.[1]

A new era was ushered in when the ancient texts were interpreted afresh. Opposed to Hindu idolatry, Tagore's father, Debendranath, being heavily influenced by Ram mohan Roy, the pioneer in the campaign against Hindu idolatry, devoted his energy to strengthen the new religious cult, Brahmoism, which, despite being based on the mainstream Hindu religious texts, was a new interpretation of Hinduism. It was thus described that Debendranath's 'thoroughgoing theism, hating all idolatry and scorning to compromise with it,

---

[1] Rabindranath Tagore, 'The Religion of An Artist,' in *Bundles of Joy*, ed. Rabindranath Tagore (Kolkata: Visva-Bharati, 2008) (reprint), 205.

or explain it away, was absolutely new'.[2] The idea was not new, as the available literature shows. Many Hindus raised their voice against Hindu orthodoxy during the late 19th century.[3] On most occasions, these views remained fragmented, which impeded their unfolding as an organized campaign. Furthermore, the Calcutta elites were not enthusiastic enough to champion the views opposing the Hindu conservatism. It was Debendranath, a true disciple of Ram mohan, who 'gave his life to the firm establishment of a Brahmo Samaj that drew its sustenance from the denial of Hindu idolatry'.[4] Debendranath's father, Dwarkanath, a rich businessman, was not pleased with his son who, being drawn to Upanishadic ideals, lost interest in worldly comforts. Evidence suggests that it was Ramchandra Vidyabagish, an expert in Vedanta, who was held responsible by Dwarkanath for 'diverting his son from material to intellectual and spiritual concerns'.[5] By 1846, he lost hope in his son and accused Debendranath of being 'misguided by [Vidyabagish and his colleagues] who had snatched his son from him'.[6] Unlike Debendranath's other sons, Rabindranath inherited the determination that his father had shown, and it is thus argued that his 'theism was of the same clear unequivocal kind like his father'.[7] For Gurudev, Brahmoism was clearly derivative, since he was raised in that environment. Being a staunch believer in theism, Debendranath was very strict with his sons, which perhaps did not allow other views to prosper in the family. It may have been likely that Gurudev's father was attracted to Brahmoism because he was vehemently opposed to the ritualistic restrictions that contemporary Hinduism epitomized, which, to him, were attempts at creating artificial boundaries among

---

[2] Edward Thompson, *Rabindranath Tagore: Poet and Dramatist* (Calcutta: Rddhi-India, 1979) (reprint of the original edition of 1948), 12.

[3] Rajat Ray provided a graphic illustration of the campaigns attacking orthodox Hindus in his *Social Conflict and Political Unrest in Bengal, 1875–1927* (Delhi: Oxford University Press, 1975).

[4] Thompson, *Rabindranath Tagore*, 12.

[5] David Kopf, *The Brahmo Samaj and the Shaping of the Modern Indian Mind* (New Delhi: Archives Publishers Pvt. Ltd, 1988) (Indian reprint), 191.

[6] Kopf, 193.

[7] Thompson, *Rabindranath Tagore*, 12.

the Hindus. Maharshi's dislike for heavily ritualistic Hinduism was ideologically supported by Ram Mohan Roy, which Tagore explained by stating

> my father was fortunate in coming under the influence of Ram Mohan Roy from his early years which helped him to free himself from the sectarian barriers, from traditions of worldly and social ideas that were very rigid, in many aspects very narrow and not altogether beneficial.[8]

Besides being a true disciple of Roy, Maharshi also 'drew from our ancient scriptures, from the Upanishads, truths which had universal significance, and not anything that were exclusive to any particular age or any particular people'.[9] Furthermore, having been born in a lower-grade Brahmin family, Pirili Brahmin, he might have suffered social ostracism by the upper-caste Hindus who had dominant influences in the then society. As per the contemporary sources, there were many instances of the Tagore family being socially looked down upon 'with a certain contempt as pirilis, ... despite their great position as zamindars and leaders of culture'.[10] Tagore referred to this aspect when he admitted that 'we were ostracized by society [because] of lower social status'.[11] For him, this was a source of strength, since, as he further mentioned, 'this liberated us [the family] from the responsibility of conforming to all those conventions that had not the value of truth, that were mere irrational habits bred in the inertia of the racial mind'.[12] Critical here is the point that Tagore's rebellious attitude was a continuity of the period in which powerful voices were articulated by many leading personalities. This was a period of change and transformation notwithstanding the counter social pressure that those who held contrary views were subjected to. With the support of some of the major social leaders, despite not being part of the mainstream, the arguments against Hindu idolatry and orthodoxy

[8] Uma Dasgupta, ed., *Rabindranath Tagore: My Life in My Words* (New Delhi: Penguin, 2006), 9.

[9] Dasgupta, 9.

[10] Thompson, *Rabindranath Tagore*, 12.

[11] Dasgupta, *Rabindranath Tagore*, 9.

[12] Dasgupta, 9.

gained momentum. It can be shown that Tagore's family stood out for being so vocally critical against the well-entrenched prejudices, being justified as drawn on the fundamental Hindu religious texts. Edward Thompson thus argued,

> [i]n no other family than that of the Tagores could all the varied impulses of the time have been felt so strongly and fully. These impulses had come from many men. Rammohan Roy had flung open doors; Deriozio [an academic associated with the Calcutta Presidency College] and other had thrown windows wide; Keshab Sen [a social reformer, famous for his views leading to the establishment of the syncretic school of spiritualism] came and [their] intellectual and religious horizons were broadened. The tide of reaction had been set flowing by the neo-Hindu school, in the battle with whom, [Gurudev Tagore] was to find his strength of polemical prose, his followers of sarcasm and ridicule; and poets and writers had established new forms, and given freedom to old ones. Rabindranath was fortunate in the date of his coming.[13]

Tagore was raised in a family that represented 'a confluence of three cultures: the Hindu, the Mohammedan and the British',[14] which perhaps explains why he was less orthodox in his views than some of his contemporaries holding more or less the same ideological beliefs. With inspiration from his father, he was also drawn to the ancient Hindu scriptures which, to a significant extent, prepared him to counter-question what was considered to be axiomatic. The available evidence suggests that in this era of neo-Hinduism, attention was drawn to the ancient Hindu scriptures as repositories of wisdom which needed to be recovered. There was hardly a dispute in this assumption that he disliked the worship of Kali since it was all about ruthless power. It was not, at all, a matter of accident that 'in his praise of Bengal, he personifies her as Lakshmi, the gentle gracious queen of beauty and good fortune … in contrast with his dislike for Kali, the capricious queen of force and destruction'.[15] Much later, in 1922, it was exemplified with the establishment of Sriniketan, a place where Sri (Lakshmi)

---

[13] Thompson, *Rabindranath Tagore*, 19.

[14] Dasgupta, *Rabindranath Tagore*, 9.

[15] Thompson, *Rabindranath Tagore*, 98.

resided. A perusal of how Sriniketan developed into a great centre of practice-driven learning also directs our attention to the concern that Tagore had for inclusive development. He always believed, like his compatriot Gandhi, that without taking the Indian villages onto the path of development, the country would continue to remain poor.

There are two points that need elaboration here. On the one hand, Tagore was a child of his time, since the transformative ideas that he inherited were derivative of the endeavours that his predecessors had undertaken. Prominent among them were Ram Mohan, his father, Debendranath Tagore, Derozio and Keshab Sen, among others. This was an era of awakening, which also led to the revisiting of the ancient Hindu texts. The growing importance of neo-Hinduism was, on the other hand, also a source of rejuvenation of Hinduism, since it drew upon the Vedas, the Upanishads and the Puranas; these were the texts that appeared to have lost their importance, largely perhaps due to the hegemonic ideas based on the easily available Western philosophical texts. The neo-Hindus, of which Tagore's family was a leading voice, contributed immensely in creating a space in which the discussion over these texts began. Hence, it is fair to argue that they played a critical role in setting in motion a process of change in which Gurudev rose as a prominent public intellectual. This is one side of the argument; another equally important aspect of the argument was his acknowledgment in a letter to his friend-cum-colleague, C. F. Andrews, wherein he stated that before he had been to the Continental Europe, he had never realized that he would be accepted by the Western Europeans as 'one of them'. This made him realize that racial prejudices against the Indians were nurtured presumably because of the inbuilt hatred that the colonizers had towards the colonized. The situation was completely different as he was welcomed when he visited the Continental Europe. As a result, there was a clear shift in his thoughts. In the letter, he thus stated that

> when I left India, I was labouring under the delusion that my mission was to build an Indian university in which Indian cultures would be represented in all their variety. But when I came to the continental Europe and fully realized that I had been accepted by the Western people as one of

themselves I realized that my mission ... was to make the meeting of the East and West fruitful in truth.[16]

It was a difficult task indeed, because, as Tagore realized, 'psychological barriers solidly built upon time-honoured tradition still stand firm, in fact, are being raised higher and more strongly buttressed on all sides'.[17] He realized this when he instituted Visva-Bharati in 1921 as an alternative seat of learning. It was a shock for him when he was ridiculed, mostly by a powerful section in Britain, since he was critical of the Raj for not being true to the Enlightenment values on which the British Empire claimed to have rested. It did not appear to be unusual to him, because it reinforced the fact that he belonged to 'a subject race'[18] that hardly had freedom which the British citizens enjoyed in Britain. Two points deserve attention here. On the one hand, Tagore was a product of a confluence of ideas that had emerged in India and also in the West; multiple religious traditions of India had left an imprint on his thoughts, and the egalitarian ideas that he had imbibed from the West had also had their impact on what he expressed through his creative writings. Being sensitive to the context, he also realized, on the other hand, that as India was a British colony, the denial of freedom, which was naturally available to his counterparts in Britain, was not unusual. Nonetheless, the withholding of freedom was a source of strength to Tagore, who appears to have been inspired to demonstrate the full potential of one belonging to the colonized. It was evident when he, despite situational difficulties, started Visva-Bharati in 1921, which, in course of time, became an important centre of higher learning in various fields of knowledge.

The purpose here is to understand Tagore's persona as a public intellectual who, through his innumerable writings, created and also firmly established a new wave of thinking, which also received severe criticism because he turned many of the prevalent ideas upside down, since they were contrary to his commitment to humanism

---

[16] Rabindranath Tagore to C. F. Andrews, 17 December 1921, reproduced in Dasgupta, *Rabindranath Tagore*, 195.

[17] Rabindranath Tagore, 'National Unity,' reproduced in Dasgupta, 195.

[18] Dasgupta, *Rabindranath Tagore*, 194.

and universalism. There should be a caution here: Tagore was not a nationalist as the term is generally understood. A patriot *par excellence*, Tagore wrote the text of *Nationalism* in 1916 to defend the argument that freedom meant the absolute, unfettered right of the people to control their own destinies, and at the same time, he also opposed the endeavours towards homogenizing them disregarding their socio-cultural distinctiveness, as they had evolved in the European nations. Being inspired by his own design of *swadeshi samaj*, he both deprecated the excessive dependence on government and also criticized the Gandhian mode of opposition, namely, boycott, since it instilled negativity in the people. His politico-ideological goal was different from that of his colleagues who were either pro-government or supported the anarchy that the anti-government opposition tended to create. While seeking to decipher Tagore's sociopolitical views, Prasanta Mahalanobis, who was close to Tagore, said:

> he believes in serving his country in constructive work; hence his emphasis on village work, sanitation and social reform. He believes in India, in her future possibilities as well as in her great past, but does not believe in nationalism. India's greatness consists in her recognition of human values – in her message of social civilization. He believes that the only permanent solution of international conflicts lies in the recognition of this fact that socialization is the way out. He has always insisted that this been India's message throughout her history. He does not believe in political freedom as an end in itself. *Swaraj* is desirable because it will accelerate a more intimate socialization – a more organized unification of India.[19]

It is evident from the above that Tagore was never appreciative of nationalism, as it devastated the distinctive socio-cultural characteristics of a people by seeking to essentialize them in terms of certain preordained criteria. This was also reflective of an evil design of taking humanity out of human beings, since it was certain to be coercively imposed on those who decided not to fall in line. So, the nation-building design was immoral because it caused obvious heartburn to those who were determined to cling to their own distinctive socio-cultural traits. In his assessment of Tagore, Mahalanobis further stated that

[19] Prasanta Mahalanobis, *Rabindranath* (Bengalee) (Kolkata: Ananda, 2002), 34–5.

he believes in protesting against injustice in the name of humanity, not in the hope of gaining concessions or as a political weapon or to create race-feeling, but simply because it is a fundamental moral duty.[20]

Being emotionally attached to the urge for political freedom from the British rule, he was never an activist like Gandhi and his Congress colleagues, though he wrote in favour of freedom in an unambiguous way. On two occasions, however, he confronted the British ruler by being integrally connected with the campaign against the alien rule. By participating in the agitation to revoke the first Partition of Bengal (1905–1908), he revealed his politico-ideological preferences for a united Bengal, which, he felt, was needed to avoid further deterioration of communal bonhomie between the Hindus and Muslims. The Partition was withdrawn in 1908, and the role of Rabindranath was immensely significant. In 1919, with his return of his knighthood to the British queen, he again openly attacked the government which, by privileging 'the passion of vengeance' over 'the nobler vision of statesmanship', completely lost its moral credibility of governing India. It was clearly stated in his letter of 31 May 1919 to Viceroy Lord Chelmsford, in which he, while criticizing the government for being 'terribly cruel', stated:

> The enormity of the measures taken by the Government in the Punjab for quelling some local disturbances has, with a rude shock, revealed to our minds the helplessness of our position as British subjects in India. The disproportionate severity of the punishments inflicted upon the unfortunate people and the methods of carrying them out, we are convinced, are without parallel in the history of civilised governments, barring some conspicuous exceptions, recent and remote. Considering that such treatment has been meted out to a population, disarmed and resourceless, by a power which has the most terribly efficient organisation for destruction of human lives, we must strongly assert that it can claim no political expediency, far less moral justification. The accounts of the insults and sufferings by our brothers in Punjab have trickled through the gagged silence, reaching every corner of India, and the universal agony of indignation roused in the hearts of our people has been ignored by our rulers—possibly congratulating themselves for what they imagine as salutary lessons. ... Knowing that our appeals have been in vain ... the very least that I can do for my country

[20] Mahalanobis, 62.

is to take all consequences upon myself in giving voice to the protest of the millions of my countrymen, surprised into a dumb anguish of terror. The time has come when badges of honour make our shame glaring in the incongruous context of humiliation, and I for my part wish to stand, shorn of all special distinctions, by the side of those of my countrymen, who, for their so-called insignificance, are liable to suffer degradation not fit for human beings.[21]

The above letter shows an angry Rabindranath who as a nationalist, challenged the government following the 1919 Jallianwala Bagh (Punjab) massacre which led to the death of hapless people who congregated to protest the arrest of two national leaders, Satyapal and Saifuddin Kitchlew. For Tagore, it was a betrayal of the government towards its citizens, which was at variance with the core values of the philosophy of Enlightenment on which the British rule rested. Besides being deceived by those in power, he also felt terribly uncomfortable, since the present regime was neither attentive to its moral commitment of providing just rule to the people of India nor agreeing to admit that it was a design to quell the dissenting voices. A careful reading of this carefully worded letter suggests that there are two important themes that run through. On the one hand, it was an expression of anguish that was natural, as the consequences were disastrous. The government might have served its purpose for the time being, Tagore noted, since the brutal killing was likely to dissuade people from undertaking protest or any other campaign affecting the British sociopolitical interests adversely. On the other hand, that perception was bound to be proved wrong, Tagore felt, since it was enough to ignite an emotional fervour in a situation in which the idea that the British government was authorized to do whatever its decision makers wanted to do at the cost of the hapless Indians gained ground. As history had shown, Tagore further hinted in this letter, no regime was spared which drew its sustenance from coercion and brutality.

Tagore's May (1919) letter was not just a warning but also a clarion call to the nationalists for mobilizing the anti-nationalist forces. The poet became a rebel, though in his critical writings he often castigated

---

[21] Krishna Dutta and Andrew Robinson, eds., *Selected Letters of Rabindranath Tagore* (Cambridge: Cambridge University Press, 1997), 223–4.

the government in a language that was not as clear as the one the above letter demonstrates. The abdication of his knighthood was a powerful statement from a poet who expressed his opposition to the alien rule in an apparently indirect manner to possibly avoid the government's wrath. It was strategic, perhaps, because once he openly fought the government as the mainstream Congress nationalist, he would have had to face many difficulties while pursuing his mission for creating an ambience in which the goal of making Indian villages self-sufficient would be easily realized.

III

Tagore was primarily a poet of global repute who also wrote many critical essays where he articulated his politico-ideological priorities. His literary texts were not independent of what he wrote in the form of essays; in fact, they were statements, the purpose of which was to provide a design of a social compact by taking into account the prevalent socio-economic peculiarities. In a nutshell, Tagore's ideas were both context-driven and derivative of his own understanding of the ancient texts to which he had had access since his childhood, presumably because of having been born and raised in a family appreciative of the free flow of ideas. It is therefore fair to argue that Tagore's sociopolitical thoughts had a unique texture, since they were drawn on what he learnt by being receptive to the ideas that he came across. As is well known, he was fortunate to have had interactions with the prominent public intellectuals of the period. Prominent among them was Ram Mohan Roy, who mentored his father, Debendranath Tagore. That the latter shifted his allegiance from Hinduism to a new religion, Brahmoism, was largely due to Roy's persuasion; Debendranath realized that Hindu idolatry was anything but religiously justified in view of the inherent limitations that Roy and his colleagues in the Brahmo Samaj had exposed. Once Debendranath was introduced to the Vedas and Vedantic texts, he claimed to have had access to the storehouse of wisdom that had remained hidden to him so far. The tradition continued. So, for Rabindranath Tagore, it was not unusual since he was born in a family that nurtured interests in these texts for, they were believed to be repository of knowledge that had not been adequately explored. But that does not mean that the Tagore family was anathemic to the

Western influences; contrarily, there was also an equally enthusiastic keenness in being acquainted with the fundamental texts that evolved newer philosophical discourses on which the Western civilization rested. In his *Atmaparichay* (Autobiography), Tagore gave us enough inputs in this regard when he candidly mentioned that

> there was something remarkable about our family. It was as if we lived close to the age of pre-Puranic India through our commitment to the Upanishads. As a boy I grew up reciting *slokas* [hymns] with a clear enunciation. We had no experience of the emotional excesses prevalent in Bengal's religious life. My father's spiritual life was quiet and controlled. Along with that there was a genuinely deep love of English literature among my elders. Shakespeare and Sir Walter Scott had a strong influence over our family.[22]

Explicit here is the claim that the Tagore family was characteristically cosmopolitan, at least in thinking since the family members were exposed to India's traditional wisdom, and also had access to the well-established conceptual texts from which the Western philosophy drew its intellectual lineage. A unique blending of the ideas emanating from the East with those from the West, the philosophical discourses that the Tagore family had privileged had their roots in the free flow of ideas that had begun with the initiatives of Tagore's grandfather, Dwarkanath Tagore (1794–1847). A loyalist to the core, Dwarkanath believed that India's happiness was linked with the material well-being of the Empire, which does not seem to have been deviant from the prevalent ethos in colonial Bengal. Nonetheless, by creating an atmosphere in which the ancient texts of Indian civilization were allowed to be taught, the senior Tagore generated an ideational confidence in what contributed to India's rich intellectual traditions. It was therefore not surprising that both his son Debendranath and his grandson Rabindranath appreciated the role that Dwarkanath discharged in augmenting interests in Vedantic texts, especially the Upanishads. The trend that Dwarkanath had set in motion in the mid-19th century received a boost from Debendranath Tagore when he started the Brahmo school in 1888 in Santiniketan in the district of Birbhum, Bengal. What was initiated by his father Debendranath

---

[22] Rabindranath Tagore, *Atmaparichay* (Autobiography), 78, cited in Dasgupta, *Rabindranath Tagore*, 4.

who was baptized in Brahmoism was fully blossomed at the best of Rabindranath Tagore once he founded Patha Bhavana in 1901 and Visva-Bharati, as a centre of higher learning in 1921.

The story, however, shall remain incomplete if we stop here, because to understand Tagore's distinct approach to nation, nationalism and national identity, one needs to pay attention to the sociocultural views that became prominent in the late 19th century with the organization of political agitations, though sporadically, in various parts of India. These attempts were just initial attempts at raising clearly a feeble voice against the British authority, because the idea of mass mobilization for the nationalist cause was still rudimentary in form and character. Nonetheless, the Tagore family was, as evidence shows, intellectually drawn to the exhortations for freedom, which were not exactly a clamour for freedom but an articulation of the difficulties of being kept in an atmosphere of unfreedom. As Tagore elaborated, poems like Rangalal Bandyopadhyay's *Swadhinata-hinatay Key Bachitey Chai* (Who Wants to Live Without Freedom) and Hemchandra Bandyopadhyay's *Bingshoti Koti Manusher Bas* (A Nation of over 200 million) had provided him with a true picture of what unfreedom meant.[23] Still, the elders in the family, argued Tagore, did not seem to be very enthusiastic in associating with the campaign that drew its inspiration from these literary interventions. However, the family stood out for having undertaken various steps to instil patriotism in those who expressed their keenness to contribute to India's self-sufficiency. Tagore was explicit when he mentioned:

> our family was at the centre of plans for establishing the patriotic Hindu Mela,[24] a national fair, whose principal organizer was Nabagopal Mitra [the founder-editor of the newspaper, *National Paper*] along with [the other

[23] Rosinka Chaudhuri dealt with how Hemchandra articulated his feeling of nationalism in her 'Hemchandra's Bharati Sangeet (1870) and the Politics of Poetry: A Prehistory of Hindu Nationalism in Bengal,' *Indian Economic and Social History Review* 42 (June, 2005): 2.

[24] It was a fair for the congregation of people seeking to generate togetherness that some members of the Tagore family had organized in the late 19th century; it was not a grand success, though it was always hailed as perhaps the first serious attempt on the part of a nascent 'nation' to raise its voice against the visible discrimination that the colonized were subjected to in colonial India.

members of the Tagore family] with the purpose of fostering a sense of unity among those attending the Mela.[25]

Besides trying to conjure a sense of unity on the basis of vaguely, if not loosely, defined Indianness, the Tagore family contributed to the popularization of Hindu Mela, founded in 1867, which was a socio-cultural endeavour seeking to rally people, particularly the educated youth, around India's distinctive cultural traits. It was, in other words, a platform for mobilizing support by drawing attention to India's rich cultural heritage. Although Nabagopal Mitra was the one who conceived the idea, the Hindu Mela gained momentum with the support from some of the members of the Tagore family. Interests in the activities of the Mela receded by the early 1890s, presumably because of its obsession with typical Hindu ethos which alienated the Tagores, leading to its final eclipse in 1898 once most of the patrons seceded to join the Indian Association, presumably because of its secular character.

The above description is useful to show that Tagore's sociopolitical ideas were an outcome of multiple influences. On the one hand, he was fortunate to have had a family which was open to newer ideas, which was possible because of the relatively welcoming nature of the Tagores since the days of Tagore's grandfather, Dwarkanath Tagore. There were also societal impulses, on the other hand, which also the family had access to. It was therefore not surprising that Tagore had had a chance to get acquainted with the poems championing an urge for freedom. Similarly, the Hindu Mela had had an impact on the evolution of his sociopolitical ideas that, however, underwent changes as he confronted newer socio-economic circumstances and myriad political challenges.

IV

Sociopolitical Thoughts of Rabindranath Tagore is a long analytical state-ment to understand that his creative writings (literary and otherwise)

---

[25] Tagore, *Atmaparichay* (Autobiography), 79, cited in Dasgupta, *Rabindranath Tagore*, 4.

were articulated as an extension of a compact of ideas based on his dialectical interconnection with the prevalent socio-economic and political realities. This perhaps persuasively explains why one notices visible changes in his attitude to the nationalist endeavour from being a staunch opponent to one who appeared inclined to endorse the nationalist agenda, of course, in a qualified manner. It is now well established that his exchange of views with Gandhi contributed to newer ideas on education as a mode of social transformation, which Tagore sought to implement in his Visva-Bharati project. That Gandhi's Nai Talim and Tagore's *ashramite siksha* (education in residence) were complementary to each other is therefore not coincidental. Similarly, the three novels *Ghare Baire*, *Char Adhyay* and *Gora* can also be read as 'a record of Tagore's attempt to grapple with his ambivalence toward the complex, melodramatic personality'[26] of Brahmabandhab Upadhyay (1861–1907), the editor of *Sandhya* and also a contemporary who evinced much of the poet's ideas that he nurtured in the days of the campaign against the first partition of Bengal (1905–1908). His original name was Bhavanicharan Bandyopadhyay. A blind admirer of Keshabchandra Sen (1838–1884), who was also known as Bhavanicharan, he renamed himself as Brahmabandhav, presumably to identify himself as a Bandhav (friend) of Brahmananda (that is, Keshabchandra Sen). Later, in 1894, he also added a new surname, Upadhyay, since Bandyopadhyay did not seem to be then socially respectable.[27] Two important ideas made Brahmabandhab stand out among his peers: on the one hand, he was a proud Hindu, which he declared unhesitatingly; he also did not hide, on the other hand, his fascination for the revolutionary nationalist method as perhaps the only effective means of removing the British rule from India. Sandip in *Ghare Baire*, Indranath and Atin in *Char Adhyay* and Gora in *Gora* acquiesced with one another because they all appreciated violence as an effective means to get rid of foreign power. Side by side, there also existed the role of Nikhilesh (*Ghare Baire*), Ela (*Char Adhyay*) and

---

[26] Ashis Nandy, *The Illegitimacy of Nationalism* (Delhi: Oxford University Press, 1994), 51.

[27] I owe these inputs to Prof Ashis Nandy of the Centre for Studies of Social Development, New Delhi, who also referred to this in Nandy, 61.

Paresh Babu (*Gora*), who represented the dilemma that Tagore evinced while developing the narratives. It is clear that the former characters were persuaded to cling to violence, while the views of Nikhilesh, Ela and Paresh Babu were extremely tempered, presumably because of the contextual constraints in which revolutionary nationalism, instead of being persuasive, led to mass alienation from the nationalist politics—more so, with the advent of the Gandhian mode of non-violent struggle in the early 1920s. The ambivalence that Tagore brought out through these characters was actually reflective of the dilemma that he himself was facing. His emphatic belief that 'inner Hinduism', that is, true Hinduism, was not separate from Brahmoism suggests that it was perhaps difficult for him to segregate the two. Gora at his later stage, when he was told about his Irish lineage, is illustrative here. Hence, Upadhyay may have been a strong influence when the poet started building the character of Gora, which however underwent a noticeable change when the novel ended with Gora's realization of the values of universal humanism. This was perhaps an episodic change in Tagore's sociopolitical beliefs, demonstrating, on the one hand, his appreciation of violence, and also transcending those beliefs which he held so dear before his engagement with the revolutionary nationalist campaign for the revocation of the first Partition of Bengal (1905–1908).

V

Sociopolitical Thoughts of Rabindranath Tagore is not a biography in the sense of being a life-and-death sketch, but a political biography of Rabindranath Tagore with reference to the prevalent socio-economic and political contexts in which his views had evolved. In other words, it is a contextual study that is sensitive to the intellectual resources that the poet had access to as soon as he joined hands with those having similar politico-ideological inclinations as him. There are two important concerns which the text seeks to capture. On the one hand, the book is directed at focusing on an area of Tagore's contribution which has not received scholarly attention so far: the poet, the novelist and the playwright Tagore appears to have hogged the limelight, and his critical essays have remained bypassed, if not neglected. The book also delves, on the other hand, into the dialectical interconnection between the ideas that Tagore articulated and the context which informed them. It was clearly dialectical, since the author, being so sensitive to the inputs that he received from the context, derived his ideas, to a significant extent, from the existent socio-economic circumstances; with his powerful and persuasive writings, the bard remained a figure in the then Bengal who critically shaped the contemporary thinking on many social, economic and political issues. It will also not be an exaggeration to suggest that as one who drew heavily on the politico-ideological views of those who set in motion processes of significant social metamorphosis in Bengal, Tagore played a very significant role in highlighting those ideas that appeared to have been conveniently forgotten; these ideas were bypassed, for they laid the foundation of a powerful campaign against social orthodoxy and, for obvious reasons, were likely to be vehemently opposed to as they were potentially threatening to the thriving vested interests in a rather propitious social environment. Tagore's was a well-designed and conceptually defended set of arguments that not only charted a new course for social trans-formation but also was a source of inspiration to undertake activities challenging the hegemonic grip of Hindu orthodoxy.

As regards the ideas that acted critically in shaping Tagore's mental universe, one can safely refer to the fact that in conceptualizing his ideational preferences, he was indebted to his predecessors who helped him build his unique conceptual package. And, critical were the contextual impulses which remained an important source for an appropriate analysis. It is true that he was not a political activist in the conventional sense of the term; nonetheless, his powerful writings were important inputs to understand how he conceptualized the colo-nial rule in India. On his return after one of his early trips to England, he, in his letter to *Bharati*, one of the leading literary magazines of Bengal, brought out his feelings by saying that

> Hundreds of Johns and Thomases are found swarming the lanes and by-lanes of cities in England, whose mothers and fathers are known to none but to a butcher, a tailor or a coal porter. But the moment they set their foot on any locality in India, their names becomes a topic of everybody's discourse. The roads through which they pass whip in hand (which under-standably is used not merely for the horse), became immediately desolate,

all the passersby taking themselves off in a frantic hurry. At their slightest gesticulation trembles the throne of an Indian king. ... The fact is, you know, whenever the small is installed in high positions, it makes an ostentatious parade of its highness by exhibiting its red eyes or expanded chest.[28]

This is perhaps the most revealing of his statements on the social background of those who ruled India and how they transformed themselves once they landed in India. While expressing his anguish, a young Tagore also hinted that the changed attitude of those who came to India for better governance was also a source of his irritation, which is clear from his articulation in a language which was anything but ambiguous. It is also true that he simply drew our attention to the torturous behaviour meted out by them to the hapless Indian subjects, though he hardly had expressed his resentment in clear terms. The reason lies perhaps in his judgement of what should go in the public domain and what should be held back. Nonetheless, he was explicit enough in putting across his feeling of being disenchanted with the British rule, presumably because it was meant to humiliate and brutalize the colonized. Being aware that the roots of caste schisms were located in the archaic social practices endorsed by an equally partisan mindset, Tagore raised his voice in many of his writings, as will be shown in the book. Suffice it to refer to his dance–drama *Chandalika* (1938), which was a caustic remark on caste division that was meant to permanently segregate those who were, by the accident of birth, untouchables. Supportive of a campaign for its complete removal, Tagore helped build 'a new consciousness after ages of suppression ... to convey his message to those still governed by caste prejudices'.[29] It was a bold step, especially in a context when the caste system did not seem to have been so severely criticized, presumably because the nationalists were not in a position to counter the backlash of an attack on the caste-driven, divisive social hierarchy.

As one who realized that India was weak and remained to be so since she was brutalized internally with the consolidation of caste

[28] Rabindranath's letter to Bharati, *Rabindra Rachanabali*, Vol. X, 258–9.

[29] Krishna Kripalani, *Rabindranath Tagore: A Biography* (New Delhi: UBS Publications, 2008) (reprint), 231.

hierarchy, an artificial system of segregation which led to a permanent compartmentalization of the majority, being identified as untouchables.

That he was a vocal critic of the British rule was revealed in a number of ways. As is well known, the 1835 Macaulay's Minute introduced English education (which will be dealt with in Chapter 5 of this book) that served the British administration well, though at the cost of the Indian learners. As an educationist, Tagore devised an alternative with the formation of Patha Bhavana in 1901 and Visva-Bharati (as a centre for higher learning) in 1921. In his 'Sikhshar Her Fer' (The State of Education, 1892–1893), he, while castigating the English education, made a very perceptive comment on the nature of education that evolved at the aegis of the British government when he said:

> the education we receive is not in conformity with the life that we live; our textbooks do not contain any elevated picture of our health and home where we live till death, we do not get in the literature we are taught in any high ideal of the society in whose bosom we have to pass the days of our life; we do not find our fathers and mothers, our friends and our kith and kin, our brothers and sisters, portrayed in them; nor our actualities of our life given any place in those narratives; the sky and the earth we behold, our crystal morning and enchanting sunset, our crop-filled fields and the music of our fortune-giving rivers are not sung in them; when we deeply ponder this, we invariably feel that no genuine accord can never be established between the education we receive and the life we live in.[30]

In his assessment of the English education that the alien rulers had imposed in India for fulfilling their partisan goal, Tagore raised two fundamental points, which are useful to conceptualize his alternative form of education. To him, education was not merely the cramming of pages from books but a device which helped learners inculcate devices for comprehending their reality on their own. In other words, education was a passport to grasp the prevalent social, economic and political reality as objectively as possible. He was also aware that it was not expected of the alien rulers, given their selfish desire to thrive at the cost of the colonized Indians. One is now persuaded to believe that being terribly upset with the prevalent system of education, the

---

[30] *Rabindra Rachanabali*, Vol. XI, 539, 542 cited in Arabinda Poddar, *Tagore; The Political Personality* (Kolkata: Indiana, 2004), 51.

idea of Visva-Bharati, which was conceptualized as both an alternative and effective centre for learning, came to him naturally. Whatever idea he conveyed in this critical essay was presented in the form of a short story, entitled *Tota Kahini* (*a parrot's training*) which he published in 1877–1878. The story exposed the inherent limitations of rote learning. Fundamental here is the idea that the poet, in his own way, evolved a powerful and also persuasive critique of the foreign rule. He was not merely engaged in a task that was confined to political opposition to the British rule, as most of his nationalist colleagues were, but also undertook several steps to build a strong nation on the basis of its inner strength which needed to be built and sustained.

The most fundamental of the ideas that Tagore held so dear while evolving his uniquely devised philosophical discourse was the communion between the temporal and spiritual authority. In Tagore's mode of argument, overemphasis on temporal gain resulted in men being totally neglectful of the higher spirit of godly authority. This was also a device to create a milieu for togetherness seeking to build harmony between human beings across geographical space. The contemporary civilization, being clearly forgetful of this aspect of human civilization was an attack on the endeavours towards building a bridge which was being destroyed with the consolidation of spiteful design of human beings (in the form of colonialism) who just became pawns at the hands of the wielders of power. It was most eloquently pointed out when the poet expressed that

> in the modern civilization, for which an enormous number of men are used as materials, and human relationship have in a large measure become utilitarian, man is imperfectly revealed. ... The prevalence of the theory which realized the power of the machine in the universe, and organizes men into machines, is like the eruption of *Etna* [a volcano in Italy, famous for its capacity to cause devastation to human settlement], tremendous in its force, in its outburst of fire and fume; but its creeping lave covers up human shelters made by the ages, and its ashes smother life.[31]

What is argued here is Tagore's urge to develop togetherness involving human beings, cutting across the artificial social segregation and also

---

[31] Rabindranath Tagore, 'The Modern Age,' in *The English Writings of Rabindranath Tagore*, ed. Sisir Kumar Das, Vol. 2 (New Delhi: Sahitya Akademi, 1996), 542.

political compartmentalization of one section from another for reasons connected with one's access to coercive power. It was a critique of the politico-ideological design insisting on generating and also sustaining human chasms purely for realizing the partisan aims of those being driven by exclusive interests. The aim was to contribute to the growth of a homogenous social organism based on sharing the products of nature and also human labour, which might sound utopian in a situation being clearly torn by conflicting social, economic and political aims. Nonetheless, with his unstinted commitment to universal humanism, Tagore was persuaded to believe that the ideals of human unity and freedom were achievable at the end of the 'era of differentiation, when classes and castes and religious discords and exploitations had become the memories of the past, when inter-dependent aspirations of all me of all the nations are fused into a synchronized future'.[32] There are two points that need reiteration here. On the one hand, despite having been born and raised in colonial India, the poet continued to remain enthusiastic about his ideas for universal humanism, since he was aware that unless it was spread out as an inspiring ideal, the future of humanity was bleak, if not completely wasted. The poet also made a claim, on the other hand, that human society suffered primarily due to the neglectful ignorance of human beings from their duties as human beings. This is a profound conceptualization, since in the wake of the industrial revolution and also the spread of colonialism, the industrialized nations conveniently undermined the humanistic philosophical discourses that had contributed to the civilization that they were proud of. Being inspired by the core values of the Enlightenment philosophy, like so many of his colleagues championing national freedom, Tagore found the British colonizing endeavour to be incongruent with the fundamental principles from which the British civilization drew its politico-ideological nourishment.

VI

Comprising six chapters, besides the introduction and conclusion, this book is devoted to the analysis of Tagore's sociopolitical thoughts.

[32] Poddar, *Tagore: The Political Personality*, 293.

In view of the innumerable texts that the poet left for posterity, it is humanly impossible to deal with each and every one of them. Hence, the book selects those of his literary creations which are useful to highlight the core theme that each chapter is slated to dwell on. Within the space available, an attempt is made to elaborate those themes which are critical to grasp the distinct characteristics of Tagore's social and political preferences. Delving into his intellectual inspirational inputs along with the prevalent contextual influences, Chapter 1 is an in-depth account of what possibly led the poet to conceptualize ideas in his unique fashion. This chapter is a fundamental chapter in the sense that it provides the readers with those important socio-philosophical concerns that critically shaped the bard's thinking in a way which did not appear to be conventional in approach. Since the book pursues the argument that Tagore was a 'nationalist' in the internationalist mould, Chapter 2 concentrates on his views on nationalism. As is well known, like the Mahatma, the poet was also persuaded to support the view that India was not a nation per the conventional Western criteria that evolved in the post–1648 Westphalia Treaty era. Especially in India, which is known for its socio-cultural diversity, the idea of oneness or essentializing the multiple identities into one is always inapplicable, if not a distortion for fulfilling narrow partisan aims. With a thorough analysis of Tagore's dissection of the idea of nationalism with reference to both his creative literary texts and critical essays, the chapter seeks to enlighten the reader on a rather less explored area of Tagore's socio-political conceptualization. As will be shown, Tagore's sociopolitical views were embodied in his protagonists' lives and activities, shown particularly in his novels and short stories, which constitute the core of Chapter 3. Besides the analytical dissection of his texts, including *Swadeshi Samaj*, which he published in 1904, this chapter also focuses on some of the main characters in his novels and short stories that upheld Tagore's politico-ideological predilections. Given the fact that he was, out and out, a practitioner too, the chapter also pays adequate attention to his experiments of Santiniketan and Sriniketan. For the poet, these were not merely centres of higher learning but also designs for conceptualizing an alternative framework of comprehension and understanding of human life and deeds. That Tagore was well ahead of his contemporaries is seen in his approach to gender issues. By focusing on how he conceptualized gender parity amidst severe opposition from those who mattered then in Bengal, Chapter 4 devotes its attention to the exploration of his peculiarly textured response to gender equity. As is the case with the poet, the protagonists in the novels and short stories also speak in a language that explicates his thinking on this issue, which was clearly an out-of-the-box idea then, but with tremendous significance for reconceptualizing concerns for gender parity in the changed socio-economic environment of contemporary India as well. Bimala of *Ghare Baire* (1916), Kumud of *Jagajog* (1929), Damini of *Chaturanga* (1916) and Prakriti of *Chandalika* (1938), among others, represented an endeavour to portray the radical nature of Tagore's conception of women and their selfhood. These women characters are innovative cultural texts seeking to revisit, re-address the socially-constructed 'fixed' identity that women were forced to accept in a patriarchy-driven hierarchical society. That Tagore was an educationist of a completely different kind is too well-known to deserve a mention. On the basis of a thorough analysis of the type of education that the poet preferred to conceptualize education as a means for realizing the exalted value of education, chapter 5 elaborates the views that he put forward to support his contention. Here too, he, being a practitioner, devoted his energy to building an alternative form of education away from the hurly-burly of urban Calcutta. In his scheme, nature was an important ingredient of learning, which prompted him to experiment with his alternative approach to education in a remote area of West Bengal, which, of course, gradually became a hub of learning different from the others that existed then. The chapter, by focusing on the distinct nature of teaching and also the course curriculum in Visva-Bharati, makes the argument that Tagore was a visionary who carved a space by creating an alternative model of education that was not so easily conceivable in colonial Bengal, especially with the hegemonic influence of English education. A comparison with Gandhi's Nai Talim does not seem to be out of place. The Mahatma too devised a new system of education, being drawn to John Ruskin who, in his *Unto This Last* (1860), insisted on that form of learning which was a source of pleasure but not an imposition making the learners unhappy. The final chapter is an attempt to summarize Tagore's fundamental contribution to humanity.

Unlike his nationalist colleagues, including Gandhi, the poet was not favourably inclined to devote wholeheartedly to political freedom from the British rule, since it was not, at all, adequate to realize universal humanism. The path did not seem to be an easy one, as Chapter 6 demonstrates, since the vested interests were too well-entrenched to ignore. Here, the poet had to fight against sources of exploitation and suppression, or, in a word, sources of unfreedom. Gora in *Gora* (1910) represented a wave of thinking that Tagore articulated in his 1930 Hibbert lecture, which was published with the title '*The Religion of Man*', and in his last speech entitled '*Crisis in Civilization*'. The protagonist in *Gora* was perplexed and also intrigued when he confronted the socio-culturally divided villagers in Bengal villages despite having been living in the same villages. What is noteworthy here is Tagore's capacity to authentically elaborate on the divisive social, economic and cultural environment with reference to the unendurable suffering of the people around the axes of class, caste and ethnicity.

With these well-argued chapters, substantiated by delving into the textual articulation of the issues, the book is an elaboration of Tagore's uniquely textured sociopolitical ideas, which is just an attempt to dwell on an aspect of nationalist political thought that has not received as much attention as it deserves. This is not just a book in a conventional sense, since it seeks to convey an argument suggesting that Tagore's intervention, despite not being compatible with the mainstream politico-ideological priorities, was an intellectually refreshing endeavour to make inroads into a realm in public thinking that had so far been peripheral.

VII

Sociopolitical Thoughts of Rabindranath Tagore is an argument with the contention that Tagore inculcated those socio-cultural ideas that constituted a blueprint for India which was neither divisive nor deviant from the core beliefs of universal humanism. According to the poet, the idea of India is not just about a collectivity being protective of its existence by hook or crook, but one that coexists with other collectivities despite being spatially separate but united in terms of being human beings. What was critical in his thinking was his firm commitment to the cause of humanity, despite knowing that this was likely not to persuade his colleagues in a situation when rabid nationalism appeared to have been privileged. Nonetheless, he stood by his concern for universal humanism despite being vehemently criticized by his nationalist colleagues, including the Mahatma, who fought for national independence, holding it prior to anything else. Here, Tagore stood out since what he defended as critical to human existence was contrary to what others felt. In fact, it is argued that the Mahatma and his nationalist compatriots pursued a mode of coming together as a unit, or a nation, in the prevalent sense of the term, which was not exactly new, since it was, as evidence shows, a transmission of a constructed idea that gradually transformed into a nation.[33] It is true that Tagore was convinced that the idea of nation could never be anything but humanist, since the countries seeking to fulfil their nationalist agenda were bound to be brutally selfish, as history had illustrated. That he remained committed to this conceptualization is amplified in his corpus of writings. There is a clear indication of this in his preference for the word *Bharatvarsha* and not India while elaborating on his distinctive ideational inklings. In a creative literary piece, 'Nababarsha' (New Year), published in 1902, he expressed unambiguously what he meant by *Bharatvarsha*, saying that, to him,

> *Bharatvarsha* that will ultimately remain is not only ancient, but also concealed, vast and generous. We – who speak in English, who disbelieve, who tell lies, who boast – year by year, we shall dissipate, disappear, like the waves in the ocean. Silent, *sanatan* Bharat will not suffer any loss as a consequences.[34]

Two ideas seem prominent here. On the one hand, Tagore, a priest of universal humanism, developed an identity of *Bharatvarsha* by being drawn to the traditional social–intellectual resources that were required to be utilized to combat the nationalistic designs seeking

[33] Rosinka Chaudhuri made this point in her essay, 'Hemchandra's Bharat Sangeet (1870) and the Politics of Poetry', 2.

[34] Rabindranath Tagore, Rabindra Rachanabali, Vol. 9, 609, cited in Chaudhuri, 'Hemchandra's Bharat Sangeet (1870) and the Politics of Poetry', 2.

to undermine universal humanism. Presumably because of being an epitome of universal humanism, Tagore championed *Bharatvarsha* a model of inclusive human existence, despite knowing that his colleagues held contrarian views about it. Tagore's insistence on drawing on the Vedantic texts was not, at all, an endeavour to go back to the past, but one to derive inspiration for the present. It was therefore not surprising that Gora in the novel *Gora*, despite being a *santani* Hindu who religiously followed all the rituals to prove himself a true Brahmin, had no qualms when he vehemently criticized the divisive caste system and also the prejudicial attitudes that caste Hindus nurtured to maintain social distance with their Muslim brethren. He was clueless when he found that Madhav Chatujje, an upper-caste Hindu, was not ostracized despite supporting the torturous indigo planter and that the villagers did not extend help to the wife of Pharu Sardar, a Muslim who was jailed for attacking the British planter. It was a revelation to Gora, who, so far, had remained unaware of how 'fragmented, narrow-minded and feeble was his *Bharatvarsha*',[35] which was merely a physical description without much substance. The *Bharatvarsha* that he was looking for was not the one that existed in reality. As a result, the deeper he penetrated into the rural life,

> the more a certain thought began to trouble his mind. He observed that in these rural areas, social restrictions were far more powerful than in educated and cultured society. In every household in the villages, food, sleep, rest, work, everything was conducted, day and night, under the unblinking gaze of society. Each individual had a very simple faith in popular traditions, never questioning such things. Yet social restrictions and adherence to custom did not empower them at all in the fields of activity. ... Beyond adherence to tradition, here was no other good that they wholeheartedly acknowledged, or were willing to understand. It was prohibition, enforced through punishment or partisanship, that they regarded as supreme. The awareness of what must not be done entrapped their nature in a net from head to toe at every step, through various forms of discipline. ... There was no broad unity among them that could draw them all together in good times or bad.[36]

[35] Rabindranath Tagore, *Gora*, in *Classic Rabindranath Tagore* (New Delhi: Penguin, 2011), 400.

[36] Tagore, 575.

There could not be anything clearer than how Gora articulated his feelings when he confronted rural Bengal. Superstitious, backward-looking and ideationally disparate, the villagers appeared to have remained in a makeshift world in which they had been made to believe that they were fated to be like this because of a providential dictum. To the rationalist Gora, it was simply a ploy to keep them under chains for the fulfilment of partisan aims of those who, in the name of contributing to social well-being, actually sustained their firm grip on the prevalent social relationships involving people from various walks of life. So long as this continued along with the inherent lackadaisical attitude of the villagers in general, the unity that was required to realize the India that Gora aspired for would remain distant, if not elusive. An analytical review of these points establishes the argument that Tagore consistently pursued the idea in his creative literary interventions to justify his lifelong commitment to universal humanism. There are two levels at which the argument is made. At the micro level, by challenging what caused social, economic and cultural alienation at the grassroots, Tagore launched a crusade against these partisan designs responsible for creating and also sustaining human segregation. In view of the nationalist desire to exploit the less privileged, the poet, at the macro level, pitched his argument to unambiguously convey his feeling of being anguished, since his view was, he strongly felt, a stepping stone towards severely, if not completely, undermining universal bonhomie among human beings, since humanism was, by nature, a design for unity. To be precise, Tagore's intervention, despite not having succeeded in mobilizing support to the extent he expected, continues to remain relevant not merely as a package for intellectual rejuvenation but also as a meaningful device for socio-economic transformation for the globe as a whole. This is where Tagore stands out not only as a poet but also as a visionary who charted a course of action in tune with human betterment, cutting across all kinds of man-made barriers and customary, restrictive social, economic and political practices.

Tagore's Mental Universe

Rabindranath Tagore had a vision with ideas for change and innovation. Committed to human emancipation, he took up the cudgels against the socio-economically well-entrenched mindsets justifying social distance between human beings around axes of caste, class and religion. It was a fresh air that he brought to our thinking when the colonized appeared to have lost the zeal to explore new possibilities. Based on his experiences, Tagore created, in other words, a new genre of thoughts that allowed us to tread the unknown terrain. It is true that he was not at all, a political activist like his nationalist compatriots, including Gandhi, but his conceptual interventions generated hope for all those who were engaged in the struggle for human betterment. Amidst hopelessness, the scion of one of the culturally most vibrant families of Calcutta set in motion, through his creative writings, processes of change that were not so easily conceivable in a context of mass disenchantment. In view of the mainstream nationalist campaign being clearly devoid of steam, especially in the late 19th and early 20th centuries, Tagore's disillusionment with the political leadership did not seem to be unfounded, since the anti-British campaign, he strongly felt, lacked the sheen that it should have had. What is also unique in Tagore's conceptualization of sociopolitical ideas was his attempt to integrate his concerns for both political and socio-economic changes. Contrary to his nationalist colleagues, he was not persuaded to believe that mere political freedom was either effective or capable of bringing about radical social transformation. Being divided around caste, class and religious axes, Indians remained terribly fragmented, which needed to be addressed simultaneously along with mobilization for political freedom. To be very precise, Tagore was convinced that unless socio-economic freedom accompanied political liberation, the very endeavour for change would remain half-hearted, which was a reinforcement of the argument that the bard made in so many of his creating interventions in the forms of novels, short stories, plays and dance dramas, among others. An example will suffice here. The 1904 *Swadeshi Samaj* provided a blueprint for future India; it was also an articulation of how to govern the *samaj* by involving people from various strata of society with various kinds of skills. It was also an attempt to seek to generate the idea of being self-reliant for winning and also sustaining India's freedom. Unlike most of his nationalist compatriots, Tagore's focus was limited. As *Swadeshi Samaj* shows, he was keen to devote his energy to develop one or two villages, since it was manageable and doable. A practical man to the core, his concern here is based on what he could accomplish on his own. By following an inductive mode of reasoning, the poet built his model which was not, however, appreciated by those nationalists who appeared to be impatient and thus failed to appreciate Tagore's arguments questioning their ways of conceptualizing the nationalist voice. In novels too, he clearly brought out his preferences. The debate between Nikhilesh and Sandip in *Ghare Baire* (1916), which was based in the context of the nationalist campaign (1905–1908) for revocation of the first Partition of Bengal, is illustrative here. While Nikhilesh was keen to cement a bond between Hindus and Muslims and was opposed to the caste hierarchy as a debilitating social form, his friend Sandip thought otherwise, by privileging political freedom over any other endeavour, since it was likely to weaken the nationalist effort. One must be a little cautious while pursuing this point of view, because the period during the anti-partition campaign and its aftermath was one of uncertainty, in contrast with what had emerged with the appearance of Gandhi on the Indian political scene in 1919 when the nationalist movement was no longer confined to the metropolitan cities of Calcutta and Bombay and was also not dominated by upper-caste Hindus. Gandhi radically altered the socio-economic texture of the nationalists by bringing in people with different caste and religious identities. This was what Tagore had propagated in his *Swadeshi Samaj* and *Ghare Baire*, for instance.

Not only was Tagore a fresh air, he was also a pathfinder creating a design for the nationalist campaign, which was inconceivable when it was articulated during the Swadeshi movement that had begun with the opposition to Curzon's division of Bengal into East and West Bengal for administrative convenience. The nationalist apprehension was perhaps true when it was argued to be an outcome of the British policy of *divide et impera*. Nonetheless, the campaign, by being restrictive in character, failed to enthuse the masses, especially the Muslims of East Bengal, presumably because of the blatant religious bias of the leaders and their followers. Tagore's insistence on communal amity to build an effective nationalist campaign was logical, as the history that followed demonstrated. In a similar vein, his scathing critique of caste segmentation was untimely and led many of his upper-caste colleagues to vehemently criticize him, which however did not restrain him. His consistent opposition to the artificially created schism among human beings helped the future nationalists reconceptualize the nationalist agenda by taking the so-called untouchables within the nationalist collectivity.

The aim of this chapter is to understand Tagore's distinct conceptual universe with reference to the essays, novels and other creative writings that he left for posterity. The discussion is analytically divided into two complementary segments, since they are dialectically interconnected. The first phase ends with the rise of Gandhi on the nationalist scene when the battle for freedom underwent a sea change. The ideas of Tagore that did not receive attention during the anti-Bengal partition campaign were far more appreciated, presumably because the nationalist movement had expanded its tentacles almost everywhere in the country due to the ideological metamorphosis of the Gandhi-led Indian National Congress. The second phase of the evolution of Tagore's sociopolitical ideas needs to be understood with reference to the debates that the bard had with the Mahatma. They were intimate colleagues but not blind supporters of each other; in fact, it is better to characterize their relationship as one of two fierce critics who left no stone unturned to consistently argue their respective points of view. Nonetheless, despite not being persuaded politico-ideologically, Tagore and Gandhi remained intimate friends respecting each other as belonging to different conceptual domains. This is one section of the chapter that will discuss how Tagore's sociopolitical ideas evolved out of his interaction with Gandhi; the other section will deal with his ideas, with reference to a selected set of his creative writings. By dwelling on these ideas, the aim of this chapter is to put forward the view that Tagore's conceptual universe is both contextual and transcendental: contextual because it has clear contextual roots, and transcendental since it remains contemporaneously relevant to persuasively understand the complex unfolding of human beings' socioeconomic and politico-ideological preferences.

FOUNDATIONAL IDEAS

Tagore influenced many during his lifetime and also afterwards; he was also heavily influenced by some of his intellectually vibrant predecessors, like Vidyasagar (1820–1891), Ram Mohan Roy (1772–1833) and Debendranath Tagore (1817–1905). What was striking about them was their selfless service to the hapless people who remained socioeconomically marginalized due to the well-entrenched sociopolitical prejudices and also the obvious pernicious impact of colonialism; they stood out by being committed to the values of universal humanism for which they had to pay heavy prices, which hardly deterred them. In conceptual terms, they were primarily social reformers who did not seem to have been politically swayed to undertake anti-colonial campaigns, since they believed that political independence was not a panacea unless it was complemented by radical socio-economic transformation. The scene was not favourably disposed, given the existence of an adversarial mindset opposed to efforts towards addressing socio-economic imbalances.

Vidyasagar's sociopolitical ideas had struck an emotional chord with Tagore, since they corresponded with what he had in mind. In two ways, his contribution was of immense significance: besides his endeavour in seeking to spread education through an institutionalized system of schooling, the educationist, by being involved in the campaign for widow remarriage, radically altered the prevalent system of gender exploitation. Tagore thus wrote that with support from English colleagues, Vidyasagar helped build an environment in which the British government was persuaded to support him in this endeavour. In opposition to the contention that widow remarriage was contrary to the well-established canons of Hindu religious and canonical texts, Vidyasagar proved to the contrary, which provoked a counter-attack on him by the orthodox Hindus. Tagore most explicitly stated this, saying:

> once the applecart of Hindu orthodoxy was disturbed it resulted in Vidyasagar being abused and hit below the belt which he absorbed perhaps the goal that he attained was far more satisfactory that what he received from the fellow Bengalees. His victory was undoubtedly a source of joy and satisfaction to him because it relieved the widows of humiliation that they often suffered; the victory was complete once it was legalized with specific directions in case the law in this regard was violated.[1]

Tagore's appreciation for Vidyasagar is understandable, since he found in this endeavour a revolutionary attempt at purging the Bengalee society of an age-old and well-entrenched social evil. This was a significant step insofar as the drive towards establishing gender equity was concerned. Furthermore, Vidyasagar's contribution in allowing the untouchables to study in Sanskrit College, which, so far, had remained an exclusive domain of the upper-caste Hindus, especially the Brahmins, was complemented by his endeavour to create facilities for English learning for the local students, which was made possible with the foundation of a school, christened as Metropolitan School. He was criticized by his detractors since it amounted, they felt, to surrender to the British design of forcibly injecting the desire to be educated in English. Perhaps the response of his critics was contextual; but that Vidyasagar had foresight was proved once traditional forms of learning were entirely replaced by English education in the late 19th and early 20th centuries.

Admiring Vidyasagar for being bold and steadfastly committed to the goal, Tagore made a very perceptive comment on the nature of Bengalees who preferred to be vocal if there was a problem but remained non-committal in case they were asked to discharge their commitment through actual deeds. Being despiteful of those Bengalees who devoted 'their energy in calculations for winning the bait in horse

---

[1] Rabindranath Tagore, *Charitrapuja* (Kolkata: Visva-Bharati, Granthan Bhivag, 1405) (Bangavda), 30–1.

races but were completely indifferent if they were asked to take care of the malaria-affected villages,'[2] Tagore implored them to learn from Vidyasagar who stood out for his selfless service to humanity. A person of impeccable character, Vidyasagar instilled in Tagore, admitted the poet, 'the zeal to question what appeared to be socially inhibiting and emotionally retrogressive',[3] though he was intrigued how a person of Vidyasagar's mindset was born in a society which was 'rotten and protective of archaic values and mores justifying servility of a large sections of the population for partisan gains'.[4] What is most striking was Tagore's final statement on the basis of his assessment of Vidyasagar's fundamental societal contribution, which he articulated by saying that 'the Sanskritist will be remembered since he found out what prevented the Bengalees from accomplishing the goal'. According to Vidyasagar, the main reason was located in the consolidation of mindsets supportive of certain characteristic traits, which Tagore most succinctly articulated by stating that we are unable to address our weaknesses effectively because

> we undertake tasks but pay no attention to find out whether it was complete; we tend to show our opulence, but prefer not to work; whatever we say, we don't believe and whatever we believe we don't say; we say things and expect other to do the work while we avoid discharging our responsibilities with pretexts; we tend to find fault with others, but never practice self-introspection; we feel proud by imitating other; we enjoy surviving on others' favour; we feel proud by deceiving others which is our politics; we are satisfied by patting ourselves at the back.[5]

This is perhaps the most caustic remark that Tagore made on the basis of his own assessment of Vidyasagar, the man. This could also be the poet's own reading of the situation in which he endeavoured to create conditions for collective betterment. It was not an easy task, indeed. Nonetheless, the above comment is most perceptive and also reflective of the poet's disenchantment with the prevalent political

---

[2] Tagore, 35.

[3] Tagore, 39.

[4] Tagore, 39.

[5] Tagore, 40.

leadership that, instead of being attentive to common well-being, devoted wholeheartedly to the fulfilment of those goals which were clearly self-serving and partisan in their aims and objectives.

Like Vidyasagar, Ram Mohan Roy was also an important source for Tagore to develop his conceptual universe. Characterizing Roy as 'a luminous star in the firmament of India's history, with prophetic purity of vision and unconquerable heroism of soul',[6] Tagore also admired him as 'the great pathfinder of this century who has removed ponderous obstacles that impeded our progress at every step, and initiated us into the present era of world-wide cooperation of humanity'.[7] In two ways, Roy, the renaissance man, made an immense contribution to India's rise as a nation with respect and élan. First, being true to what he learnt from India's ancient texts, including the Upanishads, Roy created a social milieu which helped the Indians break away from mental servility. Second, it was Ram Mohan who, by being appreciative of universal humanism, provided Tagore with significant inputs to articulate his distinct approach to cooperation between human beings at the global level. It was evident when the poet further mentioned that 'he paved the path for reassertion of India's inmost truth of being, her being in the equality of man in the love of the Supreme Person, who ever dwells in the hearts of all men and unites us in the bond of welfare'.[8] Implicit here are two points: on the one hand, Tagore was drawn to Roy for his belief in the oneness of the Supreme Person, or Brahma. This did not seem to be unknown to him, since his father was a believer in the existence of one god, an Upanishadic idea that appears to have influenced the poet, to a significant extent. In fact, much of the learning of these texts came to his father from Roy, whom he knew since his childhood because he was Roy's son Ramaprasad Roy's classmate in school. Hence, Tagore's father internalized and later transmitted the idea of one god to the poet, since the latter spent most of his childhood days with the former. Second, what united

---

[6] Rabindranath Tagore, 'Ram Mohan Roy,' reproduced in *The English Writings of Rabindranath Tagore*, ed. Sisir Das, Vol. 3 (New Delhi: Sahitya Akademi, 1996), 667.

[7] Tagore, Ram Mohan 667.

[8] Tagore, Ram Mohan 667–8.

Tagore with Roy was his relentless struggle for the betterment of human beings, cutting across geographical borders. The identity of human beings as human beings was critical to Roy, who always believed that one's birth as a human being was futile unless one contributed to the strengthening of values in support of humanity. This connotes that Tagore and Roy coalesced, since they held identical views *vis-à-vis* their responsibility as human beings. In other words, by their sincere commitment to consolidate the human bond surpassing segmented geographical boundaries, the two intellectual giants held identical concerns which, again, does not seem improbable, presumably because they drew on the same intellectual lineage that India's ancient texts epitomized.

A careful decoding of Tagore's 1933 text on Ram Mohan Roy underlines how the poet justified his intellectual debt to what the poet called the first modern Indian. He was truly a renaissance man who was an Indian with clear international fervour. This was explained by the bard through reference to his firm grounding in Indian traditions without being xenophobic to the Western philosophical ideas that also complemented his conceptualization of universal humanism. In a rather long statement, he thus admired Roy by saying that

> he knew that the ideal of human civilization does not lie in the isolation of independence, but in the brotherhood of interdependence of individuals as well as nations in all spheres of thought and activity. He applied this principle of humanity with his extraordinary depth of scholarship and natural gift of intuition, to social, literary and religious affairs, never acknowledging limitations of circumstance, never deviating from his purpose lured by distractions of temporal excitement.[9]

Fundamental here was Roy's concern for bringing human beings across the world into spiritual communion in which the role of Indians was not insignificant either, because his attempts were directed to

> establish our peoples on the full consciousness of their own cultural personality, to make them comprehend the reality of all that was unique

---

[9] Tagore, Ram Mohan 668.

and indestructible in their civilization, and simultaneously, to make them approach other civilizations in the spirit of sympathetic cooperation.[10]

This was a unique blending of the East and the West as complementary to each other. Seeking to bind India with the rest of the world spiritually, Roy put forward a model that was nationally global or globally national, which upheld his concern that without compatibility of socio-cultural values, his aim of creating an ambience for human togetherness was likely to remain unrealized. Being genuinely concerned for spiritual amity across artificially created geographical boundaries, Ram Mohan was a true believer in universal friendship, which was possible since we all are human beings with the same socio-philosophical roots. It was Roy who, Tagore felt, by nurturing sincerely the idea of cooperation among human beings across borders, 'came to our aid in a genuine spirit of comradeship'.[11] With his 'comprehensive vision of mankind', Ram Mohan, Tagore expanded his point further, paved the way for a world which was not only free from narrow prejudices but also laid the foundation for a solid bond among human beings located in various parts of the world. As Roy was the one who taught him 'perfect equity of human relationship offering uncompromising fight to all forms of conventions, however ancient they may be in usage, which separate man and man',[12] Tagore had no hesitation in declaring that he owed a great deal to Roy, because it was he who helped Tagore understand the true nature of the universal or supreme being. This, in turn, contributed to his conceptualization of human amity across the globe, presumably because as human beings we remained spiritually united, given our common roots of origin, irrespective of our locations. It was thus easier for him to appreciate the view that religious schism alienating one section of the demography from another was artificially created to enable those with vested interests to fulfil their partisan aims. Tagore thus admired Roy as 'a trailblazer for new India or *Bharat Pathik*' who, despite being raised in an environment which was clearly adverse, nonetheless gave a call

---

[10] Tagore, Ram Mohan 668.

[11] Tagore, Ram Mohan 668.

[12] Tagore, Ram Mohan 668.

for universal amity regardless of religion and race. In a metaphorical way, the poet thus said that 'it was Ram Mohan Roy who, despite the unpropitious consequences, invited Muslims, Christians to share the kitchen with the Hindus to organize a feast for all'.[13] The idea had a massive impact on Tagore who thus revered Roy for showing him a path for creating bonhomie among the diverse population to generate a mass zeal for making India a place for all. On this conceptualization remained Tagore's claim of Ram Mohan being transcendental in appeal. In Tagore's words, though Roy articulated his ideas 'in the early part of the nineteenth century on this basis of experience of being in India, he raised those issues which are clearly global since they are linked with his concern for universal humanism'.[14] In other words, despite being an outcome of a specific era and geographical location, Roy's sociopolitical ideas remain meaningful even today, because they continue to inspire human beings to undertake tasks for the common well-being.

In his *Charitrapuja* (worshipping of characters that helped Tagore become what he became), Tagore included his father Debendranath Tagore, also known as Maharshi, who, being enamoured of Ram Mohan Roy's wisdom and erudition, paved the way for a new India by questioning what caused social alienation among Indians. Tagore, being the youngest son of Debendranath, was considered by his father to be a true heir of his sociopolitical ideas which gradually blossomed in him over the years. In fact, what became Visva-Bharati in 1921 as a centre for learning was an expansion of the idea that Debendranath put forward with the foundation of Brahma Vidyalaya (Brahma school) in Santiniketan in 1888. Maharshi stood out, claimed Tagore, for his seminal contribution to social well-being for all, regardless of class, caste and ethnicity. In three ways, he made his presence felt, which were a source of the poet's intellectual empowerment. First, despite being born in a wealthy family, Debendranath's vision was never clouded by the prevalent discriminatory social practices; by being immersed in the Upanishads that drew on the concern for universal

---

[13] Tagore, *Charitrapuja*, 60.

[14] Tagore, 60–1.

well-being, he never allowed himself to be restricted by narrow social ends. The poet explained why his father was different by saying that

> just like the one who was expected to eat last in feast, organized by him, Maharshi also felt that the wealth that he inherited [because of the accident of birth] does not belong to him alone; the entire society has a claim over this, and hence, he nurtured the idea that the wealth needed to be utilized for ensuring common well-being.[15]

The idea appears to have had its roots in the Upanishadic dictum of the world being a family of relatives (*vasudhaiva kutumbakam*) in the Maha Upanishad. Linked with this is the second reason which, by highlighting Maharshi's concern for all, irrespective of religion and caste, instilled in Tagore's mind the importance of togetherness for common welfare. Appreciating his father's endeavour for making people sensitive to humanism, Tagore thus wrote: 'my father provided us with values which were neither vitiated by opulence nor by the feeling of being deprived of the basic comfort for living'.[16] As a result, he further added, 'those who were poor were always welcome in their house with equal respect and care',[17] which means that the members of the family instinctively imbibed the spirit of humanism which Maharshi transmitted to his children and those who came in contact with him. Finally, that Tagore and his siblings were capable of raising their voice against injustice of any kind was possible because their father generated an atmosphere of fearlessness in the family. No restrictions were imposed, and everybody was allowed to speak freely. As Tagore stated, Debendranath believed in the free flow of ideas, which was the reason why he never privileged one opinion; believing in the conceptualization that let the hundred flowers blossomed, he also hated the hegemony of one ideological priority. Despite not being in agreement with his youngest son on various issues, Debendranath, recalled Tagore, 'never imposed his opinion on him; instead his openness instilled in the poet the urge of being open to opinions even if that

---

[15] Tagore, 76.

[16] Tagore, 76.

[17] Tagore, 77.

were contrarian in nature'.[18] Because he maintained his catholicity of views since he believed in them, he equally respected others clinging to their respective points of view, which was axiomatic since, as Tagore explained, 'a guru who holds rigid opinions is unable to generate curiosity in his pupils which was the only means of generating new ideas; the effort was always discouraged for it meant defiance to the teacher'.[19] Contrarily, Maharshi always felt that without being provoked to tread an unknown path, 'the human desire for seeking new ideas and paths for realizing truth is bound to disappear which makes us a lifeless machine and we cease to be human beings'.[20] Probably this was the reason which prevented Maharshi from institutionalizing the Brahmo Samaj as an organized effort to pursue a specific path for human salvation. It did not seem to be striking to him, presumably because 'in an institutionalized organization, the primary objective of serving humanity gradually loses its importance because what matters now was how to sustain and also expand its acceptability by propagating the view that this was the only path for salvation'.[21] Maharshi did not follow what others normally did; instead, he was benevolent in sharing with everyone what he earned through his lifelong service to humanity. Fundamental here was Tagore's own confession of how he enriched himself as a human being by imbibing the spirit which Maharshi internalized by being a curious student who learnt a lot from the Upanishads and also by way of being involved in various kinds of activities contributing to universal benefits.

A careful reading of Tagore's own text appreciating the ideas represented by Vidyasagar, Ram Mohan and Debendranath reveals that his sociopolitical ideas had an indelible imprint of what he learnt from them. What was common to all of them was their concern for all, regardless of socio-economic chasms. To attain this, Vidyasagar devoted his energy to removing the social ban on widow remarriage, Ram Mohan eradicated the most inhuman Sati practice and

---

[18] Tagore, 90.
[19] Tagore, 90.
[20] Tagore, 80.
[21] Tagore, 80.

Debendranath, by recognizing everyone as part of the same family, laid down the foundation of a society free from prejudices. While Vidyasagar and Ram Mohan generated ideas for enlightenment in a society that preferred to be guided by age-old superstitious beliefs and customs, Maharshi established a platform to experiment with these new-found ways of conceptualizing interpersonal relationships drawn on being appreciative of one another in a milieu in which segregation of people on the basis of their respective socio-economic locations was not socially stigmatized.

UNFOLDING OF A NEW GENRE OF THOUGHTS

Rabindranath Tagore is a poet with a universal message for common well-being. He was not associated with the mainstream nationalist campaign for freedom, like Gandhi and his other compatriots were, but was integrally connected with it as one who can be said to have directionally guided the nationalist thinking. In other words, he was never part of the street-fighting that usually is meant when one gets involved in movements for freedom; Tagore was integral to the nationalist voice, which he articulates in his creative writings, and also evolved a new means of serving the nation by being involved in activities for self-empowerment and self-sufficiency in terms of basic economic needs. By not being persuaded by the mainstream national-ist design, which was meant only to attain political freedom, Tagore generated a new template of sociopolitical ideas which were translated into reality by actual deeds.

This segment has two complementary components: the first part shall dwell on how Tagore evolved his ideas as he did by being dia-lectically interconnected with the prevalent socio-economic circum-stances under the colonial rule. Here, the influence of his family and friends and foes besides, of course, the ideas that he acquired on the basis of his exposure to the Western socio-philosophical predisposi-tions. Interestingly, being born in a family that was neither extremely xenophobic nor blindly imitative of the indigenous discourses of knowledge, Tagore perhaps had the best of both worlds. Dwarkanath Tagore, his grandfather, was a wealthy businessman who built his empire with support from the rulers, though he allowed his children to pursue their objectives without any kind of interference; this was perhaps the reason why Debendranath Tagore, his father, evolved his distinct way of life which was not exactly worldly but bordered on spiritualism. Based on his continuous interaction with the Mahatma, the second segment of this section deals with the relationships between the two great minds to comprehend the unique unfolding of Tagore's sociopolitical views and ideological preferences. The point here underlines the argument that both Tagore and Gandhi drew on each other; Gandhi's concern for humanism is largely a manifestation of his intellectual debt to Tagore. By contextualizing some of the debates that enriched the nationalist discourse, the section also highlights the point that Tagore, instead of being directly involved in the anti-British campaign, complemented the endeavour by enriching its conceptual foundation whenever it was required to be done.

As regards the first set of issues, there are two points that need attention at the outset. Being generally appreciative of the renaissance concern for purging Indian society of the archaic and also civilization-ally restrictive values, Tagore's ideas were an outcome of a dialogue between what he imbibed by being integral to the family in which he was born and raised and what he learnt from other influences. Hence, it is argued that at one level, Tagore was a product of 'Indian and Upanishadic tradition together with Western modernity, a mix that characterized the Tagore family of Calcutta'.[22] At another level, his ideas were responses to the British rule that he confronted by being a subject of the Empire. But if one examines his sociopolitical ideas, it is difficult to pigeon-hole them, presumably because of the complexities in which they were articulated. He was neither an uncritical admirer of the Empire nor one of those Indian nationalists who drew their sustenance by privileging the indigenous politico-ideological priorities as axiomatic. In other words, he provided a set of ideas which was an admixture of both indigenous and derivative sources of wisdom and knowledge that was both tempered and also clearly mediated.

---

[22] Sobhanlal Datta Gupta, 'Tagore's View of Politics and the Contemporary World,' in *The Cambridge Companion of Rabindranath Tagore*, ed. Sukanta Chaudhuri (Cambridge: Cambridge University Press, 2020), 279.

As argued above, Tagore was introduced to the Upanishads by his father, Debendranath Tagore, which helped him understand the complexity of human life in a civilizational context. Being agnostic at the beginning, he did not seem to have been persuaded by the claim that the Upanishads were of great use for human existence. In his words, despite being born in a family that drew on

> a monotheistic religion based upon the philosophy of the Upanishad, ... my mind at first remained coldly aloof, absolutely uninfluenced by any religion whatsoever. It was through an idiosyncrasy of my temperament that I refused to accept any religious teaching merely because people in my surroundings believed it to be true. I could not persuade myself to imagine that I had a religion because everybody whom I might trust believed it to be true.[23]

The above argument that Tagore made is useful to understand how he evolved his ideas, which were not just imitative but ones that he held once he was convinced that they were worth emulating. It is therefore conceptually inhibiting to assume that Tagore readily accepted whatever he received; instead, as the above argument shows, he endorsed those ideas which, he felt, were sources of his intellectual enrichment. By making the above argument, he however proved his point that his ideas were not exactly derivative but mediated outcomes in a specific context. It was possible for him since he was 'brought up in an atmosphere of freedom—freedom from the dominance of any creed that had its sanction in the definite authority of some scripture, or in the teaching of some organized body of worshipper'.[24] Gradually, however, he changed his stance. At the age of 18, as he reminisced, he found out how self-fulfilling 'the spiritual unity with the Supreme Being' could be. He thus felt 'as if some ancient mist had in a moment lifted from my sight, and the morning light on the face of the world revealed an inner radiance of joy [which left] ... in his memory a direct message of spiritual reality'.[25] It was 'a realization [that] was difficult

[23] Rabindranath Tagore, *The Religion of Man* (the Hibbert Lecture for 1930) (Kolkata: Visva-Bharati, 2015) (reprint), 53–4.

[24] Tagore, 54.

[25] Tagore, 55.

to articulate in words' but one that led to enormous 'joy and gladness [which] is the one criterion of truth, and we know when we have touched Truth by the music it gives, by the joy of greeting it sends forth to the truth in us'.[26] Basic here was the point that Tagore made to support the contention that unless one was happy internally, there was hardly any means to derive happiness from any of the external sources of worldly satisfaction. This was the only way, he argued further, stating 'we touch the infinite reality immediately within us only when perceive the pure truth of love or goodness, not through the explanations of theologians, not through the erudite discussion of ethical doctrines'.[27] Hence, Tagore embraced ideas which were not exactly transmitted from exogenous sources but those which gave him joy and happiness. This means that one needs to be sensitive to the processes that contributed to his ideas which he accepted as his once they enabled him to experience joy and gladness.

For a clear understanding of how he evolved those distinctive sociopolitical ideas which were neither exactly Western nor exclusively drawn on the eastern (sic) sources, but ones that were uniquely textured and persuasively argued, one needs to go for a contextual study of his view points. While they were clearly mediated, they had clear contextual roots. It was made clear by the poet himself when he said that he was born in 'a great epoch in the history of Bengal'.[28] There were three moments that he referred to while being appreciative of the age in which he was raised. One of these, the religious, was introduced by 'a very great-hearted man of gigantic intelligence, Raja Ram Mohan Roy'. It was 'revolutionary', for he devoted his energy to 'reopen the channel of spiritual life which had been obstructed for many years by the sands and debris of creeds that were formal and materialistic, fixed in external practices lacking spiritual significance'.[29] Despite being revolutionary in his approach to life, Roy had initial hurdles,

---

[26] Tagore, 62.

[27] Tagore, 62.

[28] Rabindranath Tagore, 'The Religion of an Artist,' in *Boundless Sky*, ed. Rabindranath Tagore (Kolkata: Visva-Bharati, 2008) (reprint), 205.

[29] Tagore, 205.

since it was a threat to the well-entrenched value systems supportive of equally retrogressive social·practices. Tagore had reasons to be extremely enthusiastic, since his father, Maharshi, had also imbibed those revolutionary ideas that Ram Mohan bequeathed. As a result, his family had to suffer 'ostracism and braved social indignities'. What is interesting to note here is the fact that Roy's revolutionary ideas were neither West-driven nor a derivative of exogenous sources but had drawn on Upanishadic ideals; for Tagore, it was a rediscovery of India's socio-cultural roots in our ancient texts, an endeavour, articulated in 'an atmosphere of the advent of [those] ideals [which] ... at the same time were old, older than all the things of which that age was proud'.[30] Implied here is the point that neither Ram Mohan nor Debendranath upheld any of the ideals which were new but were integral to India's rise as a civilization; these were the ideals that made India one of the forerunners in pursuing goals for human betterment in circumstances in which they receded in importance. The second movement was captured by the efforts that Bankimchandra Chatterjee (1838–1894)[31] undertook to reorient Bangla as a language by lifting it out of 'the abyss of death' and according a new prose style; it was the completion of a process that had started with Vidyasagar in a not-so-startling way. According to Tagore, Chatterjee was 'the pioneer in the literary revolution that Bengal witnessed with the publication of novels by him'.[32] His effort was uncritically appreciated by the poet when he said that being brave, Bankim 'lifted the dead weight of ponderous forms from our language and with a touch of his magic wand aroused our literature from her age-long sleep'.[33] Insofar as Tagore was concerned, it was a 'new dawn for Bangla' which was not only inspirational to new authors but also created an independent space for the language which, so far, had remained lifeless by excessive borrowing and also being imitative of the style that scholars and authors of other languages, especially

---

[30] Tagore, 205.

[31] Bankimchandra Chatterjee (1838–1894) was one of the leading literary figures of Bengalee language, who carved a distinct space for himself by relieving Bangla of its verse-oriented old style; in its place, he pioneered a new style of prose that gained momentum with the writings of other authors, including Rabindranath Tagore.

[32] Tagore, 'The Religion of an Artist,' 205.

[33] Tagore, 206.

Sanskrit, had evolved; it was, for the bard, a servility that was clearly visible in the pre-Bankim era writings. With the appearance of Bankim, Bangla received a boost, which was hailed by Tagore as having ushered in a new era in our literary style. The third moment was a moment of political awakening which gave

> voice to the mind of our people trying to assert their own personality [which was not allowed to naturally flourish due to] the humiliation constantly heaped upon [Indians] by people who are not oriental, and who had ... the habit of sharply dividing the human world into and the bad according to the hemispheres to which they belong.[34]

Here, Tagore captured the impact of colonial rule, which, by segregating us from them, created a boundary on the basis of racial differences; justifying the assessment that Indians were inferior to the whites, the British rule had a pernicious impact on Indians as a distinct socio-cultural community. What was most disappointing was also the nurturing of this servile mindset by the Indians themselves presumably, to curry favour with the colonial masters. Tagore was very blunt when he criticized such an endeavour by saying that

> this contemptuous spirit of separatedness (sic) was perpetually hurting us and causing great damage to our own world of culture [by generating] in our young men a distrust of all things that had come to them as inheritance from their past. The old Indian pictures and other works of art were [thus] laughed at by our students in imitation of the laughter of their European schoolmasters of that age philistinism.[35]

The idea is crystal clear. The colonial design was also responsible for Indians becoming servile in thoughts, which was articulated in despising all those which were indigenous. Tagore attributed the consolidation of this trend to the coercive capability of the alien authority which created conditions in which Indians preferred to imbibe the spirit that they were instructed to by various socio-cultural and political means. It was, as the poet articulated, 'the result of the hypnotism exercised upon the minds of the younger generation by people who were loud of

[34] Tagore, 206.
[35] Tagore, 206.

voice and strong of arm'.[36] In response to an engineered endeavour by the colonizers, the nationalist movement worked at two levels: at the pure political level, the nationalists organized themselves to fight the battle by mobilizing people around their ideological priorities; at the socio-cultural level, they also embarked on a series of activities to generate a voice challenging the cultural arrogance of the British that was reflected when the British rulers disdainfully rejected anything Indian or oriental. Inspired to take on the ideologues of colonialism, Tagore took a lead in generating zeal for socio-cultural independence, which was possible once 'we build our own world with our own thoughts and energy of mind'.[37] The task was made easier for Tagore since he belonged to a family which never drew a line of separation between we and they, which means that instead of being narrowly nationalistic, he was encouraged to appreciate the values of being global, with simultaneous admiration for one's own distinctive socio-cultural traits. Furthermore, it was possible because the Tagore family, by being ostracized 'because of [its] heterodox opinions about religion',[38] had the freedom of staying away from the dominant religious trends that appeared to have restricted the liberty of choice for most of those who continued to remain committed to orthodox Hinduism. The restrictions became all-pervasive with Maharshi's decision to form Brahmo Samaj as a challenge to Hindu orthodoxy. As Tagore mentioned, 'my countrymen in Bengal thought him almost as bad as a Christian, if not worse. So, we were completely ostracized, which probably saved me from another disaster, that of imitating our own past which was not always worth-imitating'.[39] The ostracism that the Tagore family was subjected to was a boon in disguise, as the poet characterized. According to him, as a result of ostracism,

> my family had to live its own life, which led me from my young days to seek guidance for my own self expression in my own inner standard of judgment. The medium of expression doubtless was my mother tongue. But

---

[36] Tagore, 207.

[37] Tagore, 207.

[38] Tagore, 207.

[39] Tagore, 211.

the language which belonged to the people had to be modulated according to the urge which I as an individual had.[40]

Instead of restricting his conceptual universe to the known philosophical terrain, ostracism gave him the freedom to tread an unknown path which, the poet felt, enabled him to explore many areas of human activities had be been taught to appreciate only the age-old values of Hindu orthodoxy just like any other family. He was thus fortunate for being born in a family in which the free flow of ideas, regardless of their socio-cultural roots, was always encouraged. Here lay the reason why Tagore had the courage to revolt against orthodox Hinduism and readily accepted those values which were clearly humanitarian and useful for regenerating faith in universal humanism. Hence, he most passionately exhorted that

> the vision of Paradise is to be seen in the sunlight and the green of earth, in the beauty of the human face and wealth of human life even in objects that are seemingly insignificant and unprepossessing. Everywhere in this earth the spirit of Paradise is awake and sending forth its voice. It reaches our inner ear without our knowing it. It tunes our harp of life which sends our aspiration in music beyond the finite, not only in prayers and hopes, but also in temples which flames of fire in stone, in pictures which dreams made everlasting, in the dance which is ecstatic meditation in the still centre of movement.[41]

The idea that resonates here encapsulates Tagore's concern for universal humanism, which he appears to have inherited from his family, of which Maharshi was one of the leading lights. A spiritualist to the core, but grounded in one's worldly existence, Tagore creatively blended many voices to evolve his own. As will be seen in Chapter 2, the poet was very critical of narrow nationalist preferences, since they ran counter to his firm belief in universal humanism. Averse to the idea of nation, as it drew on partisan aims, Tagore developed a scathing critique of nation, nationalism and national identity, since they were means for

[40] Tagore, 207.
[41] Tagore, 230.

the realization of a single collective purpose to which all social relations were subordinated and around which all its members were mobilized; the collective purpose could be world domination, war, maximization of wealth for a nationalist minority, racial purity or some other.[42]

Being critical of collective selfishness and exclusiveness and also the desire of subordinating the entire society to a single goal, Tagore carved an independent space in India's political discourse. Under no circumstances was he persuaded to sacrifice his unconditional faith in universal humanism, which, of course, does not mean that he was not for India's political freedom. In his perception, political freedom, by itself, was not enough to make human beings' shackles free; what was required was a transformation of the mindset deriving pleasure out of happiness in all sociopolitical and economic circumstances. It was persuasively argued when the bard mentioned that

> the history of man is the history of the building up of a human universe, as has been proved by the fact that everything great in human activity inevitably belongs to humanity. And we may be sure that all our religious experiences and expressions are building up from the depth of the ages one great continent of religions on which man's soul is to win its prosperity through the universal commerce of spiritual life.[43]

Disenchanted with the narrow desire of those seeking to realize their partisan goals at the cost of humanity, Tagore evolved, through his innovative design of sociopolitical discourses, a model in which universal human interests were always privileged, because he believed that

> when organized national selfishness, racial antipathy and commercial self-seeking begin to display their ugly deformities in all their nakedness, then comes the time to know that his salvation is not in political organizations and extended trade relations, not in any mechanical rearrangement

---

[42] Bhikhu Parekh, *Debating India: Essays on Indian Political Discourse* (New Delhi: Oxford University Press, 2015). 69.

[43] Rabindranath Tagore's speech on the Brahmo Samaj centenary, reproduced in Nityapriya Ghosh, ed., *The English Writings of Rabindranath Tagore*, Vol. 4 (New Delhi: Sahitya Akademi, 748).

of social system, but in a deeper transformation of life, in the liberation of consciousness in love, in the realization of God in man.[44]

What is questioned here is the narrow vision justifying the self-seeking motives of those who privileged their partisan design even at the cost of humanity. A visionary who never allowed himself to be blinded by the narrow nationalist concerns, Tagore's sociopolitical ideas were also an effective challenge to the consolidation of sectarianism, which, by upholding narrow partisan interests, was divisive and had an adverse impact on attempts at building amity among human beings. It was most unambiguously articulated when the poet mentioned that being clearly materialistic, sectarianism

> tries to build its tower of triumph with its numerical strength, temporal power and external observances. It breeds in the minds of its members a jealous sense of separateness that gives rise to conflicts more deadly than conflicts of worldly interests. It is a worse enemy of the truth of religion than atheism, for sectarianism proudly appropriates as its own share the best portion of the homage that we bring to our God.[45]

There are two significant inputs that Tagore appears to have taken into account while developing his distinct sociopolitical discourses through his creative writings. On the one hand, being firmly committed to universal humanism, he held on to this as one of the main pillars of his conceptualization. Under no circumstances, he was agreeable, on the other, to the contention that national freedom was essential to India's rise as collective unit but not necessary for the cementing bonhomie among human beings cutting across geographical boundaries. For him, *swaraj* was a stepping stone for realizing the potential that human beings possessed for ensuring common well-being, which he elaborated by saying that 'the history of man's progress is the history of the extension of Swaraj through the dominance of self-thinking,

[44] Rabindranath Tagore, 'Race Conflict' in *Boundless Sky*, ed. Rabindranath Tagore (Kolkata: Visva-Bharati, 2008) (reprint), 348–9.

[45] Rabindranath Tagore's speech on the Brahmo Samaj centenary, reproduced in Ghosh, *The English Writings of Rabindranath Tagore*, 747.

self-confidence and self-respect'.[46] It was therefore not surprising that he insisted that being an engine for bringing people together,

> Swaraj for the whole of India would begin in the village where the people have formed themselves into a united community set on improving its health and education, its economic life, and its amusement no less. That Swaraj would advance by its own power, its propulsion inherent int the organic process of its own living growth, and not in the mechanical rotation of the spinning wheel.[47]

Historically speaking, and also as the above discussion shows, before Gandhi arrived on the scene, it was Tagore who evolved a definite sociopolitical discourse which took into account his primary concern for political freedom as just a stepping stone towards a world based on his exalted mission for realizing universal humanism. Nonetheless, the inputs that the poet received from his compatriot, Gandhi, were useful to comprehend nationalism in its most complex form and manifestation. In other words, to understand Tagore's distinct sociopolitical discourses in the context of India's campaign for political freedom that Gandhi had led, the Gandhi–Tagore dialogical interactions serve a useful purpose. They were both complementary to each other and also differed radically on occasions, presumably because they held contrasting politico-ideological priorities. The differences between them are not just a matter of interpretation but are based on completely incompatible *Weltanschauungs* or world views. Since both of them contributed immensely to the conceptualization of India's nationhood, it behoves one to engage with one of the most celebrated exchanges in the recent past, which took place between a poet and a saint.

TAGORE AND GANDHI

Tagore's critiques were based on a certain reading of Indian civilization and actual political processes that unfolded in the context of the struggle against imperialism. Tagore was in a constant dialogue with the

[46] Tagore, Ram Mohan 576.

[47] Rabindranath Tagore, 'The Striving for Swaraj,' in *Towards Universal Man*, ed. Rabindranath Tagore (Bombay: Asia Publishing House, 1962) (reprint), 284.

Mahatma. Not only did they interact regularly on various philosophical issues pertaining to India as a civilization—either through personal correspondence or through the media—but they also exchanged views on the mundane political agenda of the Indian National Congress. As a poet who was not directly involved in the nationalist agitation, Tagore sought to articulate the unexpressed concerns of Indian public consciousness. Basic to Tagore's sociopolitical discourses was his unconditional faith in humanity, which he never sacrificed for 'small' political gains. In a letter to C. F. Andrews, he thus wrote:

> I refuse to waste my manhood in the lighting the fire of anger and spreading it from house to house. It is not that I do not feel anger in my heart for injustice and insult heaped upon my motherland. But this anger of mine should be turned into the fire of love for lighting the lamp of worship to be dedicated through my country to my God. It would be insult to my humanity if I use the sacred energy of my moral indignation for the purpose of spreading a blind passion all over my country.[48]

A confident Tagore set out with his philosophical discourses through which he defended his concern for universal humanism, which he never lost sight of. The idea might have been politically restrictive, since it privileged the concern for humanity over the desire for political freedom. Tagore was persuaded to believe that due to our excessive interests in liberation from the British rule, which Gandhi always upheld, the ultimate goal of creating a world in which humanity prevailed was likely to be sacrificed. It was made clear in his correspondence with Gandhi, when he mentioned that

> power in all forms is irrational, it is like the horse that drags the carriage blindfolded. The moral element in it is only represented in the man who drives the horse. Passive resistance [that Gandhi launched] is a force which is not necessarily moral in itself; it can be used against truth as well as for it.[49]

---

[48] Tagore to Andrews, 18 September 1920, reproduced in Uma Dasgupta (edited and introduced), *Friendship of 'Largeness and Freedom': Andrews, Tagore and Gandhi: An Epistolary Account, 1912–1940* (New Delhi: Oxford University Press, 2018), 223.

[49] Tagore to Gandhi, 12 April 1919, reproduced in Dasgupta, 199.

Being critical of passive resistance, since it was drawn on the enmity of Indians against the rulers, which was a clear blot on his heartfelt concern, Tagore further argued that 'India's opportunity for winning political freedom will come to her when she can prove that she is morally superior to people who rule her by their right of conquest'.[50] His message was unambiguous: under no circumstances was humanity allowed to be sacrificed, since it meant a clear deviation from his fundamental concern. It was pursued further in his letter to C. F. Andrews where he exhorted that 'humanity is large, rich and many-sided, ... and sacrifice [of humanity] ... for narrow political gain ... is a cultivation of callousness which is a form of sacrilege'.[51] Critical of the endeavour for attainment of independence from the British rule, the poet further argued that 'emancipation of human nature [involves] more fulness of life and not asceticism [because] [d]eadness of life in all forms gives rise to impunities—by enfeebling our reason, narrowing our vision, creating fanaticism through forcing our willpower into abnormal channels'.[52] The argument is a reinforcement of the point of view that Tagore upheld despite having known that it was likely to upset Gandhi, who undertook a serious campaign for political freedom though he appreciated the latter for his steadfast campaign against all kinds of artificially created slavery. Here, Tagore, being conscious of the historical processes, attributed

> the assertion of superiority of one section of mankind at the expense of another [to] ... the inhuman desire at building the stronghold of pride and superiority upon the slavish humiliation of others [that] ... obstructs us at every step of our forward march; those whom we humiliate gradually push us down the precipice of degradation.[53]

Here, Tagore was in agreement with Gandhi because the Mahatma had also the same goal, namely eradication of social prejudices segregating one section of the demography from the rest. Characterizing the well-entrenched socio-economic values supportive of a supremacist

[50] Tagore to Gandhi, 200.

[51] Tagore to C. F. Andrews, 14 July 1921, reproduced in Dasgupta, 293.

[52] Tagore to C. F. Andrews, 293.

[53] Tagore on Gandhi's fast, 10 June 1933, reproduced in Dasgupta, 423.

mindset, Tagore admired Gandhi because he raised his voice against 'the brand of ignominy by which we have deprived from elemental human pride a section of fell-country man',[54] since he understood that 'the danger of this division' was enormous and caused 'a permanent damage to our endeavour for social transformation'.[55] So, as far as social priorities were concerned, they held compatible views; the division of opinions surfaced once Tagore expressed his strong disagreement with the Mahatma when the latter privileged political freedom over social transformation for he believed that social transformation was to follow once the British left India. Being vocal in the public domain, Tagore thus said:

> I can no longer hide it from myself that we are radically different in our apprehension and pursuit of truth [which was appreciated] ... by his friends in Europe who are [his] real kindred and whose sympathy will act as a true restorative in my present state of weariness.[56]

There thus existed fundamental differences between Tagore and Gandhi: the former considered the concern for universal humanism as non-negotiable, since mere political freedom which Gandhi held as top priority was not, at all, a necessary condition for the former. The argument was made persuasively by the poet in all his public statements, which also provoked Gandhi's strong critique, as will be shown later. Nonetheless, the Gandhi–Tagore interaction provides us with significant input to defend an argument suggesting that in their passion for evolving a model for human salvation, they explored many aspects of human existences which would not have received adequate attention without their interventions.

BUILDING AND UNFOLDING OF THE ARGUMENT

Tagore was perhaps the first to emphatically argue against the contention that identity in the subcontinent was unidimensional. Challenging

[54] Tagore on Gandhi's fast, 10 June 1933, reproduced in Dasgupta, 423.

[55] Tagore on Gandhi's fast, 423.

[56] Tagore to C. F. Andrews, 23 September 1925, reproduced in Dasgupta, 279.

the concept of 'nation', as it undermines the multi-layered Indian identity, Tagore reminds us of the combined role of the 'little' and 'great' traditions in shaping what he loosely defines as the Indian nation.[57] India's diversity, Tagore felt, was her 'nature [and] you can never coerce nature into your narrow limits of convenience without paying one day very dearly for it'.[58] Not only 'have religious beliefs cut up society into warring sections . . . social antagonisms [between the Hindus and Muslims] have set up impassable barriers every miles - barriers which are guarded night and day by forces wearing the badge of religion'.[59] For Tagore, the gulf between the communities was largely due to 'the cultural forces', released by British colonialism that 'fractured the personality of every sensitive exposed Indian and set up the West as a crucial vector within the Indian self'.[60] As India's social system got distorted, '[l]ife departed', argued Tagore, 'from her social system and in its place she is worshipping with all ceremony the magnificent cage of countless compartments that she has manufactured'.[61] Interrogating the 'totalizing' dimension of the nationalist project—where a single entity, called nation, always prevails over other forms of identity—Tagore sought to provide the alternative to an 'essentialist' invocation of identity in the shape of a nation. According to him, in articulating the civilizational identity of India, the importance of underlying cognitive and ethical claims, which are invariably lodged in and emanate from contradictory social locations, could never be undermined. So, the European modular form of nation was

---

[57] With a remarkable clarity of vision, Rabindranath Tagore succinctly wrote about his views on nation in a rather small piece, entitled *Nation Ki* (Bengalee). During his lecture tour in America in 1916–1917, he elaborated some of these points, including his views on nationalism in India. See *Nationalism*, Rupa, Delhi, 1994 (reprint of the collection, originally published in 1917), 77–99.

[58] Rabindranath Tagore, *Nationalism* (Delhi: Rupa, 1994) (reprint of the collection, originally published in 1917), 89.

[59] Rabindranath Tagore to Amiya Chakraborty, no date, in Sabyasachi Bhattacharyya (compiled and edited), *The Mahatma and the Poet: Letters and Debates Between Gandhi and Tagore, 1915–1941* (New Delhi: National Book Trust, 1997), 172.

[60] Ashis Nandy, *The Illegitimacy of Nationalism* (Delhi: Oxford University Press, 1994), 89.

[61] Tagore, *Nationalism*, 90.

conceptually futile and politically inapplicable, presumably because India's civilizational identity was not singular but multiple and thus difficult to capture on a single axis.

Gandhi held identical views. Like Tagore, he rarely used the term 'nation' in the sense Jinnah referred to it. Yet, Gandhi failed to halt the historical processes whereby Indian Muslims soon became a nation and bargained successfully for a separate Muslim state. Jinnah's role was equally significant. In the penultimate year of the transfer of power, the Jinnah-led Muslim League secured parity with the Congress, and in the 1946 Shimla Conference, the League and Congress representation was equated.[62] What came in the form of the 1940 Lahore Resolution became feasible, and Jinnah's appeal to 'unsettle the settled notions ... of Muslims being a minority [that] had been around for so long'[63] was finally translated into reality. So, not only did the *Quaid-i-Azam* succeed in dramatically altering the role of Muslims in the overall constitutional settlement on the eve of the Great Divide, he also transformed the Muslim community into a nation[64] by ascertaining 'territorial sovereignty to a heterogeneous community turned homogeneous nation'.[65] The Muslim community for Jinnah was, therefore, not 'an abstract historical-political entity . . . but a

---

[62] The Congress dismissed Jinnah's demand for parity because 'in numerical terms this meant the equation of minority with majority which was both absurd and politically impossible'. To this, Jinnah retorted that 'the debate was not about numbers nor even about communities but about Nations. Nations were equal irrespective of the size'. For details of Jinnah's argument, see Diana Mansergh, ed., *Independence Years: The Selected Indian and Commonwealth Papers of Nicholas Mansergh* (Delhi: Oxford University Press, 1999), 227–30.

[63] Jinnah's presidential address in the 1940 Lahore session of the All India Muslim League. S. S. Pirzada, ed., *Foundations of Pakistan*, Vol. II, p. 337.

[64] Jinnah always insisted that 'there are two major nations in India. This is the root cause and essence of our troubles. When there are two major nations how can you talk of democracy which means that one nation majority will decide everything for the other nation although it may unanimous in its opposition. . . . these two nations cannot be judged by western democracy. But they should be treated as equals and attempts should be made to solve the difficulties by acknowledging this fact'. Jinnah's press statement, *The Dawn*, 1 August 1946.

[65] Ayesha Jalal, 'Nation, Reason and Religion; Punjab's Role in the Partition of India,' *Economic and Political Weekly* (8 August 1998): 2185.

separate nation with distinct interests [which] could not be treated only as a minority'.[66] The argument had substance, since the Hindus and Muslims remained in watertight compartments in terms of their socio-cultural preferences. The schism was made unbridgeable once the religious differences corresponded with those around class axis, especially in Bengal, where most of the Zamindars were Hindus while the tillers of the soil were Muslims, although it did not seem to have been so pronounced during the campaign for Pakistan in Bengal. As far as Jinnah was concerned, the common religious identity of a community was enough to justify that it required an independent space for itself for fully satisfying its socio-cultural dreams. It is true that the secession of East Pakistan in 1971, which led to the rise of Bangladesh, exposed the hollowness of the argument and Jinnah was proved otherwise, since religious commonality between the two parts of Pakistan failed to sustain the bond when the Muslims of East Pakistan were persuaded to champion their claim for an independent state.

Gandhi's opposition to the concept of nation was based on two specific arguments: first, he put forward a contextual argument by saying that the logic of creating a religion-based nation state was faulty because religion could neither be 'a stabilizing nor a unifying factor in humanity' but is 'divisive'. Hence, by seeking to gloss over the obvious diversities among the Indian Muslims for a sovereign state, Jinnah ignored the long-drawn historical processes in the community formations. For Gandhi, nation was hardly a criterion to conceptualize the complex and deeply heterogeneous communities in the subcontinent regardless of religion. Couched in a humanitarian fashion, the second argument dwells on the devastating consequences of conceptualizing Hindus and Muslims as separate nations. Holding politics responsible for the Hindu–Muslim schism, Gandhi pledged to 'rescue people from this quagmire and make them work on solid ground where people are people. [Therefore his] appeal [was] not to the Muslims as Muslims nor to the Hindus as Hindus, but to ordinary human beings who [had] to keep their villages clean, build schools for their children and take

---

[66] Paul Brass, *Ethnicity and Nationalism: Theory and Comparison* (New Delhi: SAGE Publications, 1991), 94.

many other steps so that they [could] make life better'.[67] To Gandhi, nation, as a categorizing device, was perhaps the narrowest in its manifestation, ignoring the inherent diversities of the communities. Conceptually non-viable and practically inappropriate, the application of nation as a category weakened the anti-British struggle, he argued, because of the clash of interests between the Hindus and Muslims once they were characterized as separate nations.

Being pragmatists par excellence, both Gandhi and Tagore drew our attention to the sources of the division that was an impediment for India's rise as a collective multitude. The divisive character of India around the axes of caste and religion was a deterrent to the endeavour that both these great men had undertaken. The prevalence of untouchability was a social infirmity that was allowed to continue and flourish as it was protective of the existing social inequities. Tagore thus rightly pointed out that it was not only an insult to us as Indians but also detrimental to the formation and also consolidation of an associative bond involving people with contrasting socio-economic and political priorities. It had dangerous outcomes, since 'the [well-entrenched] social inequities visible in our inter-personal relationships have our time-honoured loyalty making it difficult for us to uproot them'.[68] Here, Tagore put forward a scathing critique of the caste system which was devised to put one section of the population under permanent subjugation. 'The indignity with which we treat them', he argued further, 'grows into an intolerable burden to the whole country [which amounts to the fact that] … we insult our own humanity by insulting Man where he is helpless or where he is not of our kin'.[69] Fundamental here is a conceptual point that the poet offered to enable us to understand that caste atrocities needed to be understood in a socially recognized template which remained integral

---

[67] N. K. Bose and P. H. Patwardhan, *Gandhi in Indian Politics* (Bombay: Asian Publishing House, 1967), 7.

[68] Rabindranath Tagore's address to the students of Santiniketan and Sriniketan, 20 September 1932, reproduced in Das, *The English Writings of Rabindranath Tagore*, 327.

[69] Rabindranath Tagore's address to the students of Santiniketan and Sriniketan, 20 September 1932, reproduced in Das, 326.

to prevalent interpersonal relationships. It was accepted as axiomatic, presumably because the caste system served useful socio-economic purposes for one segment of the population at the cost of the rest. In a similar vein, Tagore and Gandhi expressed their anguish when they confronted the Hindu–Muslim schism. Vehemently opposed to religious chasms separating one community from another, they appeared to have endorsed the same argument to substantiate their contention for communal togetherness for the higher cause of serving humanity. But their earnest desire remained unrealized, presumably because of the well-entrenched prejudices separating the Hindu brethren from their Muslim counterparts. As Tagore most persuasively explained,

> the real difficulty is for Hindus and Moslems to give up their respective prejudices which keep them apart [because] ... to the Hind, the Mussalman is impure: for the Mussalman, the Hindu is a kafir [which did not allow them] to join hands together for the battle for Swaraj; it means that the habit of mind which religious injunctions have ingrained in us constitutes the age-old fortress which [prevents] us from coming together as one for a common cause.[70]

The honeymoon was short-lived, because soon Gandhi and Tagore came out sharply against each other once the 1919–1921 Non-Cooperation Movement was inaugurated. Gandhi's idea of burning foreign fabric, for instance, provoked much unease with Tagore, who wondered if Gandhi was not encouraging the flames of narrow nationalism and xenophobia. As he argued,

> the clothes to be burnt are not mine, but belong to those who most sorely need them. If those who are going naked should have given us the mandate to burn, it would, at least, have been a case of self-immolation and the crime of incendiarism would not lie at our door. But how can we expiate the sin of the forcible destruction pf clothes which might have gone to women whose nakedness is actually keeping them prisoners unable to stir out of the privacy of their homes?[71]

---

[70] Rabindranath Tagore, 'Striving for Swaraj,' reproduced in Ghosh, *The English Writings of Rabindranath Tagore*, 359.

[71] Rabindranath Tagore, 'The Call of Truth,' reproduced in Bhattacharya, *The Mahatma and the Poet*, 83–4.

Similarly, withdrawal from the schools and colleges never appeared to be a wise call. Tagore refused to endorse the campaign because 'the great injury and injustice which had been done to those boys who were tempted away from their career before any real provision was made, could never be made good to them'. He was not persuaded to believe that Western education 'injured' the young minds and should be altogether rejected. The root of the misconception lay elsewhere. As Tagore pointed out,

> what has caused the mischief is the fact that for a long time we been out of touch with our own culture and therefore the Western culture has not found its prospective in our life very often found a wrong prospective giving our mental eye a squint.[72]

Tagore adopted a nuanced argument *vis-à-vis* the Non-Cooperation Movement, which was a relatively successful political campaign involving a wider section of the population across the length and breadth of India.

Tagore's critique of the aim of the Non-Cooperation Movement drew on his own perception of the 'constructive work' that he experimented with during the 1905–1908 Swadeshi Movement in Bengal. He was opposed to coercion, because his experience of the Swadeshi mobilization had shown its adverse consequences. When the movement was at its zenith, Tagore denounced its reliance on coercion and the alienating impact it had on the masses it claimed to enthuse and activate. His critique of the non-cooperation techniques followed the same logic. The pervasive use of social boycott and other forms of coercion was therefore 'regarded by him as evidence of the Swadeshi activist's failure to persuade people to their cause'.[73] He thus argued that 'we have not been patient enough to work our way gradually towards winning popular consent'.[74] This was at the root of the nationalist failure to unite all Indians in 'a grand patriotic

---

[72] Rabindranath Tagore, 'Reflections on Non-cooperation and Cooperation, *Modern Review*, May 1921—reproduced in Bhattacharya, 58, 62.

[73] Ranajit Guha, *Dominance Without Hegemony: History and Power in Colonial India* (Delhi: Oxford University Press, 1998), 121.

[74] Guha, 121.

mobilization'. The debate between Gandhi and Tagore brought out the contrasting perspectives on this subject that had, as shown, its roots in the Swadeshi Movement as well. While Gandhi was confident that the non-cooperation agenda was most appropriate sociopolitically, Tagore expressed his doubts on the ground that the 'narrow political aim' of the movement was likely to jeopardize its wider goal and objectives. The debate remained inconclusive but raised certain major questions on Gandhi's social and political ideas that appeared to have decisively influenced Indian minds.[75]

Just like the debate over the strategy of non-cooperation, the exchange of views between Gandhi and the poet on *charkha* and *khaddar* was reminiscent of different perspectives in which they were conceptualized. Tagore was not persuaded, let alone impressed, by the campaign for *charkha*. As he admitted,

> the depths of my mind have not been moved by the charkha agitation … for its inherent weaknesses [and he therefore apprehended] that all intense pressure of persuasion brought upon the crowd psychology is unhealthy for it [because] it will create blind faith on a very large scale in the charkha … which is liable to succumb to the lure of short cuts when pointed out by a personality about whose moral earnestness they can have no doubt.[76]

Tagore was not in agreement simply because the basic assumption behind the argument concerning the profitable employment of the surplus time of cultivators was flawed unless the cultivators themselves spontaneously accepted *charkha*, which was most unlikely, as Tagore believed, for two reasons: first, the cultivator acquired a special skill with his hands and a special bent of mind by dint of consistent application to his particular work. Hence 'to ask the cultivator to spin is to derail his mind; he may drag on with it for a while, but at the cost of disproportionate effort and therefore waste of energy'.[77] Second, if *charkha* was imposed on the cultivators who might not have the inclination, it would lose its significance and effectiveness.

---

[75] Tagore, 'The Call of Truth,' 79.

[76] Rabindranath Tagore, 'The Cult of Charkha,' *Modern Review*, September, 1925—reproduced in Bhattacharya, *The Mahatma and the Poet*, 101–2.

[77] Rabindranath Tagore, 'Striving for Swaraj,' 115.

In other words, the acceptance of *charkha* was not spontaneous, and hence the consequence could be devastating because, as Tagore most eloquently put,

> it would be wrong to make the cultivator either happier or richer by thrusting aside, all of a sudden, the habits of body and mind which have grown upon him through his life. ... To tell the cultivator turn the charkha instead of trying to get him to employ his whole energy in his own line of work is only a sign of weakness (sic)'. We cast the blame for being lazy on the cultivator, but the advice we give him amounts rather to a confession of the laziness of our mind.[78]

According to Tagore, spinning was not creative, for 'by turning its wheel man merely becomes an appendage of the charkha; that is to say, be but does himself what a machine might have done; he converts his living energy into a dead turning movement. [In the process] he becomes a machine, isolated, companionless'.[79] Critical of this mechanical involvement in spinning that was of no consequence for *swaraj*, Tagore suggested concrete steps which were organically linked with our life. For instance, as he perceived, the village that was self-sustained economically and supported each of its inhabitants in distress could lay the foundation of Swaraj in the true sense of the term. As he most unambiguously put, 'the village of which people come together to earn for themselves their food, their health, their education, to gain themselves the joy of so doing, shall have lighted a lamp on the way to swaraj'.[80]

Gandhi responded to the poet's critique in his rejoinders in the *Young India*. Instead of countering the arguments made by Tagore, the Mahatma, in a very cryptic way, stated his viewpoints in defending *charkha* as indispensable for India's economic well-being. In response to the charge that he insisted on spinning to the exclusion of all other activities, Gandhi argued that this was far from the truth because he never wanted 'the Poet to forsake his muse, the farmer his plough, the lawyer his brief and the doctor his lancet. [Instead], he asked

[78] Tagore, 118.

[79] Tagore, 121.

[80] Tagore, 121.

the famishing to spin for a living and the half-starved farmer to spin
during his leisure hours to supplement his slender resources'.[81] He
was not opposed to machine *per se*; what he apprehended was the
consequence of machine civilization that would make human labour
redundant, a consequence most devastating where human labour was
in abundance. As Gandhi argued,

> machine must not be allowed to displace the necessary human labour. An
> improved plough is a good thing. But if by some chance one man could
> plough up by some mechanical invention of the whole of the land of India
> and control all the agricultural produce and the millions had no other
> occupation, they would starve, and being idle, they would become dunces,
> as many have already become. ... [i]t is therefore criminal to displace
> hand labour by the introduction of power-driven spindles unless one is
> at the same time ready to give millions of farmers some other occupation
> in their homes.[82]

Charkha was a symbol of involvement with the day-to-day life of
the poor and thus a powerful device to conceptualize the reality. As
he suggested to the poet, 'if [he] spun half an hour daily his poetry
would gain in richness [for] it would then represent the poor man's
wants and woes in a more forcible manner than now'.[83] Furthermore,
Gandhi replied to the charge that *charkha* was calculated to bring
about a deathlike sameness in the nation. Hence, *charkha* to him was
'intended to realize the essential and living oneness of interest among
India's myriads'. *Charkha* was not simply an economic activity. Instead,
it brought people together by involving them in an activity that was:
(a) a source of supplementary income and (b) a device to link them
automatically with the rest of India politically.[84] Spinning, for Gandhi,

---

[81] Gandhi, 'The Poet and the Charkha,' *Young India*, 5 November 1925—reproduced
in Bhattacharya, *The Mahatma and the Poet*, 123.

[82] Gandhi, 125.

[83] Gandhi, 124.

[84] According to Gandhi, 'khadi should be linked with liberty. All the time you are
spinning, you would not think in terms of your own requirements, but in terms of
the requirements of the nation. You will say, "I want to clothe the whole nation that
is naked and I must do it non-violently". Each time you draw a thread, say to your
selves, "we are drawing the thread of swaraj". Multiply this picture million-fold and

was therefore a symbolic form of identification with the masses, while Tagore, as shown, was suspicious of any such appeal that tended to gloss over the inherent diversity among the Indian people.

Apart from these major issues, an interesting debate took place following Gandhi's characterization of the Bihar earthquake in February 1934 as 'divine chastisement' for the great sin committed against those known as *Harijans*.[85] Tagore took a serious note of this by saying: 'it has caused me painful surprise to find Mahatma Gandhi accusing those who blindly follow their own social custom of untouchability of having brought down gods' vengeance upon certain parts of Bihar'.[86] Since it came out from the most revered political leader of the country, the statement, he felt, was most devastating for its obvious impact on interpersonal relationships between *Harijans* and others. So, it should not go 'unchallenged'.[87] Tagore prefaced his critique of this superstitious view of Gandhi by saying that 'it is all the more unfortunate, because this kind of unscientific view of things is too readily accepted by a large section of our countrymen'. Underlining that 'physical catastrophes [like earthquake, etc.] have their inevitable and exclusive origin in certain combination of physical facts', he further argued that

> if we associate ethical principles with cosmic phenomena, we shall have to admit that human nature is morally superior to Providence that preaches its lessons in good behaviour in orgies of the worst behaviour possible. ... What is truly tragic about it is the fact that the kind of argument that Mahatmaji uses by exploiting an event of cosmic disturbance far better suits the psychology of his opponents. ... [He thus felt] profoundly hurt when any words from [Gandhi's] mouth may emphasize the elements of unreason ... which is a fundamental source of all the blind powers that drive us against freedom and self-respect.[88]

you have freedom knocking at your door'. M. K. Gandhi, Harijan, 28 January 1939, CWMG, Vol. 68, p. 133.

[85] Gandhi's statement, 16 February 1934.

[86] Tagore's statement to the press, *Amrita Bazar Patrika*, 24 March 1934.

[87] Tagore to the Mahatma, 28 January 1934—reproduced in Bhattacharya, *The Mahatma and the Poet*, 156.

[88] Tagore's statement to the press, *Amrita Bazar Patrika*, 24 February 1934.

Gandhi retorted against Tagore's views equally strongly. Reiterating his views on the Bihar earthquake, the Mahatma argued,

> to me, the earthquake was no caprice of God nor a result of a meeting of mere blind forces. ...Visitations like droughts, flood, earthquakes and the like, though they seem to have only physical origins, are, for me, somehow connected with man's morals. Therefore, I instinctively felt that the earthquake was visitation for the sin of untouchability. [He firmly believed] that our sins have more force to ruin the structure than any mere physical phenomenon.[89]

On this occasion, both of them held diametrically opposite views. A scientific Tagore upheld reason while a moralist Gandhi privileged reason over his faith. The point here is not to ascertain the validity of their respective arguments objectively but to dig out their appropriateness in the context of India's struggle for *swaraj* that was more than mere political freedom from imperialism. Tagore's was a reasoned argument with limited application, while Gandhi's had a wider application, given his influence over the masses. It was, as it were, a Gandhian pre-emptive measure based on his wider acceptability as a political leader. What informed Gandhi was perhaps his confidence in dissuading those practising untouchability by citing god's impending wrath. For Gandhi, the linking of the Bihar calamity with the sin of untouchability, though unscientific, was a significant step in his battle against untouchability. In other words, the statement on the Bihar earthquake acquired completely different connotations which one may not comprehend without gauging Mahatma's popularity among the masses. So, given the typical Gandhian methodology of mass mobilization for freedom, it was just another method to launch an effective and meaningful campaign against untouchability.

As evident, the difference between Tagore and Gandhi was fundamental on specific political strategies for mass mobilization. Unlike Gandhi, Tagore never appreciated the non-cooperation strategy, for instance, for its inbuilt weaknesses. Similarly, on *charkha* and *khaddar*, the poet was critical of the Mahatma since they neither provided an appropriate alternative to the masses nor adequately addressed

---

[89] Gandhi, 'superstition vs. faith', *Harijan*, 28 February 1934.

the problem of poverty. It was largely 'a hollow political slogan', as Tagore believed, given the obvious adverse political and economic consequences on the masses if forced on them. Despite the validity of Tagore's argument in a wider perspective, there is no doubt that *charkha* and *khaddar* instrumentalized the Gandhi-led mass movement; they, in other words, became symbols of mass involvement in the anti-imperial struggle. While Tagore and Gandhi differed in regard to politico-economic strategies, they held uniform views on nationalism. Given the nature of disparate Indian masses, nation, to both of them, never appeared to be a viable organizing principle. Tagore was perhaps first to confront the devastating consequences of the application of the principle of nationalism in the context of the Swadeshi Movement of 1903–1908 in Bengal, when the schism between the Hindus and Muslims was articulated in a nationalist language. The growing strength of the Muslims, defined later as a separate nation by Jinnah, the architect of Pakistan, caused a permanent fissure between these two major religious communities, which ultimately led to the 1947 partition of the subcontinent. Articulating their views in a non-nationalist language, Gandhi and Tagore, perhaps the finest products of the Indo-British cultural encounter, provided the most creative and also challenging response to the nationalist 'oneness' of the Western world.

Based on dialectical interconnection, the dialogical interaction between Tagore and Gandhi directs our attention to the complexities of the nationalist interventions, which were not exactly similar in approach. They coalesced and also differed on many counts: being true to their distinct politico-ideological priorities, they hardly hesitated to express their differences. As evident, Gandhi's principal aim was first to liberate India politically before addressing the social evils based on caste distinction and religious chasm, while Tagore, by upholding his views for universal humanism as prior to freedom from the British rule, never flinched from his commitment. Hence, for the poet,

> love of one's country was an active sentiment, not a passive and self-indulgent emotion [which] … required strong associative bonds with one's countrymen at various levels and rich communal life [creating a milieu in which] … one felt bound by the overlapping ties of common sympathies,

interests, and affections, and one's love for the country grew of and was sustained by these.[90]

As the above argument stipulates, insofar as the ultimate goal was concerned, they held compatible views; while Tagore set this aim as non-negotiable, Gandhi was of the view that with the departure of the colonizers, it was likely to be easier to accomplish the mission. With hindsight, one is persuaded to argue that Tagore had the foresight, because even 70 years after independence, neither caste division nor religious prejudices had completely disappeared, though there had grown a strong opinion challenging these artificial segregations. Here is Gandhi's contribution who, like some of his illustrious predecessors and some of his nationalist colleagues with identical politico-ideological mission, undertook campaigns against the socially-divisive communal chasm. This resulted in the consolidation of a powerful opinion and the adoption of many legislative acts for eradication of these evil practices. For instance, B. R. Ambedkar was hailed by the Mahatma for his steadfast commitment to social justice which, of course, turned the apple cart of Hindu orthodoxy upside down. Nonetheless, he supported him, which was, of course, not unconditional, as the 1932 Poona Pact demonstrated when the intransigent Gandhi was not persuaded to accept a separate electorate for the untouchables[91] as it would weaken the nationalist platform. The argument has substance and Gandhi had wider support, which is why Ambedkar succumbed to the Mahatma's dictation that resulted in his withdrawal from the campaign for treating the untouchables as a separate communal entity. Although this is an indicative example, that the Mahatma remained consistent can easily be substantiated, since he never diluted his politico-ideological priorities despite being criticized vehemently by his colleagues and detractors on many occasions. Similarly, Tagore, who was not a participant in the nationalist struggle in the sense of Gandhi being a participant, remained committed to

---

[90] Bhikhu Parekh, *Debating India: Essay on Indian Political Discourse* (New Delhi: Oxford University Press, 2015), 70–1.

[91] I have dealt with this aspect of the Gandhi–Ambedkar debate in my *The Sociopolitical Ideas of BR Ambedkar: Liberal Constitutionalism in a Creative Mould* (London and New York: Routledge, 2019), 172–6.

his wider concern for universal humanism, which was evident in his creative writings and critical essays on contemporary social, economic and political scene. Whatever might have been the consequences of the differential dialogical interactions between Tagore and Gandhi, there is no denying that bereft of this, Indian nationalist discourse would have become less innovative, if not conceptually debilitating and restrictive.

LITERARY EXPOSITION OF REFRESHING SOCIOPOLITICAL DISCOURSES

There is a misconception that Tagore was a poet who avoided making political statements highlighting his politico-ideological priorities. It is true that he was not always categorical, presumably because of the colonial context in which he was constrained, given his socio-economic lineage. Nonetheless, he, in his novels, strategically put across his views in the public domain. Besides his innumerable essays on India's politico-ideological context, he elaborated them in a very poignant way in his creative writings, reinforcing the argument that Tagore devised a unique way to articulate his distinctive politico-ideological preferences in a fashion which did not immediately attract the ruler's attention. A humanist to the core, he was persuaded to believe that mere political freedom was an essential but not a necessary condition for realizing his wider concern for humanity. Before embarking on the discussion, two qualifying points need to be made: (a) it is difficult to deal with Tagore's innumerable creative writings to critically evaluate the distinctive sociopolitical discourses that he evolved during the period he remained an active public intellectual, which justifies the exercise on the basis of a selective set of novels and plays, and (b) in view of the fact that some of his creative texts had already received attention in other chapters of the book, this section will deal with the theme with reference to some of those plays which did not, so far, receive adequate academic attention. As this section seeks to defend the argument that he was consistent insofar as his politico-ideological priorities were concerned, it is directed at those selective plays which explicitly help fathom (a) his unflinching commitment to universal humanism and (b) the complexities in which interpersonal relationships among human beings evolve contextually by always privileging human sentiments over other things.

By concentrating on the storyline of *Rakta Karabi* (1925), *Tasher Desh* (1933), *Muktadhara* (1922) and *Visarjan* (1890), this section elaborates on Tagore's concern for universal humanism. Why these plays are chosen requires an explanation. Since the objective here is to grasp how Tagore conceptualized his concern for humanity, these selective plays are curated for their analytical depth and linguistic prowess.

In the play *Rakta Karabi*, by figuratively showing how a king enslaved his subjects who behaved like machines while working in a gold mine, Tagore provided a scathing critique of human existence under chains. At the back of his mind remained the socio-economic context of colonized India where freedom for the subjects was an anathema. The storyline proceeds with the leading character, Nandini, a young girl who was surprised by the eerie silence in a city which was famous for an invisible king who forced workers to work incessantly to extract gold for him only. This is a figurative presentation of an exploitative system in which the voice challenging the king and ruthless system of governance was forcibly muzzled. The king was a decisive ruler who remained unfazed by the suffering the mine workers underwent, presumably because he was not ready to even concede that his ruthlessness reduced the workers to mere inert machines, and they were thus not expected to have a voice. The kingdom was maintained with a framework of rigid rules and regulations, where human beings were reduced to mere numbers, since in this cursed kingdom that was how they were identified. It was obvious, as the poet pursued the point, because 'the cursed town (Yaksh Puri) is a city under eclipse. The Shadow Demon, who lives in the gold caves, has eaten into it. It is not the whole itself, neither does it allow any one else to remain whole'.[92] Along with this, the city was also characterized as one that remained at a standstill because the gold mine workers hardly got a

---

[92] Rabindranath Tagore, Red Oleanders (*Rakta Karabi*), reproduced in Sisir Kumar Das 9ed.), *The English Writings of Rabindranath Tagore*, Vol. 2 (New Delhi: Sahitya Akademi, 1996), 213. It is to be noted here that Tagore translated the play in English for its wider publicity, especially among his readers in England.

reprieve from what they were chained to do day in and day out, which
the poet captured by stating:

> the calendar never records the last day. After the first day comes the second
> day, after the second, the third. There is no such as getting finished here.
> We are always digging—one yard, two yards, three yards. We go on raising
> gold nuggets—after one nugget another, then more and more and more.
> In this cursed town figures follow one another in rows and never arrive at
> any conclusion. That's why we are not men to them, but only numbers.[93]

The situation was scary and did not show any indication of being
reversed. The bard was confident that this was not going to last in
view of the lessons of history suggesting that coercive state disappeared as quickly as it rose. It was articulated when Nandini, the
principal protagonist of the play, forcefully countered the invisible
king, saying, 'you take pleasure in seeing people frightened at you.
In our village plays, Srikantha takes the part of a demon; when he
comes on the stage, he is delighted if the children are terrified. You are
like him'.[94] This is one of two dimensions of the argument; the other
dimension involves the kind of deception that the king was subjected
to, because with his continuity the system survived. Nandini again
explained this by underlining the fact that 'the people here trade on
frightening others. That's why they have put you behind a network
and dressed you fantastically [which should have been] a source of
embarrassment had the king realized that he also became a pawn in
the entire exercise'.[95] The cursed town thus emerged out of a system
that was carefully crafted. Hence, in this cursed town, everybody was
identified by the tasks they were assigned to do. 'In this Yaksha town',
the playwright thus declared,

> there are governors, foreman, headman, tunnel-diggers, scholars; there are
> policemen, executioners, and undertakers—altogether a beautiful assort-
> ment. Only Nandini is out of element. Midst the clamour of the market
> place, she is turned up lyre. There are days when the eerie silence is torn

[93] Tagore, 221.

[94] Tagore, 231.

[95] Tagore, 231.

by the sudden breeze of her passing by, and through that emerges the sight of life![96]

Here, Nandini represented life even in the midst of the scary existence of a system of governance in which all the values linked with humanity were ruthlessly scuttled. Nandini's presence was a source of joy for the inhabitants of this cursed town, who realized it but were not sure whether it was the right thing for them to do, given the fear of being devastated in case the ruling dispensation was made aware of this. Scared by the king who was invisible till almost the end of the novel, the workers were glued to the work, because they knew that any deviation was certain to invite inhuman torture. There are two types of complementary concerns that Tagore endeavoured to capture. At one level, by drawing attention to the greed of the king who did not bother about the suffering of the mine workers, he forcefully expressed his resentment against the British regime that let loose violence for muzzling its opposition and challenges. This was contrary, he strongly felt, to the core Enlightenment values on which the British Empire rested. At a far more perceptive level, being critical of the unbridled mechanization that the king encouraged for extracting quickly as much gold as possible, he also pursued his critique of machine-driven acts which was a beginning of a design of shunning humanity of humanism. According to Tagore, so long as machine remained an aid to humanity, it was complementary to human civilization; as soon as it became an instrument for satisfying the greed of a section, it lost its utility to humanity. Tagore did not want a prototype of *Tasher Desh* (1933), where human beings no longer remained as they were and were conditioned into viewing themselves as playing cards. Thus, they lived in bad faith, burdened with their artificial identities that emerged by being governed by rules and regulations which were conducive to the governance of the kingdom as per the king's whims.

In *Rakta Karabi*, there are certain principles at work which we internalize but do not recognize, as they become integrally connected with our daily existence. Human beings were conditioned by

---

[96] Tagore, 235–6.

the habit of greed - greed for things, for power, for facts, with all ramifications that greed is able to set up between man and man—is arrayed against the explosive force of human sympathy, of neighbourliness, of fellowship and of love, the force which we may term good.[97]

By being critical of the habit of greed, Tagore took up the cudgels against the capitalist design of making money by hook or by crook. What Gandhi had articulated in *The Hind Swaraj* (1909), the poet said it in a literary voice in *Rakta Karabi*. According to him, those who were engaged in this venture

> use every variety of machinery to fortify themselves or their selfish ends against the dissolving power of beauty and love—trust, the company, stocks and shares, investments, machinery through which they can avoid all human connection and so cut themselves off from their fellows whilst they extract for their own benefit the very essence of the lives of their neighbours.[98]

Fundamental here was the critique that Tagore articulated in the play to vehemently oppose capitalism that was a deliberately contrived socio-economic and political design to 'make use of men and leave out the elemental touch of kindliness by which we live in harmony with our surroundings'.[99] Besides being so ruthless, capitalism also 'crushes and mutilates not merely the opponents but also the humanity'.[100] In response to his critics, especially in England, who accused the poet of being partisan and seeking to pursue selfish designs, he pointed out that it was 'a vision that has come to [him] in the darkest hour of dismay [upholding his] stronger faith in the simple personality of man than in the prolific brood of machinery that wants to crowd it out'.[101] Nandini was both a voice of protest and a ray of hope, because she knew that 'wealth and power [were ephemeral in appeal] and the

[97] Rabindranath Tagore, 'Red Oleanders: An Interpretation,' reproduced in Nityapriya Ghosh, ed., *The English Writings of Rabindranath Tagore*, Vol. 4 (New Delhi: Sahitya Akademi, 2008) (reprint), 335–6.

[98] Tagore, 337–8.

[99] Tagore, 337.

[100] Tagore, 337.

[101] Tagore, 347.

highest expression of life is in love which she manifests in the play in her love for her beloved, Ranjan'.[102] Expressed in a simple language, *Rakta Karabi* was an explicit statement on the ruthlessness of capitalism which led to the rise of colonialism as a system sustaining its divisive nature. For reasons connected with his politico-ideological priorities, Tagore was never as vocal as any of his colleagues involved in the nationalist campaign against capitalism-engineered colonialism. Nonetheless, his critique was an articulation of a well-thought-out vision which, despite being not always blatant but metaphorical, was clearer than what many of his compatriots held. With his fierce critique of capitalism, Tagore acquainted his readers with how capitalism unfolded and was sustained amidst trenchant criticism, largely because it also created a pool of supporters for its continuity. In the play, the headmen and other stakeholders joined hands when Nandini, including the king who was perhaps entrapped in the maze, raised their voice which led to their decapacitation was muzzled since the vested interests seems to have been more powerful in those circumstances. Nonetheless, that there was a voice, a powerful voice indeed, against the continuity of a system of production which flourished at the cost of the commoners, as it was organized in such a way as to ensure that a microscopic minority was benefitted at the cost of the rest. This is the fundamental lesson that Tagore imparted by metaphorically interpreting the ruthlessness of capitalism and how it was to be combatted for the sake of humanity.

Similarly, written in 1922, *Muktadhara* (*The Waterfall*) is also a powerful nationalist critique of colonial exploitation by Tagore. The narrative revolves around the effort that the despotic king of Chitrakut, Ranajit, undertook to construct a dam across the waterfall Muktadhara to seek to deprive people of water in areas beyond the waterfall. The dam was characterized as 'a monster [that] looks like a dragon's skull with its fleshless jaws hanging down; the constant sight of which would make the life within you withered and dead'.[103] Despite opposition,

---

[102] Tagore, 346.

[103] Rabindranath Tagore, *Muktadhara* (*The Waterfall*), reproduced in Das, *The English Writings of Rabindranath Tagore*, Vol. 2, p. 166. It is to be noted here that Tagore translated the play in English for its wider publicity, especially among his readers in the English-speaking world.

since it was an endeavour that deprived those outside Chitrakut of water, the king ruthlessly executed his decision in this regard, which was, for obvious reasons, a source of irritation to a large section of the population in the area. Warning the king of adverse consequences, the village schoolmaster thus candidly stated 'your majesty may rest assured that [the aggrieved persons] will one day be a terror to you [because] it is natural that those who are deprived are likely to be resentful and shall wait for the opportunity to strike'.[104] The prince, Abhijit, held views contrary to that of the king, since the dam to hold the flow of water was not desirable as it was likely to cause devastation in areas without water. It was a threat to the eco-balance of the area adjacent to Muktadhara, which he most poignantly stated when he expressed his dismay at the disappearance of birds from the area. 'I don't know', Abhijit noted, 'whether the bird that is sitting on the topmost branch of the pine tree … will go to its nest or take its journey across the night to a distant forest'.[105] This is also an exposition of how the eco-surroundings were likely to be devastatingly damaged due to the construction of the dam. So, not only did it cause disenchantment to the local populace, it was also, as the inhabitants held the view, a source of permanent damage to the prevalent ecology? With a sustained non-violent campaign against the endeavour, Dhananjoy Boiragi succeeded in galvanizing people for the cause. Finally, the dam was washed away with a gush of water, which was hailed as providential intervention against the ill motives of the king. The description of how the dam was destroyed is worth quoting here, since it brought new life to the Chitrakut area. Abhijit was dead in the process, which was emotionally captured when the playwright mentioned that the dam collapsed when the water gushed out, taking Abhijit away. It was encapsulated when the poet noted that 'Muktadhara, like a mother, took up [Abhijit's] stricken body into her arms and carried him away'.[106] Here Abhijit's death was celebrated as it contributed to the fulfilment of a mission that the people of Chitrakut undertook with the construction of the dam which was likely to cause ecological

---

[104] Tagore, 175.

[105] Tagore, 179.

[106] Tagore, 207.

imbalances in the area. With the collapse of the dam, the people who fought for its destruction attained the goal, though with a price, since Abhijit, who also supported the campaign, was washed away by the sudden gushing of water following the crumbling of the dam.

Besides being figuratively critical of the despotic British rule, *Muktadhara* also indicates the bard's admiration of Gandhi's non-violent method, which Boiragi practised in the narrative. Furthermore, this play is also illustrative of Tagore's conceptual understanding of science and nation, which reverberated in his other textual creations. Here, Tagore held similar views with Gandhi who, in his *The Hind Swaraj* (1909), provided a scathing critique of industrialization that took humanity away from those working in the industries day in and day out. Tagore seems to have made a two-pronged attack: at one level, he was scathingly critical of the savage desire of the king to extract as much gold as possible exclusively for his own gain; along with this general point, he also hinted at the colonial rule in which Indians were like 'the gold-mine-workers' of *Rakta Karabi* who existed as human beings, but without being treated as human beings—they were slaves, and avoidance of work invited brutal torture. The ideas that this play articulates need to be understood with reference to *Tasher Desh* (1933), a dance-drama, which is also a powerful critique of the obsession with rules and regulations. This is also about a regime in which rules and regulations dominate without taking care of human needs; the colonial state was hell-bent on exploiting the colonized, and various rules and regulations were promulgated to sustain the rule. This is one aspect in both the narratives. An optimist to the core, Tagore also brought out the human weaknesses for love and care. The king in *Rakta Karabi* was enamoured by Nandini who, being neither scared nor mesmerized by his omnipresent existence, introduced the king to love, which gradually brought about changes in his behaviour.

In a similar vein, Tagore figuratively expressed his views in his dance-drama, *Tasher Desh,* which, written in 1933, made its appearance in the public domain in 1938–1939. The story is about a fictitious land of cards where the inhabitants are governed by rigid rules and regulations that are highly restrictive in nature. In this land of cards, life is lifeless, since the well-established rules remain paramount in governance. Those living in this space have nothing else to bank upon except the rules and regulations which, if violated, cause devastation to their lives. Hence, adherence to these canonical designs of governance is always revered as their duty, because the contrary is harmful to their existence. Life here is highly mechanical, since it unfolds by strictly following what needs to be followed. A careful reading of the introductory pages of this dance-drama reveals that Tagore here was seeking to capture the British rule in its most brutal form by referring to those rules which never allowed the colonized to become self-driven, conscious human beings; they hardly have the rights to articulate themselves as human beings, just like their counterparts in Britain. Similar to his other creative writings, here, the poet was not hesitant in scathingly critiquing the prevalent system of administration which, being drawn on the mechanical rules and regulations, evolved a system of governance in which human beings are not allowed to expressed themselves as living entities with desires, passions and discontents. So, at one level, it was a comment on the nature of the British regime that was completely inhuman and brutal while being engaged in attaining its partisan goals; at another level, *Tasher Desh* is also a powerful statement of how human beings have ceased to become human beings, since they are forced to mechanically organize their lives as per the ruler's whimsical desires.

The scene, however, had undergone a sea change when the prince and his sailor companion who came from outside helped the mechanically nurtured members of *Tasher Desh* view life differently and also guided them to realize the value of being free and appreciative of songs as rejuvenating devices; the inhabitants discerned how, in the name of being properly governed, they were actually in chains which they habitually accepted as being beneficial to their existence and also better life. By spreading the message of being on one's own, the sailor and his companion gave the inhabitants of *Tasher Desh* a voice, a powerful voice indeed, which was both a threat to the prevalent system of rule and also an endeavour to live one's own life as per what one deemed appropriate for oneself. The following dialogue between the king and the prince is a testimony to the point being made above:

King: the two of you wander about the island of cards restlessly—you swim in the water, climb hills, clear paths through forests with an axe. Why?

Prince: you people keep sitting up, twisting to the side, turning your backs, rolling on the ground. Why?

King: such is our custom.

Prince: such is our desire.

King: That's dangerous. Desire in this lands of cards![107]

Here, Tagore put forward a powerful, and also a persuasive, critique of British colonialism and also his personal dislike for a life that was not allowed to flourish naturally. Making a distinction between 'custom' and 'desire', the bard challenged the system that privileged customs over human desires. By implication, it meant that by being mechanically coiled, human beings gradually lost their desire to live a life differently from what they were taught. In other words, being severely critical of rule-driven human existence, Tagore here conforms to his firm belief in the natural unfolding of human beings, which runs through his other novels, plays and dance-dramas, as will be shown later. *Tasher Desh* stands out also for being blunt in its critique of mandatory laws deriving their sustenance from the so-called holy books. This was explicitly articulated when members of *Tasher Desh* raised their voice against these torturous rules impeding the unfolding of humanity among them. Because of these crippling rules, they were forced to remain mere objects, and not beings with life; they wanted to live the life of human beings capable of expressing their desires or doing whatever they considered appropriate for their natural growth as living beings. In view of being forcibly kept under the chains of rules and regulations, they however were uncertain whether they could become human beings, which the queen expressed when she said to the prince 'if being as they were will inhibit them becoming human beings'.[108] The uncertainty was, however, temporary, as the prince responded positively by stating

---

[107] Rabindranath Tagore, *Tasher Desh*, *Rabindra Rachanabali*, Vol. 12 (Kolkata: Visva-Bharati, 1422) (Bangavda), 256.

[108] Tagore, 257.

that 'this is a transitional phase in their lives which will soon be over and they will become human beings in all respects; so, they have no reason to be circumscribed'.[109] What is clear here is that since Tagore's emphatic belief in humanity was unconditional, he always ended up by revealing his confidence in the journey towards realizing the finer sentiments of universal humanism. This was, as the poet's creative texts underline, axiomatic, and he, being true to his ideological leanings, always privileged humanism over anything else. A careful study of his biographical details also confirms that Tagore was vehemently opposed to restriction of any type, since he believed that human beings were unable to thrive naturally if they were subjected to unnecessary social, economic and political restrictions. One may deduce from this assumption that Tagore was an anarchist, which does not seem to be justified, given the colonial context when the colonized had hardly freedom of action, for obvious reasons. The statement of the prince in *Tasher Desh* is illustrative here: unable to live life according to his priorities, the prince conveys his disenchantment with the regime putting all kinds of restrictions on its subjects for governance. He wanted to be free and enjoy life like 'a ploughman who wanders around the piece of land that he cultivates; for them, it is a boon which they got because of the good work that their forefathers did for humanity'.[110] Here too, the message is identical: the poet's urge for freedom, if compromised, is deterrent to the realization of his lifelong mission of human emancipation. Being allegorical, *Tasher Desh* is therefore not just an entertaining dance-drama but one that puts across a powerful critique of the colonial regime in the form of a persuasive social missive drawn on Tagore's ideological commitment to universal humanism.

The other novel, *Rajarshi* (1887), which was transformed into a play, *Visarjan* (Sacrifice), published in 1890, dwells on the importance of non-violence in human life. Long before Gandhi talked about non-violence in the context of his non-violent campaign in South Africa

---

[109] Tagore, 257.

[110] Tagore, 236.

(1894–1914), Tagore dealt with this, of course in his unique way, by dwelling on the sociopolitical implications in a figurative kingdom once sacrifice of animals was declared *ultra vires*. In many ways, he created a context in which the characters delved into the issue of non-violence, by highlighting the views as being opposed to each other. While Govindamanikya, the king, banned animal slaughter, the royal priest, Raghupati, gathered support in favour of the continuity of the ritual. Despite opposition, the decree for stopping sacrifice in front of the deity was carried forward, and the novel ended with the celebration, as no life would be lost because of humans' ill motives, Tagore emphatically declared.

The storyline does not seem to be complicated; once the decision was taken by the king, two contrasting viewpoints emerged: one for appreciation of and the other for opposition to the king for a decision that disrupted the continuity of what was characterized as part of a long tradition. The king was subject to intrigues in which his close kith and kin were involved. What was striking was the message that Tagore wanted to convey by banning animal sacrifice seemingly to propitiate the local deity. Based on his politico-ideological predispositions, Govindamanikya, the king, decreed for completely eradicating a system whereby the innocent animals were sacrificed as offerings to god. It was another way of satisfying one's greed, which the king felt was nothing but a design being justified as providentially sanctioned.

As a persuasive writer, Tagore presented his argument rescinding sacrifice by exposing that it was a man-made selfish design. The animal sacrifice in the Bhuvoneshwari temple was a ritual being performed over generations. Dismayed by this inhuman practice, the king declared about a fortnight ahead of the day of sacrifice that 'no animal shall be sacrificed this year since it was justified neither by holy texts nor by any providential decree',[111] which came as a shock to the royal priest, known as Chontai in the local lexicon, since it was not acceptable to him as it was a part of a long and carefully nurtured tradition.

---

[111] Rabindranath Tagore, *Rajarshi* (Kolkata: Visva-Bharati Garanthan Bhivag, 1969) (reprint), 12.

'Was it a dream',[112] asked Chontai. In response, the king retorted that 'no, it is not a dream;[113] in fact, that it was allowed to continue was a dream to him'. To strengthen his argument, he further stated that 'the goddess Bhuboneshwari emerged before him in his dream in the form of a young girl and implored him to stop this violent act against life [since] as a mother she cannot tolerate shedding of blood of living beings'.[114] To persuasively carry forward his argument in favour of animal sacrifice, the priest questioned the king's decision, as it was deviant from the core beliefs expressed in the holy text, saying that 'as king he is not aware of the practices that can never be abdicated and he neither has the time to go through them which is why the kingdom has a fulltime priest'. Logically, the priest's contention appeared to be true, but the king offered an impassioned counter by saying that 'the heart that has been petrified into cruelty is deaf to god's command'.[115] The king then ordered the priest to return to the temple and resume his duties. He also ordered the priest to spread the message among the people that 'the violation of this royal decree against animal sacrifice would lead to exile'.[116] The discourse of non-violence had just begun, which was further expanded by him when he stated that 'animal sacrifice is nothing by satisfying one's animalistic pleasure at the cost of the hapless animals who are easily put on the altar since they do not have a voice. This is nothing but a manifestation of the fulfilment of one's selfish desire'.[117] To get rid of this cruel motive, what was required was, as the king beseeched, 'to silence the malice within the true Shastric injunction, rather than killing life'.[118] Tagore's prescient commitment to non-violence (whose most celebrated proponent, Gandhi, would not start his non-violent activities until 3 years later) manifests itself in this plot point. It is worth noting here that in the 1890s when

[112] Tagore, 12.

[113] Tagore, 12.

[114] Tagore, 12.

[115] Tagore, 12.

[116] Tagore, 1.

[117] Tagore, 31.

[118] Tagore, 31.

Rajarshi was being written, the nationalist movement was organized in a fashion which was not, at all, non-violent. Rather, militancy and killing of the so-called enemies were never questioned; in fact, it was hailed by those associated with the campaign. There is another aspect that was reflective of Tagore being an original thinker who evolved uniquely textured sociopolitical discourses. Being a rationalist to the core, the poet was never persuaded to believe in irrational ways of justifying one's partisan predispositions. For instance, in response to the priest's insistence that 'the king, since he was a temporal authority, had no right to punish him because he was, being the royal priest, free from worldly control which means that the king was not authorized to mete out punishment to him; only god can do'.[119] Being firm in his judgment, the king remained unmoved and the punishment was carried forward.

A careful perusal of the novel highlights that *Rajarshi* is complementary to the sociopolitical views that Tagore put forward in many of his creative writings. Besides highlighting the importance of non-violence and also ascertaining the critical role of temporal authority, the poet reinforced some of the core values that he held dear to him so long as he remained active in the public domain. The banning of sacrifice of animals was not just a discontinuity of a ritualistically justified act, but led to the unfolding of a sociopolitical power design that gradually engulfed the nationalist thinking in India with the arrival of Gandhi on the political scene. Non-violence was adopted by the Mahatma as a mobilizing tool in South Africa against the execution of the 1906 Transvaal Asiatic Ordinance that imposed restrictions of movement of Indians in the province.[120] In other words, almost 15 years after the publication of *Rajarshi* by Tagore, Gandhi articulated his model of non-violence, which helped him build a pan-Indian anti-British campaign against the alien rule. Tagore's model of non-violence was also complemented by his heartfelt desire for economic

---

[119] Tagore, 65.

[120] For details, see Surendra Bhana and Goolam Vahed, *The Making of a Political Reformer: Gandhi in South Africa, 1893–1914* (Manohar, 2005), Chap. 4, pp. 93–111, besides, of course, Gandhi's own articulation in *Satyagraha in South Africa* (Ahmedabad: Navajivan Publications, 2009) (reprint).

self-sufficiency, which he devised in his 1904 tract, *Swadeshi Samaj*, and also dealt with this in his novel *Ghare Baire*, among others, which, through Nikhilesh's involvement in constructive works in villages, exemplified what the poet had in mind. This was further illustrated when the poet founded Sriniketan in 1928, which was also a design for self-generated developmental schemes contributing to the inclusive growth of the area without being partial to anybody by reference to one's class, caste or ethnic identity.

CONCLUDING OBSERVATIONS

Rabindranath Tagore was a unique personality who, despite not being involved directly in the nationalist campaign, remained there to help his compatriots evolve appropriate socio-economic strategies for realizing the goal. A poet with concerns for universal humanism, Tagore remained steadfastly committed to what he believed. It was manifested when he withdrew from the militant nationalist campaign that unfolded in the wake of the movement for the revocation of the first Partition of Bengal during the period between 1905 and 1908. Nikhilesh of *Ghare Baire* illustrated how the poet conceptualized his approach to nationalism in the late 19th and early 20th centuries. A careful analysis of the critical essays and other creative writings reveals that Tagore's sociopolitical ideas were hardly articulated by the poet in any systematic manner. As a creative writer, he explicated his views through the protagonists in various novels and short stories. There are two important features in all his creative writings: first, Tagore was not always explicit but developed characters who set out with the ideas in a language which clearly stated what the poet wanted to convey. Unlike Gandhi and his colleagues who delved into the ideas which, they felt, were directional, Tagore was not always categorical in his expression; but by couching his views in the dialogues of the protagonists, he achieved the sociopolitical goal that he deemed appropriate. Second, one also notices that Tagore was a little guarded when he expressed his views, which does not seem to be unusual since the poet owed, as he himself admitted, a great deal to Western thinking. Arguing for a creative blending of the ideas emanating from the East and the West, Tagore also represented those renaissance values supportive of universal humanism. Not being restrictive in his thinking, the bard thus drew on multiple sources of conceptualizing human existence, as it was not intellectual servility since human wisdom could never be exclusive to a community or a well-guarded secret kept in the personal repository of those with coercive power at their disposal. This is an argument that complements his concern for the Upanishadic ideal of *vasudhaiva kutumbakam* (the world being one family).

That Tagore never compromised on his commitment to universal humanism is established beyond doubt, as his creative writings unequivocally demonstrate. While dwelling on the foundational ideas that informed the poet in his endeavour in the development of his distinct sociopolitical discourses, it has been argued that a large chunk of his ideas is also a derivative of what he learnt from Vidyasagar, Ram Mohan and his father, Debendranath Tagore. The outcome of his intellectual interaction was Tagore's appreciation for the healthy exchange of ideas between the present and past and also between the East and the West. Unlike the Hindu zealots who seem to be blinded in their perception of India, defining it exclusively per the Hindu cultural ethos, Tagore argued that 'India's history is not the story of the Hindu alone. We are part material in that history; and if we cannot fit ourselves into the scheme … we will be condemned to death in the court of humanity'.[121] Conforming to this conceptualization, he further mentioned that

> the objective of Indian history is not to set up Hindu or some dominance, but to secure a special kind of fulfilment for humanity, a level of perfection that must be gain for all. In the course of this fulfilment, if Hindu, Muslim and the British have to submerge the aggressive parts of their individuality, it may be hurtful to their national pride but it will not be reckoned as a loss in the scales of truth and human rights.[122]

This is an important aspect of his sociopolitical discourse, which is an unambiguous statement on any kind of socio-economic and religious discrimination. Here, Tagore, being influenced by the trio,

---

[121] Rabindranath Tagore, 'East and West,' in Rabindranath Tagore, *Towards Universal Man* (Bombay: Asia Publishing House, 1962) (reprint), 131–2.

[122] Tagore, 131.

Vidyasagar, Ram Mohan and his father, Debendranath, imbibed the spirit of human beings as one unit regardless of differences in terms of class, caste or distinctive, ethnic-driven socio-cultural features. He was for a society in which exclusive identity based on one's religious affiliation with a denomination of faith was clearly rejected, as it stood in contradiction with the aim of building the world as one.

There is also the second aspect, which is equally important to grasp, of his distinct sociopolitical predispositions, namely the voice against discriminating against those who remained socio-economically peripheral. In his essay, 'East and West', he developed this argument in clear terms by saying that

> so long as we are prompted by individual or social folly to act inhumanly towards our own countrymen, so long as our landlords regard their tenants as their personal property, so long as the strong continue to trample on the weak as part of their ancient privilege, and the higher castes look upon the casteless as worse than beast, ... we have no future as a country.[123]

Besides showing him as a vitriolic critique, the above statement is also useful to conceptually understand one of the distinctive features of his sociopolitical discourses. This was a call for setting out for a milieu in which discrimination of any kind was sought to be combatted, since without treating everybody at par with one another, his objective of creating a prejudice-free world would remain elusive. By challenging the prevalent socio-economic interpersonal relationships which were favourably disposed towards the mighty, the bard accorded voice, a powerful voice indeed, to the voiceless, again to fulfil the goal that he set out to achieve: humanity irrespective of socio-economic disparities.

There is yet another dimension which we should not lose sight of. As one who claimed himself to have been born in a family in which both indigenous and exogenous socio-cultural insights were always welcome, Tagore instinctively imbibed the idea that the exchange of ideas between the East and the West was necessary to strengthen the human bond, surpassing national boundaries. Unless socio-cultural communion was appreciated and made to happen, it was futile to

---

[123] Tagore, 139.

argue for togetherness without nurturing the feeling of being exploited and cheated. The contact between the East and the West

> will yield nothing unless we spontaneously accept the East-West bond as naturally-evolved [which] ... will help the East unite with East, country with country, race with race, knowledge with knowledge, endeavour with endeavour. Then alone the present chapter of India's history comes to an end, and a new start—one of the noblest in the story of Man.[124]

A universalist in his belief, Tagore appears to have internalized his concern for universal humanism by being born in a family which was exposed to Western influences, since his grandfather Dwarkanath Tagore (1794–1847), being one of the successful entrepreneurs during the East India Company rule, had had exposure to the British culture. So, the Tagore family had already been introduced to the West when the poet was born. Debendranath's interest in the Upanishads created an ambience at home in which the poet had also had an opportunity to be acquainted with the literature that thrived in India's ancient past. Their landed property, particularly in East Bengal, also allowed the bard to learn about the quotidian life in Bengal. As per the available evidence, it was natural for Tagore to be immersed in sociopolitical ideas that had their roots both in the East and in the West. With his clarion call for a creative blending of the sociopolitical preferences emanating from the East and the West, Tagore echoed exactly the concern that the Mahatma evinced when he said:

> I do not want my house to be walled in on all sides and my windows be stuffed. I want the culture of all lands to be blown about my house as freely as possible. But I refuse to be blown off my feet by any.[125]

Here, the poet having views, as shown earlier, contrary to those of Gandhi, held identical sociopolitical priorities supportive of the free flow of ideas, as it was enriching for India by making it sensitive to socio-cultural diversities.

[124] Tagore, 139–40.

[125] https://www.goodreads.com/quotes/575759-i-do-not-want-my-house-to-be-walled-in, Gandhi's quotes.

In a nutshell, being nurtured in a cosmopolitan family, Tagore instinctively acquired those socio-cultural values which were anything but orthodox and xenophobic. By drawing on the libertarian ideas of Vidyasagar, Ram Mohan and Maharshi, it was easier for him to appreciate them since they put before him a new perspective which helped him build strong arguments against Hindu orthodoxy and also wholescale condemnation of anything Western. Tagore's nationalism was qualitatively different in the sense that instead of essentializing the socio-culturally diverse India with disparate communities, he articulated a 'nationalistic' vision in which wider social amity was always privileged. His nationalism was not merely a political design of togetherness but one that drew on wider connectedness among people, surpassing national–geographical boundaries. A socio-culturally endorsed scheme of interpersonal relationships, Tagore's universal humanism was an endeavour to bring disparate people together for realizing the goal of common happiness. There was hardly a difference between Tagore and Gandhi, since both of them upheld identical sociopolitical preferences, though their mode of attaining the goal was different: Tagore held a non-negotiable position by privileging human emancipation over political freedom which was, to him, just a means, while for Gandhi the attainment of political freedom was prior to human emancipation, since, for realizing the latter, the role of the former was most critical, if not absolutely essential. With hindsight, one is persuaded to argue that both of them were correct, since Gandhi's mode of political struggle led to the rise of a politically free India which, itself, created opportunities for the endeavours towards fulfilling those aims and objectives that remained distant, if not inconceivable, during colonialism. By setting out on his choice for evolving a society free from prejudices and discriminatory socio-economic practices, Tagore's sociopolitical discourses were complementary to what the Mahatma stood for, because he too simultaneously undertook several measures to purge society of the age-old and archaic socio-economic designs for discrimination and exploitation of human beings by human beings. As the above discussion shows, insofar as India's 'nationalist' discourse was concerned, the poet and the Mahatma were complementary to each other, and their dialogical interaction enriched the sociopolitical discourses that became prominent at a particular juncture of India's recent political history. Their language was different too: Tagore as a creative writer expressed his views through the characters that he constructed to say whatever he chose to say, while Gandhi, a hardcore political activist, devised means and ways for politically mobilizing combative opinions against the British rule which were direct and less figurative. The Mahatma utilized conventional means for evolving togetherness, like mass meetings, sit-ins or *Satyagraha*, boycott or other means of passive resistance, including burning of clothes, for his mission; to Tagore, they did not seem to be conducive but were likely to inhibit communion as they were class-conditioned, religiously divisive and ideologically debilitating. Nonetheless, by being respectful to each other despite holding contrary points of view, they never took their differences to a level that was likely to be a source of weakness to the ongoing nationalist mission, at the behest of the Gandhi-led Indian National Congress. So, at one level, they stood apart, as they had fundamental differences; at another level, they, of course, created a new template which helped the posterity adopt steps to complete the task that they earnestly pursued even in adverse circumstances.

Tagore's Idea of Nationalism

2

A surface reading of Tagore's views on nationalism suggests that his views on nationalism contradict the support that he had extended to the nationalist campaign in India. The point lacks substance, as a careful reading of Gurudev's views reveal. What is sought to be argued here is that Tagore held views which stood in contradiction with the conventional understanding of the idea of nationalism as it evolved in the post–1648 Westphalia Treaty era. The aim was to create national identities of nations on the basis of efforts towards homogenizing a multitude in terms of religion, culture and emotional bond drawn on common memories of oppression. Being a product of the Western context, the idea of nationalism reflected and was justified by the criteria that brought together a collectivity of human beings by essentializing their sociopolitical identities, as they are integrated with one another on the basis of certain well-defined parameters. It is therefore not unnatural that due to being appreciative of a set of ideas that evolved generationally, the ideological voice is hardly fractured. It is a matter of common knowledge that, Tagore being nurtured in an environment in which multiculturalism was always privileged, his writings clearly show that he was not partisan in his views, nor had he ever endorsed any sociopolitical campaign contrary to his beliefs. In other words, in circumstances in which attempts were made towards homogenizing a 'nation' which was socio-culturally disparate, the poet hardly wavered in raising his voice for sustaining India's historically ordained multicultural identity, which, if undermined, would cause great harm to its existence as a unit of multitudes. Two points deserve careful attention here: on the one hand, Tagore was a nationalist, perhaps in the sense of being a patriot who was protective of India's identity as an extremely socio-culturally diverse society in which the well-entrenched civilizational ethos seem to have acted as a centripetal force. This is one aspect of his argument; the other aspect is revealed when one looks at his cosmopolitan upbringing. By being exposed to multiple cultural influences, since he was born in a family that was neither orthodox nor obscurantist, but was receptive to values regardless of their socio-economic origin, the bard was nurtured in a tradition which, being uniquely textured, evolved naturally, despite being contrarian to the established socio-cultural traits. In his writings, what has emerged are those views and ideas which truly created a new wave of thinking in a context which did not seem to have welcomed the bard, presumably because he was truly a renaissance man. The aim of this chapter is thus twofold: first, by drawing upon the texts, the chapter offers the argument that Tagore's views on nationalism require to be comprehended with reference to the context and also his own understanding of the theme, by reinventing those ideas which were considered to be sociopolitically axiomatic then. Second, the chapter is also directed at showing how Tagore consistently argued against parochial nationalism, which he illustrated by referring to Japan's loss of unique identity. Here, he put across two important conceptual points: on the one hand, he argued that narrow nationalistic views were not only an impediment to the rise of a healthy nation but also severely harmed its distinctive socio-cultural characteristics; on the other hand, a careful analysis of his texts also reveals that despite being a nationalist of a qualitatively different kind, the bard helped build a milieu in which universal humanism was also privileged. The aim here is to understand how Tagore evolved his distinct approach to nationalism, nation state and national identity. Based on a critical analysis of the texts, primarily his essays on the theme, the chapter seeks to dwell on the complexities of the argument that is not exactly an outright rejection of the concept of nationalism. As will be shown in the chapter, nationalism was a product of a particular phase of global history when the importance of market seemed to have undermined universal humanism to a significant extent. A poet who was also sensitive to historical processes, Tagore, while seeking to understand its complex unfolding in the industrial era, put forward those innovative arguments which created a new theoretical template to conceptually grasp the ideas of nation, nationalism and national identity. The chapter is thus an exercise to fathom the conceptual peculiarities in the light of Tagore's own assessment of how nationalism became an inspiring ideal in the contemporary global context despite being clearly discriminatory in character.

UNFOLDING OF A UNIQUE
CONCEPTUALIZATION OF NATIONALISM

It is true that Tagore was very critical of the idea of nationalism, which he extensively elaborated during his 1916 lectures on nationalism. Prominent among the arguments that he offered are two major points of intervention. First, opposed to the effort by the British government to essentialize Indians, he felt that it was certain to be suicidal, since, historically speaking,

> India does not belong to one particular race but to a process of creation to which various races of the world contributed—the Dravidians and the Aryans, the ancient Greeks and the Persians, the Mohammedans of the West and those of Central Asia.[1]

Emphasis here is on the multicultural facets that India instinctively represented. For Tagore, it was a source of strength, because it enabled India to be sensitive to socio-cultural diversity. At the behest of the European nations, the contemporary nationalist interventions were, on the contrary, endeavours at creating a milieu in which the demarcated nationalist boundaries were deliberately privileged to destroy the bonhomie that human beings historically preferred. While being severely critical of such a debasing development in human civilization, Tagore minced no words in his criticism, stating that

> the political civilization which has sprang up from the soil of Europe and is overrunning the whole world, like some prolific weed, is based upon exclusiveness. ... This civilization is scientific, not human. It is powerful because it concentrates all its forces upon one purpose, like a millionaire acquiring money at the cost of his soul. It betrays its trust, it weaves its meshes of lies without shame, it enshrines gigantic idols of greed in its

[1] Rabindranath Tagore, *Nationalism* (Delhi, Macmillan, 1985), 9.

temples, taking great pride in the costly ceremonials of its worship, calling this patriotism.[2]

Second, being a true humanist, Tagore was never persuaded to accept the hegemony of nation state which flourished at the cost of humanity only by dint of being physically empowered. Unfair as it was, it also led to the enslavement of a section of humanity by another. For Tagore, the nation state was thus

> carnivorous and cannibalistic in its tendencies [because] it feeds upon the resources of other people and tries to swallow their whole future. It is always afraid of other races achieving eminence, naming it as a peril, and tries to thwart all symptoms of greatness outside its own boundaries, forcing down races of men who are weaker, to be eternally fixed in their weakness.[3]

Here, the poet explained how the rise of the nation state contributed to the dehumanization of humanity. Human beings ceased to be human beings. It had two serious implications: on the one hand, it fuelled the urge of enslaving people to enable the powerful nation state to sustain its claim of being powerful; as an obvious consequence, it also justified, on the other hand, those socio-economic and political designs defending the exploitation of one segment of humanity by another. In view of his firm belief that nationalism was a demeaning design, Tagore thus concluded that

> nationalism is a great menace [because] it builds on the idea of making a whole people as an organized power. This organization incessantly keeps up the insistence of the population on becoming strong and efficient. But this strenuous effort after strength and efficiency drains man's energy from his higher nature where he is self-sacrificing and creative. For thereby man's power of sacrifice from his ultimate object, which is moral to the maintenance of this organization, which is mechanical.[4]

Now, the argument is far more complex, though clearly stated. According to Tagore, nationalism was anything but humanistic, since

[2] Tagore, 36.

[3] Tagore, 36.

[4] Tagore, 66–7.

it debased basic human values by making human beings mechanically tuned to the task that was useful for the nation state to thrive at others' cost. Given the mechanical nature of the task, Tagore apprehended that it was most likely to dissuade people from being creative, which was both debilitating and harmful for human civilization. In other words, being a creative thinker, the poet was never comfortable with the imposition of socio-psychological conditionalities on people, because it was not only an impediment for innovative thinking but also a firm step for justifying the 'one-size-fits-all' syndrome. Here, Tagore is nearer to the Russian pacifist Leo Tolstoy, who also raised voice against the brutal Tzar not merely for the atrocities that adversely affected the Russians, but also against the Tzarist effort for erasing the socio-cultural diversities for which Russia was famous to impose a one-nation-one-culture model. This is one side of the argument highlighting that nation state was a restraint for creativity. The other side relates to his point regarding internal colonialism, which means that even within a powerful nation state not everybody was free from exploitation. In his words,

> those who have made their gain of money their highest end are unconsciously selling their life and soul to rich persons or to the combinations that represent money. Those who are enamoured of their political power and gloat over their extension of domination over foreign races gradually surrender their own freedom and humanity to the organizations for holding other people in slavery. In so-called free countries the majority of the people are not free; they are driven by the minority to a goal which is not even known to them.[5]

A very Marxian interpretation of how the nation state became a vehicle of both external and internal colonialism, the idea is persuasive and conforms to what Tagore always felt. As one who always argued for human emancipation, the poet was very clear that the so-called powerful nation states derived their sustenance not only from external exploitation but also from forcing a section of the population to work hard for the fulfilment of the expansionists' partisan designs. While being critical of internal colonialism, Tagore made a very perceptive

---

[5] Tagore, 73.

comment regarding social slavery, which was a deterrent in evolving a compact sociopolitical unit. Here, his attention is drawn to the Indian situation, which was plagued, to a significant extent, by the well-entrenched caste system and its related age-old social prejudices. This was explicitly stated when he candidly mentioned that

> we never dream of blaming our social inadequacy as the origin of our present helplessness for we have accepted as the creed of our nationalism that this social system has been perfected for all time to come by our ancestors, who had the superhuman vision of all eternity and supernatural power for making infinite provision for future ages. Therefore, for all our miseries and shortcomings, we hold responsible the historical surprises that burst upon us from outside. This is the reason why we think that our one task is to build a political miracle of freedom upon the quicksand of social slavery. In fact, we want to dam up the true course of our own historical stream, and only borrow power from the sources of other peoples' history.[6]

With his scathing criticism of the social reality in India representing one kind of internal colonialism, Tagore combined his persuasive critique of nationalism with his own version of human emancipation. Mere political freedom, or 'national awakening', in the contemporary parlance, was not adequate for freedom in its real sense. It was partial freedom, because the nationalist salvation was only meant to remove the political shackles of British colonialism without touching the social system supportive of social slavery based on caste prejudices. Hence, political freedom did not mean much to Tagore unless it was complementary to human emancipation. In an unambiguous way, he thus further clarified that

> those of us in India who have come under the delusion that mere political freedom will make us free have accepted their lesson from the West as the gospel truth and lost their faith in humanity. We must remember whatever weakness we cherish in our society will become a source of danger in politics. The same inertia which leads us to our idolatry of dead forms in social institutions will create in politics prison houses with immovable walls. The narrowness of sympathy which makes it possible for us to impose upon a

---

[6] Tagore, 74.

considerable portion of humanity the galling yoke of inferiority will assert itself in our politics in creating the tyranny of injustice.[7]

There were many of his nationalist colleagues who felt similarly, that so long as social segregation drawn on caste division was allowed to survive, political freedom would hardly be effective in creating a compact template for India. Hence, the poet insisted on removing

those social customs and ideas which have generated a want of self-respect and complete dependence on those above us—a state of affairs which has been brought about by the domination in India of the caste system, and the blind and lazy habit of relying upon the authority of traditions that are incongruous anachronism in the present age.[8]

A sharp critic of the existent social segregation being justified in the name of anachronistic traditions, Tagore carved out a space in the first decade of the 20th century when these ideas were not usually appreciated. It is true that Gandhi began preaching these ideas in South Africa and implemented them in practice in the Phoenix and Tolstoy ashrams there in the late 19th and early 20th centuries. Some of his colleagues in the Brahmo Samaj warned Tagore of the adverse consequences, which did not deter the poet from raising his voice against the artificially created social division for partisan gains.[9] On Gandhi's appearance on India's political scene, the scene however underwent a sea change; attacks on the caste system were no longer as despised as it was the case when Tagore wrote his 1916 text, *Nationalism*.[10] According to Gandhi, 'untouchability is a curse, a blot and a powerful poison that will destroy Hinduism. It is repugnant to our sense of

---

[7] Tagore, 75.

[8] Tagore, 68–9.

[9] Tagore's admirer and colleague Shivnath Shastri (1847–1919) expressed resentment by being scathingly critical of Tagore's condemnation of the caste system, as it was untimely. Cited in David Kopf, *The Brahmo Samaj and the shaping of the modern Indian mind* (Princeton: Princeton University Press, 1979), 31.

[10] I have dealt with this aspect of Gandhi's politico-ideological campaign against caste segregation (Rabindranath Tagore, *Confluence of Thought: Mahatma Gandhi and Martin Luther King Jr* [New York: Oxford University Press, 2013], chap. 3, 122–150).

humanity to consider a single human being as untouchable by birth'.[11] The concern that Tagore and Gandhi had expressed in the early part of India's freedom struggle resonated in 1949 in the Constituent Assembly (which was constituted to frame the 1950 Constitution of India) when B. R. Ambedkar exhorted that

> the down-trodden classes [the untouchables] are tired of being governed. They are impatient to govern themselves. This urge for self-realization in the down-trodden classes must not be allowed to devolve into a class struggle or class war. It would lead to a division in the country. That would indeed by a day of disaster.[12]

The idea is very clear. The widely practised caste division was prejudicial to the rise of India as a compact social multitude. Being social reformers of different kinds, since Tagore through his writings sought to create awareness, while Ambedkar built a constitutional framework to weed out caste exploitation, both of them thought alike. Despite that after 3 years of hard work the Constituent Assembly had produced a constitution, Ambedkar did not seem to be as cheerful as he was expected to be because of the uncertainty that loomed large in an equally uncertain sociopolitical context in which untouchability was not completely rooted out. Hence, he expressed his dismay by saying that

> on the 26th of January, we are going to enter into a life of contradictions: in politics, we will have equality and in social and economic life we have inequality. In politics, we will be recognizing the principle of one man one vote and one vote one value. In our social and economic life, we shall, by reason of our social and economic structure, continue to deny the principle of one man one value.[13]

[11] M. K. Gandhi, 'Untouchability: a curse', *Harijan*, 20 June, 1936, reproduced in *Collected Works of Mahatma Gandhi* (CWMG hereafter), Vol. 63, 34.

[12] B. R. Ambedkar, Speech in the Constituent Assembly, 25 November 1949, *Constituent Assembly Debates*, Book No. 5, p. 980.

[13] Ambedkar, Address in the Constituent Assembly, 25 November 1949, *Constituent Assembly Debates*, Book No. 5, p. 979.

This was the source of his worry that bothered him even when he successfully completed the proceedings regarding the making of the 1950 Constitution. He was agonized, which came out in his statement in the Constituent Assembly when he said that though on 26 January India would become an independent country, what would happen to her independence? 'Will she', Ambedkar exhorted, 'maintain her independence or will she lose it again?'[14] The concern was not unfounded, in view of the fact that India lost the independence that it had. 'Will she lose it again?'[15] This was the thought that made Ambedkar 'most anxious for her future'.[16] Two ideas remained dominant in Ambedkar's apprehension as to whether the democratic constitution would survive: on the one hand, he was uncertain, since India as a compact was divided hierarchically in terms of the accident of birth. Those who were born as untouchables remained outside the fold of the mainstream, which was, for obvious reasons, a source of heartburn since it drew its sustenance from an artificial sociopolitical system deliberately maintained to support internal colonialism; as a corollary of this, though, the social division justified in caste hierarchy retained, on the other hand, social segmentation, which, being interest-driven, was allowed to continue, as it protected the *status quo* social system segmenting one group of people from another for partisan socio-economic and political goals.[17]

Although at the risk of digression, the above facts are placed to substantiate the point that the idea that Tagore flagged in his 1916 lecture later unfolded in its manifold forms. Gandhi took up the cudgels against caste atrocities, which, he felt, were a handicap for his political battle against colonialism as they never allowed the people to come together as a compact. Despite his earnest efforts, the results did not appear to have pleased him. Likewise, Ambedkar fought relentlessly against caste prejudices, which did not disappear to the extent

---

[14] Ambedkar, 977.

[15] Ambedkar, 977.

[16] Ambedkar, 977.

[17] I have pursued the story further in my *The Socio-political Ideas of BR Ambedkar: Liberal Constitutionalism in a Creative Mould* (Oxford, Routledge, 2019).

he expected. He had, of course, an advantage that neither Gandhi nor Tagore had: by being a critical member of the makers of the 1950 Constitution, he put forward a scheme which, by being legally endorsed, created an ambience in which those nurturing prejudices against the lower castes received a jolt. This was surely an achievement in a situation wherein caste hierarchy was believed to have been axiomatic and hence beyond challenge.

What is striking in Tagore is that he pursued the same sentiments in his creative literary works. Here, one can refer to his 1938 dance-drama, *Chandalika*. The play revolves around Prakriti (*Chandalika*), a low-caste young girl, and her mother, Maya. She was completely ostracized for being born to *Chandal* (low-caste) parents; unable to accept this, she even questioned her mother for such a plight, despite it being similar to that of others in the locality. One day, Ananda, a disciple of the Buddha, arrived and asked Prakriti to give him water, since he was terribly thirsty, which she declined by referring to the fact that she was an untouchable. Despite her reluctance, the Buddhist monk drank the water that Prakriti gave and left with the message that all were equal in the eyes of the almighty. The narrative of *Chandalika* is an evidence of how Tagore viewed the caste system which was sustained by Brahminical hegemony, and also a possible explanation of why it continued so long. When Prakriti was ignored by Ananda on another occasion, she asked her mother who tried hard to convince her daughter to accept her plight as pre-ordained and unchangeable. But Prakriti was emotionally devasted and begged her to bring him back by undertaking various means of sorcery, to which she agreed. Ananda came and blessed her, uttering that to the almighty everybody was equal.

The above storyline contains a powerful message with the same content that Tagore highlighted in his 1916 *Nationalism* lecture. Here, the message is conveyed in a very subtle manner. It was possible for B. R. Ambedkar in the Constituent Assembly to declare untouchability as a criminal offence, which was not the case when Tagore dealt with caste prejudices in this dance-drama. The reasons are not difficult to seek. The context did not seem to be propitious, and the poet appeared to have refrained from making a clear-cut choice, presumably to avoid direct confrontation with the mainstream ortho-dox social elites. Nonetheless, *Chandalika* is a reinforcement of the views that he put across in his earlier writings, especially in the 1916 *Nationalism* lecture, as is elaborated above. There are two powerful points: on the one hand, this play articulated Tagore's disdain for caste prejudices and also by showing Ananda's willingness to have water from a Chandalika he had also demonstrated that views opposed to caste prejudices were too strong to be wished away. But they cannot be completely eradicated; Tagore mentioned by highlighting, on the other hand, the sentiments of Maya when she said that untouchability was preordained and hence it was better to accept it as axiomatic. Here, Tagore hinted at a far more powerful point, that since untouch-ability was ingrained in the consciousness of the untouchables, India's social template was unlikely to change so easily. So, the opportunity that Ambedkar had in 1949 did not seem to be available to Tagore in 1916, for reasons connected with the prevalent socio-cultural and politico-ideological milieu.

ASSESSMENT

Tagore's views on nationalism pose difficult questions in a context when the idea of nationalism was seemingly accepted universally, since it was believed to have been a liberating design for the colonized. Nationalism was an ideology for rejuvenation and also socio-cultural regeneration. An idea that was inspirational to the colonized, nation-alism appears to have created a space for socio-culturally disparate people to come together to fight for a common cause. Isaiah Berlin is correct when he states that

> nationalism springs, as often as not, from a wounded or outraged sense of human dignity, the desire for recognition. This desire is surely one of the greatest forces that move human history. It may take hideous forms, but is not in itself either unnatural or repulsive as a feeling.[18]

---

[18] Isaiah Berlin, 'Rabindranath Tagore and the consciousness of nationality' repub-lished in *The Sense of Reality: studies in ideas and their history* (New York, Farrar, Straus and Giroux, 1996), 252.

By drawing on the history of the French and Russian revolutions, Berlin further commented that the lack of an adequate socio-economic status helps evolve a context in which nationalism germinates. In his perception, nationalist upsurges take place in the social context of exclusion or rejection, which he explained by stating that

> the [nationalist] revolutionaries were, as often or not, sons of capable and self-made men, who had been socially excluded or rejected or found themselves in an embarrassing or false position in the social hierarchy of their time.[19]

In such a context, what is inevitable is isolation, which is the outcome of 'the destruction of that solidarity which only homogeneous close-knit societies give to their members'.[20] The outcome is the steady dehumanization of the masses who seek to find a way to counter the sociopolitical designs responsible for such circumstances. Tagore's idea of nationalism, conceptualized in the first decade of the 20th century, needs to be grasped with reference to the growing disenchantment of the Indians in an era of uncertainty, because neither the Congress nor any other political outfit was capable of channelizing the mass energy in a result-driven direction. He evolved his views, in other words, in circumstances when there were organized groups that were heavily inspired by the ideas that the ancient texts had articulated, and simultaneously with those who, being drawn on the philosophy of Enlightenment, strongly felt that the Western nationalist ideas were a panacea for the Indians. It was an ideational pull in opposite directions in which Tagore's most perceptive comments on nationalism came, which Berlin most succinctly elaborated by putting forward the view that

> Tagore stood fast on the narrow causeway, and did not betray his vision of the difficult truth. He condemned romantic overattachment to the past what he called the tying of India to the past "like a sacrificial goal tethered to a post", and he accused men who displayed it—they seemed to him reactionary—of not knowing what true political freedom was, pointing out that it from English thinkers and English books that the very notion of

[19] Berlin, 254.
[20] Berlin, 255.

political liberty was derived. But against cosmopolitanism he maintained that the English stood on their feet, and so must Indians. [Later] he once more denounced the danger of "leaving everything to the unbearable will of the Master", be he brahmin or Englishman.[21]

Here, one discerns 'a duality'[22] in Tagore's approach to nationalism, because, at one level, he was seen to be enamoured by the progressive ideas of English thinkers and books, and at another level, he wanted Indians to be rooted well in their socio-cultural heritage. Interestingly, Gandhi expressed identical sentiments when he uttered

I do not want my house to be walled on all sides and my windows to be stuffed. I want the culture of all lands to be blown about my house as freely as possible. But I refuse to be blown off my feet by any.[23]

The purpose of both Tagore and Gandhi was to awaken the masses to the cause of freedom, which was the only option available to them to avoid being bullied and humiliated. History is full of examples that raising a voice against the predators 'heralds the dawn of awakening social self-consciousness of a class or community [which will lead to] … the emancipation of the chained communities or races'.[24] Here, Tagore stands out because he, by insisting on the sociopolitical awakening of the Indians, questioned the urge of the global leaders for internationalizing the globe. This was an absurd proposition so long as the world was divided between nations in terms of wealth and coercive capability, which Berlin very unambiguously mentioned by saying that the campaign for internationalism was likely to succeed in

a world where peoples were of approximately equal strength and status; but so long as vast inequalities existed, these sermons … would have

---

[21] Berlin, 265.

[22] The idea is borrowed from Amartya Sen, who developed this in his *The Argumentative Indian: Writings on Indian History, Culture and Identity* (New York, Picador, 2005), 105.

[23] The quotation is taken from https://www.goodreads.com/quotes/575759-i-do-not-want-my-house-to-be-walled-in, accessed June 28, 2020.

[24] Berlin, *The Sense of Reality*, 264.

achieved the unity which the kid achieved with the tiger when it was swallowed by it.[25]

Furthermore, given the arrogance of the colonizers since the inception of colonialism in India, the call for international amity was just like expecting a tiger to give up hunting deer since it caused a depletion of the deer population. In the then context, no sermon was likely to be effective, Tagore warned, because 'justice to the weak, given human being as they, is rare because it is difficult; and to change human beings so that they will not be as they are is utopian'.[26] The situation was far more complex that it appeared. It was not an easy job because the well-entrenched mindset, capable of making a large group of people dance to its tunes, had been given access to unbridled coercive power. Nonetheless, the task needed to be undertaken, and Tagore thus suggested that 'one must seek to improve mankind by available means, not by demanding of them unattainable virtue which only the saints can emulate'.[27] Being a thinker who was well acquainted with the prevalent sociopolitical reality, Tagore put forward a point which was not readily acceptable, since it was contrary to the mainstream nationalist perception. Politically, as history shows, India was under-going a metamorphosis, since the mainstream nationalist leaders, known as the Moderates, were severely criticized, if not castigated, by their followers for being excessively mild on the colonial rulers; the other group, the Extremists, preferred armed attack on the alien government and remained politico-ideologically isolated from the masses. Neither of these groups was adequate to fulfil the nationalist mission, Tagore realized. His idea of nationalism can thus be said to have been an offshoot of his time. Hence, it was articulated as a design in which appreciation for what was good in others and sensitivity to one's culture and heritage needed to be synthesized. This was the crux of the argument, which he underlined in his letter to his prospective son-in-law Nagendranath Gangulee, who was studying agriculture in the United States, by stating that

[25] Berlin, 264.

[26] Berlin, 263.

[27] Berlin, 263.

to get on familiar terms with the local people is a part of your education. To know only agriculture is not enough; you must know America too. Of course, if, in the process of knowing America, one begins to lose one's identity and falls into the trap of becoming an Americanised person contemptuous of everything Indian, it is preferable to stay in a locked room.[28]

This is a familiar warning, possibly based on the duality that he always upheld and appreciated in his textual analysis of the Indian sociopolitical reality in the context of the colonial rule. The ideas that emanated from the West were never dismissed as misfits; nor were their indigenous counterparts hailed as axiomatic. A careful study of the novels *Ghare Baire* (1916), *Gora* (1909) and *Char Adhyay* (1934) substantiates the point. In *Ghare Baire*, set in the context of the 1905–1908 campaign for revocation of the first Partition of Bengal, the three main characters, Sandip, Nikhilesh and his wife, Bimala, represented the duality that Tagore himself expressed in his 1916 text on *Nationalism*. Being inspired by revolutionary nationalism, Sandip resorted to violence in fulfilling what he considered the nationalist goal, which attracted Bimala to him. Contrarily, Nikhilesh, also the local zamindar, held the view that by applying force on the hapless Indian subjects if they declined to burn foreign cloths, the politico-ideological objectives that the nationalists were seeking to attain could never be realized; instead, it would alienate the masses from the nationalist campaign. According to him, the poor villagers needed to be made self-sufficient, and only then the aim of the revolutionary nationalists was likely to be attained. Here, Tagore made two powerful points: the first one is derived from his powerful text entitled *Swadeshi Samaj,* which he published in 1904, where he provided a blueprint for a self-sufficient village around Santiniketan. The second point, equally important and also an anticipation of the Gandhian mode of a non-violent nationalist offensive, questioned the blind imitation of the Western mode of political struggle by drawing upon violence. Unique here is the argument that Gandhi was to make soon, upon taking charge of the nationalist counteroffensive in the early 1920s. Tagore strongly felt that only by persuasion and not coercion, an effective method for political mobilization was conceivable. Perhaps,

---

[28] Krishna Dutta and Andrew Robinson, ed., *Selected Letters of Rabindranath Tagore* (Cambridge, Cambridge University Press, 1997), 67.

here lies the root of his faith in non-violence. In the novel too, Bimala, who was enamoured by the magnetic personality of Sandip when she saw him first, also realized the vacuous nature of the campaign unless it is complemented by the support of the people at large. Nikhilesh understood the mindset of the villagers far more clearly than his counterpart, Sandip, who not only failed to fathom the force of the masses but also, by undermining the villagers as illiterate and non-committal, created an impression of the revolutionary nationalists being arrogant and hateful towards the villagers, for which the later nationalists, particularly in Bengal, paid a heavy price.

The idea that the poet put across in *Ghare Baire* was very candidly expressed in his 1905 address to the students of Calcutta University, which corresponds with the principal message that the novel conveyed. As he said,

> the downtrodden and the despised who have become callous to insults and oblivious of even the rights of their humanity must be taught the meaning of the word brother. Teach them to be strong and to protect themselves; for that is the only way. Take, each of you, charge of some village and organize it. Educate the villagers and show them how to put forward their united strength. Look not for fame or praise in this undertaking. Do not expect even the gratitude of those for whom you would give your life, but be prepared rather for the opposition.[29]

His basic concern was to create a social compact based on mutual bonhomie, which, he strongly felt, was the only way for India's salvation. What is most striking is that *Ghare Baire* put forward a blueprint of India's nationalist struggle well ahead of some of the leading nationalists who rose to prominence later. For instance, in the novel, Tagore shows his opposition to the boycott of British education, which was one of the agendas of the 1905–1908 Swadeshi Movement in Bengal. One of the protagonists, Nikhilesh, found this demand of Sandip vacuous since it was likely to boomerang. History is illustrative here; the revolutionary nationalists faced severe challenges when they went around to campaign for the boycott of schools and colleges. In a very

---

[29] Cited in Prashanto Mahalanobis, *Prasango Rabindranath* (Bengalee which means About Rabindranath) (Calcutta, Mahalanobis Trust, 1985), 9.

poignant manner, Tagore wrote to Mahalanobis expressing his dismay at this development. As he wrote,

> I remember the day, during the Swadeshi movement in Bengal, when a crowd of young students came to see me, and said that if I would ask them to leave their schools and colleges, they instantly obey. I was emphatic in my refusal to do so, and they went away angry, doubting my sincerity of my love for my country.[30]

The novel is illustrative of Tagore's unique model of nationalism, which was also evident in his 1916 essay on *Nationalism*. In a significant way, he was a forerunner of many of Gandhi's modes of conceptualizing India's nationalist counter-attack on the British. Nonetheless, the textual articulation of Tagore's views in the novel provoked Georg Lukacs, who castigated the novel as being 'unimaginative' and

> propagandistic, demagogically one-sided stance [which] renders the novel completely worthless from the artistic angle. The spiritual aspect of the story ... is a petty bourgeois yarn of the shoddiest kind ... [his] wisdom was put at the intellectual service of the British police.[31]

This is not a place to assess whether Lukacs' views are worthwhile, since that is not the aim here. But it does not seem inappropriate to suggest that the reviewer, by missing the context, arrived at his conclusion, which is a little overstretched in imagination, by being a little unfair to the poet who simply, through a specific narrative, put forward a scheme for self-introspection for the nationalists, besides devising a model for indigenous initiatives for socio-economic growth and development.

If *Ghare Baire* signposts Tagore's mode of nationalizing the nationalists in a specific way, his 1934 novel, *Char Adhyay*, presents another far more nuanced version of his idea of nationalism and also those involved in pursuing the nationalist goals. Divided into four chapters, the storyline revolves around three main characters, Indranath, Ela

---

[30] Cited in Mahalanobis, 10.

[31] Georg Lukacs, *Tagore's Gandhi novel: review of Rabindranath Tagore, the Home and the world*, trans. Peter Palmer (London, Reviews and Articles, Merlin, 1983), 8–11.

and Atindra or Atin. Indranath was a devout revolutionary nationalist who believed in violent combat with the colonizers as the only
means to liberate India. Ela believed the same. Atin joined the group
because he was attracted to Ela. In course of time, Atin also endorsed
the line of thinking that Indranath epitomized which reached the
level of being obsessed with whatever the latter decreed. Unhappy
with Atin, because this makes him accept everything that Indranath
asked him to do, even at the cost basic human values, Ela expressed
her resentment openly. Despite being in love with Atin, she refused
to marry him as she had taken a vow to remain celibate in the service
of the country. The last *adahay* (chapter) is most poignant, because
it depicts the human dilemma that came out of the dialogue between
Ela and Atin when the latter was to execute the former since she was
a liability to the group.

The story is conceptualized at two levels: at the level of the poetic
expression of the contextual predicaments, *Char Adhyay* is a nationalist
narrative in which violence was privileged. Indranath favoured armed
combat with the colonizers as the only means for India's salvation. That
he was a successful leader also suggests that the ideas that he stood for
were generally accepted by those belonging to the group. There is a
historical foundation to the novel: during the 1920s and early 1930s,
the nationalists in Bengal, despite the rise of Gandhi and an Indian
icon, were drawn to the violent method, and the two revolutionary
nationalist groups, Jugantor and Anushilan, were politically dominant,
with their organization spread out in various parts of the province
with expanding support bases in major towns and also in Calcutta.
Unlike *Ghare Baire*, the narrative of *Char Adhyay* also brings out how
appeal for humanistic concerns prevailed over what went against the
characters. Ela was ready to be killed not because of her faith in the
type of nationalism that Indranath represented but because of her
unconditional love for Atin, which was not stated in so many words
in the novel but expressed through her wholehearted surrender to the
person whom she greatly loved.

Unlike *Ghare Baire,* which was more or less a black-and-white
representation of nationalism, *Char Adhyay* is far more complex, if
not highly nuanced. Here, Tagore dealt with two types of sentiments

which are also complementary in his views. On the one hand, he was articulating the new genre of the nationalist intervention in which violence was privileged. Indranath, for the fulfilment of his goal, was not even averse to kicking his erstwhile partner, Ela. His commitment to the cause, though not humane, was undiluted. That Tagore was not comfortable when basic human values were about to be sacrificed was the other side of the narrative. Despite being committed to the cause of the nation, the human dilemma that was so poignantly described by Tagore was evident when Ela expressed her love to Atin who was sent to kill her. By describing himself as *Swabhavachyuta* (fallen from natural inclination), Atin appears to have realized that what he was asked to do was anything but humane. He was made a machine because of the contextual compulsion and forgot the basic human values, largely due to him being obsessed with the ideology and its leader. Tagore expressed Atin's conceptualization of how the followers lost their capability of thinking independent of the inputs of the leader in very clear terms when the latter said

> the theoretician (mantradata) said—"all of you collectively tug at a thick rope of the chariot closing your eyes—this is your only work". Thousands of boys began doing so. Many fell under the wheels; many were maimed for life. Suddenly the theory changed; the order came to pull in a reverse direction. The chariot turned the other way. Those whose bones were broken, as a result, could not put back to health. The invalids were swept away into the dust heaps on the roadside. The faith in one's strength was destroyed so fully that everyone proudly agreed oneself after the official ideal of the leader. When in response to the leader's directions to pull the strings other way, everyone began to dance the same way thinking that was most apt at that time. The moment puppeteer loosened the strings, thousand became superfluous.[32]

Fundamental here is an ideological dilemma that Tagore himself confronted with the growing importance of the revolutionary nationalist movement in Bengal; at one level, he appeared to have appreciated the selfless sacrifice of the participants, but at another, he was equally disturbed because of the endeavours of the leaders to force their followers to follow them blindly regardless of the consequences. The

---

[32] Rabindranath Tagore, *Char Adhyay* (Kolkata, Visva-Bharati, 1934), 398.

movement had lost its mind, the confident Tagore argued. What upset him most was the decline of basic human values in the name of serving the nation. Atin was not a villain but one who had lost his soul, and as a result, he hardly feels hesitant to carry out the instruction of killing Ela, who surrendered to him since she was deeply in love with him. For Tagore, this was the dilemma of the age, in which humanness was a casualty and thus sacrificed at the slightest provocation. *Char Adhyay* is a testimony of a very clearly articulated mode of nationalism, upholding Tagore's deep belief in humanity, which needed to be protected first to develop a true nationalist mindset. The idea that this novel highlighted runs parallel with that of George Orwell's 1945 *Animal Farm,* which, by being allegorical to the brutal Stalinist regime in the erstwhile Soviet Union, endorsed the same conclusion by reinforcing that human values always remained *a priori* to any other politico-ideological goal.

The argument that Tagore provided while devising a unique model of nationalism of which appreciation for humanism is an integral part, cannot be complete without a critical assessment of the 1909 novel, *Gora.* An appraisal of his ideas in these three novels reveals that he developed complementary sets of views, both in his essays and in his novels, in support of the point that his contemporary colleagues did not always welcome. Set in 1870 Bengal, *Gora* is an articulation of a politico-ideological priority that was a little different from those of *Char Adhyay* and *Ghare Baire,* in the sense that here Tagore was far more forthright in his views. Gora is the son of a retired government official who was known for his orthodoxy, which significantly influenced him. His meeting with Binoy, who took him to Paresh babu, an erudite Brahmo who privileged personal morality and spiritual sensitivity over any ideology was a beginning of a new chapter in his life. The story gets complex when Binay falls in love with Lolita, Paresh Babu's daughter. A spirited, defiant girl with a mind of her own, Lolita did not like Binay being over-dependent on Gora because of her fear that he would lose his independence in ideas and views. This was not acceptable to Lolita because of her strong belief that without argument and counterargument no advancement of ideas and thoughts was possible. That her love for Binay was conditional was evident when she ran away with Binay on his return to Calcutta, despite the risk of the social scandal that immediately erupted as was common then. Meanwhile, Gora's idea of India had undergone a sea change when he had had a chance to visit rural Bengal. The views that he had imbibed about the country through his orthodox upbringing were severely challenged; his stereotypes about Hindus and Muslims were completely shattered. He was introduced to the more open Hinduism of the village barber who lived in solidarity with the Muslims rather than with their Hindu oppressors.

The other interesting aspect of the novel is when Gora, being enamoured by Sucharita, Paresh Babu's adopted daughter, had fallen in love with her. Unlike Lolita, Sucharita, being reticent and more absorbing, gave a different impression of womanhood to Gora. For him, she was not just a woman but a representation of Indian womanhood. After several rounds of meetings and interactions with Sucharita, Gora was now persuaded to believe that 'women do not merely symbolize the motherland, they are the motherland and it is the indifference to the humiliation of woman-as-motherland which explains the male's insecurity about thus loss of manhood'.[33] Nonetheless, Gora was torn between his commitment to the nation and his love for Sucharita, because, according to Paresh Babu, Gora's ideological mentor, it was not so easy for Gora to appreciate human emotions, given his obstinacy for his ideological commitment. The end of the novel shows a clear reversal, since Gora, once he was told that he was not even an Indian because he was born to Irish parents and was only raised by the Hindu family, realized how human sentiments prevailed over other considerations. To explicate the inner feelings of Gora, when he came to know about his Irish lineage, Tagore most poignantly wrote in the novel that

> the foundation on which, from childhood all his life had been raised had suddenly crumbled into dust, and he was unable to understand who he was and where he stood. ... He felt as though he were like the dew drop on the lotus leaf which comes into existence for a moment only. He had no mother, no father, no country, no nationality, no lineage, no God even. Only one thing was left to him and that was a vast negation.[34]

[33] Rabindranath Tagore, *Gora* (Kolkatai, Visva-Bharati, 1909), 272–3.

[34] Tagore, 278.

What is striking here is the forceful argument in favour of human-ism that Tagore so strongly believed in. Despite being enamoured by Hindu orthodoxy and the nationalist inklings, Gora was now apprecia-tive of his being as a human being, which was severely threatened, if not shattered, by the divulgence of his true lineage. It was then clear to him that neither ideological commitment *per se* nor an unconditional adherence to what was transplanted onto him as true Hinduism was adequate to one's existence as a human being. What was required was to be appreciative of (a) human values and (b) the prevalent socio-cultural context supportive of those ideas and designs which helped build a true nationalist compact.

There are three points that deserve attention here: first, as *Gora* was a continuity of the ideas that Tagore put forward in both *Ghare Baire* and *Char Adhyay,* the novel is also a context-driven articulation of the thoughts that he forcefully presented. Central to *Gora* was his unconditional patriotism, which was not very dissimilar to the one that flourished in the phase of revolutionary nationalism of the 1870s and its immediate aftermath. A group of youth who were altruistic and committed to the nationalist cause dedicated their life to fulfil their aim of removing the foreign rule. Being appreciative of their selfless sacrifice, Tagore however did not find their sacrifice worthwhile, presumably because of their reluctance to evolve a model with refer-ence to the existent sociopolitical texture of Bengal. *Gora* epitomized that concern which the poet had been pursuing in his writings. Two complementary aspects of the novel clarify the point: Gora's first-had experience of the human bonhomie in Bengal villages where a Hindu family easily accepted a Muslim barber as the member of his extended family despite being religiously different and despised a Hindu oppressor notwithstanding sharing the same religious inclinations. This was not unusual in rural Bengal, where the son of Faru Sardar, a Muslim jailed for his opposition to the British rule, was taken care of by a Hindu family. Similarly, Gora was perplexed when he found that Madhab Chatterjee, a British loyalist, planned to ostracize the Hindu family for being kind to Faru Sardar's son given his religious identity as a Muslim. What stands out here is the importance of human values which put human beings together regardless of socio-cultural differences. The second evidence comes when Gora declared, at the end of the novel, that 'Today I am free … today I am really an Indian. In me there is no longer any opposition between Hindu, Muslim and Christian. Today every caste is my caste, the food of all is my food'.[35] These are useful inputs to develop Tagore's unique ideas of universal humanism. What they establish is that Tagore, being opposed to institutionalized religion, never allowed religious parochialism to thrive, and his writings are not only exemplary but was also illustrative of a design that however did not received as much attention as was required during his lifetime. Complementary to universal humanism was also his views on how to empower women, which he illustrated in *Gora* as well. By creating the character of Lolita, the flamboyant woman who was not afraid of social scandal for love and Sucharita who, by being reticent, also taught Gora what selfless love meant and how it complemented his growth as a 'true' human being, the poet captured complexities of human behaviour. Interestingly, one finds a continuity in the thoughts that Tagore put forward while depicting Bimala in *Ghare Baire*, Ela in *Char Adhyay* and Lolita and Sucharita in *Gora*.

Gora appears to have personified Tagore himself. It was evident when he appreciated Paresh Babu who, in tune with Brahmo belief, was a 'good householder, lived simply'[36] and in his study on the wall is a coloured picture of Christ and a photo of Keshab [the social reformer] … and in a small bookcase on the upper shelf stood a complete set of Theodore Parker's [an American thinker (1810–1860) who, as an abolitionist, inspired Abraham Lincoln and Martin Luther King Jr] works arranged in a row'.[37] The uncertainty that seems to have bothered Tagore in *Ghare Baire* and *Char Adayay* appears to have gone in *Gora*, which is illustrative of an endeavour on his part to blend 'the nobler features of Brahmo heritage with the exigencies of contemporary life in Bengal'.[38] The effort was directed at challenging 'narrow nationalism that Gora epitomized [by insisting on] a self-overly well-defined and

---

[35] Tagore, 279.

[36] Kopf, *The Brahmo Samaj*, 297.

[37] Tagore, *Gora*, 31.

[38] Kopf, *The Brahmo Samaj*, 297.

exclusive ... and an authentic Indian identity'.[39] The idea was stated far more scathingly in his essay 'Towards a Universal Man', published posthumously in 1961, in which he lashed out at those who 'buried the abuses of the Hindu social order in the patriotic sloganeering of aggressive nationalist ideology'. His vehement opposition to the artificially created caste system was not new, but 'nowhere earlier did [he] attack the caste system so scathingly as a system where men are looked upon as lower than beasts'.[40] As a result, 'life departed from [India's] social system and in its place she is worshipping with all ceremony the magnificent cage of countless compartments that she has manufactured'.[41] This was an irritant to the poet, which he articulated by saying that so long as the caste system existed, even if 'we succeeded in pushing out the British by one means or another this pain [due to artificial social segregation] will still be there'.[42] The voice was heard in the Constituent Assembly when Ambedkar argued that one of the serious impediments towards realizing Indian nationhood was caste, which never allowed to develop 'the sense of common brotherhood to all Indians, or the idea of Indians being one people, an idea which gives unity and solidarity to social life'.[43] In the then circumstances when the caste order was so well-entrenched, fraternity was neither instinctive to Indians nor organic to their psyche. Hence, so long as the caste system was allowed to survive, the point about the inculcation of a sense of being one as a community seemed fruitless. This was further elaborated when Ambedkar adumbrated the view that since caste, as a system, was divisive, it was 'anti-national [because] in the first place [it] brings about separation in social life and [secondly] because [it] generates jealousy and antipathy between caste and caste'.[44] For Tagore, contrived social segmentation was an evil in itself, just like for

[39] Ashis Nandy, *The Illegitimacy of nationalism* (Delhi, Oxford University Press, 1994), 42.

[40] Kopf, *The Brahmo Samaj*, 298.

[41] Rabindranath Tagore, *Nationalism* (Delhi, Macmillan India, 1985, reprint), 70.

[42] Rabindranath Tagore, *Towards a Universal Man* (London, Asia Publishing House, 1961), 139.

[43] Ambedkar, Address in the Constituent Assembly, 980.

[44] Ambedkar, 980.

B. R. Ambedkar who realized that unless the supremacist mindset was completely abrogated, the idea of India being one solid social compact would be remote, if not improbable.

The purpose here is to piece together Tagore's ideas based on his heartfelt urge to bring disparate Indians together for emancipation in the real sense of the term. As is argued above, political salvation was an important ingredient, but not all; it needed to be complemented by socio-economic freedom in which segregation, either in the social or economic axis, was an anathema. Being exposed to the global scene and the views of those who felt alike, the poet did not mince his words while questioning the heartlessness of the Western powers and their cohorts who were causing devastations by taking out humanity out of human civilization, by privileging the heartless rat race for material gain at any cost and by coercing the subjugation of one section of the people by another. In an essay entitled 'Race Conflict' (1931), he thus wrote that

> when the organized national selfishness, racial antipathy and commercial self-seeking begin to display their ugly deformities in all their nakedness, then comes the time for man to know that his salvation is not in political organization and extended trade relations, not in any mechanical rearrangement of social system, but in a deeper transformation of life, in the liberation of consciousness in love, in the realization of God in man.[45]

Bereft of love, care, concern and empathy for human beings, the existence of humanity was at peril. The three novels, *Ghare Baire*, *Char Adhyay* and *Gora*, that we have discussed above are knitted together with a powerful voice for universal humanism. In its earlier version, Brahmo-ism was projected as an exclusive design that was extremely critical of Hinduism, which Tagore heavily detested because it led to Brahmo sectarianism. On one occasion, he thus mentioned that 'the Brahmo Samaj ... is belittling Ram Mohan Roy by judging him as a Brahmo minus the Hindu society'.[46] He appeared to have favoured the

---

[45] Rabindranath Tagore, 'Race Conflict' in Rabindranath Tagore, *Boundless Sky* (Kolkata, Visva-Bharati, 2008, reprint), 348–9.

[46] Rabindranath Tagore, *Charitrapuja* (Appreciation of four Great Men of India), (Kolkata, Visva-Bharati Granthan Bhibhag, 1405, Bangavda), 59.

idea of Hindu Brahmoism which was, besides being a serious critique of Brahmo sectarianism, perhaps directed at creating a unified social compact. In other words, his aim was to integrate the smaller units into a larger unit, while at the same time 'advocating that Hindu society integrate itself into the larger unit of Asian civilization'.[47] Furthermore, he even went to the extent of saying that 'unless Brahmos identify with Hinduism, the attempt to give it progressive leadership, the community would be committing suicide by allowing the Hindu reformation to drift into false directions'.[48] One of the stepping stones towards giving the zeal for social reform a big push was to evolve an education system which was conducive to individual freedom. Being critical of the Russian education system, since it aimed at evolving and also consolidating a mould to caste humanity in a preordained manner, Tagore warned that it would 'burst into pieces or man's mind will be paralysed to death or man will be turned into a mechanical doll'.[49] It was a powerful critique of the endeavour seeking to essentialize human beings, which was likely to be suicidal in view of the ingrained socio-cultural diversity among human beings. The outcome was disastrous, as Tagore himself most unambiguously expressed when he wrote that

> our living society, which should have dance in its steps, music in its voice, beauty in its limbs, which should have its metaphor in stars and flowers, maintaining its harmony with God's creation, becomes, under the tyranny of a prolific greed, like an overladen market-cart, jolting and creaking on the road that leads from things to the Nothing, rearing ugly ruts across the green life till it breaks down under the burden of its vulgarity on the wayside, reaching nowhere.[50]

Here, Tagore held the views that Gandhi conveyed in many of his writings. Both of the them resonated the ideas that Edward Carpenter's *Civilization: Its Cause and Cure* (1889) elaborated. Critical in Carpenter's work was the contemporary efforts towards debasing the

---

[47] Kopf, *The Brahmo Samaj*, 302.

[48] Cited in Kopf, 302.

[49] Rabindranath Tagore, *Russia's Letter* (Kolkata, Visva-Bharati, 1426, Bangavda), 27.

[50] Rabindranath Tagore, 'Civilization and Progress' in Rabindranath Tagore, *Bundles of Joy* (Kolkata, Visva-Bharati, 2008, reprint), 204.

foundational human emotions and moralities that constituted civilization. Like Tagore, he despised the beastly urge of those championing civilization by saying that

> the various theories and views of nature which we hold are merely the fugitive envelopes of the successive stags of human growth—each set of theories and views belonging organically to the moral and emotional stage which has been reached, and being in some sort the expression of it; so that the attempt at any given time to set up an explanation of phenomena which shall be valid in itself and without reference to the mental condition of those who set it up, necessarily ends in failure; and the present state of confusion and contradiction in which modern Science finds itself is merely the result of such attempt.[51]

Carpenter attributed the debasement in modern civilization to the lack of importance to the moral and emotional quotient of human beings. The growth of human civilization was not, at all, a machine-driven act, but an outcome of a creative blending of human efforts, soaked in moral uplift and emotional gratification. The concern was similar when Gandhi, in his *The Hind Swaraj* or *Indian Home Rule* (1909) wrote that

> this civilization takes note neither of morality nor of religion. Its votaries calmly state that their business is not to teach religion. Some even consider it to be superstitious growth. Others put on the cloak of religion, and prate about morality.[52]

As the contemporary civilization was hardly restrained by moral and religious shackles, it led to social degeneration, affecting the entire humanity. In other words, for gains of an absolutely temporary nature, the humanity lost, to a significant extent, its identity. Human beings ceased to be human beings. They were turned into machines and 'keep up their energy', Gandhi exhorted, 'by intoxication ... and for the sake of pittance women who should be the queens of households,

---

[51] http://www.gutenberg.org/files/44094/44094-h/44094-h.htm#Page_15, Edward Carpenter, *Civilization: Its Cause and Cure* (London, George Allen and Unwin, 1989), 80.

[52] M. K. Gandhi, *The Hind Swaraj or Indian Home Rule* (Ahmedabad, Navajivan Publishing House, 2005, reprint), 32.

wander in the streets or they slave away in the factories'.[53] Central to the argument is the adverse impact of contemporary civilization on human life, due largely to unbridled industrialization, which also created the nationalist urge for politically controlling those nations which lagged behind industrially. So, there was a logical connection between the emergence of industrialized nations and the search for markets for selling their products, which was made easier by colonizing country after country for the colonizers' partisan gains. In his last address, delivered on 14 April 1941, Tagore nurtured the same feelings. According to him, he who

> set the English on the throne of [his] heart because of the qualities that the English race represented [was] ... soon disillusioned ... when [he] began increasingly to discover how easily those who accepted the highest truths of civilization disowned them with impunity whenever questions of national self-interests were involved.[54]

While drawing attention to the pernicious impact of the British rule in India, he did not hide his resentment, because, for him, it was a disillusionment, since he held the British nation in high esteem for the contribution it had made to the welfare of humanity. As a colonial power, by abdicating those exalted values of the Enlightenment philosophy, the British nation was no longer the one that he admired. One of the reasons, he further added, reiterating the language of Carpenter and Gandhi, was that

> the mastery over the machine, by which the British have consolidated their sovereignty over their vast empire, has been a sealed book, to which due access has been denied to this hapless country.[55]

The result was obvious, as 'India smothered under the dead weight of British administration, lay static in her utter helplessness'.[56] Emotionally disturbed, Tagore also warned that though India

---

[53] Gandhi, 33.

[54] Rabindranath Tagore, *Crisis in Civilization* (Kolkata, Visva-Bharati, 2014, reprint), 14.

[55] Tagore, 15.

[56] Tagore, 18.

was suffering now under the machine-driven British rule, 'it was symptomatic of a global problem', because, as he articulated,

> the demon of barbarity has given up all pretence and has emerged with unconcealed fangs, ready to tear up humanity in an orgy of devastation. From one end of the world to the other the poisonous fumes of hatred darken the atmosphere. The spirit of violence which perhaps lay dormant in the psychology of the West, has at last roused itself and desecrates the spirit of Man.[57]

Here is also an ideational connection between Tagore, Carpenter and Gandhi: they all felt that industrialization was responsible for debasing humanity. The narrow desire of expanding their sphere of influence by deploying coercive powers led the industrialized nations to unhesitatingly subjugate the less powerful people. By being protective of their industrial know-how, the British regime deliberately pursued a partisan design for keeping India industrially backward so that their rule continued uninterruptedly. With the increasing power of these industrially advanced nations that hardly bothered about humanism, there was little hope, Tagore rued, for the vast humanity in the colonies that reeled under unbridled violence and brutality. The increasing importance of nation was an attack not only on humanity but also on its unshackled unfolding. By championing narrow and rabid nationalism, Japan lost, argued Tagore, her traditional glory. Similarly, Gandhi also found that the British nationalist project was doomed to be a failure as it was derivative of narrow motives and the wilful ignorance of basic human values.

CONCLUDING OBSERVATIONS

For Tagore, nationalism was 'a menace',[58] since it was based on the wild urge of fulfilling partisan missions of a collectivity, selfishly appreciative of its distinctive socio-cultural existence. This was most unambiguously stated by him when he said that

---

[57] Tagore, 21.

[58] Tagore, *Nationalism*, 67.

the idea of nation is one of the most powerful anaesthetics that man has invented. Under the influence of its fumes the whole people can carry out its systematic programme of the most virulent self-seeking without being in the least aware of its moral perversion—in fact can feel dangerously resentful if it is pointed out.[59]

Implicit here are two very perceptive comments that Tagore made to sharpen his arguments against nationalism: on the one hand, nationalism is ideologically directed at creating a self-obsessed concern for clearly communal interests; this is dangerous, on the other hand, because the idea of nationalism contributes to the generation of a most virulent campaign towards attaining the goal at any cost. By referring to the radical transformation of the British race from being a champion of humanism to one that pursued a policy of ruthless governance at the cost of core human values, he justified his claim. He elaborated his argument, saying:

I have a deep love and a great respect for the British race as human beings. It has produced great-hearted men, thinkers of great thoughts, doers of great deeds. It has given rise to great literature. I know that these people love justice and freedom and hate lies. They are clean in their minds, frank in their manners, true in their friendships; in their behaviour they are honest and reliable. The personal experience which I have had of their literary men has roused my admiration not merely for their power of thought or expression but for their chivalrous humanity.[60]

Here, he can be said to have been enamoured by the British race for its contribution to universal humanism through creative designs benefitting the human race. Based on his own experience with many men of letters in Britain, Tagore neither had hesitation nor was constrained in expressing his admiration of the British race as a whole for being so noble in its mission and also its accomplishments. The race had however degenerated, claimed the poet, once Britain became a nation and pursued her narrow nationalist goal at all costs. The same Tagore who commended 'the greatness of the British race'[61] as the contribution

---

[59] Tagore, 25–6.

[60] Tagore, 9–10.

[61] Tagore, 10.

of the sun to Mother Earth was very critical, since Britain as 'a Nation [became] … a thick mist of a stifling nature covering the sun itself'.[62] For Tagore, the stark deviation of Britain from the values of the Enlightenment philosophy that drew on care, concern and empathy for fellow human beings was attributed to her being transformed into a nation. He was now far more caustic in her criticism, which was evident when he stated that

> [t]his government by the Nation is neither British nor anything else; it is an applied science and therefore more or less similar in principles wherever it is used. It is like a hydraulic press, whose pressure is impersonal, and on that account completely effective. The amount of its power may vary in different engines. Some may even be driven by hand, thus leaving a margin of comfortable looseness in their tension, but in spirit and in method their differences are small. Our government might have been Dutch or French or Portuguese, … its essential features would have been the same.[63]

Like Gandhi who condemned the Empire since it followed policies which were contrary to the core principles of the Enlightenment philosophy, Tagore held the same logic in the sense that he chided the British government in India for being deviant of these ideas on which the British civilization rested. Similar to the Mahatma, the poet also attributed the civilizational crisis to rabid industrialization that, regardless of human consequences, created a milieu in which human beings became ruthless in pursuing partisan goals. In other words, industrialization was responsible for a situation that took creativity away from human beings, which Tagore articulated metaphorically by stating that

> in the products of the hand-loom the magic of man's living fingers find its expression, and its hum harmonises with the music of life. But the power-loom is relentlessly lifeless and accurate and monotonous in its production.[64]

[62] Tagore, 10.

[63] Tagore, 10.

[64] Tagore, 10.

His scathing critique of industrialization was complemented by his earnest endeavour at developing indigenous handicrafts, which he conceptualized in his *Swadeshi Samaj* (1904) and put into practice in Sriniketan with adequate support from his colleagues. Fundamental here was Tagore's conceptual point that he made by being critical of the ruthlessness of Britain being a nation. By implication, it means that had Britain not been a nation in its most limited sense, she would not have been appreciative of these considerations justifying the exploitation of human beings by their counterparts elsewhere. This was surely a blot, felt Tagore, on human civilization that needed to be deplored and effectively countered for the sake of the existence of human beings as human beings. His critique is persuasive, because the explanation that he provides to defend his point of view is crystal clear. This is evident when he argued that

> the nation with its paraphernalia of power and prosperity, its flags and pious hymns, its blasphemous prayers in the churches and the library mock thunders of its patriotic bragging, cannot hide the fact that the Nation is the greatest evil for the Nation, that all its precaution are against it, and any new birth of its fellow is the greatest evil.[65]

It was natural for Tagore to vehemently oppose the eulogization of nation, since it was contrary to the core values of universal humanism that he always upheld. He emphatically believed that 'my country-men will truly gain their India by fighting against the education that teaches them that a country is greater than the ideals of humanity'.[66] The belief was well-entrenched, as far as Tagore was concerned. The poet strongly felt that under no circumstances was humanism to be sacrificed. Being endowed with coercive power, the Western nations, in the name of their civilizing missions, created a milieu by instituting an institutionalized system of hierarchy among human beings which, instead of sustaining humanity, was responsible for a general decadence in human society. Since Indian culture was not receptive to this idea, stated Tagore, the countrymen were instinctively averse

[65] Tagore, 17–18.
[66] Tagore, 64.

to this endeavour. In other words, a blind imitation was anything but conducive to the growth and consolidation of universal humanism on which the Indian civilization rested. With his great sense of history, the bard firmly believed that the jingoist nationalism had emerged in the European contextual peculiarities which were completely alien to India. Hence, his advice was to

> make up our minds that we cannot borrow other people's history, and that if we stifle our own, we are committing suicide [because] ... when you borrow things that do not belong to your life, they only serve to crush your life.[67]

This is one aspect of the argument that he offered to condemn nationalism as an organizing principle, because it was a socio-culturally imposed design in India following the consolidation of British colonialism. The other aspect highlighting the constraints for India to rise as a unit drawn on her own socio-cultural strength was the artificially generated caste segmentation deriving its sustenance from 'the recognition of differences, but not the mutability which the law of life'.[68] As a result, 'Life departed from her social system and in its place she is worshipping with all ceremony the magnificent cage of countless compartments that she has manufactured'.[69] The caste system was thus nothing but a contrived social division which helped build a mindset supportive of its continuity for mere partisan gains. A humanist to the core, the poet raised his voice challenging the very socio-religious foundation of the caste system; he also warned that unless it was completely done away with, the campaign for political freedom was doomed to be a failure. According to him,

> the social habit of mind which impels us to make the life of our fellow-beings a burden to them where they differ from us even in such a thing as their choice of food, is sure to persist in our political organization and result in creating energies of coercion to crush every rational difference which is the sign of life.[70]

[67] Tagore, 64.
[68] Tagore, 70.
[69] Tagore, 70.
[70] Tagore, 75.

Social division was an impediment that needed to be eradicated to realize freedom in its real sense. Mere emancipation from political bondage with the withdrawal of the Raj was futile, Tagore further noted, unless it was complemented by systemic politico-ideological changes liberating the socially ostracized section of the society. The freedom that one should aspire for was one that created conditions for human emancipation. Here, the bard was very emphatic in expressing his views. As he strongly argued,

> those of us in India who have come under the delusion that mere political freedom will make us free have accepted their lessons from the West as the gospel truth and lost their faith in humanity. We must remember that whatever weakness we cherish in our society will become the source of danger in politics. The same inertia which leads us to our idolatry of dead forms in social institutions will create in our politics prison-houses with immovable walls. The narrowness of sympathy which makes it possible for us to impose upon a considerable portion of humanity the galling yoke of inferiority will assert itself in our politics in creating the tyranny of injustice.[71]

Here too, there are two fundamental points that deserve attention. First, questioning the Western emphasis on materialism at the cost of humanity, the poet reiterated his faith in universal humanism. Resonating the ideas of Edward Carpenter and Gandhi, as discussed above, Tagore strongly felt and also persuasively argued for humanism to thrive, and the Western endeavour at development at any cost was accordingly questioned. Second, being severely critical of the highly divisive social fabric of India due to caste segregation, the poet attributed the failure of India as a unit of human collectivity to the prevalence of separation between communities of the basis of the accident of birth. As it was a man-made device to sanction social authority to some to oppress the rest, it could be neither logical nor humanitarian. For the bard, just like the racial segregation justified by a supremacist mindset, caste division was a social ailment that needed to be cured to evolve a healthy India. Here too, Tagore reiterated the views of Gandhi, who fought a relentless battle against caste hierarchy, and also B. R. Ambedkar, who stands out for his lifelong crusade against endeavours

---

[71] Tagore, 74.

towards separating the majority of the population from the rest on the basis of one's caste identity.

To conclude, Tagore's assessment of nationalism is one of the persuasive accounts of the idea which was both contextual and transcendental: contextual because the idea evolved in a milieu wherein the mainstream nationalists in India made an effort to galvanize the people towards a nationalist goal, to which Tagore objected, and transcendental since the bard's conceptualization helps us comprehend the unholy nexus between nationalism and the pursuit of self-interests. Nonetheless, a question is usually raised as to whether Tagore believed in nationalism, since he endorsed the nationalist campaign that held political freedom as its principal goal. A surface reading suggests that he was not nationalistic in his belief and endeavour, yet, he appreciated the selfless sacrifice of those who fought against the British for political emancipation. To address this issue persuasively, one is tempted to argue, as a commentator did, that Tagore was seeking to clearly

> separate patriotism from nationalism so to create an intellectual and psychological base that would allow the "natural" territoriality of a political community to avoid the European-style nationalism ... since he foresaw the devastation towards which European nationalism was pushing Europe and the world.[72]

Hence, one can be a patriot without being a nationalist, argued Tagore. The idea is simple: a patriot can be a nationalist, but a nationalist may not always be a patriot in the sense Tagore understood. There is a caveat here: for the poet, 'patriotism cannot be our final shelter; my refuge is humanity', which he reinforced unambiguously by stating that 'I will never allow patriotism to triumph over humanity as long as I live'.[73] The argument conforms to Tagore's widely publicized point of view privileging humanity over any other consideration, which means that if humanity was sacrificed by being patriotic, the poet was not hesitant to raise his voice against this. The argument was

---

[72] Ashis Nandy, 'Genuine and Spurious: mourning two early post-nationalist strains', *Economic and Political Weekly* 41, no. 32 (August, 12–18, 2006): 3501.

[73] In a letter to Ababla Bose, wife of the famous scientist, Jagadish Chandra Bose, Tagore made this point. The letter is cited in Sen, *The Argumentative India*, 108.

further extended when the bard was critical of the attitude insisting on oneness, which the nationalists demanded while pursuing their goal, which was not unusual, presumably because he upheld India's socio-cultural diversities as a source of inner strength. Nationalism in India, as Tagore felt, should not be exclusive but a politico-ideological design to bring together socio-culturally disparate people. It is conceptualized at two levels. At one level, it is merely a label seeking to unite one with another for a cause; in the case of Tagore, it was the urge for political emancipation from the British rule. At another, far more perceptive level, nationalism is one of the cementing factors along with, for instance, religion, cultural distinctiveness and regional visibility in terms of some distinctive features, among others. The reasons are not difficult to seek. In South Asia,

> nationalism as an ideology has a thin presence in most citizens [presumably because] ... not only are the religions alive and kicking in this part of the world, so are many aspects of the traditional cosmologies aligned or associated with religions.[74]

What is hinted here is the fact that besides nationalism, there are other ideational modes in which fraternity develops. Appreciation for the nation does not necessarily mean endorsement of the argument seeking to essentialize the multiple socio-cultural traits which are ingrained in India. Here, nation refers to a unity comprising people who are instinctively respectful to the multiple socio-cultural identities that they inherit by being born and raised in different social, economic and political environments. So, nation, as Tagore consistently argued, has a wider connotation that cannot be comprehended if it is sought to be conceptualized in the Western prism highlighting the boundary-driven national identity. Here, one notices Tagore being a little flexible in his approach to the idea of nation. At one level, he was clear that 'Nation ... is the organized self-interest of a whole people where it is least [humane] and least spiritual'.[75] At another, rather perceptive level, he appears to have deviated from this stance, as he clearly welcomed the design of the nation for fulfilling his concerns for rural well-being. In

---

[74] Nandy, 'Genuine and Spurious', 3503.

[75] Rabindranath Tagore, *Nationalism*, 8.

Swadeshi Samaj, where Tagore put forward an alternative model in sharp contrast to nation-driven human existence, he did not seem to be hesitant in borrowing nationalist mechanisms for organizing people on a larger scale. This appears to be logical, since it was easy to manage 'a small village given the intimate contact that existed between people in small villages [which was] ... implausible in Tagore's Swadeshi Samaj comprising a cluster of villages'.[76] Hence, what was required was a nation-state-derived mechanism to build cohesion, which Tagore saw as a necessary condition for the proper functioning of the *samaj.* In such circumstances, argued the poet, borrowing was not unjustified. Being practical in his approach, the bard did not feel hesitant to learn from the West of how to cement a bond among many for the sake of a common cause. He thus metaphorically suggested that 'unless one installs the instruments for production, the factories shall not work'.[77] Likewise, by accepting the borrowed mechanism, he upheld his primary concern for achieving the goal. Here is a caveat in his argument, because he, despite having accepted the derivative mechanism, as it was necessary, was not, at all, inclined to give up his commitment to the humanist ideal of fraternity on which Indian civilization rested. It was evident in his elaboration of the structure of the *samaj* and also the mechanism that enforced its democratic character. Most of the ingredients in Tagore's recipe for the *samaj* had been structural and ideological pillars of Western state systems. Being sensitive to the Indian socio-psychological reality, he adapted these elements and mechanisms with an eye for the diverse and specific requirements of the Indian peoples. Hence, the arguments that the poet offered in defence also delve into the roles of religion and other traditional rites and rituals associated with the community, and also region; their roles cannot be wished away, since they also help cement and sustain the bond among the members of a multitude. That religion, Hinduism in particular, has ritualistically different manifestations in different parts of India is a testimony to the argument that it is not adequate to keep people together, since they hold identical religious inclinations. Fundamental

---

[76] Rabindranath Tagore, 'Swadeshi Samaj' in *Collected Works of Rabindranath Tagore* (Rabindra Rachanabali) (Kolkata, Visva-Bharati, 1410, Bangavda), Vol., 643.

[77] Tagore, Vol. 2, 643.

to Tagore's perception on nationalism is the qualified acceptance of some of the Western criteria for nation-building, which substantiates the claim that the *swadeshi samaj* was simultaneously indigenous and also derivative in its ideological and structural characteristics. Unity or togetherness in diversity remained the core assumption on which the arguments that the bard put across drew their sustenance from. Critical here is also the point that Tagore, being born and nurtured in an environment of cross-cultural influences, evolved as a model in which nationalism or the nationalistic design had not emerged in the European way but had been articulated by being sensitive to India's socio-cultural peculiarities. This was therefore a uniquely conceptualized mode of nationalizing people, because though it did not hinge on othering, it was not prone to uncritically accepting exogenous influences either.

Tagore on Socio-economic Reconstruction

3

Similar to Gandhi, Rabindranath Tagore evolved a unique model for inclusive development. There are many texts which are illustrative of Gandhi's concerns. In his *Constructive Programme* (1946), Gandhi laid out a scheme of socio-economic rejuvenation for the country as a whole, which was put to test in the ashrams in South Africa and later in India. Critical of dependence on outside help, the Mahatma stressed the need for being self-sufficient to realize the socio-economic needs of the people. He insisted on people becoming neither completely independent nor dependent but inter-dependent on one another. Tagore's views coalesced with those of Gandhi to a significant extent, though in one respect the former was a little different, since he translated his ideas with the formation of Sriniketan (abode of wealth) in 1928. Interestingly, not only was he involved with the evolution of Sriniketan from the very beginning, he also devoted his energy to its development by resorting to various means for augmenting the income of the rural folk who had no alternative source of income besides agriculture. With his own initiatives, the village handicrafts had a market in Bengal and elsewhere, which was surely of great help to the villagers who found a new source of income to take care of their needs. That he had concerns for rural reconstruction was evident in his 1904 tract entitled *Swadeshi Samaj*, which literally means an indigenous society, though it was meant to develop a model of change for betterment in a context when neither the ruler nor the Bengalee elites seem to have paid much attention to this aspect. *Swadeshi Samaj* is Tagore's manifesto for rural development. His choice was based on the consideration that without making Indian villages self-sufficient economically, the campaign for political freedom was, at best, a self-gratifying rhetoric and, at worse, a design for permanently segregating the villages from the towns and cities. Here too, Tagore was not much different from Gandhi, who held the views that 'India lives in the villages'. For the Mahatma, the village remained the core of the development strategy that he proposed in his *Constructive Programme*. A package of how to bring about inclusive development, Gandhi's *Constructive Programme* was not merely a checklist of what was required to be done in this respect but also an appropriate design for development by involving the stakeholders; it was a well-thought-out plan to evolve a people-centric design for growth and significant socio-economic change. A little probing into the programme reveals that the Mahatma was interested in a scheme that would be attractive to the people who would be willing partners in its implementation in reality. So, for Gandhi, it was not just a meaningful model of economic progress; it was, at the same time, a mechanism for social togetherness, since by being involved in numerous collective ventures the villagers would have had a platform to be together for a common socio-economic mission. In other words, the Indian villages that were divisive because of the well-entrenched segregation around the caste axis had an opportunity to combat the forces supportive of sustaining the socio-cultural hierarchy among the villagers based on the accident of birth. Unlike Gandhi, Tagore had a first-hand knowledge of Bengal's village life, being a landlord who had regular interactions with the villagers. For him, this was his primary source of knowledge of the nature of poverty that the rural folks confronted in their daily existence due to: (a) the government's indifference to them; (b) the lack of interest shown by the local landlords for the redressal of their genuine socio-economic grievances; and (c) the well-entrenched caste prejudices separating the higher castes from the lower castes, which was an impediment for the development of fraternity among the villagers despite them being part of the same village.

As argued so far, Tagore had a specific plan of rural reconstruction which he developed out of his interaction with the villagers and also the knowledge that he derived from various other sources. It is evident that whatever ideas he held, he exemplified them in his novels, short stories and critical essays. Given the enormous quantity of writings on this theme, it is difficult to develop the narrative by referring to each and every text. By being selective, the chapter deals with those texts which are very useful to comprehend Tagore's distinctive approach to rural reconstruction. Keeping this aim in view, the chapter is divided into two complementary segments. The first segment dwells on the conceptual framework that Tagore generated to evolve his own distinct model of understanding the rural poverty and the possible ways of mitigation. Hence, this segment provides a threadbare discussion of the 1904 *Swadeshi Samaj* and the 1928 *The Cooperative Principle* to acquaint the readers with the ideas that he held so dear to him. These tracts are conceptually relevant, because while the latter identified the foundational principles to bring people together, the former is about the model, derivative of these principles, which is actually the blueprint for the inclusive development of rural Bengal. The second segment dwells on the experiment of Sriniketan, or the abode of wealth, since it was established to put into practice the principles that, according to Tagore, helped reconstruct Bengal villages that were free from hunger, poverty and other associated miseries. Sriniketan was actually a training ground for learning new devices for agricultural development and also to improve the skills of rural folks by putting them under the care of experts. This was a remarkable experiment in the early part of the 20th century which was tried first in the United States during the 1880s with the initiative of Abraham Lincoln. Whether Tagore was aware of this 19th century experiment is not known, but there are uncanny similarities between what Lincoln had in mind for rural development in the United States and Tagore's thoughts in the context of 20th-century Bengal. Hence, it is fair to argue, as the chapter offers, that Tagore had evolved his model of inclusive development out of his own unique experience first at his zamindari estate, Silaidaha, and later at Sriniketan.

CONCEPTUALIZING A MODEL OF RURAL RECONSTRUCTION

A practitioner himself, Tagore appears to have developed his own conceptual framework in his 1916 novel, *Ghare Baire*. His methodological technique is fascinating. He deals with the issue at two levels: first, at the ideological level, he drew our attention to the nature of nationalism that emerged during the 1905–1908 Swadeshi movement which, by being blind to the prevalent socio-economic texture of Bengal, did not seem to have inspired the bard. Being a pragmatist, the poet, at the level of practice, also justified why he undertook the task for rural reconstruction, which he explained through a long statement by one of the main characters of the novel, Nikhilesh, made while delineating why he should do what he had already contemplated. He thus elaborated his point by saying that

> I believe that when you can't summon up the enthusiasm to serve the country by thinking of her merely as the country and its people as mere human beings, when you need to scream and shout out mantras and call her a goddess and go into a trance, then you love the craze more than you love your motherland. The need to place an obsession about Truth is an indication of our innate servility. When we set our mind free, we are no longer as strong. Unless we place an illusion, or an image or some framework of the establishment upon our listless consciousness as a rider, we cannot function. As long as we don't acquire a taste for the plain truth, as long as we need an obsession, it is obvious that we haven't acquired the strength to receive our country in all the glory of its freedom. Until then, whatever state we are in, either imaginary spectre or a genuine presence will continue to trouble us.[1]

For Nikhilesh, the love for the motherland should not be reduced to the mere chanting of *Vande Mataram* as Sandip, the self-acclaimed devotee of Mother India in the novel, did. This is Tagore's own thinking, which he expressed through Nikhilesh. Fundamental here are two points which will help us understand his conceptual inkling. On the one hand, he was fiercely critical of those who, instead of doing something concrete for the people, discharged their responsibilities by being mere rabble-rousers. By seeking to empower the ordinary villagers to being economically self-sufficient, Tagore always avoided being part of those nationalistic endeavours that were devoid of substance, since they were merely demonstrative and not, at all, directed to make the hapless people of India stand on their own. The second

---

[1] Rabindranath Tagore, *Ghare Baire* (Home and the World), trans. Classic Rabindranath Tagore (New Delhi: Penguin, 2011), 689–90.

part of this perceptive statement is most illuminating because it helps us grasp how to revitalize a moribund nation reeling in poverty and ignorance. One needed to have an imagination for one's future. It had to be 'an obsession', Tagore strongly felt; otherwise, the goal remained remote. In other words, what he perhaps had in mind was an inspirationally effective human urge to create an alternative which was far more emotionally gratifying and tuned to the attainment of commonly held goals and objectives.

On another occasion, the poet most graphically illustrated the daily routine of a poor villager, Panchu, just to demonstrate (a) how he organized his day for mere survival and (b) despite being heavily occupied during the day, which left little time for himself, how Panchu hardly cribbed, presumably because of the well-entrenched mindset, already referred to in the above paragraph, justifying that since it was preordained, there was no escape from this. These ideas are exemplified when Nikhilesh described Panchu's plight by saying that

> every morning [Panchu] wakes at dawn and takes a basket filled with paan [betel leaf], tobacco, coloured strings, mirrors, combs etc, which appeal to the farmer women, wades through the knee-deep pond and goes to the area where the lower castes live. Over there, he trades his wares for paddy, which fetches him a little than a purely monetary exchange. On the days, he can return early, he finishes his meal quickly and goes to make sweetmeats at the sweet shop. When he returns from there, it's late at night. Even after working so very hard, he and his family get two square meals a day only a few months of the year. His manner of eating is thus: at the very outset, he'll fill his stomach with a jug of water and a large portion of this mean consists of the cheap variety of banana. At least four months in a year, he only gets to have one meal a day.[2]

Here, Tagore dealt with the drudgery of life that villagers in Bengal underwent, presumably because they had accepted this plight as predetermined and thus there was hardly a relief from this. That Panchu and his family were deprived of even two square meals a day was, to Tagore, an outcome of colonialism, which thrived on the exploitation and deprivation of people of their basic needs for survival. Being poor

---

[2] Tagore, 724.

was not natural; it was deliberately contrived to make one section of the population richer at the cost of the other section that continued to reel in poverty and misery. What was thus required to be done, felt Tagore, was to raise a voice against the exploiters simultaneously with the creation of a milieu in which the urge for being self-sufficient was to be made as widespread as possible. Making everybody self-sufficient was the only viable option, because giving financial support to the poor might only help mitigate the misery temporarily. Hence, Tagore suggested that 'you may spoil people with your charity, but you can't end their misery. In Bengal', he further added, 'Panchu is not alone'.[3] Then came the most profound statement which the teacher in the novel *Ghare Baire* made to Nikhilesh by stating that 'the breasts of the entire land are dry. You will never be able to pour in money from the outside and make up for the milk which isn't there'.[4] This is a philosophically charged idea highlighting that the poor shall remain poor unless a device is generated to help them get out of this environment in which they instinctively imbibe the view that they are poor because that is providentially bestowed on them. In order to bring them out of this unjustified plight, Tagore, through his Sriniketan experiment (to be discussed later in this chapter), stressed the need for providing skills to the villagers which would make them stand on their own feet.

The third important lesson that Tagore imparted in *Ghare Baire,* which appears to have theoretically defended his scheme of *Swadeshi Samaj,* relates to his idea of gender equality. The argument for equal space for women that the poet pursued as early as 1916 was revolutionary and path-breaking. Bimala of *Ghare Baire* represented the urge to break the artificially created social shackles which kept the women permanently in chains. She was proud to have married Nikhilesh because not only was he appreciative of Bimala's sociopolitical rights as a human being, he also helped develop her personality by creating an environment in which she was allowed to speak her mind. This is illustrated when she said that her 'husband always claimed that men and women have equal rights over one another and hence their love

---

[3] Tagore, 724.

[4] Tagore, 724.

is also on an equal footing'.[5] On another occasion, when Bimala characterized women as being 'narrow and crooked',[6] Nikhilesh retorted by exhorting that

> just like the feet of Chinese women which are crooked and narrow, ... the entire society has squashed our women's minds from all sides and made them narrow and crooked. Fate gambles with their lives—their lives depend on the turn of the dice; do they have any powers of their own?[7]

This is also a very insightful statement which shows that Tagore was far ahead of his time insofar as the ideas concerning gender equality are concerned. Subjugation of women was a societal disease which was never effectively treated, presumably because of the powerful, well-entrenched vested interests flourishing under the cloak of protecting the so-called traditions and socially justified prejudices. Hence, 'it is not always possible to hand the [women] whatever their heart desires',[8] Nikhilesh stated to support the contention that unless the prevalent mindset underwent a sea change, the talk of women's liberation would appear to be a clamour bereft of substance. Given the deep societal roots of gender discrimination, it was not so easy to completely weed out the sources instantaneously. Women were also held responsible for its continuity, as Nikhilesh pointed out when Bimala complained that 'women are very coy [and] ... they never admit the truth and resort to pretences',[9] which she justified by referring to the 'mis-behaviour' that she was subjected to by her elder sister-in-law. In response, Nikhilesh retorted that

> you have enough sympathy for yourself when your own feelings are bruised, and you have none to spare for those whose lives have been ripped to shreds by the cruel arrows of society? Should the loser be made to pay a fine for losing?[10]

[5] Tagore, 671.

[6] Tagore, 673.

[7] Tagore, 673.

[8] Tagore, 674.

[9] Tagore, 674.

[10] Tagore, 674.

This is also an axiomatic truth, as Tagore corroborated, since women appear to have internalized that they need to follow certain societal restrictions despite being aware that they are artificially constructed to justify the patriarchal hegemony. Things might have changed marginally in response to the rebellious voice challenging the discriminatory social format rationalizing gender inequality as a perfectly settled fact. However, on the whole, as Tagore adumbrated in *Ghare Baire*, the feminist voice was too feeble to combat the social tendencies in favour of legitimizing gender discrimination for fulfilling the partisan interests.

Ghare Baire is one of those Tagore texts that was clearly based on his own conceptual thinking on various socio-economic and politico-ideological issues. The above detailed discussion of the issues raised in the novel is justified, since the narrative is drawn on his own experience of the 1905–1908 Swadeshi Movement in Bengal that finally annulled the first partition of the Bengal of 1905. A careful analysis of the dialogues and the description that Tagore provided reveals that most of the ideas that he put forward in his 1904 tract, *Swadeshi Samaj*, resonated in *Ghare Baire*. The ideational similarity is too vivid to ignore. As shown above, the novel is a powerful comment on three important aspects of a specific kind of sociopolitical voices that Tagore had articulated on the basis of his own unique ways of understanding the existent socio-economic and political reality. Of the three issues that the novel highlights, the first one is a scathing criticism of the contemporary nationalist campaign which was derailed because (a) it was almost alienated from the common mass of people, and (b) the leadership was highly partisan, since it neglected the demographically preponderant Muslim community. The selfishness of the leaders was also a source of concern for Tagore, because it meant that their love for the motherland was a stepping stone for attaining partisan goals. The second aspect dwells on how the poor survived in Bengal by dint of being involved in all kinds of menial jobs, which hardly left any time for them for self-gratification. Here, Tagore made a theoretically profound statement when he said that financial support to the poor was not, at all, a device to eradicate poverty: they needed to be given skills for self-sustenance; once they started earning their livelihood, they would realize their potentials, which would give them the much-desired self-respect. The third aspect is about Tagore's concern for gender equality, a concern that did not receive as much attention as was required, presumably because of the well-entrenched patriarchal prejudices. This is one side of the argument; the other side is epitomized by the instinctive imbibing of women of their inferior social existence by being willingly subservient to their male counterparts. Taken together, these three aspects constitute a persuasive theoretical paradigm which steers us through the cobwebs of society-governed human nature and relationships in a colonial context when the exogenous influences were too powerful to be so easily ignored. Being keen to promote a seamless exchange of views, values and ideas between the East and the West, which Tagore exemplified by founding Visva-Bharati as a university in 1921, he mapped out a conceptual framework in the novel in which he situates his arguments for universal humanism. *Ghare Baire* thus not merely stands out as a historical account of the Swadeshi movement (1905–1908) but also provides directional inputs to understand the theoretical inclinations that Tagore evinced in so many of his creative writings.

THE MODEL OF RURAL RECONSTRUCTION

Core to Tagore's thought of rural reconstruction was his concern for villages, which were, according to him, 'fatally neglected'.[11] As a result, he further elaborated, 'they are fast degenerating into serfdom, compelled to offer to the ungrateful towns cheerless and unintelligent labour for work carried on in an unhealthy and impoverished environment'.[12] Hence, Tagore warned that

> there cannot be any escape from our sense of frustration and growing discontent as long as we are not able really and truly to stand by our brethren of the village, as long as we do not bring them the light of knowledge or

---

[11] Uma Dasgupta, ed., *Rabindranath Tagore: My Life in My Words* (New Delhi: Penguin, 2006), 209.

[12] Dasgupta, 209.

dedicate ourselves whole-heartedly for their betterment, whatever the sacrifice.[13]

The above statement was perhaps the harshest critique of Tagore of the prevalent socio-cultural context in which the tribal population and those at the lower rungs of the caste structure always remained outcastes. Determined to bring about a radical change in the existent system of human existence, Tagore was hardly diplomatic in his criticism of those who drew advantages by being the self-declared custodians of the then socio-cultural texture. Presumably because of his helplessness in fulfilling the goal that he assiduously championed, he was anguished, which came out very clearly in his statement that

> at the present time, we are imbibing three different kinds of intoxicants in the three social strata to which we severally belong: spirituous liquor plain and simple, the liquor that corrupts the mind and morals; and finally—the liquor that puts conscience to sleep. There is a brand to suit every taste— that of the [lower castes and tribal people] at the lower strata, of the more privileged middle class of the village society, and finally the educated gentry of our towns and cities. That this has happened is solely because each of these three limbs of our body-politic is languishing for the lack of its own proper nourishment.[14]

The statement is Tagore's own assessment of the prevalent socio-cultural texture of India which was responsible for its decline as a polity. In other words, India's political weaknesses were attributed to the social fragments deliberately maintained for protecting the partisan interests of a few who, in Tagore's lexicon, remained intoxicated so much so that their conscience hardly reacted even when their countrymen suffered heavily due to hunger and poverty. For him, it was a source of agony, which he clearly articulated by being fiercely critical of those who were not only indifferent but were also agonizingly selfish. Had they had a sense of belongingness, it would not have been possible, felt Tagore. Whether this sharp criticism of the then 'privileged middle class of the village society' was enough to change

---

[13] Rabindranath Tagore's speech, reproduced in Leonard K. Elmhirst, *Poet and Plowman* (Calcutta: Visva-Bharati, 2008) (reprint), 162.

[14] Rabindranath Tagore's speech, 163.

the well-entrenched mindset in favour of class and caste hierarchy is debatable. Nonetheless, through his scathing remarks, Tagore, being a powerful public intellectual in the then India, rose to become society's conscience keeper.

The 1904 tract, *Swadeshi Samaj*, was a significant text, since it was an articulation of Tagore's ideas that, he felt, were a stepping stone towards rejuvenating Indian villages. Setting out the responsibility for each and every individual in fulfilling the mission, he thus stated that

> what I wanted to say that we did not have to think of the whole country; we could make a start with one or two villages. If we could free even one village from the shackles of helplessness and ignorance, an ideal for the whole of India would be established.[15]

Based on his determination to ensure that villages were socio-economically adequately equipped, Tagore, while starting the Sriniketan campus, prepared a blueprint for inclusive development by adopting 50 villages around the vicinity of Santiniketan. What struck him was the socio-economic decadence of the villages around the campus, which was worrisome to the poet because 'their culture is failing, their social life is deteriorating [and] their economic base is disintegrating'.[16] In order to secure a healthy India, besides 'non-cooperation with the foreigner, … we must coexist with our rural brethren'.[17] It was a matter of great shame to the bard, who castigated his countrymen by saying that

> few among us know or realize the sad state of affairs that are allowed to flourish in the village: some of the communities there indulge in atrocious travesties in the name of their ancient faiths and religions—a tragic fact which does not even bear talking about.[18]

[15] Rabindranath Tagore, 'City and Village,' reproduced in Rabindranath Tagore, *Towards Universal Man* (Calcutta: Asia Publishing House, 1962) (reprint), 322.

[16] Rabindranath Tagore's statement is quoted in Elmhirst, *Poet and Plowman*, 16.

[17] Rabindranath Tagore's conversation with Leonard K. Elmhirst, 18 July, 1921, reproduced in Elmhirst, 161.

[18] Rabindranath Tagore's speech, reproduced in Elmhirst, *Poet and Plowman*, 161.

Besides showing concerns for providing the villagers with a source of livelihood, the poet was also keen to develop a healthy society immune from prejudicial beliefs; for him, the lack of education was perhaps one of the major reasons for the villagers being steeped in superstitious beliefs and religious prejudices. The socio-cultural texture in the areas around Sriniketan (located in the district of Birbhum) was remarkably different from that in other parts of Bengal, presumably because a large section of the population comprised the Santals, the indigenous local tribe, and also because the demographic strength of the Muslims was not negligible. Given the peculiar demographic composition of the area, Tagore undertook steps to create sources of livelihood for all and also an awareness, by developing opportunities for their education. Insofar as the first step was concerned, the role of Leonard K. Elmhirst, an Englishman who was trained at Cornell University in the United States in agriculture, deserves special mention. In response to Tagore's request, Elmhirst came to Sriniketan and took up the challenge of building a bridge between those in the campus and the villagers around the campus. Being a student of agriculture, he utilized his knowledge to extend help to the local cultivators to augment the production of paddy and vegetables for their own consumption and also to sell what they did not require to earn an extra amount of money for the family. Elmhirst's success in increasing agricultural production attracted Tagore's attention and was appreciated by the poet, who said that 'the way he is going ahead with the work among the peasantry of a country strange to him—is a marvel to watch.'[19] Elmhirst was dismayed when he came to Birbhum for the first time in early 1921, which he articulated in his own written tract entitled *The Robbery of the Soil*, noting that

a journey through the district of Birbhum will show even to the casual observer that all is not well [in view of the] ... increasing death rate, the all-powerful sway of malaria and other kinds of diseases, the grinding poverty and the frequency of famine in this area.[20]

[19] Elmhirst, 157.
[20] Elmhirst, 27.

The reason for all these deficiencies was located in the poor quality of the soil, which was surprising to Elmhirst because 'the Birbhum area was once the richest district of Bengal, and supported upon the cultivation of the soil a large and flourishing community'.[21] With his hard work and by involving the local Santals, he contributed immensely to the improvement of the soil, which not only became far more productive but also defused the widely accepted view that since it became barren, no cultivation was possible. Being impressed by his capabilities, Tagore candidly admired the hard work that he put in to realize what had been inconceivable earlier, saying that

> my whole heart is with you in the great work you have started. I wish I were young enough to be able to join you and perform the meanest work that can be done at your place, thus getting rid of that flimsy web of responsibility that shuts me off from the intimate touch of mother dust.[22]

Being keen to get involved in the work that Elmhirst was pursuing in Sriniketan is illustrative of the contention that Tagore meant what he stated in his texts. As India was a village-centric civilization, his lifelong mission of making the country self-dependent, at least regarding food, was unlikely to be realized unless the villages were made agriculturally strong enough to stand on their own. Besides the immediate economic gain with the development of agriculture, it would also create a bridge of integration between the men and the soil. In his letter to Elmhirst, he elaborated his feelings by saying that

> the small beginnings which you have made ... in a remote corner of the world carries in it a truth for which men today are groping in bewilderment. It is the truth of Peace. Real peace comes from a wealth which is living, which has the blessings of nature's direct touch, which is not machine-made—let us seek humbly, coming down to the soil, dealing with forces of life which are beautiful and bounteous.[23]

[21] Elmhirst, 27.

[22] Rabindranath Tagore to Leonard K. Elmhirst, 31 March, 1922, reproduced in Dasgupta, *Rabindranath: My Life in My Words*, 211.

[23] Rabindranath Tagore to Leonard K. Elmhirst, 211.

Here, Tagore approached rural reconstruction at two levels. At a very mundane level, Elmhirst's contribution yielded positive results, which was certainly a source of encouragement not only for the poet but also for those who drew sustenance from agriculture. There is also a level of thinking at which the bard clearly philosophized his approach to the agrarian issues. Being integrated with the soil was a step to realize peace in its absolute sense, an argument that the poet justified in two complementary ways. On the one hand, not only did it link human beings with Mother Earth, it also gave them a sense of fulfilment by their being associated with the activities greatly contributing to human survival; it was a definite means to satisfactorily take care of the brutality of hunger and poverty. On the other hand, like Gandhi, Tagore also raised his voice against machine-driven cultivation because the more the human beings were involved in agriculture, the stronger would be the argument against the deployment of machines in this regard. Basic here is the point that Tagore offered for bringing people closer to nature. Sriniketan therefore created a space for experimenting with newer techniques of agricultural production with support from his colleague, Elmhirst, besides endorsing the wider philosophical concern of linking human beings with Mother Earth.

ELABORATION OF THE MODEL

As mentioned above, the 1904 tract, *Swadeshi Samaj,* was Tagore's manifesto for inclusive growth. Delivered as a speech, this text is a clear statement of what he had in mind to contribute to the well-being of India's villages, because without their all-round development, no welfare measure was likely to succeed. Fundamental here are two core points which were explicitly made in his talk. First, unlike Europe, which privileged state over society, in India, it was just the other way round, namely, society upheld the state and set out rules and regulations for governance; in this sense, society was prior to state. In Tagore's words, India, like China, was socialist, which meant that the rule of society was always preferred: it was society that arranged for 'education, water to the thirsty, food to the hungry, shrine to the pilgrim, punishment to those breaking laws, the homage to the venerable'.[24] On the whole, the society retained India's distinctive character despite the change of rulers now and then, which meant that the country belonged to the people and the ruler was just a part of the whole. While reinforcing this point, the poet thus argued that since India was 'a society-centric unit, its core driving force happens to be the people'.[25] The second point is a critique of the British rule, since with its advent in India, the golden principle of society-led governance had already been reversed by putting the state ahead of society. As he argued, 'the British government has, by giving priority to the state, adversely affected the core sentiment on which India, as a country, has always rested which devastatingly upset the social-balances'.[26] As soon as the state-centric governance was allowed to prosper, the society had withdrawn from what were its core responsibilities. The consequences were disastrous: villages became a hub of 'fraud, forgery and false litigation and also the country went to dogs due to diseases, ignorance, poverty and crime'.[27] In clear terms, Tagore drew attention to the devastations that the British rule had caused by contributing to the decline of the society-centric existence of the Indians. Hence, his advice was also crystal clear: instead of wasting time on the nature of British governance, the Indians should concentrate on bringing back the past well-entrenched tradition of serving each other regardless of expectations, which was also a reverberation of the Upanishadic talis-man, namely, those who serve humanity serve God. The objective was to organize the masses by instilling 'the idea of service to mankind'[28]; otherwise, there was no hope to get out of this quagmire that the alien authority had deliberately created for its partisan interests.

With the elaboration of the model in broad terms, the poet now provided the minor details of his approach to *Swadeshi Samaj*. What is striking was his constant endeavour to justify theoretically that the

---

[24] Rabindranath Tagore, *Swadeshi Samaj*, (Bengalee) (Kolkata: Visva-Bharati, 1908) (reprint), 1–2.

[25] Tagore, 2.

[26] Tagore, 2.

[27] Tagore, 2.

[28] Tagore, 3.

model of governance that had evolved in the West was hardly applicable to India, because (a) our history had followed a different path and (b) as the history was different, the same formula highlighting the widely hyped positive role of the state in development was bound to fail. Fundamental here is his critique of Western governance, which was also synonymous with the state. A perusal of India's past reveals that this was not the case, because the responsibility of the monarch was confined to certain specific areas, whereas the society had a wider sphere of activities covering almost all parts of human existence. Hence, Tagore argued that irrespective of whether the monarchy was sensitive to its duties to the subject, there was hardly

> a brake to the activities of the teachers or Gurus in imparting education to their students, the digging of pond to take care of the demand of the people for drinking water, the dissemination of religious instructions in various places in the villages and looking after those who needed to be looked after.[29]

A pragmatist to the core, Tagore graphically illustrated the difference between what India was and what she became after the imposition of foreign rule. The above description is theoretically important, because it also justifies the distinction that the poet made between a liberal system of governance and socialistic (sic) ways of taking care of social needs. Drawn on the fundamental tenets of liberalism, theoreticians uphold individuals over the collectivity, while in 'socialism' society remains the core and government does not seem to be so important in extending the help that is required for social well-being. The reason is not difficult to seek, as Tagore himself gave enough inputs to provide a persuasive explanation. In the West, the state or government is responsible for ensuring individual pursuits for happiness; in India, the state or the king's domain of functioning is well-demarcated, and lack of support from the ruler will hardly make a difference to the life of people, since they themselves are instinctively trained to take care of their basic needs for which they do not depend on outside help. From this, it is clear, as the bard further argued, that

---

[29] Tagore, 5.

diverse civilizations develop their life wires differently. The heart of the country is that spot which contributes to the nourishment of the people as a whole and if that is adversely affected, the country shall severely be devastated. Hence if the state is doomed in Europe, it will have its manifestation in the society as a whole; similarly, if the society is seriously impaired, it would cause irreparable damage to the human existence in India. What it means is that the survival of Europe rests on the protection and strengthening of the state whereas in India, our existence and well-being are dependent on the retention of socio-ideologically justified rules and regulations or habit-building devices (*anusashanas*, in Sanskrit).[30]

The above long statement is about the processes leading to the consolidation of togetherness among the people, despite their being socio-culturally diverse. It did not seem to be difficult, as various designs of bringing people together evolved in Bengal historically. One of the most effective designs happened to be, as Tagore himself identified, regularly held rural fairs (*melas,* in Bengalee) in various parts of the province. According to Tagore, 'when rural folks feel the need of being connected with the wider world, they organize Mela … which is an earnest call to invite the external world to [their] footsteps'.[31] With their congregation in one location, not only did the villagers get an opportunity to interact with people from outside, but it also enabled them to exchange their views on various issues, which helped them learn and also widen their perspectives of thinking, argued Tagore. This was one of the objectives; the other goal of *melas* that was reflective of the poet's contextual concerns related to the deteriorating communal relations between Hindus and Muslims. As is so well known, during the 1905–1908 anti-Bengal partition campaign, Muslims were alienated due to the pronounced Hindu bias of the movement. Moreover, the steps, particularly the *bonfire* of foreign clothes and boycott of foreign goods, that the revolutionary nationalists had adopted alienated a large section of Muslims, because it affected them adversely since they were forced to give up foreign clothes which were cheaper and, in their place, buy clothes other than 'the Manchester-made-products' which were expensive. Hence, the

---

[30] Tagore, 7–8.

[31] Tagore, 12.

movement became a class war. In order to address this serious concern of the poor Muslims, Tagore suggested organizing a *mela* in which the educated and sensible men 'helped build bonhomie between Hindus and Muslims since Mela, by bringing them together, would create an opportunity to interact with the members from both the communities'.[32] This was not a difficult task, believed Tagore. He illustrated this, though a little sarcastically, by referring to the care that was always extended to guests. While narrating his experience of being part of two Congress annual conferences in the province of Bengal, he mentioned that these congregations served no nationalistic purposes, because 'those who attended the conferences expressed their resentment only during those three days and conveniently forgot their commitment to the nation for the rest of year'.[33] Nonetheless, Tagore was impressed by the care to the guests during those three days which knew no bounds, because they were treated so well not only by being offered the most sumptuous food but also by having arrangements made for their stay to give them maximum comfort. It was surprising to Tagore, because

the ritual of hospitality was more conspicuous than the zeal for work. It was like a bridal party: the demands for food and entertainment, comforts and pleasure were so excessive that they must have spent a fortune.[34]

Being critical of the extravaganza that always accompanied the Congress-organized annual conferences, Tagore further added that 'this aspect in the Congress which is truly national—its hospitality—has always been active, even though its work ends with a three-day annual session and it gives no signs of life for the rest of the year'.[35] Here, Tagore expressed his feelings in two contrasting ways: on the one hand, he condemned the so-called nationalists who remained non-committal to the nationalist cause throughout the year except on those three days when the conferences were held, which, to the poet, was hypocritical and also disrespectful to the people who had faith

[32] Tagore, 13.

[33] Tagore, 18–9.

[34] Tagore, 18.

[35] Rabindranath Tagore, 'Society and State,' in *Towards Universal Man*, ed. Rabindranath Tagore (Calcutta: Asia Publishing House, 1962) (reprint), 58.

on them; on the other hand, by being appreciative of the care that the organizers extended to the participants, Tagore also highlighted the instinctive human nature of Indians *vis-à-vis* guests. Here too, Tagore found this response as the most natural because he argued that, we instinctively learnt that warm hospitality to the guests was as good as serving the God. This also meant that human relationships were always privileged despite one being lackadaisical in one's politico-ideological commitment to India's emancipation from the foreign rule. Implicit here is also a fundamental philosophical assumption which, according to the bard, guided the Indian mindset then: providing hospitality to even a stranger did not seem to be unusual, because

> the innermost creed of India is to find the one in the many, unity in diversity. [As a result], India does not admit difference to be conflict, nor does she espy an enemy in every stranger. So, she repels, none, destroys none, and strives to find a place for all in a vast social order. She acknowledges every path and recognizes greatness wherever she finds it.[36]

Historically, India has always kept her door open for outsiders. It would thus not be an exaggeration to suggest that India epitomized a mode of socio-cultural togetherness. Even before the British rule, various religious communities arrived in India, which also created a milieu in which people with different religious inclinations merged together to form a pan-Indian identity that Tagore explained as 'unity in diversity'. For the poet, it was great experimentation which led to a completely different kind of identities where the original socio-cultural identities might not have been so salient in one's socio-cultural responses. 'It is as though Providence has opened', Tagore argued further, 'a vast laboratory on Indian soil for the purpose of a massive social fusion'.[37] What was to be done, Tagore expressed his concern. The response was unequivocal:

> the truest way of protecting oneself is to rouse one's inherent powers [and] … not to hide oneself at a distance. Britain is bound to hold our souls in subjection until we forsake our inertness. To sit in a corner and

---

[36] Tagore, 65–6.

[37] Tagore, 62.

bewail our losses will bear no fruit. To imitate the British and try to save ourselves by adopting a disguise is mere self-deception. We can never be real Englishman, and we can never trick them by turning into imitation Englishman.[38]

This is Tagore's unique way of awakening the people and also to make them sensitive to what they should do under the present circumstances. It was now clear to him that political freedom was a distant goal so long as the countrymen remained mesmerized by the British way of life, which represented a failure on the part of the colonized Indians to comprehend the true nature of the British rule in India. It was, in other words, a servility of mind that was a natural outcome of long colonial subjugation. In such a context, it is easily comprehensible why the desire to emulate the British and also the deliberate avoidance of attack on the British rule became part of the Indian psyche. By being so caustic to those clinging to such an understanding of the British rule, Tagore set in motion a powerful critique of colonialism that flourished in India not merely through state-sponsored coercive measures but also through the generation of a strong support base with the help of those who appeared to have accepted the British rule as providentially good for the country.

Even at the cost of a little digression from the main theme, the above discussion is useful for two complementary reasons. First, unlike so many of the nationalists, Tagore never supported the claim that political freedom was prior to the social empowerment of the people. His endeavour for social empowerment was constantly threatened and also effectively challenged, on many occasions, presumably because the oppositional forces, being socially well-entrenched, were hardly meaningfully countered. This was, felt the poet, demonstrative of mental servility to the colonial rule, because that ensured worldly gains for those who uncritically accepted the prevalent system of governance. As history shows, the scene had undergone a sea change with the gradual acceptance of the view that colonialism was a bane to the colonized. Second, for the poet, the social awakening of India was a necessary condition for the success of the political campaign for freedom. So

---

[38] Tagore, 65.

long as the battle for freedom was confined to a narrow segment of the population, as was the case before the arrival of Gandhi on India's political scene, its future was bleak. What was therefore needed was to involve the masses by erasing the socio-economic boundaries separating one section of the population from another. *Swadeshi Samaj* provided a scheme that was Tagore's answer to the socio-economic ills crippling the endeavour towards making India politically free. As argued above, being vehemently opposed to the European state-centric civilization, the poet was always in favour of purging the society of deficiencies which were an impediment towards bringing people socio-culturally closer to one another. Here is located the reason why the bard focused more on society: it is because he believed that a healthy society was a necessary precondition for healthy people. A perusal of history also confirmed, argued Tagore, that 'India always considered saving its religion and society as the only means to self-preservation'.[39] Besides the well-entrenched systemic restrictions connected with the contrived socio-cultural practices segmenting people which were allowed to survive, if not flourish, the cause of Indians being intellectually servile to the British was certainly the English education, the product of Macaulay's 1835 minutes on education. As Indians were overwhelmed 'by being trained in English education, ... they [appear] to have lost their faculties for independent thinking which helped build conditions in which Indians are not even keen to objectively assess the circumstances that resulted in such a hopeless situation'.[40] This is suggestive of Tagore's frustration, since he never understood how the Enlightenment ideas that the Indians had an easy access to by being part of the British colony 'created a group of mindless Indians [for] ... Enlightenment philosophy is an instruction for evolving a creative mind ... and also a society which is free from socio-cultural prejudices'.[41] It was a novel argument which impressed his colleagues. For instance, Hirendranath Dutta, who presided over the meeting in which Tagore presented his model of *Swadeshi Samaj*, appreciated his endeavour as 'intellectually persuasive and impregnated with fresh

[39] Tagore, 35.

[40] Tagore, 39.

[41] Tagore, 43.

ideas'[42]; he also criticized the mode of opposition that the Congress preferred as being 'overactive for three days of the year when its members meet for the annual congregation',[43] which was hardly effective in generating a powerful voice against the colonial rule. Reiterating Dutta's sentiment, Bipin Chandra Pal, one of the members of the trio Lal-Bal-Pal[44] who represented the revolutionary segment of the Congress in the early part of the 20th century, also supported Tagore by saying that 'instead of being dependent on the alien government, Indians need to stand on their own for fulfilling their sociopolitical and economic goals'.[45] By characterizing Tagore's ideas 'as most innovative and contextually-relevant in view of the growing opposition against the Moderate mode of nationalist campaign',[46] Pal gave a clarion call to the youth to get involved in those activities that the poet had suggested in *Swadeshi Samaj* for effectively addressing the concerns of the rural folks which would be a great service to the motherland.

THE MODEL

The conceptualization of *Swadeshi Samaj* is based on two persuasive arguments that Tagore offered when he delivered the speech. The first one is both a critique of the contemporary nationalist campaign at the behest of both the Moderates and the Revolutionary Nationalists and also attempts at articulating an alternative mode of nationalist mobilization. He was critical of the Moderates because their campaign was exclusively confined to the elites, which did not allow the campaign that they had launched to go beyond the metropolitan cities of Calcutta and Bombay. His opposition to the Revolutionary Nationalists was

---

[42] Tagore, 53.

[43] Tagore, 53.

[44] With the consolidation of the revolutionary nationalist group (also known as the Extremists in the government parlance) against the Moderates, led by Surendernath Banerjee, the trio, Lal-Bal-Pal (Lala Lajpat Rai of Punjab, Bal Gangadhar Tilak of Maharashtra and Bipin Chandra Pal of Bengal) became a powerful ideological voice within the Congress.

[45] Tagore, 55.

[46] Tagore, 55.

based on their failure to rise above their religious prejudices against the Muslims that caused an unbridgeable gulf between them and the majority of Bengal's population, and also on the indiscriminate use of violence for fulfilling their goals; like their Moderate counterparts, they, despite their selfless commitment to the nationalist aim, also nurtured an antipathy against the Muslims, which was an inherent weakness of the campaign at their behest. The second argument focuses on how to rejuvenate the moribund nation. Here, in his own unique style, Tagore insisted on a design of self-empowerment by being involved in activities contributing to the generation of the nationalist zeal among the masses. Hence, he argued that 'the work of the motherland should not turn into a pompous external ceremony',[47] which is a caustic remark against the Moderates who discharged their loyalty to the nation only by participating in the meetings. Instead, the poet insisted on their involvement in activities leading to the rural well-being. By referring to Indian's mental servility to the British rule, which was obviously retarding, he explained his point by saying that 'we have now discovered the treasure—the trove of *Atmashakti* (the self-power) which would contribute to the generation of our capability for fighting our own battle'. To be more explicit, he used a metaphor by saying that

> instead of waiting for the invitation by the British to have food with them, isn't it better to cook our own food at home; this will not only be tastier but also give us confidence that we are able to prepare our own food by dint of our own strength.[48]

This was a call for being self-dependent or capable of fulfilling the basic socio-economic needs of the people through own endeavours. In order to accomplish the goal, a methodical Tagore set out certain rules and regulations for those who agreed with him. As a preface to these, he mentioned that

> we shall remove our wants and perform our duties as far as possible with out combined effort. We shall create a system of administration to attain the

[47] Tagore, 57.
[48] Tagore, 57.

goals that we will set out ourselves for Samaj's well-being. We will dutifully follow the rules and regulations and if there is a violation, we will accept whatever punishment is given for this.[49]

Before the constitution of the *samaj* was placed for collective approval, the poet announced certain rules that were mandatory for the members, which are as follows:

1. For any social issue of our Samaj and for the Indians as a whole, we shall not crave for favour of the government.
2. We shall not voluntarily use foreign garments and other foreign goods.
3. Except for official purposes we shall not write to any Bengalee in English.
4. At the ceremonial gatherings, we shall avoid British food, British dress code, British music, wine and avoid inviting British people for ostentation. If for reasons of friendship we have to invite any Britisher, we shall arrange for him and Indian feast.
5. So long as we do not ourselves establish Swadeshi schools, we shall send our children to schools run by the Indians as far as possible.
6. If there is any internal feud among the people of our Samaj, then instead of going to court we shall first try to sort it out through judicial measures laid down by the Samaj.
7. We shall buy goods for everyday needs from Swadeshi shops.
8. Even if there are differences of opinion leading to mutual discord, we shall not take it out in the open.[50]

This checklist of items is illustrative of the urge for being self-dependent. Seeking to fulfil the objectives, Tagore suggested some measures which were governed by his desire to make the villages draw on each other for satisfying the basic economic needs; the primary aim was to develop a collectivity based on common concerns. This was nothing new, he felt. As India's past had shown, the village-based Indian society was governed by the idea of cooperation among those

[49] Tagore, 58.
[50] Tagore, 58–9.

living side by side in the villages; the villagers, being compassionate towards one another, were hardly selfish when their neighbours
required help of any kind. This had evolved instinctively among the
villagers, who, being together spatially, evolved by being appreciative
of concerns for common well-being. By 1934, the scene had become
worse, as Tagore warned, and it was attributed to the radical change
in people's mindset which, instead of being concerned for others,
tended to be overprotective of partisan interests. This was likely to
disturb 'the natural balance in Indian society for which the British
rule was certainly responsible along with the failure of the Indians
to sustain their distinctive socio-cultural inclination, nurtured over
generations'.[51] What is striking here is the idea that Tagore's nationalist attitude is conceptualized with two complementary goals in view.
On the one hand, it was certainly anti-British, since the alien rule
was a hindrance to realizing India's full potential as a socio-economic
and political compact. This argument was complemented, on the
other hand, by also insisting on the self-driven designs for economic
uplift, which was, in Tagore's views, possible with the development
of a *swadeshi* enterprise. To sustain these enterprises, a complementary mindset was required to be put in place, which also means that
Tagore's idea of inclusive growth was not merely conventional, since
it also needed to be supplemented by creating and nurturing a milieu
in which the nationalists shared identical concerns. Presumably to
generate a shared mindset, Tagore also stressed the importance of
an education in which the values supportive of being economically
independent were promoted. It is also true that Tagore's clarion call
for *swadeshi* schools had hardly been effective in the context of the
Swadeshi campaign (1905–1908), though it had inspired the later
nationalists to a significant extent. The national schools that C. R.
Das developed in the context of the Non-Cooperation Movement
(1921–1922) were based on what Tagore developed in his written
tract, *Swadeshi Samaj*, of 1904.

---

[51] Rabindranath Tagore, 'Neglected Villages,' 6 February, 1934, printed in Rabindranath
Tagore, *Pally Prakriti* (*Nature of Villages*) (Kolkata: Visva-Bharati, 1817) (as per Bengalee
Calendar), 84.

In order to create a *samaj* of his priorities, Tagore prepared a constitution to set out the rules and regulations for its governance. Besides devising the nature of governance, the poet also stipulated the aims for which the *samaj* was constituted. Primarily seeking to develop a cluster of villages into a compact, he also suggested forming rural communities which were to function in accordance with the socio-economic and political objectives that the members of this cluster of villages decided to pursue. It was, in other words, an endeavour to evolve a platform of togetherness by bringing the villagers under one umbrella.

Based on the rules, enumerated above, the constitution provides broad guidelines, which Tagore characterized as aims of the *samaj*. There were 15 aims.[52] which can be categorized into three sets of aims, which are discussed below.

Since the primary source of income was agriculture, the first set of aims dwelt on how to improve agriculture and augment agricultural production. To take care of the needs of the people, Tagore suggested constructing granaries to store paddies with utmost care. Along with this, the poet also insisted on finding out alternative sources of income by reviving traditional handicrafts, which would receive adequate attention soon with the establishment of Sriniketan on 1928. The second set of objectives focused on the importance of taking ample care for health. He was aware that lack of concern for hygiene remained an important source of worry, because it was the source of all kinds of ailments that the villagers suffered. His emphasis was to provide pure drinking water, because water carried germs affecting one's health most adversely. Once this was done, the villages, Tagore strongly felt, would be free from water-borne diseases. In his constitution, the bard also stressed the need for qualified medical doctors and paramedical experts to take adequate care for health in the villages; furthermore, they were expected to teach the villagers how to protect themselves from diseases by being alert to the consequences of the outbreak of contagious diseases like cholera and malaria, in particular. According to Tagore, one needed to put all preventive measures in place, but what was most important was to take care of one's health,

---

[52] Tagore, *Swadeshi Samaj*, 65–7.

for which the bard suggested the creation of gymnasiums and play-grounds. As he believed health was wealth, he started sports facilities in his estate immediately after the Swadeshi Movement got over; these ideas developed later into their full form at the aegis of Sriniketan. The third set of directions related to education, because Tagore always held that education was an effective instrument to acquire knowledge, which was a stepping stone to build a society free from superstitious beliefs. An educationist par excellence, Tagore always worked hard to disseminate knowledge by institutionalizing the system through which it was transmitted. Santiniketan was a model, and so was Sriniketan, which followed the founding of the former in 1921. Disappointed with book-based knowledge, which the British had created to help them in running the administration, the poet never lost sight of the system that laid the foundation for practice-driven knowledge. Sriniketan, as we will see in the following section, was founded with this purpose in mind.

The above is an elaborate narration of how to develop a system of governance leading to the fulfilment of the socio-economic needs of the people. But the system was likely to function well only provided those who lived in the villages were linked with one another by the spirit of togetherness. In other words, the villagers needed to develop bonhomie among themselves, which was possible by generating a supportive mindset seeking to ensure a common well-being. Tagore had in mind the social distance between the Hindus and Muslims and also that between the rich and the poor. The gulf was required to be abridged; otherwise, the entire edifice of social equilibrium that the poet sought to develop was likely to collapse. Simultaneously, he also paid attention to popularize Swadeshi goods; here too, the concern was to evolve and sustain the belief of being capable of surviving on what the people had at their disposal. The character Nikhilesh in *Ghare Baire* is illustrative here: Nikhilesh always favoured the endeavour towards producing the basic goods that the villagers required for daily survival. What is most striking was Tagore's insistence on collecting informa-tion, following the census format of the government, which would help create a solid databank at the disposal of the *samaj* regarding the size of the population, including the number of males and females, number of deaths and births, the population ratio in terms of religion, number of victims and death due to malaria, cholera, small pox and other epidemics, among others. The purpose was to codify the nature of the village, which was to help not only to understand the village and its socio-economic texture but also to identify the weaknesses that needed to be addressed effectively.[53]

THE MECHANISM

Tagore stands out as a public intellectual who always argued for self-sufficiency in our basic economic needs. Dependence on others for the fulfilment of basic needs was tantamount to slavery, he felt. In the preface to his *The Co-operative Principle* (1928), he thus noted,

> from the land have vanished health and beauty, knowledge and joy, and even of life itself little remains. Today in the village the tanks are dry, the air pestilent, the roads impassable, the granaries empty and social bonds lax. Envy and malice, squabbles and misdeeds hasten the decay of the crumbling society. The end seems near, for in this squalid, uncared-for land the fearful rule of Yama [the death God] grows more powerful every day.[54]

This is perhaps the most revealing explanation of the state of affairs in Indian villages. Besides being very explicit, Tagore also conveyed his feelings of being disenchanted, presumably because the hapless villagers, who, being instinctively tuned to be fatalists, had hardly undertaken steps for rejuvenating the village economy which would also address effectively most of the social ills crippling the villages. In other words, what he wanted was to regenerate the village life as one compact where everybody, regardless of class, caste and religion, came together for common well-being, which was possible only when they were self-dependent in terms of what they required for their day-to-day needs and survival for the future. It was indeed a challenging task.

---

[53] These points are summarized of the points elaborated by Tagore in the Samaj's constitution. Tagore, 65–7.

[54] Rabindranath Tagore, *The Cooperative Principle* (Calcutta: Visva-Bharati, 1963), Preface.

What mechanism did he devise to translate his ideas into practice? As he clearly noted,

> I had always felt that the attainment of human welfare and prosperity, in the true sense of these words, by means of mutual aid and cooperative striving was of the very essence of civilized life. It is by such endeavour that Science has achieved its triumphs, and while so doing has been able to knit mankind more closely together. The same is to be seen in the civic and political fields, not to speak of that of religion.[55]

Cooperation was possible by means of mutual aid and cooperative striving, which means that it was attributed to an ideational change governed by the need for fulfilling a common goal. Historically, the human race survived by being appreciative of common concerns, which appeared to have evaporated with the consolidation of the urge to satisfy one's needs at the cost of others. There were many reasons; the British rule was one of the major factors which further consolidated the already existing socially discriminatory and also hierarchical human existence around the caste and class axes. Philosophically, the reasons for social degradation were attributed to the loss of harmony, Tagore argued. In his words,

> whenever harmony is destroyed, passions become violent, anti-social disorder prevails, the few destroys the sustenance of the many, seeking to use them as tools for their self-aggrandizement. Then crushed under the burden of the misery of the masses, thus reduced to slaves, society either becomes moribund or, to save itself, prepares for revolution.[56]

Fundamental here was his concern for creating a milieu for harmony to flourish, because without being concerned for one another, human society was likely to perish. The lesson was transmitted from one generation to another, though the scene did not seem to be propitious then, since the tendencies towards creating schisms among human beings became prominent. This was explained by Tagore in categorical terms when he mentioned that 'the life of the villages began to be impoverished when the social nervous system that formerly knit

---

[55] Tagore, *The Cooperative Principle*, 53.
[56] Tagore, 25.

together the rich and the poor, the learned and the unlettered, by a simple and universally recognized arrangement, was torn to pieces by this blow from outside'.[57] Here, the primary concern of Tagore was articulated by his heartfelt desire to evolve symbiotic relations between the haves and have-nots. Unless this mindset to contribute to the well-being of others was developed, the goal of attaining common welfare would remain both distant and elusive. In pursuance of this argument, the poet further stated that

> the welfare of the individual as well as the community is achieved only when there is scope in the community for each member to work for the good of all [and this is obstructed] ... whenever a man resolves to excel others in wealth or power [which causes] harm to himself, ... [since] no one is complete in himself.[58]

On the basis of his own philosophical leanings, Tagore now proposed his model of a cooperative which he fully put into practice in his Sriniketan project. Drawing on examples from Europe, he realized that 'the abject poverty of [India is due to the fact] that we keep ourselves segregated, trying to bear all our heavy burdens by ourselves'.[59] Those who worked in agriculture needed to come together because

> the combined effort many hands will do miracle [which is possible] if each cultivator did not regard his small holdings as an independent unit, it all adjoining strips were reckoned as one, fewer plough-shares and bullocks could do the tilling and much wasteful labour would be eliminated. There would again be a great saving of energy and expense if, after harvest, the farmers collectively stored and marketed their produce.[60]

Reiterating the need for cooperation among the people, Tagore defended his model, which was also drawn on his experience of how the Europeans developed themselves by being involved in whatever was required to be done for common well-being. Industrial development was a deterrent, since machines made the handicraft workers

---

[57] Tagore, 21.

[58] Tagore, 15–6.

[59] Tagore, 10.

[60] Tagore, 11.

redundant. Nonetheless, instead of putting them under dire stress, the European society created opportunities for them to utilize their skills differently. It was possible because the concern for others remained well-entrenched in the European mindset, which did not seem to have been clouded by the selfish motive of fulfilling only partisan aims and objectives.

In his *The Cooperative Principle*, he elaborated how he conceptualized his goal by saying that

> the village in the country must be built up to be completely self-sufficient, and able to supply all their own needs. For this, village groups should be formed—a few villages going to form each such group—and the headman of each group should make it self-sufficient by providing work for all, and seeing that all their wants are met. Thus, only can self-government become a reality all over the country.[61]

This argument has two integrated concerns: on the one hand, the poet insisted that to fulfil his goals, the villagers needed to be self-sufficient to take care of what they required for their day-to-day survival. He also suggested a system by putting in place a structure, village groups, in his parlance, or a cluster of villages, led by a headman. Here, headman is a coordinator which explicitly mentions the functions that he is expected to discharge to sustain the bonhomie among the villagers. So, the idea of self-government in Tagore's conceptualization is illustrative of a design of togetherness for fulfilling well-set-out plans and programmes, directed to achieve common goals which were also well-defined. According to the poet, 'the villages must be educated, assisted and encouraged to establish primary schools, centres for training in arts and crafts, centres for religious activities, cooperative stores and banks'.[62] As a social reformer, Tagore believed that one of the reasons for Indian villages being socio-economically backward was the lack of education and also absence of centres for imparting education. To take care of this need, he insisted on the establishment of primary schools in each and every village. Given his concern to

[61] Tagore, 19.
[62] Tagore, 19.

provide technical skills to the villagers, he also paid adequate attention to the building of centres capable of training men and women
with skills in pottery, weaving, woodworks and also ironworks.
For him, religious activities were equally important for sustaining
the bond among people; here, his idea was to utilize religion as an
instrument of building togetherness and not social segmentation,
which can easily be explained by referring to his bitter experience
during the 1905–1908 anti-Bengal partition campaign when religion,
instead of being a cementing device, became divisive. He was unique
in his approach in another respect: following the European model
of cooperatives, he also felt the need for banks to support farmers as
and when they needed liquid cash as a loan. Furthermore, he also
took ample care to create facilities for helping cultivators in need.
Two specific modes were suggested: (a) he favoured the creation of
cooperatives for the distribution of seeds and (b) his idea of *dharma-
gola* [silo] epitomized his endeavour towards common storage of the
products, to be distributed among those, again as a loan, who needed
to come out of a crisis of survival, if any.

Drawing from what he learnt from the West, *The Cooperative
Principle* is a long statement of measures that are required for inclusive
development. Formatted in the European style of cooperatives, these
principles helped Tagore articulate his thoughts on how to inject life
into the moribund Indian villages that remained highly backward,
not merely due to the application of an old mode of cultivation but
also due to internal squabbles among the villagers because of social
segmentation. A poet who was also politico-ideologically committed
to India's socio-economic growth, Tagore helped develop a mindset
supportive of his aim, despite steep opposition from his colleagues
and friends nurturing contrary views. Apart from essays defending his
socio-economic concerns, he wrote novels, short stories and dance-
dramas with identical objectives. For instance, his *Ghare Baire* (1916)
is a powerful statement explaining what he meant by *swadeshi* which,
besides having a clear political message, was also an endeavour for
creating centres for the indigenous production of basic household
goods. With his contribution to the development of a soap factory in
the zamindari that he controlled, Nikhilesh of *Ghare Baire* illustrated

what Tagore had in mind. These ideas were reinforced in the scheme that C. R. Das evolved in the context of the non-cooperation campaign (1920–1922) when the endeavour towards developing indigenous industries gained momentum. Gandhi's *Constructive Programme* (1946) echoed the same concerns of Gurudev. In view of the series of efforts that had begun with the publication of *Swadeshi Samaj* in 1904 and *The Cooperative Principles* (1928), there is no denying the fact that Tagore set in motion initiatives which helped the future nationalists spell out their socio-economic concerns in specific politico-ideological designs for: (a) regenerating self-confidence among the Indians and (b) countering the mental servility impeding the growth of the strong nationalist sentiments.

THE SRINIKETAN EXPERIMENT (1928)

Tagore's model of rural reconstruction was translated into reality with the inauguration of the Sriniketan campus of Visva-Bharati in 1928, though the idea was articulated in detail in his *Swadeshi Samaj* (1904). In simple terms, the Sriniketan campus provided a platform which Tagore utilized to experiment with the modes in which he conceptualized rural development. As argued above, according to Tagore, mere political opposition to the British rule was not enough; what was required to be done was to stand on our own so that we did not have to depend on the British government to take care of basic needs. Hence, he argued that

> Our ills cannot be cured by treatment of the symptoms. The causes have to be removed. Frist, the people must cease to be parochial; they must feel that they are part of a world society. Secondly, in the economic sphere, their efforts have to be coordinated to the efforts of men elsewhere. In other words, like tall trees they need wide spaces to spread out their roots under the earth and their branches in the air and light.[63]

Two ideas seem to have coalesced here: on the one hand, the poet insisted on widening one's vision, which was possible only by being educated in tune with one's responsibility for attaining common good;

[63] Tagore, 14.

there was also, on the other hand, the need for sharing the fruit of one's labour with the members of the community—only then would his exalted aim of creating a society free from hunger and poverty be attained. 'Thus, we see that the welfare of individual as well as the community', argued Tagore, 'is achieved only when there is scope in a community for each other to work for the good of all'.[64] Keen to develop a bridge of understanding among the members of the community regardless of socio-economic barriers, the poet's primary concern was to create a communally integrated compact of human beings who remained united despite provocations of any kind.

Furthermore, Tagore's approach to poverty was qualitatively different from the conventional understanding which revolved around techniques for augmenting production by any means. So, it was basically an attempt to address the question of poverty eradication purely in mechanical terms. By linking his concern for poverty alleviation with his distinct philosophical inclinations, Tagore differed from those who attributed poverty removal to the availability of plenty of material goods. While elaborating his point of view, he thus commented that

> most of us who try to deal with the poverty problem think of nothing else by of a greater intensive effort of production, forgetting that this only means greater exhaustion of materials as well as humanity, and this means giving a still better opportunity for profit to the few at the cost of the many. ... But we forget that it is fullness of life which makes us happy and fulness of purse. Multiplying materials intensifies the inequality between those who have and who have not. This is the worst wound from which social body can suffer. It is a wound through the body is bled to death.[65]

A humanist to the core, Tagore never privileged mere material comfort over what allowed human beings maximum happiness. For him, a self-contented individual was a source of strength for the society, while a frustrated one was a burden by being a source of nuisance. It is true that industries contributed to enormous production which helped a few to amass wealth at the cost of many; this was likely to cause resentment among those who remained deprived despite having

---

[64] Tagore, 15.

[65] Rabindranath Tagore's introduction to Elmhirst, *Poet and Plowman*, 25.

had a role in the augmented production. Hence, huge production also led to a social imbalance which, as a consequence, created a fissure among those who were wealthy and those who toiled hard to make both ends meet. The inevitable outcome of this schism was 'unhappiness'; its hydra-headed nature would affect the entire society adversely by generating 'inequality', which was neither desirable nor easy to eradicate. It was a source of concern for the bard, because unless it was addressed effectively, inequality was sure to cause unhappiness by disturbing social amity. An optimist in his belief, Tagore also found a solution because his object was to try

> to flood the choked bed of village life with streams of happiness. For this, the scholars, the poets, the musicians, the artists as well as the scientists have to collaborate, have to offer their contribution. Otherwise they live like parasites, sucking life from the country life, and giving nothing back to them. Such exploitation gradually exhausts the soil of life, the soil which needs constant replenishing by the return of life to it, through the completion of the cycle of receiving and giving back.[66]

Reinforcing the point that mere focus on increasing production at any cost was harmful for human civilization, Tagore provided a mechanism to generate happiness in human existence through being collaborative with one another. What he sought to develop was a model of cooperation among those who, with their capabilities, were keen to contribute to the progress of humanity as a whole and also acted as a shield against exploitation of human beings by human beings. For Tagore, this not only was absolutely necessary for our survival as human beings but also was expected of all of us to give in return whatever we could to Mother Earth, since she gave everything at her disposal to us for our healthy existence.

UNFOLDING OF THE PLAN

Tagore was clear about the aims of the Sriniketan experiment, which were explained in his 1939 text entitled *Sriniketaner Itihas O Adarsha* (the history and ideals of Sriniketan). He sought to achieve the aims

---

[66] Rabindranath Tagore's introduction to Leonard K. Elmhirst, 24–5.

at two levels. At a very mundane level, he argued that cooperative farming was the only means for alleviating the sufferings of those living on agriculture, and once this was meaningfully addressed, most of the sources of human discomfort were likely to disappear. Hence, the stress was on cooperation involving the villagers at large for various kinds of economic activities, including agriculture. It was a stepping stone, which Tagore argued at a philosophical level, towards creating an awareness among the people for participation in collective activities leading to social and economic development. In a nutshell, the poet reinforced his belief in cooperation, which he wanted to institutionalize in the case of agricultural farming because it was bound to be beneficial to all and also supported the idea that with this the urge for cooperation was likely to get strengthened. It was far more explicitly codified in his 1928 *Visva-Bharati Bulletin*, in which he summarized his aims in unambiguous terms. According to him, what inspired him to undertake the Sriniketan project was his desire to make villagers 'self-confident, self-dependent, healthy and also to generate faith in the mutual give-and-take policy in case it is required for the betterment of the village as a unit of collectivity'.[67] Aghast at the political feud which, in his opinion, was a deterrent towards building an economically self-sufficient economy, Tagore also insisted on creating a milieu in which hatred shown by upper-caste Hindus towards their lower-caste counterparts disappeared. He was also disappointed with the general concerns for obtaining rights without performing one's respective social duties. It was achievable, the bard was persuaded to believe, once the villagers joined hands to work together for a common cause which also included a regular cleanliness drive in the villages, because it would not only prevent the outbreak of epidemic diseases like malaria and cholera but also instil in their mind the importance of cleanliness as a shield against these fatal ailments. Primarily, there were three objectives that Tagore sought to attain with the foundation of Sriniketan as an inspirational model in the nationalist context when parallel attempts were being made to make India stand on her own. First, Sriniketan symbolized a

---

[67] Rabindranath Tagore, 'Sriniketaner Itihas O Adarsha,' reproduced in Rabindranath Tagore, *Palliprakriti* [Indian villages] (Kolkata: Visva-Bharati, 1417) (Bangavda), 100.

concern for self-confidence and generating *atmashakti,* or the capability of attaining our goal on our own; second, it was also an application of the cooperative principles that he elaborated in his 1928 publication, *The Cooperative Principle.* Finally, with cooperative efforts, he also felt that local handicrafts were likely to be made viable sources of income or livelihood. In short, Sriniketan was both a sharp comment on how the distance between the educated and uneducated, upper castes and lower castes and urban and rural inhabitants was a serious impediment for socio-economic changes for the betterment of villages as well as a scheme for rural development drawn on indigenous resources. With the inauguration of Sriniketan, Tagore also reiterated one of the core principles of his philosophy that drew on the concern for common well-being. It was not easy to achieve, because of the well-entrenched vested interests which were responsible for the alienation between the haves and the have-nots. The task became far more difficult also because of the superstitious belief that the 'poor became poor due to the sins that they had committed in their earlier birth'[68]—that one was poor or born as an untouchable because it was believed to be 'pre-ordained'. This mindset made them, Tagore lamented, 'helpless and dependent on providential grace [which was possible, they further believed] by accepting what they have been fated to do in this life for survival'.[69] The scene had not, however, been as debilitating in the past as it was then, since the rich in the villages were connected with their poor counterparts in a symbiotic relation, because the former was willing to support the latter, as the rich believed it was 'a service to God and [and was] a virtuous act'.[70] With their departure for the towns for a relatively hassle-free life, the relationship of the villagers became sour with those who acted as caretaker of the property of these rich men. The villagers were, as a consequence, left on the lurch. For Tagore, the Sriniketan project was, therefore, a device for generating an awareness among the villagers and their ability to accomplish the goal of being self-sufficient and self-dependent once they were confident of their capabilities. Towards fulfilling this aim, Tagore insisted on

[68] Tagore, 101.

[69] Tagore, 101.

[70] Tagore, 101.

educating the poor to enable them to judge issues rationally; that they were misled by their unconditional acceptance of the conventional arguments attributing their miseries to sins committed in previous births needed to be effectively countered, which was possible only by inculcating rational thinking through education. It was most succinctly stated by an analyst when he stated that

> [i]n Sriniketan, Tagore wanted to fuse together the role of education with an ideology of cooperative life, betterment of economy, health, linking science and rural reconstruction simultaneously. He wanted education to act as a stimuli of development, enabling people to translate their knowledge for the betterment of life and usher in economic well-being ... to play not only a constructive but a creative role in making the life as completely as possible.[71]

This was easier said than done, given the well-entrenched social prejudices that flourished, presumably because they were never challenged meaningfully to the extent of rooting them out. Nonetheless, in Sriniketan, Tagore laid out a socio-economic design for transformation, which was put into practice by his colleagues with identical aims and objectives. One of his most trusted co-workers who contributed immensely in this regard was Leonard K. Elmhirst, who arrived in Santiniketan in 1921. The first step which he took was to locate those individuals who were willing to 'live among the villagers ... in such a way that the cultivators will welcome everything that these men can give them [which was possible if] ... if they work with their devotion and without expecting anything in return'.[72] What caused an uncertainty in Elmhirst's mind was how to approach the villagers who, being oppressed by the local rich and upper-caste people, lost their faith in them and whose faith in outsiders had also been considerably weakened by the failure of the government to address their concerns. This was evident when Elmhirst wrote that

---

[71] Dikshit Sinha, *A Poet's Experiment in Rebuilding Samaj and Nation: Sriniketan's Rural Reconstruction Work, 1922–1960* (Bolpur, West Bengal: Birutjatio Sahitya Sammiloni, 2019), 131.

[72] Elmhirst to Tagore, 8 September, 1921, Elmhirst Collection, Rabindra Bhawan Archive, Viswa Bharati – cited in Sinha, 167.

our problem was, therefore, first to make a definite contact with a village, any village, then to prove that we were not oppressors, and then to show that we were not foolish. We had to convince them that we had one chief object, to prove to them, after winning their respect, that there were quite a number of ways in which they could, by helping themselves, keep and increase their own self-respect and slowly achieve a new and more potent command over their generally tragic and poverty-stricken environment.[73]

What was attempted was to create a milieu to develop a sense of interdependence between the villagers and those who were to work among them for their self-enrichment by creating a rational mindset. The situation did not seem to be familiar to Elmhirst, presumably because he was born and raised in the West, which was relatively free from the prejudices linked with one's birth in India. Furthermore, in view of the democratic structure of governance that had emerged in the West, the government there appeared to be more sensitive to the poor, making them stakeholders of the system. The scene in India was thus clearly at variance with that of the West, which Tagore was reported to have clarified to Elmhirst when he said that

in India, the real cause of the weakness that cripples our spirit of freedom arises from the impregnable social wall between the different castes. These check the natural flow of fellow feeling among the people who live in our country. The law of love and mutual respect has been ignored for the sake of retaining an artificial order. This only serves to promote a sense of degeneracy and defeat. The people of India in this way have built their own cage; but by trying to secure their freedom from one another, they only succeed in keeping themselves eternally captive.[74]

Here, Tagore attributed the socio-economic decadence of Indian villages to 'the outdated [but well-entrenched] caste system',[75] which held back many villagers from participating in his project, because they were too scared of the outsiders and also sceptical of their activities, given his identity as an upper-caste zamindar. But it was Kalimohon

---

[73] Leonard K. Elmhirst, *Rabindranath Tagore: Pioneer in Education* (London: John Murray, 1961), 24–5.

[74] Elmhirst, 23.

[75] Elmhirst, 23.

Ghose, a trusted aide of Tagore who had wide experience, who 'laid the foundation for the work in the villages'[76] by being respectful to each and every villager, which immediately created a space for the work that the poet had in mind for rural well-being. Appreciating Ghose for his immensely important role, Tagore further clarified his approach in a letter to Elmhirst, saying that the task was made easier because the Elmhirst-led team generated an environment in which the villagers accepted the challenge as their own. It was possible for the team to accomplish the mission, because they dealt with the villagers as human beings, which was graphically illustrated by the bard when he expressed his confidence that the team was highly capable by underlining that

> the villages are waiting for the living touch of creative faith ... and, with the instinctive humanity of [the team members], they came into the closest touch with the living being which is the village. ... They had human sympathy in abundance ... which was the principal motive power that carried [them] across all the difficulties that stood against [them] in their congregated might.[77]

A humanist to the core, Tagore upheld those values and principles which were critical to the protection of human beings as human beings. His model of Sriniketan was based on this. He was persuaded to believe that no endeavour towards attaining inclusive development for the country was possible unless Indian villages were rejuvenated, which was not achievable without involving the villagers; this was a distant goal, he further noted, so long as they remained indifferent to the activities that Tagore undertook in Sriniketan. Elmhirst, one of the significant members of the team that was devoted wholeheartedly to this task, thus noted that 'Tagore's idea was always to illustrate a few basic principles by winning the confidence of a few village at first',[78] which was a stepping stone towards generating mass zeal for village reconstruction beyond the village in which the work was first undertaken. To sustain the villagers' concern for common

[76] Elmhirst, 25.

[77] Elmhirst, 28–9.

[78] Elmhirst, 41.

well-being, Tagore also underlined the importance of education, which was meant to blossom individual personality in all spheres of human activity. Contrarily, the British system of education was devoid of substance, since it was directed at producing a pool of clerks trained to defend the system of exploitation engendered by the colonial rule. Hence, Tagore castigated those 'charitably-minded, city-bred individuals when they talk of education [because] their sole aim is to create a servile nation [bereft of] an independent voice'.[79] The aim was therefore to generate an interest in education that was not merely a passport for jobs in government offices but one that was potentially an effective means to ensure individuals' all-round development. Being practical to the core, Tagore also knew that it was a Herculean task to spread education throughout the country. Hence, his advice was to begin with

> one or two villages … hoping that our efforts will touch the hearts of our village neighbours, and help them in reasserting themselves in a new social order [and] … if we can give a start to a few villages, they would perhaps be an inspiration to some others.[80]

Logically, it was a plausible argument, since the result-driven activities easily persuaded others, given the fact that the means that were effective on one context were likely to be the same in another.

As argued above, Tagore's prescribed model of development drew inspiration from what he thought of education—that it was a time-tested device for creating a prejudice-free mindset. His education was not confined to books or tests but was meant to nurture those qualities which made human beings also be involved in activities meant to contribute to common well-being. Based on this concern, he thus suggested a course curriculum that included performance of 'a variety of duties, in dormitory, kitchen, poultry-run and dairy'.[81] In addition to these activities, they learnt, noted Tagore, 'games, songs and plays, carpentry and some other craft, and their sums and writing were

[79] Elmhirst, 37.
[80] Elmhirst, 38.
[81] Elmhirst, 35.

focused on their daily experience'.[82] Out of this training grew Tagore's idea 'of an education basic to the needs of any child in a rural society'.[83] So, Tagore conceived education in its widest possible connotations, as something which was not only innovative but also provided an alternative scheme to offer a powerful critique of the prevalent mode of learning that flourished in the wake of the British rule.

The Sriniketan model is an elaboration of Tagore's ideas on rural construction. As mentioned above, complemented by his colleagues, including Elmhirst, it was possible for the poet to lay out a solid foundation for an alternative scheme of development which drew on both theoretical learning and practice-driven exercises. For him, mere learning of 3 Rs might have its relevance to the colonial masters; but it was of no use for India's socio-economic development. The idea is persuasive because this is linked with the view that the artificial social segregation based on the accident of birth was meant to defend a social order in which one section of the population always remained·socio-economically peripheral. Being vehemently opposed to a deliberately pursued divisive social design such as the caste system, Tagore felt the need for education as an effective means to expose the fault lines of this logic in its defence. On the whole, Tagore's Sriniketan project was a package, certainly a new package, that he unpacked by putting in place a persuasive alternative mode of rural reconstruction with the primary goal of bringing about inclusive development in the country.

CONCLUDING OBSERVATIONS

What is striking in Tagore's approach to socio-economic reconstruction is the shifting of attention from the cities to the villages, just like that of Gandhi, who also believed that 'India live in the villages', which primarily means that neglecting Indian villages would be hara-kiri for the country as a whole. The schemes that Tagore developed in his *Swadeshi Samaj* of 1904, which he put into practice in Sriniketan in 1928, are illustrative here. He was primarily concerned with

[82] Elmhirst, 35.

[83] Elmhirst, 35.

community development and village welfare by infusing into villages 'a new pulsation of life'.[84] Based on the twin principles of self-reliance and enlightenment, Tagore created a milieu in otherwise moribund villages (located in the district of Birbhum of Bengal province) in which the villagers were inspired to participate in the schemes that he evolved by being interactive with them. It was possible for him to undertake this gigantic task since he was assisted by equally enthusiastic colleagues like Kalimohon Ghose and Leonard K. Elmhirst, among others. Not only did they emotionally align with the objectives that Tagore had laid out, but they also ensured their day-to-day involvement in activities that drew on his concern for common welfare. Presumably because of this, there emerged a unique system of cooperation among the stakeholders in the villages. The primary aims were to (a) make the villagers integral to the schemes that were meant to create fraternity among them regardless of class, caste and ethnicity; and (b) generate interests in vocational training which enabled them to utilize their leisure hours in weaving, carpentry, dairy, pottery and book binding, among others. As a result, the villages that were 'even a decade ago shabby and lifeless slowly regained their life and became agog with activities and villagers shook off their stupor to take part in village reconstruction programme'.[85] Innovative was Tagore's idea of agricultural cooperative banks which, by supplying credit to villagers when they required it, removed moneylenders from the scene; similarly, the establishment of *dharmagolas* (cooperative grain banks) helped the villagers tackle crises due to natural calamities and famine by creating a permanent source of supply of grain in case it was needed.

Tagore's approach to rural reconstruction can be said to have evolved historically. *Swadeshi Samaj* was written in 1904, just before the outbreak of the anti-British campaign following the bifurcation of Bengal in 1905. As elaborated above, here, the poet developed a model which was meant to ensure common well-being in Indian villages, because he believed that mere political freedom would be of no consequence unless it was complemented by socio-economic freedom

---

[84] Ajit K. Neogy, *Santiniketan and Sriniketan: The Twin Dreams of Rabindranath Tagore* (New Delhi: National Book Trust, 2015) (reprint), 266.

[85] Neogy, 267.

for the people. Hence, he raised his voice against artificial social segregation based on caste and the failure of the well-off sections of Bengal to carry with them those who remained socially and economically peripheral. The Sriniketan model was an articulation that drew on what he conceptualized as his own brand of rural reconstruction. It became an achievable goal since Tagore was fortunate to have around him a group of selfless individuals who also had identical missions. For his colleagues who participated in fulfilling the objectives, it was not just a step towards the social well-being of the people, it was also a service to mankind. Thus, Elmhirst emphatically declared that

> Sriniketan must itself be training ground, a home into which the homeless idealist can come and find new paths of self-expression ever held out to him, new ideals of freedom, of friendship in service, of attitude to the simple villager.[86]

Reverberating the ideas that Tagore nurtured and articulated in his written texts and speeches, Sriniketan, as Elmhirst saw it, symbolized not only a hope to the villagers who had nothing to cling to, especially during the crisis, but also allowed them to be integrally connected with the schemes meant for their socio-economic well-being. In other words, Sriniketan was not just an academic model but also a powerful voice based on Tagore's concern for inclusive development of the people as a whole. Inspirational in nature, the Sriniketan experiment was imbued with ideas that became prominent during the nationalist struggle, when it was strongly felt that political freedom bereft of economic well-being was futile. Hence, it is not surprising that Elmhirst insisted on the emulation of the experiment by those sharing his concern. As he conveyed in his letter to the editor of the *Modern Review*, Ramananda Chatterjee,

> each district should have its own Sriniketan. I am inclined to think that each portion of a district should duplicate certain of our activities and this reason I would like to see a little branch of Sriniketan set up by two or

---

[86] Leonard K. Elmhirst to Ramananda Chatterjee, the editor of the Modern Review, 25 December, 1924—reproduced in Neogy, 271.

three of our workers in some villages in another part of Birbhum ... where a little land, a house and funds are available.[87]

What is important to remember is the fact that based on his conceptualization of *Swadeshi Samaj*, the poet put in place a realistic model that ushered in a new wave of thinking. Inspirational in nature, the idea of *samaj* stood for cooperation among those willing to work for the betterment of the villagers, which was, according to Elmhirst, the best model to have brought about radical socio-economic transformation in similar circumstances. It was undoubtedly Tagore's unique approach to rural reconstruction, which, to a significant extent, drew on what he saw in Russia. As he pointed out, rather enthusiastically, his trip to Russia in 1930 was a source of emotional satisfaction when his 'mind was filled with dark despair'. Why was it so? The poet himself explained that

> ostentation of wealth in other European countries ... is so Olympian that, poor as we are, even our envy fails to reach its height. In Russia, the display of luxury is wholly absent; probably that is why it was easy to catch a glimpse of her true being. [There] I saw mighty efforts being made to provide universally everything of which India is deprived.[88]

There is an interesting connection between Tagore's visit to Russia in 1930 and the spurt of activities that had begun in Sriniketan following his return. In a discussion with Elmhirst immediately after he came back to Sriniketan, he insisted on learning from how Russia addressed the issues of poverty and socio-economic discrimination most effectively, which was soon to be implemented for realizing his goal of common well-being. He elaborated his point by developing his views at two levels. At the level of practice, what was required to be done was to inspire the mind to enable the body to act in accordance what the former sought to fulfil. It was necessary because 'in the bloodless body of our country the mind has suffered an eclipse: there is no joy

---

[87] Leonard K. Elmhirst to Ramananda Chatterjee, the editor of Modern Review, 271.

[88] Rabindranath Tagore, *Letters from Russia* (Calcutta: Visva-Bharati, 1984) (reprint), 106.

in life: we are dying in mind and body'.[89] So, a design was needed to be developed to reverse the situation. At the level of conceptualization, he was thus insistent on creating a social milieu in which discriminatory practices had no place, because so long as discrimination of any kind was allowed to exist, social harmony would remain an elusive goal. The goal was to evolve a milieu that would obstruct the social tendencies destroying social harmony

> by the increasing distance between the strong and the weak, ... leading to disease owing to bloated indulgence on the one hand and anaemic emacia-tion on the other. In all civilized societies today', the poet argued further, 'the messenger of death finds entrée through this opening. In our country, the gate of his (sic) entrance seems opened wider than elsewhere.[90]

Implicit here are two complementary arguments of Tagore that he put forward continuously, since his ideas were basically context-driven. On the one hand, he was aware that much of India's socio-economic imbalances was artificially created, which meant that attempts at reversing the prevalent socio-economic order were certain to receive staunch opposition, since they would affect the vested interests adversely. Nonetheless, by referring to this, he clearly had shown his politico-ideological priorities by providing a persuasive critique of what he perceived as a distorted form of one's social existence. A practitioner par excellence, Tagore did not stop there. He devised, on the other hand, a model which, he thought, was appropriate to bring about the social and economic metamorphosis by involving the villagers as stakeholders in the process. An optimist to the core, he further mentioned that only through cooperation was the nature of interpersonal relationships likely to undergo transformation; the idea of drawing on each other was a time-tested mechanism to initiate and also sustain the processes of change. There was, of course, an uncer-tainty that the bard showed once in a while, which was evident when he admitted that 'we ourselves do not have the ability to continue with the activities that we have undertaken [to improve the villages]

[89] Tagore, 107.

[90] Tagore, 147–8.

because our resources are limited'.[91] Nonetheless, he showed his optimism because he also believed that the Sriniketan experiment stood as a class apart by demonstrating that their efforts had yielded results and the villagers had joined hands in sustaining the activities that he and his colleagues had started with its inauguration in 1928. It was far more explicitly stated in his letter to Elmhirst, when he wrote that

> the small beginning which you have made ... at a remote corner of the world carries in it a truth for which me today are groping in the bewilderment. It is the truth of Peace. Real peace comes from a wealth which is living, which has the blessing of Nature's direct touch, which is not machine made; let us seek it humbly, coming down to the soil to deal with those forces of life which are beautiful and bounteous.[92]

The Sriniketan experiment was Tagore's articulation of how to achieve universal humanism; availability of plenty which was made possible with industrialization might not be enough for peace for which we needed (a) communion of human beings irrespective of one's socio-economic location and (b) willingness to erase the distinction between we and they. This was his message when he uttered that 'I nourish my faith in the last survival value of friendship, of love and of the spirit of cooperation fed by constant delight of sacrifice'.[93] So, the goal for the bard was much bigger than mere socio-economic change; the Sriniketan project was complementary to what he was so assiduously seeking to achieve. Elmhirst graphically illustrated what Tagore had in mind when he laid out his plan for Sriniketan, stating that

> [c]onstantly he [Tagore] used to remind us that our practical achievements, our clean milk, our fresh eggs, our flourishing co-operatives, were all useful means, but still only means, toward the achievement of much greater ends [by drawing upon] ... all the resources, in music, song, drama and dance, drawing and design ... to enrich our lives, to liven our aspirations, to inspire our leisure and to increase our delights in every kind of artistic

[91] Rabindranath Tagore, 'Palliseva' in Rabindranath Tagore, *Palliprakriti* (nature of villages) (Kolkata: Visva-Bharati, 1417) (Bangavda), 113.

[92] Rabindranath Tagore to Leonard K. Elmhirst, 31 March, 1922—reproduced in Elmhirst, *Poet and Plowman*, 125.

[93] Elmhirst, *Rabindranath Tagore*, 43.

expression, until we and [those who are engaged with us] … could produce a richness and a wealth of cultural life of our own, and a rejuvenation of those ancient art forms that still survived, but so tenuously, in the village around us.[94]

A careful study of Tagore's approach to socio-economic reconstruction reveals that it was both contextual and innovative. It was contextual because his long association with Bengal villages brought before him the hapless conditions of the villagers despite their having toiled ceaselessly for bare survival. Of course, his approach had its roots in the contemporary socio-economic imbalances which, felt Tagore, needed to be addressed. As an innovative thinker, he also suggested various devices to take care of the villagers' requirements. For instance, the idea of cooperative agriculture, which was drawn on the example that Europe had already set out, was an innovative design insofar as Bengal agriculture was concerned; it was a design that was soon to be emulated elsewhere. What is most important and striking was his emphasis on building *samaj*, or amicable collective existence. The 1904 tract, *Swadeshi Samaj*, was clearly directional in this respect. This was also an ideational essay that seems to have influenced Nikhilesh in *Ghare Baire* who, while being critical of armchair revolutionaries like Sandip for being indifferent to the prevalent socio-economic disparities due to caste and religion, expressed the poet's sentiments in clear terms. In a similar vein, his 1928 text entitled *The Cooperative Principle* represented the bard's preference for a specific kind of togetherness which, he felt, was necessary to effectively combat the poverty in rural Bengal. The aim was to develop and strengthen the *samaj*, which was a time-tested design, to address most of the troubling issues that seriously debilitated efforts towards achieving inclusive development. In other words, *samaj* was not just an articulation of the cooperative principles but was also a seriously undertaken endeavour to evolve and consolidate social amity among those living in the villages as friends, neighbours and compatriots. As argued above, unlike so many of his nationalist colleagues, Tagore was also a practitioner, which was evident with the inauguration of Sriniketan in 1928; his effort, complemented by his co-workers, including Leonard K. Elmhirst and

94 Elmhirst, 43.

Kalimohon Ghose, among others, yielded results with the establishment of Sriniketan as a laboratory to experiment with the ideas that he nurtured. Similar to Gandhi, who devised a design in his 1946 tract, *Constructive Programme,* which was also directional and an endeavour to involve the stakeholders in what was appropriate for their socio-economic well-being, the poet provided both a model and its articulation in practice. Rather than insisting on mere political freedom, which was futile bereft of socio-economic transformation, Tagore was keen to bring about human emancipation based on social geniality, cultural bonhomie and adequate economic prosperity to create conditions for building a *Swadeshi Samaj.* This is what separates the bard from most of his nationalist colleagues and makes him transcendental as a social thinker who neither was swayed by political gimmicks nor accepted the privileging of political freedom over others but remained committed to his visions for radical socio-economic changes as the only means to have a value-driven, socio-culturally vibrant, politically innovative and globally oriented India.

Tagore's Understanding of Gender Issues

Rabindranath Tagore was not a feminist in the sense of champion-ing an exclusive identity for women but was vehemently opposed to gender discrimination, since women constituted an integral part of humanity. As a humanist to the core, patriarchy which drew on gender discrimination was thus not acceptable to him. It was a revelation that despite being nurtured in an environment where prejudices against women were never considered unusual, the poet boldly pursued his arguments for freedom for women. By referring to many Upanishadic tales, he put across the point that neither the ancient texts which were generally cited to justify gender inequity nor the practices that they supported rationalized the bias against women. For the poet, vari-ous devices that had emerged later were largely constructed to fulfil partisan aims. Tagore's claim that women remained discriminated due to specific socio-economic and political processes is based on his exposure to (a) the ancient texts and also (b) the Western experiences, which were also an important source of his belief in gender equal-ity. Furthermore, the experience of being raised in an environment in which women were encouraged to be part of the outside world, appeared to have had a natural appeal in an otherwise unfavourable social, economic and political circumstances.

Historically speaking, concern for gender equality had hardly swayed the mainstream thinking in Bengal until Ram Mohan Roy (1772–1833) emerged on the scene. With his initiative, the cruel Sati custom was abolished once the 1829 Bengal Sati Regulation was adopted during the reign of Lord William Bentick as India's Governor-General. Besides the rescinding of the Sati customs, Roy was also instrumental in mobilizing opinion against caste rigidity, polygamy and child marriage. It is argued that Roy 'attributed social evils in Hindu religion and society to the poisonous effect of idolatrous notions'[1] which were contrary to most of the Vedic beliefs. He appeared to have prepared the ground for Vidyasagar (1820–1891), who introduced the practice of widow remarriages notwithstanding the steep opposition of the Hindu mainstream. By effectively challenging the polygamy that the upper-caste Brahmins happily practised, the Sanskrit scholar set in motion a campaign for women being treated at par with their male counterpart regardless of caste. Based on his understanding of the ancient texts, like the Vedas, which were always cited by the then orthodox Hindus to justify gender discrimination, Vidyasagar raised his voice against the deliberate distortion of the ideas codified in these tracts to substantiate his claim that it was a design that drew on the desires of a section of the population for their partisan gain. These were surely powerful steps which helped build a strong movement in Bengal, especially at the aegis of the Brahmo Samaj. Rabindranath Tagore's father, Debendranath Tagore, also known as Maharshi, was one of the Brahmo Samaj leaders who, along with his colleagues, not only initiated several new measures but also consolidated the campaign for gender equality. Not only did he encourage women to go to schools and colleges for formal education in an institutionalized set-up, but he also created a milieu for the women to come forward to participate in activities which had so far remained a male bastion. Tagore's compatriot Keshabchandra Sen also stood out for his significant contribution in this regard; he also played a key role in generating zeal for education among the women, since he felt that only by being educated would they be capable of questioning the age-old superstitious beliefs that kept them in chains. So, for Sen, sending women to schools and colleges was one of the most effective ways of combatting the social tendencies supporting degradation and humiliation of women. It is true that the campaign that the Brahmos undertook was largely confined to Calcutta, which meant that the rest of Bengal remained untouched; nonetheless, the initiatives that unfolded with the Brahmo Samaj campaign for women's

---

[1] David Kopf, *The Brahmo Samaj and the Shaping of the Modern Indian Mind* (New Delhi: Archives Publishers Private Ltd., 1988), 14.

empowerment left a legacy for the future; it was a legacy on which Rabindranath Tagore defended and also strengthened his arguments for treating women as equal to their male counterparts. In other words, what we see in Tagore's creative texts was a continuity of a trend that gained momentum as history progressed. In view of Tagore's concern for gender equality, the chapter, by dwelling on the creative texts that he articulated to support his point of view, argues that his intervention not only strengthened the campaign for socio-economic changes but also contributed immensely to the conceptualization of women's issues in a completely different theoretical format. As mentioned above, the ideas that the poet put forward were drawn on what his predecessors in the Brahmo Samaj, including his father, stipulated, but were also an expansion of those ideas which they failed to pursue due to adverse social reactions. The chapter has thus a twofold aim: on the one hand, by delving into what Tagore developed, particularly in his essays, novels, short stories and dance-dramas to persuasively argue his point of view, the chapter reinforces his arguments in favour of gender equality; on the other hand, the chapter demonstrates the strong women characters in his creative texts who represented what Tagore prescribed for ushering in a world with gender parity. Basic here is the point that Tagore, similar to some of his nationalist colleagues, took up the cudgels for ending sexist oppression and exploitation of a section of the demography by another due to their gender identity.

CONCEPTUAL PATHWAYS

By the time Tagore was a powerful voice, the Enlightenment values championing equality regardless of sex seem to have developed organic roots in Bengal. The idea of gender equality became part and parcel of the campaigns for social reform, which was clearly an intellectual aid to the poet when he focused on issues relating to gender discrimination. For him, it was a social disease which needed to be treated firmly to create a society free from gender prejudices. There was hardly an escape, because the social context supportive of gender discrimination was constructed deliberately. The idea was most persuasively argued by Simone de Beauvoir in her *The Second Sex* when she stated that 'feminine reality has been constituted [in which] they [women] have been defined as the Other', with the consequence of being denied 'a legitimate space in the human *Mitsein* [communal existence]'.[2] The point was graphically illustrated by the author when she further added that

> men's economic privilege, their social value, the prestige of marriage, the usefulness of masculine support—all these encourage women to ardently want to please men. They are on the whole still in a state of serfdom. It follows that woman knows and chooses herself not as she exists for herself but as man defines her. She thus has to be described first as men dream of her since her being-for-men is one of the essential factors of her concrete existence.[3]

Critical here is the idea that women do not exist as an agency independent of men; their entire being is structured, governed and shaped as per the social context which is a male creation. There are many authors, such as Kate Millett[4] and Carole Pateman,[5] among others, who pursued the point by touching on various aspects of gender issues in the contemporary context. The scenario continues to remain the same as long as 'men and women do not recognize each other as peers, as long as femininity, [as it is conceptualized now,] is perpetuated'.[6] What it means is that unless the prevalent mindset representing specific kinds of social, economic and politico-ideological preferences is transformed, 'the new woman cannot appear'.[7] An analytical perusal of the principal texts on gender reveals that women remain discriminated presumably because of the existent socio-economic circumstances that drew on politico-ideological support from a set of preordained ideas which are required to be changed. The task is easier said than done, since these ideas are not only socio-economically well-entrenched but have also evolved as integral to one's social existence. There have been protests against the best of feminist scholars who genuinely felt

[2] Simone de Beauvoir, *The Second Sex* (London: Vintage Book, 2011), 17.

[3] de Beauvoir, 159.

[4] Kate Millett, *Sexual Politics* (New York: Doubleday, 1970).

[5] Carole Pateman, *The Sexual Contract* (Stanford: Stanford University Press, 1988).

[6] de Beauvoir, *The Second Sex*, 771.

[7] de Beauvoir, 777.

the need for change for the sake of building an egalitarian society in which discrimination around social, economic and political axes is an anathema.

The admittedly straightforward discussion above is useful when arguing the point that Tagore's endeavour was an integral part of the concern that many authors who focused primarily on the theme of gender parity dealt with to persuasively conceptualize the theme. Being a creative writer, the poet put forward his views through the characters that appeared in many of his texts. It is not possible to deal with each and every character which represented the thematic concern that he sought to articulate. By discursively analysing the nature of the character with reference to the socio-economic context in which they emerged, the chapter provides useful inputs to graphically present Tagore's socio-economic and politico-ideological preferences as well. The aim here is to understand his approach to gender equity, which was both contextual and transcendental: contextual because his views were an offshoot of the milieu in which he was raised and nurtured; transcendental since the ideas that he propounded remain relevant in similar socio-economic and political circumstances.

FORMULATING THE GENDER QUESTION

A universalist, Tagore was a crusader against any kind of discrimination, whether on the basis of religion or archaic mindsets. Drawing on the experiences of being raised in a family that welcomed the values of Enlightenment, his condemnation for anything artificially compartmentalizing human beings was a natural response. Discriminatory practices, thus argued the poet, had their roots in deliberately created socio-economic designs for segregation. In his opinion, 'it is a symptom of our egotism, this clinging with fanatical fervor to all that is accidental [to our civilization], making it ... a source of discrimination [which] is the greatest calamity, in the present age, for peace and welfare of all'.[8] Being persuaded to believe that the supremacist

---

[8] Rabindranath Tagore, 'Brahmo Samaj Centenary,' in *The English Writings of Rabindranath Tagore*, ed. Nityananda Ghosh, Vol. 4 (New Delhi: Sahitya Akademi, 2008) (reprint), 747.

mindset was an impediment for universal humanism, the bard linked his concern for gender parity with his principal socio-economic objective, maintaining that gender parity would remain distant so long as women were kept in chains. This was stated most persuasively when he mentioned that

> the history of man is the history of the building up of a human universe, as has been proved by the fact that everything great in human activity inevitably belongs to all humanity. And we may be sure that all our religious experiences and expressions are building up from the depth of the ages one great continent of religions on which man's soul is to win its prosperity through universal commerce of spiritual life.[9]

There are three perceptive points that deserve attention here: first, according to Tagore, religion that was purely ritualistic was futile insofar as human welfare was concerned. Instead, religion, for him, represented a way of life directed to achieve universal well-being. Being disenchanted with the narrow vision that contemporary religion embodied, the poet raised his voice, since it was responsible for generating and also consolidating various forms of socio-economic discrimination. Second, as a practitioner, he always devised a means to translate into reality his conceptual ideas. Based on his concern to build a universe drawing on concern for one another, he built Visva-Bharati, which was also a laboratory for executing some of his plans for universal well-being. The twin campuses of Visva-Bharati, Santiniketan and Sriniketan, created an environment in which Tagore's concern for gender equity was translated into many designs, which, he felt, was a stepping stone to bring about the desired change in the prevalent mindset among those associated with this place of learning. Finally, universal prosperity was possible only through cooperation regardless of gender, class and ethnicity, which meant that goal-driven endeavours were to be undertaken to root out the deliberately designed socio-economic segregation. Here too, the examples of Santiniketan and Sriniketan will suffice to prove the point. By promoting co-education, Tagore sought to create an atmosphere of bonhomie among the inmates of the two schools, Patha Bhawana and Siksha Satra, which

---

[9] Tagore, 748.

he founded to put into practice what he felt so strongly—to evolve togetherness among the students regardless of their gender identity.

A very insightful thinker, Tagore also analysed how the present socio-economic priorities contributed to segregation around the gender axis. In his well-thought-out argument, he proposed a model which explains how views opposed to gender parity evolved historically, presumably because of the prevalent socio-economic context in which they always received approbation. While seeking to explain why man-woman discriminatory segregation emerged at the first place, the bard attributed the biological difference between sexes 'to the inequalities fostered by circumstances'.[10] Women seem to be naturally constrained because of their inherent nature which did not allow them to be fit for all kinds of work. This was what gave man, argued Tagore, adequately justified reasons to draw the line. As Tagore articulated,

> man is not handicapped by the same biological and psychological responsibilities as woman, and therefore he the liberty to give her the security of home. This liberty exacts payment when it offers its boon, because to give to withhold the gift is within its power.[11]

Hence, naturally endowed biological differences created an imbalance which instilled in women the idea of men being superior. This was the source of 'unfreedom', noted Tagore. According to him, 'it is the unequal freedom in their [man-woman] relationships which has made the weight of life's tragedies so painfully heavy for woman to bear'.[12] This is a profound conceptual statement which is illustrative of how women, by being instinctively receptive to this unequal freedom, accepted their socially degrading position as inescapable. Nonetheless, it was a suffering for them which was likely to cause disruptions in inter-gender bond, if any. Tagore explained the obvious outcome of such imbalances by saying that

[10] Rabindranath Tagore, 'Woman and Home,' in *The English Writings of Rabindranath Tagore*, ed. Sisir Kumar Das, Vol. 2 (New Delhi: Sahitya Akademi, 1996), 552.

[11] Tagore, 552.

[12] Tagore, 552.

all great suffering indicates some wrong somewhere. In the present case, the wrong is in woman's lack of freedom in her relationship with man, which compels here to turn her disabilities into attractions, and to use untruths as her allies in the battle of life, while she is suffering from the precariousness of her position.[13]

The idea is crystal clear: women continued to remain subjugated in view of the socially defended restrictions which they accepted as given; or, in other words, it was predestined for a woman to endorse what she received as soon as she was born as a woman. There were occasions when they were seemingly treated at par with their male counterparts, but that was a subtle way of sustaining the socio-economic imbalances. Tagore articulated this, saying that by being instinctively tuned 'to perform their services in such a manner that they ... may be raised from the domain of slavery to the realm of grace ... women have tried to prove that in the building up of social life they are artists and not artisans'.[14] Condemning the paternalistic male attitude towards women, Tagore also drew our attention to the processes whereby women were reduced to an instrument for carrying forward the dictated instructions of their male counterparts. In a very scathing tone, he now articulated his viewpoints by exhorting that

> when necessity drives women to fashion their lives to the taste of the insensitive or the sensual, then the whole thing becomes a tragedy of desecration. Society is full of such tragedies. Many of the laws and social regulations guiding the relationships of man and woman are the relics of a barbaric age, when the brutal pride of an exclusive possession had its dominance in human relations, such as those of parents and children, husbands and wives, master and servants, teachers and disciples. The vulgarity of it still persists in the social bond between sexes because of the economic helplessness of woman. Nothing makes us so stupidly mean as the sense of superiority which the power of purse confers upon us.[15]

Between genders there existed a clear demarcation in which women were clearly disadvantaged. Their role was socially determined, which

---

[13] Tagore, 553.

[14] Tagore, 553.

[15] Tagore, 553–4.

also reinforces the argument that they hardly had freedom of action in accordance with what they deemed appropriate. For Tagore, one of the primary reasons needed to be located in the milieu in which women did not have independent sources of income or they were not allowed to work for generating income for themselves. This was certainly plausible, though the lack of income was one of the many factors that impeded the rise of women as independent agencies. For instance, as recent studies have shown, women were being subjected to various kinds of constraints due to various kinds of socially transmitted devices of segregation around multiple axes. From this stems the idea of intersectionality, which is a framework for conceptualizing a person, a group of people or a social problem as affected by a number of discriminations and disadvantages. This is a theoretical endeavour to account for people's overlapping identities and experiences in order to grasp the complexities of the prejudices that they face. Conceptually persuasive, the theory of intersectionality iterates that people are often subjected to multiple sources of oppression: their race, class, gender identity, sexual orientation, religion and other identity markers. It emphasizes that identity markers (female or any socio-economically disadvantaged group) do not exist independently of each other and each informs each other, often creating a complex convergence of oppression.[16] It is true that one does not get an explicit reference to the idea of intersectionality in Tagore's conceptualization of gender issues, though one gets an idea that he was aware of this aspect if one contextualizes his viewpoints by referring to the prevalent colonial context. Indians were socio-economically and also politically marginalized with the onset of colonial rule; women, being part of the same system, had hardly escaped the shackles of colonialism, which was the backdrop in which the poet intervened to comprehend the complexities of gender discrimination. What is worth pointing out here is Tagore's courageous stance to create a milieu for women to break free from the chains of oppression. It was evident when he stated that

---

[16] Kimberle Williams Crenshaw, *Mapping the Margins: Intersectionality, Identity Politics, and Violence Against Women of Colour*. https://www.racialequitytools.org/resourcefiles/mapping-margins.pdf.

the present age has sent its cry to women, asking her to come out from her segregation in order to restore the spiritual supremacy of all that is human in the world of humanity. She has been aroused to remember that womanliness is not chiefly decorative. It is like that vital health, which not only imparts the bloom of beauty to the body, but joy to the mind and perfection to life.[17]

The above conceptual points help us comprehend the foundational theoretical ideas on which Tagore based his approach to gender and socio-economic discrimination that people were subjected to during British colonialism. Whether it was Nandini in *Rakta Karabi*, Bimala in *Ghare Baire*, Ela in *Char Adahay*, Damini in *Chaturanga* or Sucharita in *Gora,* the idea does not seem to be different; they represented an urge to break the social constraints justifying women's 'enslavement' in a male-dominated patriarchal society. Basic to his argument are two conceptually innovative points. On the one hand, by identifying the sources of intersectionality or multiple sources of society-driven oppression that women failed to escape, Tagore, like some of his colleagues, highlighted, in the public domain, those issues which hardly received serious attention, presumably because of the available socially validated constraints. He however did not stop with simply flagging the issues; by creating bold characters in his creative writings, the poet devised, on the other hand, a design for socio-economic metamorphosis which set a tempo for significant attitudinal changes in the course of time.

Tagore's argument remains incomplete unless one is drawn to the other aspect highlighting what he specified as 'self-introspection' by women themselves. As argued above, that women needed to be conceptualized differently was the outcome of wider socio-economic changes across the globe. Despite being a deterrent, colonialism also introduced Indians to the liberating Enlightenment values, which set in motion processes of impactful socio-economic changes in India. Ideas for gender equity were rooted in these values which came to India in the wake of colonialism. It was easier for Ram Mohan Roy or Vidyasagar to accomplish their objectives presumably because of the

---

[17] Tagore, 'Woman and Home,' 555.

support that they received from the rulers. Core to this argument is the point that concerns for gender parity had their roots in the philosophy of Enlightenment which was a natural gift to the colonized. Tagore was, however, a little uncertain, because influences from the outside might not be adequate to remove internalized misogyny in women. Here, the poet had in mind the well-entrenched prejudices (which were justified as given) that women nurtured instinctively in view of their socialization in a socio-economic and politico-ideological milieu in which they became integral to their existence as women. In other words, that women were meant to fashion their socio-economic preferences in accordance with the patriarchal priorities appeared to have been axiomatic. Hence, there was no escape route. In view of the well-entrenched mindset in support of large sets of debilitating social mores and economic designs, it was not easy for the women to get out of what they had been taught to follow since their birth. These ideas survived without much difficulty, since they were transmitted from one generation to another. In *Ghare Baire*, Bimala's elder sister-in-law's condemnatory attitude towards Bimala's seemingly unfeminine behaviour is a perfect example of the kind of finger-wagging that progressives had to confront in their engagement with the old guard. Here, Tagore delineated the tortuous path towards feminist enlightenment that the Bimalas of the world must traverse. On this journey, 'radical and critical questioning serves as a roadmap, which one uses to examine one's own preconceived notions and prejudices, as well as the socio-cultural forces that determine one's relation with the world'.[18] Tagore readily admitted that this path was not free of obstacles, but he rejoiced in the power of questioning to overcome all such obstacles on the road to freedom. Despite the sorrows and dangers involved in this process of radically transforming attitudes, Tagore was confident in the inevitability of change, for he believed that 'the tides of time cannot be reversed'.[19] Unlike some of this orthodox nationalist colleagues whose politics hinged on a nostalgic yearning for the past, Tagore was aware of the oppressive underpinnings of such a stance.

[18] Rabindranath Tagore, 'Nari' (woman), in *Kalantar*, ed. Rabindranath Tagore (Kolkata: Visva-Bharati, 1425) (Bangavda), 365.

[19] Tagore, 366.

In modernity, he saw opportunities for progress, social justice and widespread enlightenment. It is this relentless optimism that formed the bedrock of his women characters' unshakable faith in modernity.

VOICING THE VOICE OF PROTEST

As argued above, there is a correspondence between Tagore's concern for gender parity, which he articulated in his critical essays, and the characters that he developed in his novels, short stories and dance-dramas. By selecting some of the major characters from his texts, this section provides an elaboration of the views that the poet propounded to defend the politico-ideological priorities in favour of gender parity. In other words, what is most striking is the fact that the characters that Tagore designed spoke in an identical language championing his concern for a society free from gender discrimination. There is another aspect that also deserves sedulous attention, namely, in order to spread the message, he did not merely talk about the middle-class woman but also dwelled on how the marginalized sections of society suffered due to gender prejudices. The main character, Prakriti, in the dance-drama *Chandalika* (Untouchables) had a powerful voice that she raised against the established social practices denying her a rightful place in society; being a *Chandal* (untouchable), she remained ostracized primarily due to constructed values and mores permanently segregating the lower castes from the rest simply because of the accident of birth. Basic here is the point that Tagore delved into gender issues at two levels: at the contextual level, he endeavoured to capture gender discrimination which drew sustenance from the well-entrenched social and economic practices and complementary ideological priorities detrimental to the evolution of a level playing field for all; at the conceptual level, he, being inspired by the ideas of the Enlightenment philosophy, graphically explicated the tensions between the context-centric indigenous ideas and those derivative from the Western sources. On occasions, Tagore resolved the tension himself, and on others he left it unresolved. Bimala in *Ghare Baire* is illustrative here: it was Nikhilesh who introduced her to the Western liberating ideas which helped her understand why caste segregation was a debilitating influence. Here, she was a liberated woman, but the sudden death of her husband, Nikhilesh, radically altered her perception about life, and she readily accepted that her apparently deviant behaviour provoked divine retribution; here, Bimala was not different from her elder sister-in-law who, being blind to the prevalent social restrictions for a widow, never appreciated the former for being zealously receptive to the transmitted Western values.

UNFOLDING OF THE IDEAS

Tagore held revolutionary views insofar as gender was concerned. The characters in his novels, plays and short stories were protagonists of ideas that did not receive the approbation that the poet had expected, which confirms that despite being progressive in nature, the well-entrenched socially justified prejudices were strong enough to easily dismiss these ideas. Nonetheless, these characters epitomized a format of thinking which helped build persuasive arguments in favour of gender equity. The following text is an elaboration of how Tagore developed his point of view through those characters who spoke in a language that the poet evolved to set in motion processes leading to women's empowerment.

BIMALA IN *GHARE BAIRE*

Set in the context of the campaign to annul the first Partition of Bengal (1905–1908), *Ghare Baire* (1916) is a historical novel which primarily deals with the nationalist question in an alternative format of ideological priorities that Tagore represented. Disenchanted with the way the campaign evolved, the poet gradually dissociated from it, since it was contrary to what he thought was conducive for national awakening. Our purpose here is not to dwell on this issue. What is noteworthy here is the articulation of the bard's concern for gender parity mainly through the character Bimala, though he also brought out the two principal male characters, Nikhilesh (Bimala's husband) and his friend Sandip, the firebrand nationalist, who led the campaign against partition.

At the outset, Tagore's Bimala appeared similar to any other woman in Bengal, since she nurtured all those feminine qualities which are associated with womanhood. This was evident when Bimala expressed her happiness on being married to Nikhilesh, who belonged to an aristocratic family. She was a little disappointed because her husband did not match the picture that she had painted before her marriage. Nonetheless, she came to terms with this because of her husband's views on gender equality, though she did not always appreciate them, presumably because of the socialization processes that instilled in her the idea of the husband always being superior to his wife. Tagore very succinctly put forward his point, highlighting the tension between what he felt and what Bimala, being a woman, internalized. In the novel, Bimala thus noted that

> my husband always claimed that men and women have equal rights over one another and hence their love is also on an equal footing. I have argued with him on this [though] … my heart says that devotion doesn't stop people from being equals. It tries to equalize people by elevating them. Hence, the pleasure of becoming equal is ever-present in it and it never turns into a thing of indifference. On the tray of love, devotion is like the light of the lamp in the ritual of worship—it falls the same way upon the worshipper and the worshipped. Today I know for sure that a woman's love is sanctified only through her own veneration—or else it's worth noting. When the lamp of our love glows, the flame rises upwards and only the burnt-up oil remains at the bottom.[20]

The idea is crystal clear. Bimala set out her femininity at two levels. At one level, she conformed to the misogynist trope of marriage necessarily fostering contentment among married women. It was therefore natural that she expressed her devotion for Nikhilesh, who deserved to be venerated by virtue of being her husband. Here, Tagore seems to have echoed the conventional views on gender. But the statement highlighting Nikhilesh's more feminist stance laid, at the level of conceptualization, the foundation of his theoretical design for gender equity. The stance was undoubtedly revolutionary, though for Tagore

---

[20] Rabindranath Tagore, *Ghare Baire*, reproduced in *Classic Rabindranath Tagore: Complete and Unabridged*, (English translation of selected novels and short stories) (New Delhi: Penguin, 2011), 671.

it did not seem to be unusual, presumably because of the socialization that he had undergone by being part of a family in which women were hardly discriminated against. As the available sources delineate, the Tagore family, being baptized in Brahmoism, helped create a milieu of sociopolitical equality regardless of gender. Having been raised in this environment, Rabindranath Tagore can thus be said to have instinctively embraced these ideas supportive of gender parity.

Bimala became 'a modern woman', since Nikhilesh wanted her to be one; here, Tagore failed to go beyond the conventional ideas, making the male the agency of change. She was transformed into a modern woman by Nikhilesh, which means that the latter became an agency of change; it further means that Tagore conformed to the core values of patriarchy wherein the man was considered to be the primary agency for change. Nonetheless, the point seems persuasive in view of the well-entrenched social prejudices governing woman's life in general. The poet very clearly articulated his ideas when Bimala stated that her husband 'dressed [her] up in contemporary fashions'[21] which made other members of the family, especially her sisters-in-law, jealous. Despite being aware of this, Nikhilesh was, as Bimala described, unperturbed. According to her,

> my husband was well aware of all this. But his heart brimmed over with sympathy for women. He would always advise me, don't be upset. I remember, once I had said to him "women's minds are very crooked, very narrow". He had replied, "just like the feet of Chinese woman which are crooked and narrow. The entire society has squashed our women's minds from all sides and made them narrow and crooked. Fate gambles with their lives—their lives depend on the turn of the dice; do they have any powers of their own?[22]

In a dialogical format, Tagore expressed his preferences very clearly. The views of Bimala were familiar, since they corresponded with what was very common to women of the era. As an author, however, Tagore put forward contrasting views to firmly argue what he sincerely believed in. Here, he was categorical in his choice, which was

[21] Tagore, 673.

[22] Tagore, 673.

evident when Nikhilesh condemned the social mores denying the rightful place to widows, including his elder sister-in-law, by saying that 'law or society has not supported my sisters-in-law; it was a great humiliation for them to have to beg for what they once knew to be rightfully theirs, by virtue of their husband's legacy'.[23] Not annoyed with his sisters-in-law's envy of Bimala, he, instead of characterizing it as 'unfair', mentioned that 'there is a grain of truth embedded in envy [because] whatever brings happiness should ideally be received by every individual'.[24] Bimala seemed to have found an answer and thus asks her husband to get whatever was required for their happiness. Now, Nikhilesh expressed his helplessness, because 'it isn't possible to hand them whatever their heart desires';[25] this is a statement that reinforces the inherent power of the well-entrenched social prejudices which were difficult to neutralize in the then socio-economic circumstances. So, being angry and envious was natural to them because 'when someone is deprived, this is the only way they know to conquer their deprivation—it is their only consolation',[26] argued Nikhilesh. The point was elaborated further when Bimala's husband made a caustic remark in response to her accusations that the manipulative behaviour of her sisters-in-law created an unpleasant situation in the family, affecting her adversely. Nikhilesh condemned his wife for her selfishness, since she had 'enough sympathy for [herself] when [her] own feelings were bruised, and [she] had none to spare for those whose lives [had] been ripped to shreds by the cruel arrows of society'. 'Should the loser be made to pay', he continued, 'a fine for losing?'[27] The views that Tagore had articulated in his concern for gender equality were grounded on his faith in the enlightenment values supportive of equality, fraternity and togetherness regardless of class, caste and ethnicity. There was also the feeling of being restrained, due to the archaic social fabric in which women were denied of all worldly comforts as soon as they became widows. Women's behaviour was socially

[23] Tagore, 673.

[24] Tagore, 674.

[25] Tagore, 674.

[26] Tagore, 674.

[27] Tagore, 674.

conditioned, which underlines the argument that as women they were expected to behave in a particular fashion, which was axiomatic and thus inescapable. Hence, Nikhilesh expressed uncertainty regarding Bimala's love for him: 'did it stem from the deep well of her heart or was it driven by social pressures like the fixed ration of municipal water that one receives daily?'[28] Implicit here was his concern for the freedom of choice of women; he was not comfortable if a woman was forced to love someone whom she was married to, since it was a love that emerged mechanically, which was contrary to how equality was conceptualized in a free society. This was most likely to happen, because while choosing a groom for a woman, her views were never taken into account; hence, women were denied any role in the entire process—they were told to love whom they married. This was not acceptable to Nikhilesh. Hence, he was not hesitant to admit that 'it is obvious to me that in [Bimala's] life, I am incidental; the person who [Bimala's] entire being can truly complement, is [the firebrand nationalist leader], Sandip'.[29] A true renaissance man, Nikhilesh was neither annoyed nor upset for Bimala was not given a choice to select her husband which was clearly stated when he noted that 'no point getting angry; … instead [Bimala] should be mad at her destiny [because she] didn't really pick [him] out in a *swayambara* (an ancient practice which allowed women to pick up her husband among the probable suiters); [she] had to take whatever [she] got with [her] eyes shut'.[30] Here too, being very categorical, Tagore put forward another powerful argument to support gender equality in a social context wherein it was unheard of. By raising his argument seeking to ensure that the views of the bride while choosing her groom were considered, the poet stated his preferences in unequivocal terms.

DAMINI IN *CHATURANGA*

Serialized in four consecutive issues in a monthly magazine, *Sabujpatra*, between December 1914 and March 1915, *Chaturanga* (Quartet) was

---

[28] Tagore, 688.

[29] Tagore, 707.

[30] Tagore, 715.

published as a novel in 1915. Damini, the female protagonist of gender issues in the novel, represented Tagore's ideas of sexuality and gender freedom in a fashion that was simply inconceivable in the then Bengal. She was a woman with a voice asserting her individual preferences for what she deemed appropriate for her in social circumstances which were not exactly in her favour. In a nutshell, Damini was a vision that Tagore articulated in *Chaturanga* to argue for women's independence as an agency even if that disturbed the social equilibrium. What is also striking is that Tagore ventured to unambiguously put before his readers the inner feelings of women who were forced to accept the conditionalities as inescapable. Like Bimala in *Ghare Baire*, Damini was also rebellious in expression. While Bimala, on occasions, did not appear to have been sanguine in communicating what she preferred, Damini was confident in explicitly raising issues of sexuality which were usually avoided in the then public discourses. A change was thus visible. The reason may be identified in the locations of these two novels: the fact that Bimala was not always categorical in expressing what she wanted was presumably because the novel was set in rural Bengal, where the idea of gender equality did not seem as prominent as in the metropolitan cities like Calcutta and Bombay. The issue of sexuality was frankly discussed by Damini as she was a city-based woman. It was very unequivocally stated by Tagore when Sachish, one of the main characters, stated that there were two forms of universal feminism: one was articulated by

> the woman who takes upon herself the stigma of sin, who sacrifices her life for sinner's sake, who, dying adds to the contents of life's cup of ambrosia. [In Damini], the universal feminism assumes another form. She has no truck with death, she is a celebrant of the vital force. Like a spring garden she is always brimming with waves of lovely fragrance. She doesn't want to renounce anything in life; she is unwilling to play host to ascetics; she has sworn not to pay a single paisa in homage to the cold north wind.[31]

By creating Damini as a fearless woman hardly restrained by social shackles while seeking to fulfil her desires, the poet carved an

---

[31] Rabindranath Tagore, *Chaturanga (Quartet)*, reproduced in *Classic Rabindranath Tagore*, 633.

independent space in the discourses championing gender equity. Damini was a free woman who, in other words, represented a new wave of thinking that Tagore very clearly articulated by contrasting it with the conventional notions of feminism, which were clearly restrictive and also repressive. Within this conceptual format, the poet expanded his argument by graphically illustrating what Damini undertook to fulfil her carnal desires when she totally surrendered to his beloved, Sachish. In his diary notes, Sachish very frankly expressed what he felt when Damini initiated an intimate interaction with him in a desolate place. As he elaborated:

> then something clasped my feet. At first, I thought it was a wild animal [because the incident took place in a cave surrounded by deep forest]. But a wild animal is hairy, this creature wasn't. My entire body shrank at the touch. It seemed to be an unknown snake-like creature. I knew nothing of its anatomy—what its head looked like, or its trunk or its tail—nor could I imagine how it devoured its victims. It was repulsive because of its very softness, its ravenous mass. I was speechless with fear and loathing. I began pushing the creature away with both feet. It seemed to place its face on my feet—it was breathing heavily—I didn't know what sort of face it was. I began to kick at it. Eventually I came out of my trance. At first, I thought the creature was hairless; but suddenly I felt a mass of hair, as from a mane, fall on my feet.[32]

Hence, Damini was not afraid, though Sachish had not been as forthcoming as she had been expecting. In Sachish, Tagore had shown how two contrasting pulls arising out of the prevalent social context put him in a dilemma. To him, surrender to a woman did not seem to be desirable, given the social context, though he did not seem to be absolutely disinclined to respond to Damini's call. Being sensitive to the contextual constraints, the poet was perhaps unable to think differently. It is also possible to argue that in view of his primary concern, namely to deal with suppressed women's sexuality, Tagore opted for this: Sachish was made less forthright than Damini. There are reasons to persuasively argue this point if one refers to the confession that Damini made to Sachish when he met her alone. She did not appear to hide her desire as a woman when she mentioned that as 'a woman, … it is our

---

[32] Tagore, 637–8.

nature to devote ourselves body and soul to caring for the body. The task is entirely the responsibility of women. That's why when we see the body being neglected our hearts cry out'. The hint was subtle but clear; Damini's desire for Sachish was attributed to her responsibility to care for her beloved. It also provoked Sribilash, another character, who held the conventional notion of being desirous of sex being a taboo, to be drawn to Damini, who castigated him for being indifferent to the importance of the body in human relationships, which she characterized as 'weird'.[33] In response to Damini's questioning, Sribilash felt what he lost, when in a soliloquy he admitted that 'the longing of your sex for the weird is boundless. ... O Sribilash, earn enough merit in this world so that you can be reborn as one of those weirdos'.[34] This is one aspect of the argument suggesting that human carnal desires can be suppressed as it is socially-conditioned and also justified; the other aspect is highlighted when Sribilash was asked to be restrained by being drawn to the fact of women being calculative and also cunning when it concerned the pursuance of their personal goals and objectives. Characterizing his weakness for Damini as surrender to 'Nature's fatal charm',[35] Sachish endeavoured to hold him back by saying that

> the beautiful form with which it has bewitched you will disappear like a mask as soon as she has realized her purpose; when the time comes, she will remove this very desire which has clouded your vision and made you see as greater than anything else in the universe. When the trap of illusion is clearly laid, why walk straight into it with bravado?[36]

Sachish and Sribilash depict those characters who, being largely governed by social mores and values, were not clearly persuaded to appreciate gender parity unconditionally. They, clearly being favourably disposed, did not always express their priorities unambiguously, presumably because of their inability to break the social barriers. There was no way one could be very sure of one's stance,

[33] Tagore, 656.

[34] Tagore, 656.

[35] Tagore, 643.

[36] Tagore, 643.

since it had its roots in the prevalent socio-economic circumstances. Women could be deceptive, though Tagore was confident that once they made up their mind with regard to what was appropriate for satisfying their needs, they hardly wavered. In view of her unconditional love for Sachish, Damini's womanly concerns made her 'most intolerable'[37] when he was made to suffer by others. Furthermore, the fact that 'she would try to thrust herself forward to take Sachish's task on herself'[38] also suggests how deeply she was in love with her. Implicit here are two important points that figure prominently in Tagore's thoughts on designs for ending sexist oppression. On the one hand, by strongly arguing that Damini was right when she expressed her desire and also undertook steps for its gratification the bard strongly argued against the well-established social practices. In other words, this was a significant advancement insofar as gender equality was concerned. It was not one-way traffic, since Damini's effort was likely to succeed once the socially engendered practices and values were effectively challenged and, if possible, discarded. The task was easier said than done, which Tagore vividly described, on the other hand, by outlining the nature of the dilemma that Sachish and Sribilash underwent.

Chaturanga was a powerful statement that Tagore made to elaborate and also justify his unique conceptualization of gender parity, which drew on the spirit in which his predecessors, especially Ram Mohan Roy and Vidyasagar, strongly argued against gender discrimination. This novel was set in an urban locale, which was reflected in the differentially structured responses to the gender questions. Contrasting Damini with Bimala of *Ghare Baire* will illustrate the point. Bimala was less vocal, though she dealt with sexuality in a way which was satisfactory to her. Having been raised in Calcutta, Damini had a completely different take on this issue; she was not only uninhibited but also expressive in her choices. It was evident when she completely surrendered to Sachish in the cave; she was shackle-free and courageous when she decided to go ahead with the plan regardless of the consequences. Here, the gender freedom was shown to have been

[37] Tagore, 648.

[38] Tagore, 648.

won by her fearlessness and also the willingness to pay the price, if any, for this.

ELA OF *CHAR ADHYAY*

Published in 1934, *Char Adhyay* is one of those novels that dealt with revolutionary nationalism as an alternative to the mainstream, Gandhi-led nationalist campaign. The story revolves around three characters: Indranath, a revolutionary leader, Atindra or Atin or Ontu, the scion of an impoverished aristocratic family and a new recruit to Indranath's groups of revolutionary nationalists, and Ela, an attractive girl who was associated with Indranath and was in love with Atin. The plot became complicated once Ela refused to marry Atin despite being deeply in love with him, since she had taken a vow not to get married to avoid being diverted from the cause for the nation that she always privileged. Atin, with Indranath's guidance, became a ruthless but committed soldier of the group, which, as Ela mentioned, 'dehumanized him' to a significant extent. The relationship between Ela and Atin was thus stressful. Ela's love for Atin and vice versa was thus not shackle-free, since neither of them was willing to fulfil their objectives by paying a price. The story took a different turn when Atin was given the task of eliminating Ela because she was considered 'a burden' to the group. Being so much in love with Atin, Ela allowed herself to be killed by her beloved, since it meant the fulfilment of her unfulfilled desires, due to peculiar circumstances in which they were placed.

The storyline does not appear to be as complex as that in *Chaturanga*; nonetheless, it also dwells on Tagore's own take of gender issues, which is fascinating for two reasons: first, it is a reiteration of the priorities that the poet clearly articulated in his other novels; and second, it also suggests that Tagore put forward a discourse on gender that was consistently argued and persuasively adumbrated. Unlike *Ghare Baire* and *Chaturanga*, *Char Adhyay* stands out, because here Tagore appears to have developed a format of argument that is less complex or far more clear.

There are two interrelated aspects in the novel *vis-à-vis* the gender question. First, the leader of the group, Indranath appreciated Ela's feminine attraction to gather around him a set of dedicated men for the cause. Atin joined the group because it allowed him to be with Ela who was, as he admitted, 'a paragon of beauty'. Here, the gender of Ela was utilized by Indranath to pursue a goal which was justified, since it contributed to the nationalist cause. While talking about Atin, Indranath also confessed that it was 'Ela's beauty that brought Atin to the group'.[39] It was true to a great extent, since Atin had fallen in love with her and wanted to marry her, which Ela refused, given her apprehension that being married would be an impediment to the fulfilment of her nationalist commitment. There was no other reason for her refusal except her declared commitment to the group devoted to national liberation. Here, Atin was conventional in his thinking, while Ela was not. Being impressed by Atin, who left no stone unturned to carry out the groups' directions which were meant to liberate the country from its chains, Ela was gradually drawn to Atin and was desperate to be with him, either through the nuptial bond or otherwise, which he declined citing the same reason that Ela had cited while refusing to marry him. The last page of the novel poignantly expresses Ela's love for Atin, who was ordered by the group leader, Indranath, to kill her, as she was alleged to have been responsible for a plot against the group. Here, Ela came out openly to express how deeply she was in love with him. Ela thus exhorted:

> don't have any qualms; am I not yours, wholly yours, even in death. Take me,... this body belongs to you. ... Ontu [as Atin was fondly addressed by her], my Ontu, my king, my god, I have not been able to show you how much I love you. By this love I charge you to kill me. ... Let the last bit of my consciousness be for you. ... Let me die awake in your arms; let our last kiss be eternal.[40]

Ela's exhortation does not seem to be striking, since it was natural for someone who had fallen in love. In the first part of the novel, it was Atin who surrendered to Ela, who was a little apprehensive and hence did not respond to his passionate urge. As days passed on, Ela was also found to have nurtured the same feelings, which made her

---

[39] Rabindranath Tagore, *Char Adhyay* (Kolkata: Visva-Bharati, 1418) (Bangavda), 35.

[40] Tagore, 115–6.

surrender completely to Atin when he was asked to kill Ela. The narrative does not appear to have any particular dimension that shows Tagore in a different light. However, a careful reading of the text reveals the subtlety of the message for gender equality that the poet unambiguously articulated. In Chapter 2 of the novel, Atin was vocal in support of protecting women's rights as integral to the society; so far, it had been dominated by the male which was reflective of the usual patriarchal hegemony. By challenging the excessive dominance of the male in governing women's lives, Atin, the protagonist of gender equality, thus declared that 'women need to come out of their shell and also challenge whenever attempts are made to put them under chains by reference to the age-old restrictive practices, justified as appropriate by the so-called religious texts'.[41] There are two levels at which the argument is made: at one level, it was a reiteration of the concerns that Tagore had expressed in so many of his creative texts, namely, women were required to be bold enough to raise their voice against injustice of any kind; at another level, he also made the male counterparts responsible partners in altering the accepted social practices which were inhibiting in character. Besides this, the poet also referred to a situation in which the holy texts were suitably distorted to defend the archaic mores and values seeking to put women in chains.

There is another aspect of concern that Tagore talked about in the novel which is a reinforcement of the argument that he kept making. It is true that he attributed most of the gender-driven restrictive practices and values to patriarchy. Nonetheless, by highlighting the contribution of women in sustaining the system, he did not spare them either. While highlighting the role of women in continuing with the decadent practices, Atin felt the need for strong condemnation by women, who were held responsible for this kind of state of affairs. It was very categorically stated when Atin insisted that despite being women, mothers-in-law helped continue the system putting women in chains. Once a woman became a mother-in-law, she was a different individual, interested

---

[41] Tagore, 44–5.

in expanding her sphere of influence by hook or crook; the first casualty happens to be the daughters-in law who, by being submissive to the dictates of her mother-in-law (as she was nurtured to behave that way), help create circumstances in which the hegemonic control is allowed and sustained.

This was nothing unusual, as it had been a practice which had gone unchallenged, Tagore exhorted. While explaining why it continued, he thus mentioned that the sons who remained 'captive of mothers' influence neither questioned nor challenged them despite having realized that it was unfair and uncalled-for'.[42] Here too, Tagore put in words the nature of a reality which had emerged due to the failure of those who, notwithstanding having accepted their wives as partners, lost their independent voice by being scared of their mothers, presumably because it was a convenient design for protecting their self-interests. Being annoyed with those who abdicated their responsibilities towards their wives, the poet was most caustic in his remarks, saying that 'those who are incapable of supporting and protecting their wives from being unfairly tortured by their mothers should not get married, at all [because] … it is neither humanly-justified nor socially admissible in view of the adverse social consequences that it results'.[43] This is one part of the argument; the other part is equally important, where Tagore also castigated those henpecked husbands who were also responsible for such a deplorable milieu. The argument is two-dimensional: on the one hand, it is critical of the role of the mothers-in-law, since the so-called obedient sons do not disturb the apple cart by being reverent to the prevalent system of social control by their mothers; on the other, it is critical of the husbands who, by their unconditional surrender to their wives, also helped build a situation in which they preferred not to raise their voice, which did not seem to be fair either. Seeking to convince Ela when she refused to marry Atin, the latter made these arguments which reflected Tagore's point of view that he adhered to in so many of his creative texts. Accusing Ela of being a 'coward since she decided not to go ahead with nuptial

---

[42] Tagore, 57.

[43] Tagore, 57.

bond with him',[44] Atin endeavoured hard to persuade the former to revise her stance *vis-à-vis* marriage.

Char Adhyay was a continuity of the viewpoints that Tagore developed in his *Chaturanga*, where he dealt with Damini's suppressed sexuality. In this novel, he delved on both the aspects of human behaviour. Being devoted to the nationalist cause, Ela restrained herself when Atin proposed to her for marriage; the radical behavioural manifestation of Ela at the end of the novel brought out a nuanced picture since Ela, being deeply in love with Atin, was willing to go ahead which is not an unusual human feelings though the situation is reversed since Atin was not keen to accept Ela as his wife. The story had not been narrated in black-and-white terms; instead, it had epitomized the complex tensions that human beings underwent in a real situation. Tagore was not free from these, which came out very clearly through the characters, Atin and Ela, who had shown how human decisions were made, and to understand them as based on the peculiar socio-economic contexts, one needed to be receptive to the influences which were not static but were outcomes of an equally complex interplay of social, economic and political processes. What is striking in Tagore's creative writings is the fact that despite him being an author who remained sensitive to the milieu in which he was born and raised, they are transcendental in appeal, because the messages that he had sought to convey continue to be relevant even after the lapse of more than a century.

SUCHARITA OF *GORA*

Published in 1909, *Gora* is perhaps one of most complex of Tagore's novels, which stands out as a commentary on some of the topical social, economic and political issues prominent in that era. Since the chapter is confined to the elaboration of Tagore's ideas of gender equality, it delves into one of the major woman characters of *Gora*, Sucharita, who represented the views that the poet articulated *vis-à-vis* gender equity. Serialized in a literary magazine, *Probasi*, between 1907 and 1909, *Gora* is another long statement of Tagore's concern

---

[44] Tagore, 57.

for evolving designs for ending sexist exploitation. Set in the prevalent socio-economic tapestry, *Gora*, the novel put across the points through the main protagonists, Gora and Sucharita, which support the poet's inner conviction for gender balance in the country in a context of multiple contradictions that grew in importance largely due to socially entrenched archaic values and mores. It was a persuasive comment on the nature of Indian nationalism that did not become nationalistic in the true sense, presumably because of the nationalist failure to create a template of togetherness irrespective of religion and one's socio-economic location.

As far as gender parity was concerned, India's record was clearly appalling, exhorted the poet, since there were hardly any voices against gender discrimination. It was stated very unambiguously by the bard when Gora mentioned that 'we see only half of *Bharatvarsha* [because] we see *Bharatvarsha* only as a land of men; we don't notice women at all'.[45] Appreciating the English for have created a milieu in which women were treated at par with their male counterparts, Gora further added that 'like the English, we would like to see women everywhere, indoors and out, on earth, in water and in space, at meals, feasts and work, everywhere'.[46] The reasons were not difficult to find, since

> when members of a household gaze with long familiarity at women performing domestic chores, they don't really see the women at all. If we could view our nation's women outside our domestic needs, we would perceive our nation in its beauty and wholeness. We would see an image of the nation easy to die. At least we would never behave mistakenly as if the women of our country are nowhere to be found. ... We need to create a milieu [in which] ... our women can appear in public without loss of dignity [and we must be aware that] ... the seclusion of women has reduced our swadesh [country], our own nation, to a half-truth, incapable of infusing our hearts with love and power in their complete forms.[47]

The concern for gender parity is explicitly stated here: by not recognizing women as integral to human existence, the prevalent views were

---

[45] Rabindranath Tagore, *Gora*, reproduced in *Classic Rabindranath Tagore*, 357.

[46] Tagore, 357.

[47] Tagore, 357.

clearly prejudiced, Tagore unambiguously stated. Women were indispensable for running a home, though their role was hardly socially acknowledged. This conceptualization of women being ignored despite having a critical role in domestic life is reflective of a part of wider prejudices, which Tagore articulated by underlining that we saw 'the peasant only as farm-labour and the weaver only as fabric producer, we dismiss them as lowly and uncouth, not recognizing them as complete beings, and this rich-poor divide weakens the nation'.[48] Following this argument, he now linked the gender-abuse with our attitude to demean women which was articulated when the poet argued that 'if we imprison the women of our country within their routine of cooking and grinding regarding them reductively as merely the female sex'.[49] This was the root of our decadence as a nation, since one important half of our population was not only ignored but also reduced to social entities without substance. Once he identified the root cause of India's downfall as a country, the bard put forward a persuasive conceptual framework through Gora's friend, Binoy, to meaningfully generate ideas for common well-being; under no circumstances, women's contribution could be belittled, since, Tagore argued,

> Man and woman represent two aspects of social power; man is power manifest, but the magnitude of his strength does not lie in its visibility; woman's power remains unexpressed, and to try constantly to express this secret power is to propel society towards swift bankruptcy by expending all its stored-up capital. That is why I say, if we perform the holy sacrifice while women take charge of the grain-store, the yagna ritual will be successful, despite the woman's invisibility. Those who try to expend all forms of power for the same purpose, at the same place and in the same way, must be insane.[50]

Implicit here is a fundamental point in defence of gender equality which was possible to achieve, the poet felt, only once women were recognized as an integral segment of society that needed to be taken into account most seriously. In other words, the aim here was to evolve

[48] Tagore, 358.

[49] Tagore, 358.

[50] Tagore, 358.

a supportive environment where gender discrimination disappeared. It was easier said than done. Nonetheless, the main protagonist of the novel, Gora, an orthodox Hindu with all the prevalent prejudices against women, realized that given their immense importance in society, it was not logical to dismiss them as just an appendage. In other words, with Binoy's intervention, Gora imbibed the concern for gender parity, given 'women's special presence and influence in society'.[51] Gora appeared to have conceptualized his approach to gender issues at two levels: at the level of values, that women remained integral to human society was acknowledged; at the level of practice, he felt that this was a stepping stone for unifying India, for it consolidated the foundation of *Bharatvarsha,* drawing on socio-cultural diversity, which came out very clearly in his statement insisting on

> a vast, profound unity in many manifestations and multiple endeavours of *Bharatvarsha,* a unity that drives [him] wild with joy. Rejoicing at such unity, [he had] no hesitation in mingling with the most ignorant of *Bharatvarsha's* inhabitants, taking [his] place beside them in the dust. Some understand this message of *Bharatvarsha,* others don't, but never mind [he was] with everyone in *Bharatvarsha*—they are all my own people—within all of them [he had] no doubt, eternal *Bharatvarsha's* concealed presence is constantly at work.[52]

What is striking here is Gora's awareness of India or *Bharatvarsha* being one, regardless of socio-cultural diversity; he was able to mingle with everyone, since he belonged to a nation that decried discrimination of any kind, as it was a threat to the unity that had evolved over generations. The exhortation—'my own people'—appears to have captured the feelings of Gora that were unambiguously expressed. It was further clarified by Gora in his dialogical interaction with his compatriot, Binoy. According to him, since 'Hindus are a community, ... it is impossible to express its essence by confining to any label, ... just as the ocean can't be described by its waves, Hindus can't be described as one either'.[53] Being vehemently opposed to the design

---

[51] Tagore, 358.

[52] Tagore, 377.

[53] Tagore, 522.

of conceptualizing *Bharatvarsha* as one, he further elaborated on his stance by adumbrating the view that it would be conceptually wrong to imagine that 'there is no diversity among human beings'.[54] The socio-cultural divide was a source of strength, because it allowed people to learn how to survive and also flourish as a community amidst diversity. The bard believed that the forcible unity was harmful to the existence of human beings as because the muzzling of diverse socio-cultural voices, sealed their natural growth. Tagore's Gora thus spoke that

> the brigand races who believe it's best for the world if they vanquish all other races to extend their sole empire, who are too arrogant about their own power to admit that the distinctiveness of other races is of priceless benefit to the world, who spread only slavery across the world—how are you people different from them.[55]

This digression is not futile, since it puts forward Gora's *Weltanschauung* or world view, which was an aid to comprehend his approach to gender equality. It is true that that the argument is a little convoluted, because Gora's concerns for gender parity were part of these entire sociopolitical priorities which stemmed from his own experiences as 'a Hindu' and also out of his constant dialogue with the Brahmos, especially other protagonists in the novel. The role of Sucharita was also significant because her direct or indirect encouragements helped him find a course of thoughts in a persuasive way. A thoughtful woman herself, Sucharita adored Gora for his

> utterance which was no mere discourse, it resembled a new creation. It was so tangible over time that it could dominate one's whole mind and body ... and she no longer retained the strength to determine how far her opinions coincided with Gora's.[56]

Gora thus not merely articulated a persuasive message of treating human beings as an equal multitude regardless of division, but he also endeavoured to develop a design for all on the basis of his firm

---

[54] Tagore, 523.

[55] Tagore, 523.

[56] Tagore, 524.

commitment to humanity. Not only did he object to gender discrimination, but he was also strongly opposed to socio-economic schisms
segmenting one section of the multitude from another. His exalted
goal was to awaken the nation as one set of people with multiple
socio-cultural preferences. He thus declared:

> by professing my respect, I want to awaken the nation's heart to the great-
> ness of our sacred philosophy, the profundity of our devotional tradition.
> I want to arouse its pride in its own riches. I shall not let the country bow
> its head in shame, nor make it blind to its own reality by generating self-
> hatred. That is my vow. ... I constantly feel that *Bharatvarsha* cannot be
> completely represented through masculine perspective alone. It existence
> will be fully realized only when manifest to the eyes of our women. I have
> thus no doubt that one a communion between man and woman remains
> a future, a strong future, for *Bharatvarsha*.[57]

There was not an iota of doubt that without man–woman partnership,
the future of *Bharatvarsha* was bleak. It did not seem to be an easy task,
given the well-entrenched socio-cultural prejudices. Nonetheless, his
earnest call for radical changes in the social, economic and cultural
fields created a template to build a model for furthering the goal
that Gora held so dear to him. Despite being an orthodox Hindu by
upbringing, Gora's endeavour towards attaining common well-being
was the outcome of two major sources: Sucharita's influences, which
were supplemented by Paresh Babu's powerful intellectual inputs,
and the experience he gained by extensive travelling across villages.
Hence, Tagore noted that

> the deeper he penetrated into the world of [the villagers], the more a certain
> thought began to trouble his mind. He observed that in India's rural areas,
> social restrictions were far more powerful than in educated, cultured soci-
> ety. In every household, food, sleep, rest, work, everything was conducted,
> day and night, under the unblinking gaze of society. Each individual had a
> very simple faith in popular traditions, never questioning such things. Yes,
> social restrictions and adherence to custom did not empower them at all in
> their fields of activity. It was doubtful whether such timid, helpless beings,
> so incapable of judging what was good for themselves, existed anywhere
> in the world. Beyond adherence to traditions, there was no other good

---

[57] Tagore, 537.

that they wholeheartedly acknowledged, or were willing to understand. It was prohibition, enforced through punishment or partisanship, that they regarded as supreme. The awareness of what must not be done entrapped their nature in a net from head to toe at every step, through various forms of discipline. ... There was no broad unity within them that could draw them all together in good times or bad.[58]

In a rather long argument, Tagore very grudgingly referred to the prevalent sociopolitical and cultural environment to argue that it was an impediment towards fulfilling the objective of ensuring common well-being; the root cause was the mindset that was opposed to even recognizing human beings as human beings. The well-entrenched caste segregation and also the religious chasm between Hindus and Muslims remained a constant source of irritation to those seeking to create an ambience for ideologically justified socio-economic and political equality. In other words, *Bharatvarsha* was not only divided along the gender axis but also following segmentation on the basis of one's caste identity. These were not new claims, since Tagore had already elaborated some of them in his earlier creative texts. *Gora* was perhaps the most clearly articulated version of Tagore's oppositional politics seeking to reinforce his views for equality for all. Nonetheless, what is little perplexing was the nature of the approach that Tagore upheld to put his ideas in such a way as to generate support for the project that he proposed to carry out for ensuring good to all. Seeking to identify the roots of our failure to bring about radical socio-economic and cultural changes, Gora was aghast when he noticed that

humans were using the archaic practices as weapons to suck the blood of other human beings, brutally robbing them of their selfhood. How often he had observed that in performing social rituals, nobody showed the slightest compassion for anybody else! [He was appalled] ... when the father of a poor man was seriously ill, ... the villagers, instead of helping him, [attributed his illness] ... to an unknown sin [forgetting that] the poor man had neither the resources nor any help that was forthcoming.[59]

[58] Tagore, 575.

[59] Tagore, 575.

Here too, Tagore expressed a general concern which was linked with his aims for gender empowerment. It was difficult to achieve the goal, presumably because of the widely held ideas in favour of ritual-based social behaviour. In a cruel society, as he noticed, there was hardly space for compassion, empathy and care. As a result, human beings, in general, and villagers, in particular, suffer immeasurably. Gora thus stated that 'this society did not help a man in times of need, nor supported him in times of trouble; it only used discipline as a threat to subdue him'.[60] The idea here is very explicit: unless a society is compassionate enough to engender the feeling of togetherness among fellow human beings, our existence is neither humane nor worthwhile. A powerful exhortation indeed, it was directed, at one level, at creating conditions for evolving a level playing field in which discrimination of any kind was an anathema; at another level, along with a scathing critique of the prevalent socio-cultural practices upholding supremacist mindsets, implicit here was also a call for change by involving those with like-minded attitudes and missions.

Unlike Damini in *Chaturanga* and Ela in *Char Adhyay*, who were not hesitant in displaying their sexuality, Sucharita in *Gora* was a voice that was tempered but firm, decisive but polite and self-generated but contextual. Here, Tagore articulated his views on gender differently, though the foundational concerns remain the same: by characterizing Sucharita as a fearless voice, he raised those issues which he felt needed attention. One of the distinct manifestations was the participation of the female protagonist, Sucharita, in discussions on sociopolitical and nationalist issues which, in the then Calcutta, were exclusively a male domain. By encouraging her to speak out while debating on these concerns, Gora also represented a voice which was complementary to the processes of women's empowerment. Here, Tagore's views were formed by being raised in an environment in which views and also practices supportive of gender equality were always appreciated and attempts were constantly made to recognize them as integral to the family. As such, the Brahmos were pathfinders for many progressive endeavours such as promoting women's education, championing views against the purdah system of secluding women and involving

[60] Tagore, 576.

women in events outside home, among others. Tagore was also a pioneer in many respects, as his experiments in Santiniketan and Sriniketan show.

A careful analysis of Sucharita also reveals that Tagore was not free from being paternalistically biased. While Damini and Ela were primarily guided by their instinctively-nurtured desires to justify their acts, Sucharita was encouraged to speak out by Paresh babu, Gora and also her dislike of Haran Babu, her suiter, created an ambience which enabled her to say unhesitatingly what she felt. It is also true that, Damini and Ela being products of an environment in which gender parity was the norm, their fearlessness was also context-driven. But in the case of Sucharita, the male protagonists in the novel are seen to have encouraged her to share her views in their deliberations, which was certainly a persuasive input that helped her build an independent personality and also create conditions favourably disposed to her. In other words, by giving her a respectful place in forums for discussion, the poet created for her not only an opportunity to express her views but also a design seeking to institutionalize the processes of sustenance for the future. This also means that, for Tagore, it was not a one-time device but one that was likely to contribute to the generation of a mindset in support of gender equity and a voice against gender discrimination. Gora's highly prescriptive approach to moral issues led him to espouse an unusual marriage of views; his Hindu orthodoxy bloomed alongside his abiding commitment to gender equality. This was one of the main reasons that brought Sucharita out of her patriarchally mandated shell over the course of various fiery deliberations on sociopolitical issues that she participated in at home. Sucharita's character arc is therefore, to a significant extent, a product of various paternalistic influences on her life, which was typical of the era, and by being sensitive to them in the novel, Tagore, in *Gora*, also created a legitimate space for the progressive voices regardless of gender.

GENDER ISSUES IN SHORT STORIES

There are two important features of Tagore's creative texts. On the one hand, he was consistent while articulating his views on gender.

Similar to views that the protagonists in his novels held, the characters in the short stories had also, on the other, echoed the sentiments in an unambiguous way. A common thread running through all his gender-based short stories is the need for gender parity, as conceptualized by the Brahmo Samaj, of which Tagore was one of the main proponents. Since the message is the same, it does not seem essential to deal with each and every short story. Hence, this section will explore the feminist underpinnings of three of Tagore's characters: Mrinal of 'Strir Patra' (Wife's Letter), Anila of 'Poila Number' (Number One) and Sohini of 'Laboratory'.

MRINAL OF 'STRIR PATRA' (1914)

Published in *Sabujpatra*, 'Strir Patra' is about Mrinal, a housewife who held conventional views regarding family and other commitments that went with those of a typical daughter-in-law in the then Bengal. When she joined her husband's joint family after marriage, she hardly gave any inkling to the radical views that she articulated in her letter to her husband, which were hard-hitting insofar as patriarchy was concerned and were an unambiguous articulation of her own identity as a woman. The storyline was simple: Mrinal left her adopted home and took refuge in a faraway place near the sea. The letter was a poignantly expressed piece of a note which was pregnant with views upholding a critique of the prevalent anti-feminist practices and views. In short, the letter dealt with the fundamental problem of patriarchal oppression in its different forms, such as dowry, denigration of women and denial of their rights as human beings, inhuman stance *vis-à-vis* providing accommodation to women, restraints on their education and the virulent outbursts against women's endeavours for asserting their independence, among others. Although the tone of the letter was not, at all, abusive or attacking, it helped us understand the agony that a married but childless woman underwent because of her sex. Being born a girl was a source of humiliation, which Mrinal illustrated by drawing attention to what her neighbours, particularly the women, expressed when her brother died. Mrinal was abused for her survival though here she had no role; the neighbours thought that had she been a male, she would have escaped death. Even when her in-laws' family came for fixing her marriage with a man (who later became her husband), she was not consulted at all, which meant that whatever the seniors decided upon was mandatory for her. She had not had the courage to challenge it, though she had accepted the decision as preordained or fated to be complied with. After she was brought in as a daughter-in-law, she was openly discriminated vis-à-vis other male members and she had no alternative but to accept without being displeased. The situation underwent a sea change once Mrinal lost her daughter immediately after her birth. She lost a chance of being a mother, which probably would have given her 'a respectable place in the family because a childless woman was always despised since she was considered a bad omen for the family'.[61] Yet, she absorbed the taunts that others hurled at her, simply because she was taught to be non-confrontational for the sake of marital peace. For Tagore, this was a kind of 'idealism' that Bengalee woman internalized by being raised in circumstances in which this was zealously pursued.

The second part of the letter dwelt on a peculiar relationship that Mrinal had with Bindu, another woman with the same fate who took refuge in her in-laws' house to avoid the physical and emotional torture meted out to her by her cousin brother. She was allowed to join the family as she was related to Mrinal's elder sister-in-law. Initially, she was welcomed as an extra helping hand for which no payment was necessary. Later on, feeling compassionate for the hapless Bindu, Mrinal came forward to extend a helping hand to her, since she felt that it was her duty as 'a human being'. She became close to her, since there was none to support her, including her elder sister-in-law who abdicated her responsibility once her husband withdrew his support. Bindu was in a serious predicament in view of her being an unwanted burden in the family. With Mrinal's intervention, Bindu was allowed to stay. Here was another twist in the story. Tagore treaded a difficult path through human relationships which were unconventional and highly tabooed. Bindu's excessive love for Mrinal was a source of happiness and also irritation at the same time: happiness because her love for Mrinal reinforced Mrinal's faith in human values which

[61] Rabindranath Tagore, 'Strir Patra,' in *Rabindra Rachanabali* (Bengalee), Vol. 12 (Kolkata: Visva-Bharati, 1422) (Bangavda), 331.

were articulated through love, care and compassion; irritation because Bindu's passion for physical proximity (though not clearly stated) scared Mrinal, as it was socially stigmatized. Mrinal was unambivalent while expressing what she felt about Bindu when the latter became obsessed with her. As she noted,

> Bindu began to love me with such fervour that I was scared. I have not seen a comparable face of love. I have only read about it and that also between man and woman. ... She would gaze upon my face as it she could not have enough of it. ... The girl was obsessed with me. ... At times, I was exasperated with her, I admit, but through her love, I could get a glimpse of my own self, of which I had not been aware. This is unencumbered self.[62]

Here, Tagore dealt with a theme highlighting a relationship based on a romantic involvement of a woman with another woman, which was socially tabooed and despised. Even Mrinal admitted that she was only aware of this kind of relationship on the basis of her reading of books; but by analysing her immensely compassionate feelings for Bindu she was not persuaded to believe that it was not only conceivable but was also possible. Tagore's courage to put the nature of this socially unusual relationship made him a class by himself, because he sought to not only articulate but also conceptualize lesbian interactions (though in a guarded manner) ahead of the feminist scholars who were to theoretically defend the theme in the early 1970s.[63] This was a reciprocal relationship, Tagore hinted, which helped Mrinal to rediscover her individuality and assert her independence. In view of the well-entrenched prejudices against the same-sex relationship, Mrinal was reluctant to continue, which was evident when she agreed to Bindu's marriage with an insane man. Here, Tagore made a very caustic remark by contrasting women with men in a society appreciative of patriarchal norms and values. Women were objects of entertainment and also exploitation, and men, by being men, were allowed to enjoy a shackle-free existence. In other words, no voice was raised when Bindu was married to a madman, simply because this was not

---

[62] Tagore, 332–3.

[63] Martha Shelly's seminal text entitled *Lovers and Mothers* (New York: Sefir, 1981) is one of the most cited intellectual interventions on the theme.

a cause for his disqualification, while Bindu being a woman had no other alternative but to accept the dictates of the family. For Mrinal, it was unacceptable and a crime against humanity. Nonetheless, it was not easy for her to halt the juggernaut in a situation which was not exactly in her favour. What upset her most was the support that her elder sister-in-law extended when the proposal came, because she justified Bindu's marriage with 'a mad man by saying that since she was born as a woman, she had to accept the decision because by agreeing she got what women aspired for'.[64] What does it imply? The poet, seeking to explain the predicament of the era, suggested that, with women being raised in an environment in which patriarchal values were well-entrenched, the response of Mrinal's elder sister-in-law did not seem to be unnatural; what is implied here is also Tagore's warning that so long as women tended to think in this fashion, their liberation would be a distant goal.

'Strir Patra' stands out in another respect: Tagore appears to have addressed the dilemma that women in Bengal underwent. Bindu escaped the torture by committing suicide; she set herself on fire, which was very common for women of that era, mentioned Tagore. Mrinal was sceptical, since it could have been a murder, because this was 'a fashion', she sarcastically said, saying that it hardly happened 'with Dhoti-clad men in Bengal'. 'No answer was expected because, she further added, it was man's domain in which women were considered to be an appendage (lifeless too) that was meant to be utilized as per men's requirements'.[65] The liberated Mrinal had the courage to break the socially engineered barriers and socially justified design of a shackled life; she thus had the valour to declare that 'she will never return to where she lived in Calcutta with the members of her adopted family because she saw, in her own eyes, how women were forced to accept those inhuman and tortuous means to survive despite being anguished and left-out'.[66] At one level, 'Strir Patra' was an elaboration of how women were brutalized, given the well-entrenched patriarchal

---

[64] Tagore, 'Strir Patra,' 334–5.

[65] Tagore, 337.

[66] Tagore, 337.

prejudices; at another level, it was also a clarion call for a radical societal transformation which empowered women as they were and allowed them to independently pursue the course of action which they deemed appropriate for their well-being. The last paragraph of 'Strir Patra' most poignantly illustrates Tagore's optimism, when Mrinal declared that

> she was not going to die since she, like mythical Mira Bai [who spent her life by worshipping Krishna knowing well that it was not going to give what she wanted], she would continue to live like a woman by being committed to what she preferred to do on her own. This is the mantra that she learnt on the basis of her experience. So, she will live a life by imbibing the spirit of being alive despite the torture that she underwent.[67]

Implicit here are two core points that Tagore made in defence of his concern for creating an independent space of women. First, despite being paternalistic on occasion, the poet did not allow his bias to cloud his opinion. Mrinal, representing the bard's views for human emancipation, agreed to lead an independent life away from the familial environment. This was an articulation of a design in which women created and also defended their own space without being aided by their male counterparts. In other words, it was not just a call for independence but also an attempt at institutionalizing the space that was created as a result. Second, Mrinal also referred to the brutality that a woman underwent by being married, which not only uprooted her from the familiar environment in which she was born and initially raised but also placed before her new sets of problems that she had to negotiate. The new life, instead of becoming exciting, was reduced to mere physical existence, since the adopted family did not seem to be generally forthcoming in accepting daughters-in-law. The latter were welcome as they contributed to the family through their physical labour; they were usually subjected to torture in view of the well-entrenched patriarchal impediments. The husband, the only person who was to be their saviour, was generally restrained, presumably because of the age-old ideas justifying servility of the newly married. Furthermore, that women without a child were an easy prey was again due to the

---

[67] Tagore, 338.

rootedness of the superstitions that generated hatred for them. There were, of course, exceptions in some families, which, however, does not invalidate the proposition based on experiences of women in general in the then Bengal. Mrinal of 'Strir Patra' was thus an eye-opener in the sense that she fearlessly articulated what she wanted despite being challenged, since the environment was not exactly in her favour. Having been exposed to the Enlightenment values and also the ideas that the Upanishads held, it was possible for Tagore to be confident of what he preached in favour of gender parity despite being vehemently criticized by his compatriots, since they were persuaded not to disturb the apple cart supportive of gender disparities.

SOHINI OF 'LABORATORY' (1940)

Being fundamentally creative, Tagore always conveyed unique messages with a clear socio-economic and political meaning through his innovative literary outputs. 'Strir Patra' and 'Poila Number' were imprints of a system of relationships in which gender issues were debated; the main protagonists raised their voice against discrimination around the gender axis amidst well-entrenched contrarian social, economic and political forces. The poet's aim was to evolve a mindset which was to be positively tilted in favour of gender parity. 'Laboratory', published in 1940, is dissimilar from his other creative texts on many counts. First, it is a story in which the main character, Sohini, was a Punjabi woman who represented a different kind of mindset, presumably because of being a non-Bengalee raised in a milieu that was hardly similar to that of Bengal. Second, Sohini was ready to accept any challenge for defending what she deemed justified to her. In other words, she expressed her commitment to fulfil the objective that she accepted as complementary to her goal. Finally, she hardly wavered in stating 'unpleasant truth[s]' regardless of the social consequences. That she had a baby out of wedlock notwithstanding the fear of being ostracized, she had shown her courage to challenge soically-justified norms to conduct human behaviour and was likely to suffer. In a nutshell, with his focus on an unusually uncommon situation, especially from the point of the Bengalee psyche, Tagore here introduced the readers to themes, relationships and mindsets which were not exactly familiar. Hence, Sohini, treading a completely unknown path, was Tagore's endeavour to capture a reality in which the male–female interaction was conceptualized differently. Nonetheless, there was a common thread of thinking that characterized women in general; Sohini, despite being a Punjabi, wanted to carry forward the tradition that her Bengalee husband bequeathed, simply because that was the only way to express her unconditional love for him who, unlike other males, never treated her as 'a doormat' but treated her as a companion for fulfilling jointly desired missions.

The storyline is unconventional. Tagore dealt with one's zeal for being self-independent and was also keen to show that women were equally competent to be able partners if they were convinced of their role in fulfilling the mission. Sohini met Nandakishore, her future husband, when the latter travelled to Punjab in connection with his professional needs. The marriage between Sohini and Nandakishore, though unusual in the conventional sense, was based on the common desire to do something good for society. Nandakishore had the intellectual prowess, while Sohini complemented him when he began his laboratory as a business venture. Drawing on his desire to be self-dependent, Sohini's husband nurtured the concern of making India scientifically independent, and he was confident that it was not difficult, since 'Indians have the brain though they lacked the initiatives [presumably because] of the alien regime that, by being severely restrictive, inhibits Indians' natural desires'.[68] Furthermore, his intelligence allowed him not to be misled or cheated by those who endeavoured to that effect. It was evident when Sohini observed how 'the well-established businessmen of Punjab failed to deceive which they usually do with a non-Punjabi'.[69] This was one of the reasons which endeared Sohini to Nandakishore to the extent of being deeply in love with him that finally led to their marriage. In other words, being swayed by Nandakishore's intelligent ways of handling those who were cunning and deceitful, Sohini admitted having the right kind of person for her. Implicit here are two fundamental points

---

[68] Rabindranath Tagore, 'Laboratory,' in *Rabindra Rachanabali* (Bengalee), Vol. 13 (Kolkata: Visva-Bharati, 1410) (Bangavda), 270.

[69] Tagore, 271.

that are integral to Tagore's wider concerns. First, 'Laboratory' is a story in which the urge to become economically self-independent is explicit. This was a concern that Tagore had clearly articulated in the 1904 text, *Swadeshi Samaj*. Nikhilesh of *Ghare Baire* epitomized the concern, which ran contrary to the nationalist design justifying the application of force in case the nationalist dictates for both discarding foreign clothes and burning them in bonfires were violated. As shown in chapter (chapter 1), it had boomeranged during the 1905–1908 anti-partition campaign in Bengal. With the sole purpose of creating indigenous facilities for developing scientific knowledge, Nandakishore represented a heartfelt desire that Tagore had epitomized as one who held views, different from his nationalist colleagues, for self-independence. Second, this is a story which also drew on the poet's concern for gender equality. By being candid even in expressing her choice of Nandakishore as her husband, Sohini presented herself as an independent agency who did not seem to be bothered by what others would say because of her decision to marry a person from a different kind of socio-cultural milieu. Sohini was different from both Anila of 'Poila Number' and Mrinal of 'Strir Patra' in the sense that unlike them, she was engaged in an endeavour that was complementary to the mission that her husband had. The storyline is explicit here: Sohini was involved in the work not because she was forced to but because she wanted to, which is a recognition of Sohini, a woman, as an independent agency who became so in socio-economic circumstances which were not favourably disposed towards gender parity. The role of Nandakishore was significant here, since he devoted his energy to prepare the ground for Sohini to be independent and capable of thinking on her own. In his words,

> incompatibility is likely to arise if an engineer husband keep his wife confined to the kitchen which is normally the case in most of the households; the implication is disastrous because unless both husband and wife are united with the desire to realize identical objectives, the married life will be everything by self-fulfilling; so, what is required to done is to create a milieu in which husband and wife meets each other as compatriots which will make wife responsible to her husband and vice versa.[70]

[70] Tagore, 272.

Here, Tagore not only elaborates but also defends the argument supporting why an interdependent man–woman relationship was critical for social well-being. So long as an interpersonal relationship is clouded by gender equations, the man–woman bond is likely to be fragile; however, if it is based on recognizing each other as integral to the relationship, it is immune to being adversarial. What is important for any relationship, Tagore felt, is respect for each other, because hierarchy is anything but conducive to a healthy understanding between individuals. This is more the case in a wedlock, because the woman joins the adopted family by being completely uprooted from the environment in which she was born and raised. Here, Nandakishore talked in Tagore's language, supporting the point that no conjugal bond survives, let alone flourish, unless it is cemented by respect for each other. So, Sohini was not an exception, since she corresponded with the characters that the poet created to pursue his concern for gender equity.

Nandakishore's sudden death came as a plot twist. Many sought to take advantage of her widowhood by attempting to coerce her into selling the laboratory. However, this is where Sohini came into her own by dishing out emphatic refusals to such manipulative proposals. Her fight to save the laboratory led her to a young scientist, Rebati Bhattacharjee, who she thought would be of assistance. This decision was governed by Sohini's firm belief that ensuring the continued existence of the laboratory that was the result of her late husband's hard work was the only way for her to express her love and gratitude for him. That she owed her transformation to her dead husband was a constant refrain, which also reminds us of Bimala of *Ghare Baire*; like Bimala, who became what she became largely due to Nikhilesh's initiatives, Sohini kept remembering that it would not have been possible for her to be a different person had Nandakishore not encouraged her to be immersed in studying books and texts for scientific knowledge along with him. She was always protective of the laboratory, so much so that she refused to hand it over to anyone, including her daughter who had, she was persuaded to believe, no emotional attachment to its continuity, and hence even if the laboratory had folded up, it would hardly have had any impact on her daughter. So firm was Sohini's belief that she even disclosed that her daughter had been born out of wedlock,[71] which completely ruled out the latter's claim of being a legal heir to Nandakishore. This is also illustrative of how protective Sohini was of the laboratory that had evolved out of the hard work that she and her husband jointly put in for a cause. Besides her unconditional love for her deceased husband, which did not seem unusual, that she was a different kind of human who was compassionate towards living beings was also evident when she was found to be extra caring towards 'a stray dog which was almost dying due to malnourishment', 'that symbolizes her idea of devotion to god', as the author stated, 'in contrast to the ritualistic Hindu tradition of sacrificing animals at the altar for providential blessings'.[72] Here, Sohini was Tagore's voice questioning the established rituals which were, he felt, deceptive since they, instead of being socially conducive, bred superstitious beliefs and prohibitive mindsets.

Sohini is an articulation of Tagore's concern for (a) self-reliance, (b) women empowerment and (c) universal humanism. As far as self-reliance is concerned, there is a historical continuity, because what he argued in the 1904 text, *Swadeshi Samaj*, and articulated in *Ghare Baire* was also manifested in Sohini. In other words, it was a reiteration of the concern that poet held so dear throughout his life. As regards universal humanism, Sohini represents a new woman who was so devoted to her husband not just because of his being her husband but because of his contribution to make her capable and free from prejudices supportive of social hierarchy. Linked with this was also Tagore's firm belief that unless women were adequately empowered to fight their battle on their own, the endeavour towards establishing gender parity would remain vacuous. What also requires to be highlighted here is Tagore being paternalistic in his attitude towards women, presumably because this was the tradition that was handed over to him since the days of Ram Mohan Roy. Hence, it was not surprising that Sohini, who was grateful to her husband for being so confident in her, thus declared that

---

[71] Tagore, 297.
[72] Tagore, 276.

in relation to the qualities that he [her husband, Nandakishore] found in me, he regarded my shortcomings as insignificant. He reposed his complete trust in a non-descript woman like me, as I have never betrayed his trust. My being incapable did not stand between him and me [because] ... my smallness he always ignored, but gave me unstinted support where he found that I was worthy. Who knows to what level I would have sunk, had he not valued my good qualities which remained hidden when he met me for the first time.[73]

This was an unqualified confession that Sohini made to express unambiguously her gratitude to the deceased Nandakishore. What the bard conveyed here was his belief in humanity that was a casualty presumably because human beings privileged mere material gain over this civilizational ethos supportive of basic human values. In that respect, the message that Sohini delivered was not uncommon but a reinforcement of what Tagore strongly felt and sincerely propagated. There is another aspect which appears to have been revolutionary in the then context, namely, the open declaration of being involved in physical intimacy leading to the birth of a baby out of wedlock. This was candidly admitted by Sohini when she said that

I feel ashamed to confess that I had been involved in relationships which were socially-unjustified. The very thought that I have been close to a number of men still ruffles me. ... Our temptations remained hidden under our flesh and bones, but flares up at the slightest provocation. It does not inhibit me to [disclose] that very early in my life I went to the bed with many men. We, women are not chaste all our life though we pretend to be so. ... Let me tell ... that I had not clear perception of what was right and what was wrong [and] there was nobody to guide me. So, I plunged into evil ways (sic) as I have been able to come out of it. Yes, my body was tainted, but not my soul.[74]

Here, Tagore treaded into unconventional terrain, since Sohini's forthright disclosure of infidelity was indeed unthinkable in a context when Victorian morality was always privileged. For the poet to put this in black-and-white was clearly an endeavour to not only challenge the well-entrenched patriarchal prejudices but also to boldly say that

[73] Tagore, 287.

[74] Tagore, 278.

women's body was her domain and nobody else had any right over this. In a sense, Tagore foresaw the conceptualization of the idea that Carole Hanisch developed in her pathbreaking essay entitled 'The Personal is Political', published in 1969.[75] The idea that Hanisch conveys is about women being independent agencies for doing what they deem appropriate. Challenging the claim that women needed to be guided, she further maintains that the so-called exhortation that men, through their revolutionary struggles, brought about radical changes in the plight that women were subjected to due to the well-entrenched socio-economic prejudices, was far from being true. This is not the place to argue either for or against the contention. What is striking in Tagore's 'Laboratory' was the bold confession of the main protagonist, Sohini, that she, by being involved in 'an illicit relationship', had had a baby, which was inconceivable then. There are two aspects that need attention here: on the one hand, Tagore was forthright in stating about a socially unrecognized relationship and supported it openly as perfectly justified on the other, by accepting Sohini's baby as his, her husband, Nandakishore also demonstrated that he was not, at all, guided by the archaic Victorian morality championing the hardcore Catholic predispositions. So, Sohini, in the short story 'Laboratory', is both a pathfinder and a harbinger of a new era of conceptualizing gender relations afresh.

ANILA OF 'POILA NUMBER' (1920)

'Poila Number' (Number One), published in 1920, is another short story in which Tagore pursued his thoughts on gender issues. The storyline revolves around Anila and her husband. Later in the story, Sitangshu appears after he shifts to the house number 1, or *poila* in Bengalee. 'Poila Number' is primarily an elaboration of how Tagore negotiated with prevalent socio-economic circumstances in which gender equality was an anathema. Unlike 'Strir Patra', wherein Mrinal expressed her views categorically, the main protagonist here, Anila, approached the concern completely differently. At one level, she, a married woman, was a voice, a powerful voice indeed, against gender

[75] Carole Hanisch, *The Personal is Political*. https://webhome.cs.uvic.ca/~mserra/AttachedFiles/PersonalPolitical.pdf.

exploitation, which did not seem unusual so long as patriarchal hegemony continued. She was a good wife, since she discharged her responsibilities towards the family in an impeccable manner; everybody was happy. At another level, she, unlike Mrinal, articulated her response differently; Mrinal left home and expressed her views, in a strong language, while being away from home. Anila was silent in her protest, for she was hardly vocal, and left the family without leaving any clue to her whereabouts. Here, Tagore conceptualized his approach, rather heuristically, by drawing on the arguments that her male companions offered on the basis of their interaction with her.

In the story, Anila is introduced to the reader by her husband as a very mature and intelligent person, with an example. That her father-in-law trusted her more than his son, who was Anila's husband, was referred to by her husband to prove that she was honest and reliable. The dying father of Anila's husband gave her a portion of his savings for bringing up Saroj, the son by his first wife since he apprehended that his second wife might not look after her step son after his demise. He thus said: 'please take care of my son, Saroj who is likely to suffer since my second wife may not be as concerned for his well-being as she will naturally do her children'.[76] Although her husband was terribly annoyed with the decision, he, however, later understood that by choosing Anila for this task his father actually had shown how prudent he was.[77] Anila took an independent decision when she engaged a private tutor for Saroj, which made her husband angry, though he immediately realized that since he was academically unfit, what his wife did in this regard was perhaps the best deed.

A new dimension is added to the narrative when Anila gets a neighbour, Sitangshu, who occupied the first building with the address *poila* number, or number one in English. The family was rich and had an opulence that caused a sense of anger in Anila's husband. Not only was Sitangshu well-off, but he was also a connoisseur of music and games, which attracted many of the neighbours to him. Anila appeared

[76] Rabindranath Tagore, 'Poila Number,' in *Rabindra Rachanabali* (Bengalee), Vol. 12 (Kolkata: Visva-Bharati, 1422) (Bangavda), 377.

[77] Tagore, 377.

to have been disturbed by the sudden spurt of activities in the neighbourhood, which was likely to be a cause of irritation to others in the locality, though her husband had apprehended that she was swayed by Sitangshu's opulence and also multifaceted personality. It was made clear by the author when Anila's husband expressed the feeling of being relieved when she asked him to change their residence, which was however delayed because of Saroj's impeding school tests. His joy knew no bounds when he came to know that Sitangshu was going out of the city for two weeks for an excursion in South India. His sense of relief came out very clearly when Tagore stated that 'with his imminent departure for south India, the threat (sic) that disturbed him disappeared completely'.[78] The delay in the proposed shift to a new place became a source of agony when Anila left home without informing any of the members of the family. It was a bolt from the blue when her husband discovered a letter under the pillow which stated: 'I am going away; don't try to search for me and even if you do, I won't be found'.[79] In view of his suspicion that Anila was perhaps emotionally involved with Sitangshu, he immediately concluded that she had eloped with Sitangshu, since the latter had also left the city in the morning of the same day. He also realized that whatever the authors wrote about extramarital relationship was true when it happened to him. It also dawned on him that he had had 'his contribution too because he neglected her to a great extent which created an emotional vacuum leading to search for her fulfilment of emotions'.[80] A wife at home was considered to be 'an appendage and was expected to discharge her responsibilities as efficiently as possible and as her husband he was to enjoy the comfort without extending any help whatsoever'.[81] The story took a sudden turn when Anila's husband discovered 25 letters from Sitangshu to his wife expressing his admiration for her. Sitangshu was so enamoured by Anila that he characterized her as 'a paragon of beauty and epitome of knowledge and wisdom though he did not

[78] Tagore, 381.

[79] Tagore, 382.

[80] Tagore, 383.

[81] Tagore, 383.

want her as partners in the conventional way'.[82] Being respectful to her, he further wrote: 'don't misunderstand me; I am your admirer and my admiration for you is based on my appreciation of your devotion to the family despite being denied a rightful place there',[83] which was justified, her husband felt, since she had never been allowed to be part of the gatherings that took place often in his residence at his behest. Nonetheless, accusing his wife of being an 'infidel', Anila's husband followed a familiar path of thinking. Here the story line conforms to the explanations, based on patriarchal understanding of women which however had undergone a sea-change soon when Sitangshu who was shown to have stolen his wife, and Anila mentioned that she received a letter with the same message that her husband received when she left him. The message was the same: 'I am going away; don't try to search for me and even if you do, I won't be found'.[84] Through this skilfully rendered plot twist, the poet presented his views on gender in a remarkably creative manner.

'Poila Number' is a uniquely textured response that Tagore had articulated to pursue his concern for gender equity. In three complementary ways, the text stands out. First, here the poet had left many things unsaid but had given enough indications to comprehend the urge for destabilizing the available social format defending gender discrimination in a persuasive manner. The narrative is an endeavour to grasp how the existing social mores created a vacuum in women, which had its manifestation in different forms. Being left out even in her adopted family, Anila underwent the suffering without ever raising her voice. Second, this short story is also a graphic rendering of how silence can be a powerful weapon to ventilate one's grievances. This is, in other words, an exploration of an area of human endeavour seeking to chart out a meaningful course of action without stating anything to that effect. In this respect, Mrinal of 'Strir Patra' and Sohini of 'Laboratory' are different, for, by articulating their views in black and white, they expressed unambiguously what they felt. Contrarily,

---

[82] Tagore, 383.

[83] Tagore, 383.

[84] Tagore, 384.

Anila, by being silent, articulated a voice which was as powerful as the ones that the other protagonists of gender equality had raised with an identical objective. Finally, 'Poila Number' introduced a new literary style in which the unsaid became a powerful medium of equally powerful messages addressing the primary concern that the poet had. Being dutiful to everybody in the family, Anila built her image as 'an ideal daughter-in-law who devoted all her energies and time for the benefit of the members of her adopted family'.[85] While she was hailed as an ideal daughter-in-law or wife, nobody seemed to have been bothered to find out whether she was contented or not being sincere to her assigned role. It was thus not surprising that Anila's husband was overjoyed when he found out that his wife prepared the food items that his friends liked the most, though he never enquired whether that made her happy. She was considered to be the one who was always to give without expecting anything in return. With her one expression, 'I won't be found', Tagore said many things which probably would not have come out so poignantly had he explained the emotional turmoil that Anila had been undergoing while performing the socially endorsed roles for wives and daughters-in-law. The poet is thus not merely a storyteller but also an innovative thinker who endeavoured hard to put across his message for gender parity, which clearly deviated from the mainstream thinking on this theme.

As argued above, 'Poila Number' may have adopted a different literary style, but the message that it conveyed is similar to other of Tagore's texts on the same theme in nature and also texture, because (a) it is about Tagore's concern for parity regardless of sex and gender, and (b) the narrative delineates a space in which 'the unsaid' became a powerful device to convey and establish his views for the cause of gender equality. In other words, by drawing our attention to 'the silent zones' of human behaviour, the bard can be said to have evolved new yardsticks to understand human emotions, which one can feel provided one has the compassion and inkling for the same. 'Poila Number' stands out, for it is illustrative of a new literary design that Tagore experimented with to articulate the familiar voice against gender

---

[85] Tagore, 382.

disparity, which he raised here in a different fashion. Hence, this is a story with a message at one level; at another, it also demonstrates an endeavour towards realizing the goal that the poet aspired to achieve with his steadfast commitment to the cause of gender equality.

CONCLUDING OBSERVATIONS

A thorough analytical scan of Tagore's creative texts reveals that his concern for gender equity was not derivative but one that he imbibed rather instinctively. As mentioned at the outset of this chapter, it is difficult to deal with each and every text where the poet delved into gender parity as part of his wider project on human emancipation. Persuaded by the efforts that his predecessors like Ram Mohan Roy, Vidyasagar and also his father, Debendranath Tagore, undertook, the poet took upon himself the responsibility to carry the tradition forward. Being critical of the prevalent social system drawing on patri- archal prejudices, Rabindranath remained committed to this cause till the last days of his life. To the poet, the social design ignoring one half of the demography required to be replaced to create conditions in which women were treated at par with their male counterparts. The poet who established his fame as an author in Bangla attributed his reputation to the spontaneous willingness to read the texts that he wrote in the vernacular language. Being candid in his appreciation, he thus said that

> Bangla has become a respectable language of expression largely due its massive female readership; even those male readers who bought Bengalee novels [even written by him] were ashamed to say it publicly because it would bring them bad name. Despite being neglected by the male read- ers, the books in Bangla language were fondly nurtured by their female counterparts which helped books written in Bangla gain respectability and wider acceptance in due course.[86]

Hence, for Tagore, women were harbingers of a new era wherein Bangla was no longer as despised as in the past. With this preface,

[86] Rabindranath Tagore, 'Atmashakti' (self-confidence), in *Rabindra Rachanabali* (Bengalee), Vol. 2 (Kolkata: Visva-Bharati, 1410) (Bangavda), 685.

Tagore now embarked on a bigger project, namely, to express his views to radically alter the widely practised socio-economic norms and politico-ideological predispositions which were clearly disposed against the womenfolk. As shown above, by drawing on a selective set of his writings (novels and short stories), the chapter substantiated the point referring to how the female protagonists raised their voice against being discriminated merely due to the accident of birth and the socially justified patriarchal system. Based on his understanding of the Upanishadic messages and also his absorption of Enlightenment values, he initiated a new literary genre, viewing women as respectable members of society, in opposition to the mainstream conservative outlook drawing on gender disparity. A pattern is visible—whether it is Bimala or Ela or Damini or Anila or Mrinal or Sohini, they all were attempts at establishing their independent identities as women. Interestingly, this was the pattern if one draws attention to Binodini of *Choker Bali* (1903), Nandini of *Rakta Karabi* (1925), Kumudini of *Jogajog* (1929). It is true that these characters espoused the same cause, though differently. In *Rakta Karabi*, Nandini, the young girl, destroyed, with her feminine charm and attraction, the well-entrenched restrictions that the invisible king had so far maintained for fulfilling his partisan aim of becoming rich at the cost of those working in the gold mines. It was Nandini who helped the king and also those who were associated with the extraction of gold from the mine realize the charm of life. The message that Tagore conveyed was about the women power in bringing about a sea-change in their behaviour which resulted in appreciation of the basic human values of equity that, so far, remained an anathema. Binodini, or Bali, as she was fondly addressed by Asha, another character in the novel, raised certain other issues. At one level, she was a conventional woman who expressed her unconditional love for her beloved, Behari, by saying that 'my life is empty, my heart is empty, there is emptiness all around me—come unto this emptiness, even if, for an instant, you have to come. I won't let go of you'.[87] Questioning the social norms depriving widows of worldly comforts and charms, Binodini was a voice, a

---

[87] Rabindranath Tagore, *Chokher Bali* (A Grain of Sand), reproduced in *Classic Rabindranath Tagore*, 107.

powerful voice indeed, which was difficult to conceive in the context of the mainstream conservatism that flourished in the 19th and early 20th centuries. Here is another dimension of gender question that we will deal with in chapter no (Chapter 5), in which Tagore attributed gender freedom to education; being educated, it was easier for her to carve out an independent space amidst the other female members in the family. Here, the letters that figured in the novel are illustrative. While depicting Kumudini, Tagore juggled with two contrasting views: one that is desirous of gender freedom and the other that deals with the impediments towards women being treated as equal to their male counterparts. When Kumudini left her husband's home, since she had found him entangled with a prostitute, Shyamasundari, nobody appeared to have appreciated the decision, and she was accused of being 'an arrogant woman [because] she did what she was not expected to do'.[88] By virtue of being a man, the argument was elaborated further, Kumudini's husband 'was naturally superior to her—a fact that was unarguable'.[89] This was tantamount to

> slavery [though] there does not seem to be an escape route [because] the wife becomes a property in a sacramental marriage. The day you go around the sacred fire seven times with the groom, your body and mind are bound to him for ever. There is no escape. It is worse than death. Once you are born a woman you may not reverse the course of a woman's fate.[90]

The argument is familiar, at one level, that with marriage women lost their independence completely; they just became a stooge at the beck and call of their husband and other members of their adopted family following the marriage. At another level, the poet draws our attention to the processes supportive of the patriarchal grip over women which they themselves support and nurtured. Kumudini's decision to leave her husband's home was condemned by her aunt and others who were not persuaded by her argument, presumably because they had lost their independent thinking after having been nurtured in an

---

[88] Rabindranath Tagore, *Jogajog* (Nexus), reproduced in *Classic Rabindranath Tagore*, 935.

[89] Tagore, 935.

[90] Tagore, 935.

environment in which patriarchal prejudices seemed to have clouded their vision in such a way as not to allow them to judge issues independently. Patriarchy survived and also thrived because

> women themselves valued women the least. They were not even aware that this was the reason why it was so easy for men to dishonour women in every home. The women themselves had put out their own light. And then they lived in perpetual fear and anxiety, oppressed by unworthy men, and accepted the highest attainment in a woman's life was to bear all of this silently, without protest.[91]

Here, Tagore talked about a wider social constraint that was primarily due to the unavoidable impact of the societal values that had been nurtured over generations. Women, instead of being an independent agency for social metamorphosis, became entrapped in the maze. Contrary to what was naturally expected, they unknowingly became an agent for patriarchy to remain unaffected. In other words, that women tended to argue for defending patriarchal prejudices was thus a natural outcome of being born and raised in an environment in which the torture that women suffered did not seem unusual. Nonetheless, Tagore, being one who always remained an uncompromising crusader for gender justice, warned his compatriots championing gender-based social imbalances through Biprodas, Kumudini's brother and a protagonist for gender equity, who declared that 'so much violation of human rights could not be allowed any longer. Those whom society had degraded so much were now pulling the society down with them'.[92] This was the silver lining, since this contains a powerful message that Tagore articulated to establish the point that incessant struggle for gender equity was certain to bring about radical social transformation leading to gender equality by considerably undermining the age-old patriarchal hegemony justifying various restrictive socio-economic and politically-restraining practices.

In a nutshell, Tagore's approach to the gender question draws on his concern for according proper recognition to women, who, despite

---

[91] Tagore, 935.

[92] Tagore, 936.

comprising half of the population, remained socio-economically marginalized and denigrated. This is a significant part of the package of ideas that he developed while being engaged in the wider struggle for human emancipation. Unlike his nationalist colleagues, including Gandhi, he was not persuaded by the argument that political freedom was necessary for eradicating much of the social ills inhibiting equality of the sexes. In fact, Tagore's argument was, as the above discussion shows, just the reverse. According to him, unless one's social prejudices were eliminated, freedom of any kind was futile. In other words, so long as the artificial but socially engineered designs controlling human behaviour were allowed to survive, no endeavour for radical social transformation was likely to succeed. *Ghare Baire* is testimony of his heartfelt concern for erasing the Hindu–Muslim social distance; *Chandalika* is a scathing critique of the caste system justifying social divisions between high-caste Hindus and their 'untouchable' counterparts; *Jogajog* is an elaboration of how the male–female social divide subjected Kumudini, one of the main protagonists in the novel, to severe emotional torture which she had absorb since she had been born a woman. By raising his voice against oppression around the caste, class and gender axes which had, so far, been considered to be axiomatic, the poet was ahead of his time. Furthermore, in his writings, gender and sexuality in various figurations become 'an expressive device in exploring certain aspects of a power relationship'.[93] His novels, in particular, are illustrative here. Bimala in *Ghare Baire* expressed her sexuality in both familial and political contexts; in *Char Adhyay*, Ela articulated here womanhood in the arena of violent nationalist struggle, Kumudini of *Jogajog* represented a completely different kind of sexuality when she expressed her displeasure at her husband, since he had been physically intimate against her will. In *Chaturanga*, Ela was explicit in her statements for the fulfilment of her womanly desire, which might have been immoral if it was conceived in the conventional thinking. In fact, the arguments that Tagore offered in defending his specially textured point of view for gender equality

---

[93] Himani Banerji, 'Women, Gender and the Family in Tagore,' in *The Cambridge Companion to Rabindranath Tagore*, ed. Sukanta Chaudhuri (Cambridge: Cambridge University Press, 2020), 244–5.

contributed to a new genre of literature, both in India and abroad. In other words, the model that he built remains a source of inspiration for future writers regardless of national boundaries. Hence, the bard can be said to have ushered in a new era pregnant with possibilities for radical social metamorphosis. His creative texts on social issues thus continue to inspire generation after generation seeking to develop new conceptual tools for capturing the zeal and also urge for noticeable change within interpersonal/inter-group power dynamics.

Tagore's Approach to Education

A perusal of the nationalist movement suggests that the nationalists paid attention to the development of an alternative education system in India, since the British system of education was there to create a set of clerks to help the foreign ruler govern the country in accordance with their politico-ideological priorities. As a mayor of Calcutta, C. R. Das (1870–1925) endeavoured to set out a scheme of education in contrast with that of the British system of learning in 1921. Gandhi also provided a blueprint of education through the articulation of Nai Talim in his *Constructive Programme* in 1946. In line with his thinking, Tagore also put forward his ideas of a model of learning which was conducive to character-building and also generation of care, compassion and empathy for fellow human beings regardless of their socio-economic identities and locations. The British rule did neither, because its primary aim was to strengthen the Empire at any cost. The public sapping of ethical ideals slowly unfolded with the dwindling of values which had been considered sacred not so long ago, the immediate outcome of which was revealed when the exploitation of one section of humanity by another was privileged without being bothered at all. Besides making the new learners insensitive to the prevalent socio-economic reality, the new education system that came out of the famous 1835 Macaulay's Minute on education making English learning a passport to employment led to the rise of a new educated class on the basis of rote learning. According to Tagore, education was both a means of learning and also character-building; the former seemed more important, because mere learning, through rote learning, was of no use unless it contributed to the consolidation of the human values of care, compassion and empathy. This was, for him, the need of the age when human beings, obsessed with the fulfilment of material gains at any cost, created an artificial world by being terribly partisan in their goals and aims. For Tagore, this was the beginning of the rise of the new world, because the foundation of modern civilization, that is, Western civilization, had been shaken, and the Enlightenment values had been happily bypassed to justify colonization as desirable for the colonized, as it was a device for them to be 'civilized' out of their barbarian existence. The rule by others was, therefore, a panacea, as it were, for those who lost the battle due to a complex set of factors. That it was not so was revealed soon with the consolidation of the voice of the opposition by the colonized. Seeking to break the shackles, the voice represented a serious questioning on the basis of intellectual inputs from both indigenous and derivative sources. A perusal of how this voice developed also underlines the contention that education and learning, Siamese twins, cannot be seg-regated. Unless one's learning contributed to the common well-being, it was futile. The model of Visva-Bharati that Tagore so carefully built directs our attention to areas of human activities which are meant to create harmony, togetherness and empathy for one another regardless of class, clan and ethnicity. This was the need of the hour, since the great civilizations of the past had collapsed with the growing strength of sociopolitical forces that hardly paid attention to the foundational values which contributed to their rise and consolidation in the course of time. In his endeavour towards bringing back those values that were critical to humanity, Tagore founded Visva-Bharati in 1921, which was built upon the ideal of the spiritual unity of all races in consonance with the inspirational Upanishadic ideal, *Yatra Vishvam Bhavati Eka Needam,* which means that this is the place 'where the whole world meets in a single nest'. Visva-Bharati was a place of learning for those who believed in divine humanity; education here was not merely a medium of instruction but one that drew on concerns for universal humanism or the instinctive desire for self-emancipation. Implicit here was Tagore's lifelong mission for devising a system of education leading to a learning that privileged socio-economic values seeking to erase discrimination of any kind. A revolutionary idea in the context of the nationalist movement indeed, which was complemented by his critic-cum-compatriot, Gandhi, the projects Patha Bhavana, Siksha

Satra and Visva-Bharati, founded in 1901, 1924 and 1921, respectively, stood out also in the global reckoning, since they set in motion a campaign which was enriched by an urge for universal well-being.

A visionary himself, Tagore devised a design for education in the colonial context which was innovative, a source of joy and a platform for fulfilling one's sociopolitical and cultural mission. The chapter, besides dwelling on what he did to provide an alternative system of education, is also an endeavour towards grasping the conceptual foundation on which his approach to education rested. This is pursued in two complementary ways: on the one hand, the chapter dwells on how he viewed education and its role in building a nation of independent-minded individuals who also had a wider concern for human emancipation; on the other, by concentrating on the unique models that he constructed according to his preferences, this is also an elaboration of the design and its functioning in a context when the government-sponsored English education appeared to have been hegemonic.

UNFOLDING OF A CONCEPTUALLY INNOVATIVE DESIGN

As a creative writer, instead of only writing critical essays championing his unique voice, Tagore put forward his views through short stories, novels, dance-dramas and plays. Here, there is no exception. Of all the creative tracts, his approach to education was most hilariously articulated by Tagore in his satirical short story *Tota Kahini* of 1918 in which a king's effort to educate a parrot, called Tota, ended in disaster because the king felt that by forcing the bird to swallow the written papers, the bird's education would be complete; in the end the bird died because of too much of papers that it had been forcibly fed. There was a plot twist in this short story because the desire to make the bird forget how to sing and instead learn how to read the scripture which needed to be done even by application of force.[1] The end of the

---

[1] In his short story of 1918, 'The Parrot's Training', Tagore thus wrote, 'once upon a time, there was a bird. It was ignorant. It sang all right, but never recited scriptures. It hopped pretty frequently, but lacked manners'. Rabindranath Tagore, 'The Parrot's

training of the parrot was also very poignantly articulated when the poet wrote 'the bird was brought to [the king], guarded by the Kotwal and the sepoys and the sowars. The King poked its body with fingers. Only its inner stuffing of book-leaves rustled'.[2] It was an allegorical story signifying how Indian kids evolved as *totas* (parrots) due to just rote learning. As a counter to that, Tagore started a school, Patha Bhavana, in 1901, followed by another school in 1924. The goal was to provide education to young minds differently, for their inculcation of values, morals and compassion for others, besides being intellectually inquisitive for knowledge that was useful for the humanity. In 1921, Tagore laid the foundation of a university Visva-Bharati, which figuratively meant a creative blending of knowledge from all over the world. It was Gandhian as well, because the Mahatma held an identical view as far as education was concerned. Based on the motto, *Yatra Vishvam Bhavati Eka Needam*, 'where the world comes together in a single nest', Visva-Bharati was sought to be made an alternative centre of learning in contrast with what was being transmitted by the alien ruler. Contrary to the British education which was based on rote learning and was responsible for making the young learners insensitive to innovation, Tagore concentrated on developing a centre where the aim was to build socio-cultural bonhomie among those coming to Visva-Bharati for education. As he believed, 'education must enable every child to understand and fulfil the purpose of the age, not defeat by acquiring the habit of creating divisions and cherishing national prejudices'.[3] For him, education was a source of empowerment which needed to be utilized for attaining political freedom by our own strength. His argument was very precise and well-clarified when he stated that 'the countrymen ... should not beg for [their] rights, [they] must create them for [themselves] because ... to depend on gains from the outside

---

Training,' reproduced in Sisir Kumar Das, ed., *The English Writings of Rabindranath Tagore*, Vol. 2 (New Delhi: Sahitya Akademi, 1996), 272.

[2] Tagore, 274.

[3] Rabindranath Tagore, 'A Poet's School' reproduced in *Rabindranath Tagore: Pioneers in Education (Essays and Exchanges Between Rabindranath Tagore and LK Elmhirst)* (London: John Murray, 1961), 65.

is to hurt one's true self'.[4] His primary concern was to make Indians aware of their own capability, which was likely to bring independence to India. But that was not enough; the education that we imparted was required to instil in the learners a sense of ownership of their country among them. As Tagore mentioned:

> we may try to hunt down the monster of alien rule with lethal weapons, but it will baffle us every time by changing its skin and complexion. Only when we feel within us that our country exists, that it is real, then, it leads to fruition.[5]

Implicit here are two fundamental points that Tagore never lost sight of in his critical essays and creative writings. On the one hand, he was insistent that only by being economically self-reliant would the country acquire the capability to stand on its own. His *Swadeshi Samaj* (1904) and also *Ghare Baire* (1916) are illustrative here: while in the first he prepared a blueprint for future India, showing how it was to be achieved, as discussed in Chapter 3. The scheme of economic development that the poet evolved were put into practice by Nikhilesh of *Ghare Baire*. The argument is, on the other hand, a testimony of Tagore's concern for building a society free from social prejudices against people with different religious and caste identities. The *swadeshi samaj* that was laid out for rural reconstruction was a scheme in which people from all strata were given specific roles for its success. Because he always felt that Indians became alienated from one another largely due to the construction of social barriers around the caste and religion axes, he raised his voice against these artificially designed schisms segregating one section of the population from another. This was a deliberately fashioned endeavour which was an impediment towards social amity. Unless this was completely eradicated, no design for India's socio-economic upliftment was likely to reach fruition. It was very unambiguously articulated by the bard when he said that

[4] Rabindranath Tagore, 'Striving for Swaraj,' in *The English Writings of Rabindranath Tagore*, Vol. 4, ed. Nityapriya Ghosh (New Delhi: Sahitya Akademi, 2008) (reprint), 357.

[5] Rabindranath Tagore to C. F. Andrews, 9 July 1921, cited in Uma Dasgupta, ed., *Rabindranath Tagore: My Life in My Words* (New Delhi: Penguin, 2006), 359.

the inmost creed of India is to find the one in the many, unity in diversity. India does not admit difference to be conflict, nor does she espy an enemy in every stranger. So, she repels none, and strives to find a place for all in a vast social order. She acknowledges every path and recognizes greatness wherever she finds it.[6]

In view of social division among the people, being responsible for cementing the bonds, Tagore had taken up the challenge to bring them together regardless of their sociopolitical identities. The concern here was to, in other words, devise a design of togetherness cutting across social, economic and cultural barriers. Gandhi had the same mission, but it was desirable to the Mahatma for politically mobilizing the Indians for the anti-British campaign that he had launched. Unlike him, Tagore's aim was conditioned by his concern for universal humanism, which was likely to be severely impaired unless social division among the people was completely eradicated. Here too, the poet's ideas were exactly innovative, since the Upanishadic dictum of *vasudhaiva kutumbakam* (the world being one family) drew on this aspired socio-ideological aim. As shown in Chapter 1, the debate between Tagore and Gandhi hinged on whether political freedom was prior to the former's mission to accomplish universal humanism. Despite not having agreed with the Mahatma, who always privileged political freedom from the British rule, Tagore however considerably tempered his opposition to the extent of not harming the nationalist platform that evolved in the wake of the campaign against the colonizers. The point needs little elaboration, since both Tagore and the Mahatma held human emancipation as the ultimate aim of their politico-ideological mission. The difference that was visible was regarding the method to be deployed for attaining their exalted aims. A careful scan of the text that the Mahatma left for posterity reveals that he was equally concerned for building social harmony regardless of differences due to class, caste and ethnic identities. His battle for the eradication of untouchability is too well known to be mentioned separately. Nonetheless, as a politician, he was not persuaded to sacrifice the immediate political goal which was to be realized with India's liberation from colonial rule. As

[6] Rabindranath Tagore, 'Society and State,' in *Towards Universal Man*, ed. Rabindranath Tagore (Bombay: Asia Publishing House, 1962) (reprint), 65–6.

shown in Chapter 2, Tagore held strong views in this regard, since he emphatically believed that nationalism was ideologically restrictive and always led to the generation of enmity between one section of humanity and another. In other words, as nationalism was a device for fulfilling narrow interests of the powerful, the poet felt that it could never be a tool for human emancipation. Hence, the concern for political freedom did not attract the poet's attention to the extent it did to the Mahatma.

PHILOSOPHIZING THE NEED FOR EDUCATION

There is a similarity between the poet and B. R. Ambedkar, since both of them felt that education was an empowering device. It is well known that Ambedkar's famous slogan was 'educate, organize and agitate', which entails that education, organization and agitation constitute the pillars of his campaign for the recognition of untouchables/Dalits as equal with their upper-caste counterparts. Education was needed to understand how they were misled by the social leaders to believe that the inhuman treatment that they were subjected to was providentially endorsed. So, for Ambedkar, education was an important source of empowerment for the socio-economically marginalized and politically peripheral sections of the population. Tagore also held identical views emphasizing the importance of education as an enabler for those who remained socio-economically left out. He also justified his argument by assessing the nature of education that flourished during colonialism which was clearly an aid to the British rule. Instead of being a device for becoming enlightened, the English education was one of those means which consolidated the foreign hegemony in India. It was a system to produce sets of loyalists for running the system of governance supportive of the alien design. In a very fierce but persuasive manner, the poet thus mentioned that

> since our education bears no relation to our life, the books we read paint no vivid picture of our homes, extol no ideals of our society. The daily pursuits of our lives find no place in those pages, nor do we meet there or anything we happily recognize as our friends and relatives, our sky and earth, our mornings and evenings, or our cornfields and rivers. Education and life can never become one in such circumstances, and we are bound to

remain separated by a barrier. Our education may be compared to rainfall on a spot that is a long way from our roots. Not enough moisture seeps through the intervening barrier or earth to quench our thirst.[7]

Core here is the point that the education that was imparted at the aegis of the empire was futile, since it hardly equipped us to comprehend the social, economic and political contexts in which we were born and raised. This was an instrumental design directed at fulfilling objectives exclusively for the furtherance of the colonizers' partisan interests. As a result, there had emerged a schism between education and those who were at the receiving end. Tagore beautifully captured his sentiments by saying that the education that we received was never adequate since it neither provided us with a tool for understanding the surrounding reality nor generated enough curiosity for knowledge. Once the limitations were identified, Tagore engaged himself in locating the reasons. In a very perceptive manner, he thus suggested that one of the principal reasons for such an appalling outcome was the hiatus between what we learnt and the thoughts that informed the processes of learning. According to Tagore, 'the reason why we are never on intimate terms with English literature is to be found in the dissociation of language and thought that takes place at the outset of the teaching-learning phase of our life'.[8] As a result, the interest in learning both English as a language and the literature that evolved in the specific socio-historical milieu disappeared. The consequence was disastrous, since this disjuncture created a mindset that also remained indifferent to Bengalee as a language and also its literature. 'They have become', lamented the poet, 'strangers to Bengalee [by developing] … an aversion for it [though] … they do not, of course, openly admit it that they do not know it, and they cry it down as unsuitable for thoughtful work and unworthy of cultivated people like themselves'.[9] The argument is crystal clear. With the forcible endeavour for spreading English education that was devoid of the scope for its contextualization, the

[7] Rabindranath Tagore, 'The Vicissitudes of Education,' in *Towards Universal Man*, ed. Rabindranath Tagore (Bombay: Asia Publishing House, 1962) (reprint), 45.

[8] Tagore, 47.

[9] Tagore, 48.

British government created circumstances in which Indians were not only deprived of being acquainted with the thoughts that accompanied the English literature, but they also remained, in the process, completely 'uneducated'. What disappointed the poet further was that their inability to grasp the English language and literature was further compounded by their disdain for Bangla and Bangla literature. But one is also surprised because it was the same Tagore who opposed a complete boycott of British education. As he wrote in a letter to C. F. Andrews on 5 March 1921, when a crowd of young students came to see him at the onset of the 1920–1922 Non-Cooperation Movement to seek his advice on whether they should leave schools and colleges, in response, he was 'emphatic in [his] refusal to do [which] made them angry and also doubt [his] sincerity to the nationalist cause'. [10] The reason was simple, Tagore felt, and needed to be located in the widely hyped fanfare in Gandhi's zealous call for non-cooperation, which was articulated by him when he stated that 'the reason for my refusing to advise those students to leave their schools was because the anarchy of a mere emptiness never tempts me, even when it is resorted to as a temporary shelter'.[11] There is hardly a contradiction here, since, for Tagore, the young minds were likely to be easily misled unless they remained engaged with something or the other. With the call of Gandhi for boycotting British education, the possibility of being engaged completely disappeared, which was likely to create circumstances in which the kids had nothing to do. This was to be avoided, since the 'idle brain is the devil's workshop', warned Tagore.

What alternative did the poet have in mind? As is well known, he was the one who founded two schools, Patha Bhavana and Siksha Satra, and a university, Visva-Bharati, to articulate a system of alternative education. Guided by his idea to free children's mind from the death grip of a mechanical method and a narrow purpose, Tagore designed an alternative format of education based on generating

[10] Tagore to C. F. Andrews, 5 March 1921, reproduced in Krishna Dutta and Andrew Robinson, *Selected Letters of Rabindranath Tagore* (Cambridge: Cambridge University Press, 1997), 260.

[11] Tagore to C. F. Andrews, 260.

sympathy for all, including the environment in which they learnt. This is a stage of education which one reached

> not through following any reasoned-out system but through an inner life growth in which the subconscious has ever been bursting up into the conscious plane [leading to the consolidation of] ... a creative force which is acting in the bosom of the present age passing through repeated conflicts and reconciliations, failure and readjustments making for the realization of the spiritual unity of human races.[12]

Here, Tagore put forward his argument at two levels. At a very mundane level, he expressed his resentment against the system of education which did not allow the children to develop naturally. In other words, an instrumental education was of no use insofar as realizing the goal of education in its real sense was concerned. At a conceptually creative level, the poet devised a design which, through processes of trial and error, helped us link education with the goal of human emancipation. A humanist to the core, Tagore always upheld the view that under no circumstances was it to be undermined. After having laid out the conceptual foundation, the poet was now in a position to elaborate the scheme that he had in mind, which was fructified with the establishment of the schools and university at his behest.

As the above discussion demonstrates, there were two inputs that appeared to have inspired the poet to undertake his educational projects. On the one hand, he was of the firm belief that the prevalent system of education was an endeavour seeking to mechanically train young minds towards the fulfilment of pre-decided goals; this was therefore not a space where one could experiment with intellectually challenging projects. The children became the parrot of his *Tota Kahini*. Convinced that the English education was clearly mechanical in character, Tagore, on the other hand, was persuaded to embark on this project to seek to create facilities for the development of the mind as well. Drawn on children's curiosity for knowing the unknown, his schemes were directed to put in place a system which was both

---

[12] Tagore to Sir Patrick Geddes (a professor of Sociology and Civics, Bombay University), 9 May 1921 reproduced in Dutta and Robinson, 292.

innovative and enabling. While elaborating his views on 'my school', he thus mentioned that since

> children's minds are sensitive to the influence of the great world to which they have been born ... [t]heir subconscious mind is active, always imbibing some lesson, and with it realizing the joy of knowing. This sensitive receptivity of the passive mind helps them, without their feeling any strain, to master language, that most complex and difficult instrument of expression, full of ideas that are undefinable and symbols that deal with abstractions. And, through their natural gift of guessing they learn the meaning of words which we cannot explain.[13]

What stands out in the above statement is Tagore's insistence on children being allowed to be free from restrictions of chains in the form of fixing what they should learn. Instead, Tagore felt that if they were allowed to move around like free birds, they would acquire the training of learning from nature, which was always full of resources for curiosity. So long as the system of rote learning prevailed, warned Tagore, the natural creativity of the human mind was certain to be muzzled, which would neither be self-fulfilling nor contain any excitement for learning. This was most scathingly stated when in the same essay he further maintained that when children's minds were most inquisitive, they were brought to

> the educational factory—lifeless, colourless, dissociated from the context of the universe, within bare white walls staring like eyeball of the dead. We had the God-given gift of taking delight in the world, but such delightful activity was fettered and imprisoned, stilled by a force called discipline which kills the sensitivity of the child mind, the mid which is always on the alert, restless and eager to receive first-hand knowledge from mother Nature. We had to sit inert, like dead specimens of some museum, whilst lessons were pelted at us from on high, like hailstones on flowers.[14]

Out of his own experience, Tagore had learnt that bookish knowledge was not, at all, a useful device to learn; in fact, not only was it responsible for the rise of constricted minds, but it would also lead to

---

[13] Rabindranath Tagore, 'My School,' in *The English Writings of Rabindranath Tagore*, Vol. 4, ed. Nityapriya Ghosh (New Delhi: Sahitya Akademi), 518.

[14] Tagore, 518–9.

sterile thinking, since the children were tied up with routinized sets of activities which gave them no joy but sadness. Because he himself had realized this when he had been sent to a conventional Bangla-medium school, he did not want to subject the children to the emotional torture that he had undergone. What was most important was to create 'an environment' in which the development of children's mental faculty was not allowed to be undermined. With this, learning was to be a source of fulfilment and gratification, which was not conceivable in view of colonialism being a strong determinant of human behaviour in India. This was not the case. The prevalent education system was a deterrent to the evolution of the natural self of the children. This was attributed to the inherent weakness of the system which

> refuses to admit that children are children; [they] are punished because they fail to behave like grown-up people and have the impatience to be noisily childish. Their educators do not know, or they refuse to acknowledge that this childishness is Nature's own provision and that the child through its restless mind and movements should always come into touch with new facts and stumble upon new information. Thus, the child becomes the battle-ground for a fight between the school master and mother Nature itself.[15]

As a perceptive thinker who understood the Indian mindset far more clearly than any of his contemporary colleagues, Tagore hit the bullseye by drawing our attention to one of the intrinsic limitations of the education system that flourished in the wake of the British rule. Being raised in an atmosphere in which they accepted the system as axiomatic, the teachers failed to understand that the system of learning that they imparted might be useful for the rulers but was futile insofar as the taught were concerned, because it was not only restrictive but also a device to permanently damage their capability of thinking. How and why did it happen? According to the bard, by generating those values on which colonialism safely rested, the British rulers gradually developed a system which was nourished by the ser-vile mindset that had emerged in colonized India. So, the behaviour of the schoolmaster, nurtured in the atmosphere of servility, did not

---

[15] Rabindranath Tagore, 'The School Master,' in Das, *The English Writings of Rabindranath Tagore*, Vol. 3, p. 504.

seem to be an aberration. It was manifested when it was found that the schoolmaster

> wants to mould the child's mind according to his ready-made doctrine and therefore wants to rid the child's world of everything that he thinks will go against his purpose. He [thus] excludes the whole world of colour, of movement, of life, from his education scheme and snatching the helpless creature from the mother heart of Nature, shuts it in his prison house, feeling sure that imprisonment is the surest method of improving the child mind. This happens only because, ... as a grown-up person he thinks that this is the time-tested method [and was thus] not willing to [accept that] the adult mind in many respects not only differs from, but is contrary to the child mind.[16]

By being so candid in his assessment of the situation in which the teaching of children was pursued, Tagore left no doubt that the system was not only debased but was enough to completely kill the inquisitiveness that a child was privy to by being a child. The system that generated servility of the mind had its roots and drew its sustenance from colonialism. Despite being aware of how it developed, Tagore, being conscious of how debilitating it was for the children, embarked on his project of finding an alternative to the sterile system of education that was in existence. There were two serious constraints that he found which acted as a deterrent to the development of a child as a grown-up aware of his/her responsibilities. One constraint was linked with the environment in which freedom was denied to the child. As Tagore felt, so long as the children were not allowed to fulfil what they wanted freely, education continued to be mechanical. According to him,

> only through freedom can man attain his fullness of growth and when we restrict that freedom it means that we have some purpose of our own which we impose on the children, and we have not in mind Nature's own purpose of giving children its fulness of growth.[17]

In his perception, children failed to blossom naturally since in the prevalent system of education they were asked to mechanically follow

---

[16] Tagore, 505.

[17] Tagore, 508.

the instructions given by the schoolmaster which, being always directional, did not allow them to flourish in their natural forms. Associated with this was the second constraint, which was very scathingly articulated, referring to how the school teachers behaved when they interacted with their students. Disappointed with those who perpetrated torture in the name of being strict disciplinarians, Tagore was far more caustic when he condemned them as 'tyrant[s]'. These schoolmasters, in order to give 'outlet to their inherent lust for tyranny … make use of these helpless children and impose on them their own code of behaviour. They try to crush', he further added,

> their minds with tasks which are lifeless, which are mechanical, which kill the intellectual mind, the fresh mind. They impose all kinds of torture because these tyrants take pleasure at the very sight of it, and such a great opportunity for such enjoyment they can never hope to attain outside their school premises.[18]

Perhaps his own brief experience of being in a school in Calcutta was so nightmarish that his painting of schoolmasters as tyrants can be said to have emerged out of this. This might have been an important source of his conceptualization of schoolteachers, though one cannot totally ignore the wider concern for humanity which remained a critical influence insofar as his views on education were concerned. It was explicitly stated when he mentioned that the tyrannical behavioural manifestation of schoolmasters 'causes the greatest mischief possible in the human world',[19] since they expressed their professional commitment not with 'imagination and sympathy and understanding'[20] but with 'the machine-like behaviour of an executioner or a prison warden'.[21] It did not come to the poet as a surprise, because 'the tyrants, … of the educational administration … want the children to grow up according to the pattern that they have set for themselves

---

[18] Tagore, 508–9.

[19] Tagore, 509.

[20] Tagore, 509.

[21] Tagore, 509.

[in accordance with] the government's administrative directions'.[22] In two ways, it was complementary to what Tagore conceptualized as his form of education that eventually was articulated with the inauguration of Visva-Bharati, in particular, in 1921. First, he was convinced that without allowing students to think independently it would be difficult to realize the goal of education; he was opposed to rote learning, which he most scathingly demonstrated in his *Tota Kahini*. The tyrannical ways of functioning of the teachers was an impediment in creating an atmosphere of free and critical thinking, though it was obvious given the colonial context in which the government set the priorities for the colonized. Second, despite being aware that the scene did not seem to be very encouraging, Tagore was also confident that its reversal was always possible with the zeal and commitment of those who were persuaded to believe that they needed to be proactive in transforming the otherwise sterile system of education. What he emphasized was an ideational change to instil in the public domain that so long as the existent system of education was allowed to survive Indians would remain slaves to the colonizers, since in it lay the strength of the administration. In other words, as soon as independent thinking became part of the learning, the loyalty to the British government was likely to be seriously questioned, since it was meant to sustain Indians' political slavery to the British. In such circumstances, Visva-Bharati had emerged, in 1921, which not only set in motion a new system drawing on Tagore's own ideas but also illustrated how self-initiatives by the poet and his colleagues led to fruition. Seeking to realize the goal that Tagore had set for the institution, Visva-Bharati was not just an academic centre for learning, but it was also an attempt to structure human life in terms of the exalted value of universal humanism that appeared to have considerably lost its appeal, presumably because of the prevalent socio-economic and political context privileging human selfishness over the rest. This was most persuasively described in a 1924 public address in Calcutta by the bard, who stated:

> Visva-Bharati [does not base] its ideal upon any ulterior expectation, political or otherwise. Its one object is to help each student to realize his

[22] Tagore, 509.

personality, as an individual representing his people, in such a broad spirit, in such an unobstructed sunshine of spiritual expansion of consciousness, that he may know how it is the most important fact of his life for him to have been born to the great world of man'.[23]

Even at the risk of iterating the same point, it is worthwhile to explicate the concern that Tagore expressed when he founded Visva-Bharati as a centre of learning. Questioning the existing system of education, which Macaulay's Minute (metaphorically characterized as Macaulay's poison tree[24]) brought about in the early 19th century, Tagore put forward a meaningful alternative, which he articulated with the establishment of two schools, Patha Bhavana (in 1901) and Siksha Satra (in 1924), and a university, Visva Bharti, in 1921. The narrative of the evolution of Tagore's ideational world is symptomatic of a wider concern that Tagore evinced along with his like-minded colleagues. It was he who captured 'the nationalist-global' moment of a particular phase of his ideational growth in which he devised a specific scheme of education as perhaps one of the most effective means of developing an alternative amidst hopelessness. Unlike his nationalist compatriots, the poet contributed constructively to the consolidation of a nationalist voice which flourished not out of hatred towards others but by generating bonhomie surpassing one's narrow identity with partisan aims and objectives. The idea was not new, since it was being championed since the early 19th century, especially with the rise of Vidyasagar, Raja Ram Mohan Roy and Tagore's father, Debendranath Tagore. In their efforts, they drew on the glorious Indian past and also the newly acquired ideational inputs of the Enlightenment philosophy. The invented renaissance consciousness of the politico-ideologically alert section of the Indians appeared to have created a new template for thinking. It was informed by the memory of India's ancient and glorious civilization, as articulated by those who, along with their appreciation for the derivative Western discourses, also felt the need for unearthing the golden voices of the

---

[23] Rabindranath Tagore, 'Notes and Comments,' in Das, *The English Writings of Rabindranath Tagore*, Vol. 3, p. 494.

[24] Partha Chatterjee, 'The Fruits of Macaulay's Poison Tree,' in *The Present History of West Bengal*, ed. Partha Chatterjee (New Delhi: Oxford University Press, 1997).

ancient sages that the Upanishads and other Vedic texts epitomized. Hence, the Indian thought was multidimensional in the sense that not only did it contain elements of the ancient texts, but it also allowed itself to be enriched by engaging with the transmitted Western wisdom which came to India along with colonialism. This was a unique phase of India's rise as a voice representing a creative blending of 'liberal, conservative, rationalist, romantic, westernizing, revivalist, forward-looking ideas [that] all became part of the story of [India's] modern rebirth'.[25] By being born in a family which was one of the pioneers in appreciating the modernizing zeal of the era, Tagore imbibed this spirit which he gradually internalized. His effort towards creating an alternative system of education had its roots in his father's endeavour, which was translated into reality with the institution of a Brahmo school in 1888 in Bolpur, West Bengal. The course curriculum, it was not for a conventional school which paid a greater attention to the Vedic texts since it was believed that Indians forgetfulness of the past wisdom was at the root of their being reduced to non-existence in contemporary world. The trend continued with the inauguration of the two schools Patha Bhavana and Siksha Satra in 1901 and 1924, respectively. Based on his distinct ideas about educating young minds, the poet transformed the Brahmo *vidyalaya* into an 'Ashram Vidyalaya', which later became Patha Bhavana. Being a little disenchanted with the school as it became a refuge for the children of well-off parents, primarily those of Calcutta, Tagore felt the need for another school to educate the rural children, which was articulated with the inauguration of Siksha Satra in 1924. According to the poet,

Siksha Satra is the natural outcome of some years of educational experiment at Santiniketan and at the Institute of Rural Reconstruction at Sriniketan. Here an attempt is being made to give an all-round education to village children and provide them with training which will not only enable them to earn a decent livelihood but also to equip them with the necessary training and creative imagination with which they help to improve the rural life of Bengal in all respects.[26]

[25] Chatterjee, 91.

[26] Rabindranath Tagore, 'The Aims of Siksha Satra,' *Visva-Bharati Bulletin*, no. 36 (1936).

That Tagore was conscious of his role and true to his commitment is evident here. What he had articulated in the 1904 text, *Swadeshi Samaj*, was translated into practice once Patha Bahvana and Siksha Satra came into existence, though nobody took him seriously when he broached the matter, as he himself admitted. What inspired him to go ahead was his belief: 'if nobody comes in answer to thy call, walk alone'.[27] Furthermore, his critical evaluation of the prevalent system of education which was geared to serve the alien power also helped him build his alternative. While creating his conceptual framework for an alternative education, Tagore drew inspiration from the Renaissance thinking and also the obvious negative character of the English education that the British introduced for realizing their partisan goals. So disgusted was he with the prevalent system that Tagore compared the schools with factories. In his brief exposition on the nature of education, he thus stated,

> what we now call a school in this country is really a factory, and the teachers are part of it. At half past ten in the morning the factory opens with the ringing of a bell; then, as teachers start talking, the machine starts working. The teachers stop talking at four in the afternoon when the factory closes, and the pupils then go home carrying with them a few pages of machine-made learning.[28]

This was the most revealing statement that captured the equally dilapidating system of education that drew its sustenance from the colonial masters. As argued above, it was a systemic problem that needed to be addressed at the societal level, since the type of education that evolved in the wake of colonialism was largely due to the fact that it was complementary to colonial rule. It was obvious that the English education was, by nature, heavily tilted in favour of the colonial government for survival, and those who were associated with its functioning were unlikely to raise their voice, since their survival was also linked with its continuity. So, it was expected that

---

[27] Rabindranath Tagore, 'On Constructive Work—A Letter,' *Modern Review* (March 1921), Calcutta, p. 356.

[28] Rabindranath Tagore, 'The Problem of Education,' in Tagore, *Towards Universal Man*, 67.

there would hardly be a voice against the English education. On the contrary, on its existence depended the strength of colonialism, since it was the education system that provided the necessary intellectual nourishment and also support to the regime. The result was obvious: the Indian school system remained totally disconnected from India's human reality. As Tagore mentioned,

> the schools in our country, far from being integrated to society, are imposed on it from outside. The course they teach are dull and dry, painful to learn, and useless when learnt. There is nothing in common between the lessons that pupils cram up from ten to four o'clock and the country where they live; no agreement, but many disagreements, between what they learn at school and what their parents and relatives talk about at home. The schools are thus … turning human beings into robots.[29]

A clearly articulated vision, the above assessment represented how Tagore viewed the contemporary system of education that developed at the behest of the colonial government. The school system was clearly at variance with the societal needs but was organized with a narrow motive of making it useful for the continuity of the foreign hegemony in India. Visva-Bharati and its associated schools were formed with a view to creating a system which was not a factory but one that helped build an organic link with the surrounding milieu by being sensitive to the socio-economic needs of the people living there. It was an attempt to bridge the gulf between the city and village, since, for their survival, they needed to be dialectically interconnected. Tagore was drawn to his belief that an inclusive development of the country was possible only

> so long as the spirit of cooperation and self-sacrifice is a living ideal in society. When some temptation defeats this ideal, when selfish passion gains ascendancy, a gulf is formed and goes on widening. City and village then stand as exploiter and victim.[30]

That Tagore had a wider concern than merely imparting different kinds of learning is evident here. An organic thinker, he always believed that

---

[29] Tagore, 68.

[30] Rabindranath Tagore, 'City and Village,' in Tagore, *Towards Universal Man*, 315.

unless there was a radical transformation of the mindset, the socio-economic metamorphosis that he had in mind would remain a distant goal. Like Gandhi, who believed in village *swaraj*, which was a conceptual formulation of inclusive development involving people from both the cities and villages, Tagore too upheld the same view, because he was also persuaded to believe that without being interdependent, neither cities nor villages would flourish. This is one side of the argument suggesting that for inclusive economic development villages and cities needed to draw on each other for their well-being. There is another aspect that is equally pertinent to conceptually understand Tagore's socio-economic priorities, namely, the critical importance of being happy. As he mentioned, 'unhappiness, rather than poverty is the greatest problem'.[31] There were many sources, some of them were visible, some of them were not. Tagore might have hinted at the social separation between the villagers around the axes of caste, class and ethnicity that appeared to have compartmentalized human existence in India, which needed to be eradicated; otherwise, the clamour for the rise of all on an equal footing would remain elusive. Hence, the bard declared that the objective of Visva-Bharati was

> to try to flood the silted bed of village life with the stream of happiness. For this, scholars, poets, musicians and artists have to collaborate and offer their contributions. Otherwise, they too must live as parasites, sucking life from the people and giving nothing in return.[32]

A practitioner to the core, Tagore built a model that drew on his concern for common well-being. Implicit here are three significant points showing how Tagore's wider concern for universal humanism seems to have governed his politico-ideological preferences. First, it was true that poverty was required to be effectively addressed, but that was not enough to bring about happiness, which draws our attention to the prevalence of an archaic and also inhibiting mindset supportive of the socio-economic prejudices of a section of human beings against their fellow counterparts. Second, the task the poet had undertaken

[31] Tagore, 316.
[32] Tagore, 316.

needed cooperation from people from all walks of life. In other words, it was to be a joint venture in which participation by all was required. Since his goal was to bring happiness for all, the poet felt the need for involving those who had the capacity to make life happy. Given the poet's focus on human emancipation, mere fulfilment of physical requirements would not be sufficient by itself for the growth of a happy society; hence, he left a space open for all those involved in creative activities, like the scholars, musicians and playwrights, among others. Finally, Tagore believed that given what we received from society, we were also required to give it back in return. In concrete terms, what he meant was that only through contribution to social growth and transformation would human beings have a chance to be of help in society's all-round development. This was a scathing comment on those selfish individuals who always privileged their gain at others' cost. In a nutshell, being a staunch believer in cooperation, Tagore nurtured those ideas which, he felt, were tuned to create (a) an awareness among all regarding the importance of being interdependent on one another as perhaps the best option to meaningfully address serious socio-economic challenges, and (b) concern for those socio-economically marginalized and hapless sections of the population who needed to be helped. Only then would social progress no longer remain a mere conceptual expression but become a reality that was comprehensible.

While seeking to capture the complex argument that Tagore put forward in building his unique model of education, one is persuaded to argue that his ideas in this regard were not independent of his wider concern for human emancipation, in the sense that the latter was possible if the former was tuned to its attainment. In other words, education was critically important, but its role was considerably conditioned by the wider societal considerations supportive of or discarding the value from which they derive their sustenance. Being an important tool for socio-economic transformation assisted by similar kinds of politico-ideological priorities, education, for Tagore, was an important vehicle for human progress, and that was the principal reason why he established Visva-Bharati and its allied schools in a place which was away from the metropolitan city of Calcutta. Why did he do so? The reasons are not difficult to seek: Bolpur, the place where he founded Visva-Bharati, was a remote area with perhaps a very distinctive socio-cultural characteristic, in view of the presence of a large contingent of tribal people—Santals, in particular. This allowed him to understand the peculiar socio-economic problems confronting this area; further-more, the surrounding villages that he adopted once the university came into being were strikingly poor, which also gave him an open field to experiment with many of his schemes for common well-being.

The idea that education was meant to create a level playing field for all was consistently pursued in his creative writings, which insisted that unless the rural masses were taken out of abject poverty, the political campaign for freedom was anything but inspiring. Nikhilesh in *Ghare Baire* and Gora in *Gora* put forward this argument which the contemporary nationalists paid no heed to, as Tagore showed. Not only was he subjected to trenchant criticisms for his conviction in the need for human emancipation, but he was also challenged because of his firm belief that India was never a nation in the Western sense. 'India has never had a real sense of nationalism',[33] thus argued Tagore. With his firm belief in 'the ideals of humanity', he further mentioned that 'my countrymen will truly gain their India by fighting against the education which teaches them that a country is greater that the ideals of humanity'.[34] His unconditional faith in universal humanism was justified by his reference to his own conceptual universe which drew on a creative integration of finite and infinite; they were in

> harmony pervading not only my personality but my entire environment—something which cannot be grasped within the prison of sectarian intel-lect; in my father's heart, *Hafiz* (Quranic verses) and *Upanishads* were in confluence, a union of two opposed elements, as is necessary for the creation of beauty.[35]

[33] Rabindranath Tagore, *Nationalism* (Madras: Macmillan, 1950) (reprint), 64.

[34] Tagore, 64.

[35] Rabindranath to Brajendranath Seal (one of the famous philosophers of modern India), 31 October 1921, reproduced in Dutta and Robinson, *Selected Letters of Rabindranath Tagore*, 283.

Hence, education was meant to generate harmony by being respectful to humanity. Unfortunately, what caused disillusionment to the poet was the adoption of those means which were potentially dangerous to the rise and consolidation of values supportive of humanism. In the context of India's nationalist campaign, humanity was the first casualty, which was clearly articulated by Tagore in his letter to C. F. Andrews in which he expressed, most frankly, his disenchantment with the nationalist politico-ideological design. According to him, 'the same processes of repression and curtailment of humanity is often advocated in our country under the name of patriotism. Such deliberate impoverishment of our nature seems to me a crime. It is a cultivation of callousness which is a form of sacrilege'.[36] Here too, that Tagore was consistent in his commitment to humanity was reinforced. This also confirms that his views were articulated as a package in which education was an important component. As the above discussion establishes, Tagore never deviated from his politico-ideological allegiance to universal humanism, which remained supreme in his conceptual universe. Visva-Bharati and its associated school system were complementary to the goal that Tagore set for himself and those who thought alike. Qualitatively different and emotionally gratifying, the system of education that evolved with the foundation of Visva-Bharati, Patha Bhavana and Siksha Satra thus not only was a pathfinder but also set in motion a campaign contributing to and consolidating the ideas seeking to firmly establish a template for universal humanism.

EDUCATION IN ITS NEW FORM

As mentioned above, education was an effective mode of transmitting knowledge. This was evident with the importance that the foreign ruler accorded to imposing English education in India. In order to counter the insidious political motivation of the British, Tagore felt the need for an appropriate education to instil in young minds concerns for national well-being, which, the poet felt, was complementary to universal humanism. Keeping this in mind, Tagore thus set out a plan 'to save

---

[36] Rabindranath Tagore to C. F. Andrews, 14 January 1921, reproduced in Dasgupta, *Rabindranath Tagore*, pp. 344–5.

children from such vicious methods of alienating their minds which are fostered through books, through histories, geographies and lessons full of national prejudices'.[37] Aided by his friends from the West with identical concerns for humanity, Tagore further argued that this was a stepping stone towards building human amity cutting across social, economic and political barriers. As the aim was to build a centre for learning with the goal of ensuring 'the spiritual unity of all races',[38] the building of a platform where people, regardless of racial differences, joined hands for the cause was of utmost importance, claimed the poet. Here, Tagore had two purposes to attain. On the one hand, keen to create conditions for fulfilling his primary objective of universal humanism on the basis of racial fraternity, the poet challenged the clichéd understanding of the Western people who were prejudiced against the colonized, since there were many scholars and ordinary fellow human beings who came forward to be with Tagore on the same platform for realizing the goal. This conceptual design was also, on the other hand, an endeavour to generate zeal for creating an alternative centre of higher learning that came into being with the establishment of Visva-Bharati in 1921. The objective of education that Tagore had unambiguously elaborated upon was articulated when he argued that

> [o]ur education must enable every child to grasp and fulfil the purpose of the age, not to defeat it by acquiring the habit of creating divisions, and of cherishing national prejudices. There are, of course, natural differences in human races which should be preserved and respected and the mission of our education should be to realize our unity in spite of them, to discover truth through the wilderness of their contradictions.[39]

The aim was to develop a centre of learning where the concern for universal humanism was fully realized in circumstances where learners learnt with joy and pleasure. Hence, Visva-Bharati was not just a university, as far as Tagore was concerned, but also 'a great meeting place for individuals from all countries who believe in [India's] spiritual

---

[37] Rabindranath Tagore, 'My School' in Ghosh, *The English Writings of Rabindranath Tagore*, Vol. 4, p. 522.

[38] Tagore, 522.

[39] Tagore, 522.

unity and who have suffered from the lack of it, who want to make atonement and come into human touch with their neighbours'.[40] Not only was he clear about the socio-ideological goal that Visva-Bharati was expected to achieve, but his opinion regarding how it was to be realized was also well-articulated. According to the poet, in Visva-Bharati, 'our endeavour has been to include the ideal of unity in all the activities in our institution, some educational, so that comprise different kinds of artistic expression, some in the shape of service to our neighbours by way of helping the reconstruction of village life'.[41] This is how he conceptualized the institution that was tuned to the fulfilment of those human values which were conducive to the consolidation of humanity. Being committed to universal humanism, Tagore therefore wanted 'the institution to be inter-racial', for which he invited some of the great minds from the West. As a result, Visva-Bharati became 'a place where men of all nations and countries may find their true home, without molestation from the prosperous who are always afraid of idealism or from the politically powerful who are always suspicious of men who have the freedom of spirit'.[42] The task was made easier because of the enthusiasm with which students, Tagore underlined, worked for common well-being. They did not be seem to be 'nationalistic' but were certainly patriotic. For Tagore, it was a source of great hope, as 'our students were always in readiness to help others, always cheerful and equipped with a real human interest, in which as a rule our people are lacking'.[43] The distinction between being nationalistic and patriotic, discussed in detail in Chapter 2, is of profound conceptual significance. Nationalism bereft of concern for human well-being is like human existence without a purpose, which represents a clearly escapist mindset. Tagore was caustic in condemning those who in the name of serving the nation engaged in activities which were guided primarily by the desire for fulfilling partisan desires. Hence, he argued that the lack of human interests

---

[40] Tagore, 522.

[41] Tagore, 522–3.

[42] Tagore, 523.

[43] Rabindranath's address to the students of Santiniketan, 4 August 1938, reproduced in Ghosh, *The English Writings of Rabindranath Tagore*, Vol. 4, p. 602.

'has made our spirit of nationalism greatly unreal. Our nationalism is like a special dress', he further mentioned,

> which we don or doff according as there be or be not ceremonial or sensational occasions. We often clamour for things of no account whatsoever. Three hundred and sixty-four days we are unmindful of the true interests of our own country, and one day in a year we wake up to find that a great servant of the nation had died that day and we array ourselves and make speeches and hoist flags and then relapse into our own selfish pursuits.[44]

In his address to the students of Visva-Bharati at Santiniketan, Tagore, in an unambiguous manner, charted out a course of action to create togetherness on the basis of plans and programmes towards ensuring common well-being. He was upset since the so-called nationalists, instead of being committed to the nationalist goal, were busy seeking to fulfil their exclusive interests. The above 1938 speech is thus a directional input in assessing the nature of Indian nationalism that flourished in circumstances in which Gandhi reigned supreme as a leader. A careful reading of the speech reveals how Tagore linked the goal of education with national well-being. How was it possible? Tagore's vision was crystal clear. While developing Santiniketan as a centre for learning, he also associated the university with the surrounding villages which required to be taken care of for the socio-economic well-being of the villagers. Being a landlord himself who saw the suffering of the villagers from very close quarters due to the well-entrenched socio-economic prejudices besides, of course, colonialism, Tagore thus emphatically declared that 'I understood that unless the poor villagers were provided with decent means of existence, unless they were taught self-respect, unless their minds were strengthened, there was no chance to realize true independence. I could never appreciate the unreality and insipid demonstrativeness of platform patriotism'.[45] There are two levels to this argument that need attention: at one level, Tagore devised a design for inclusive socio-economic development with active grassroots engagement by the students; at another, he condemned the armchair activism prevalent at the time and exposed

---

[44] Rabindranath's address to the students of Santiniketan, 603.
[45] Rabindranath's address to the students of Santiniketan, 603.

the difference between rhetoric and activism. For him, Visva-Bharati was a platform to actualize his heartfelt desire for development for all. Hence, he argued that

> I have provided for you an agency for village improvement work which should go hand in hand with cultural development. I would wish you to come close to the simple life of the primitive people and poor peasants in the surrounding villages, to know their needs and thus gain experience of truly helping that part of your nation whose needs should be palpable to you, if only you would care to look round and see.[46]

By laying out a design of education that was clearly different from the English education, the activist Tagore created an alternative format which helped students learn by being actively engaged in activities directed at ensuring mass well-being. As India was village-centric, the poet held views which were identical with those of the Mahatma. The objective of Visva-Bharati was to accomplish 'the mission of realizing the fundamental unity of humanity through cooperation and love'.[47] Conceptualizing Visva-Bharati in the mould of the ancient ashram, Tagore devoted his energy to build the institution by imitating the spirit in which students had been taught then by their gurus in their homes, who accepted the former as integral to their families; the purpose was to make the students fit for any role that they were expected to discharge after the completion of their studies. For Tagore, education seeking to generate love, care and empathy for one another could never be

> a mere mechanical contrivance to spread literacy or a commercial investment in the name of enlightenment; [it was meant] ... to stimulate human interest and not to insist upon the clock-work precision of efficiency. With that idea in view [the poet] ... had made provision[s] not only for academic courses of teaching, but also for other elements of culture: music and art and dancing, seasonal festivities and opportunities of helping the neighbouring villages.[48]

---

[46] Rabindranath's address to the students of Santiniketan, 603.

[47] Rabindranath's address to the students of Santiniketan, 603.

[48] Rabindranath's address to the students of Santiniketan, 603–4.

Being critical of the mechanically devised education that the English education was, Tagore's alternative involved not merely academic training in various courses but also engagement with work in the villages, which would expose the students to the reality of life. Reminding us of the system of education that Plato devised for his gymnasium in Athens, Tagore, by insisting on including music as part of the curriculum, had shown how critical music could be in the development of human personality, since music had a soothing effect on the human mind.

ARTICULATION OF A RESPONSE

The formation of Visva-Bharati and its allied schools was a response, a powerful response indeed, which the poet articulated to develop an alternative template for education. As history shows, the nationalists, during the Non-Cooperation Movement (1920–1922), devised national schools and colleges, especially with C. R. Das' initiatives. The enthusiasm that the nationalists had shown was based on their genuine concern for building an alternative model of education, since it was education that was an important aid for consolidating a conducive voice for the campaign for nationalist rejuvenation. Given the well-thought-out plan of the colonial government to create a pool of clerks to keep the government machinery functioning, the need for an alternative education was strongly felt, since it was presumed to be a helpful device to realize the nationalist goal. It was also preferred because of its contribution to generating a design in support of the nationalist politico-ideological preferences. Tagore's experiment at Santiniketan was part of this endeavour, which put in place his ideas of an appropriate system of education most conducive for India to rise as a collective unit aware and respectful of its distinctive socio-cultural identity. It was an awareness of India being capable of being independent in every respects that was missing or not allowed to be appreciated as it stood in contradiction with the colonizers' selfish designs.

Being inspired to develop a system of education with completely different politico-ideological preferences, Tagore also laid out the objectives that he wanted to attain by way of developing Visva-Bharati as an alternative centre of learning. First, the location of the campus in a faraway place was deliberately chosen, as Tagore mentioned. According to him, he established the institution in a beautiful spot away from the noisy city of Calcutta, 'where the children had the greatest freedom possible under the shade of ancient trees and the field around open to the verge of horizon'.[49] It is not surprising that Patha Bhavana has been functioning since it was inaugurated in 1901 in an open mango orchard known as Amra Kunja. Why did he choose to do so? Tagore himself explained by saying that learning amidst nature was far more effective than learning in a classroom. As he felt, the atmosphere in which learning was imparted was critical than the content of the teaching. He believed that learning in a natural surrounding was effective since internalization of what was seen came to the students naturally and stayed there permanently. The bountiful nature was there to liberally share her wealth, and by being blindfolded by the English education, we were conveniently ignoring her presence. This was considered to be 'a sin to the poet ... if we pay our dutiful attention to mathematics ... while [ignoring that] the kiss of rains thrills the heart of the surrounding trees'. Clouds gathered and announced their arrival without any previous notice, which was a source of sustained enjoyment for those were privileged to have 'an intimate contact with nature'.[50] In order to reinforce his point, Tagore further said that 'to alienate our sympathy from the world of birds and tree is a barbarity which [was] not allowed in the institution'.[51] In a nutshell, Tagore's idea of alternative education was one that was nature-driven, since he believed that learning was most enjoyable when it was imparted in a natural environment in which the learners had a chance to see how nature behaved and also changed independently. The second feature of Tagore's unique conceptualization of education was articulated when the poet insisted that Visva-Bharati was to be a confluence ground for the meeting of ideas, values and impulses from the East as well as

---

[49] Rabindranath Tagore, 'The Educational Mission of the Visva-Bharati,' in *Boundless Sky*, ed. Rabindranath Tagore (Kolkata: Visva-Bharati, 2008) (reprint), 293.

[50] Tagore, 293.

[51] Tagore, 293.

the West. It was far more important then, since a wall of differences had been erected by the narrow nationalist zeal nurtured by most of the nations. This was most suffocating because, as the poet believed:

> the man who entertains no guests, living solely for himself, is petty-minded; this applies to a nation too [which, instead of nurturing narrowmindedness] should have guest houses where it will entertain visitors from all parts of the world, and national educational institutions are its best guest houses.[52]

This was the aim of Visva-Bharati, which he very unambiguously articulated by stating:

> we are building our institution upon the ideal of spiritual unity of all races [which will help us create] a great meeting place for individuals from all countries who believe in divine humanity and who wish to make atonement for the cruel disloyalty displayed against men.[53]

To avoid being misunderstood, Tagore clarified that by 'unity' he did not mean 'uniformity'. Unity was possible only once the differences were acknowledged. 'Only those', argued Tagore, 'who are different can unite'.[54] Reiterating this idea during his many addresses in China in 1924, Tagore thus insisted that despite

> natural differences in human races which should be preserved and respected, the mission of our education should be to realize our unity in spite of them, to discover truth through the wilderness of their contradictions. [Hence,] our education must enable every child to grasp and to fulfil this purpose; [that is] not to defeat it by acquiring the habit of creating divisions, and of cherishing national prejudices.[55]

His principal aim was to generate sentiments supporting the argument that human society flourished only through mutual exchange of ideas

---

[52] Rabindranath Tagore, 'The Unity of Education,' in *Towards Universal Man*, ed. Rabindranath Tagore (Bombay: Asia Publishing House, 1962) (reprint), 250.

[53] Tagore, 'The Educational Mission of the Visva-Bharati,' 294.

[54] Tagore, 246.

[55] Sisir Kumar Das, ed., *Rabindranath Tagore: Talks in China* (Santiniketan: Rabindra-Bhavana, Visva-Bharati, 1999) (reprint), 70.

and values cutting across geographical boundaries. It was forcefully argued when he mentioned, during his 1924 trip to China, that

> in Asia, we must unite, not through some mechanical method of organiza-
> tion, but through a spirit of true sympathy. The organized power of the
> machine is ready to smite and devour us, from which we must be rescued
> by that living power of spirit which grows into strength, not through mere
> addition, but through organic assimilation.[56]

Here, his argument is based on two interrelated concerns: on the one hand, he was opposed to machine civilization since it set in motion processes whereby human sentiments were easily sacrificed. He was also convinced that machine civilization separated one from another which was contrary, on the other, to his heart-felt desire to evolve together out of mutual love and respect.

With the establishment of the schools in Santiniketan, Patha Bhavana in 1901 and Siksha Satra in 1924, that the poet meant what he said became evident. The reason for starting a school, at the outset, stemmed from his concern to prevent young minds from being viti-ated, as he witnessed among the children who were being taught in the English education system. According to him,

> the minds of these children are shut inside prison houses, so that they
> become incapable of understanding other people with different languages
> and customs. This causes us, when our growing souls demand it, to grope
> after each other in darkness, to hurt each other in ignorance, to suffer
> from the worst form of blindness of this age [resulting in] a situation when
> children lose their freedom of mind.[57]

Here too, he provided a scornful critique of the English education which, being devoid of life, transformed human beings into machines by taking out their capability of independent thinking. Unless this was halted, it would be difficult, if not impossible, for the bard to accomplish the mission that he nurtured as one who was conscious of his role as a social being.

[56] Das, 51.

[57] Das, 71.

Appreciative of the unity of ideas through processes of creative synthesis, Tagore did not reject Western ideas as some of his militant nationalist colleagues did; instead, he was in favour of borrowing from 'the people of the West—their treasure of intellect which is immense and whose superiority we must acknowledge'.[58] Borrowing, however, did not mean total ignorance of the indigenous wisdom, which he very confidently argued by saying that 'it would be degradation on our part, and an insult to our ancestors, if we forgot our own moral wealth of wisdom, which is of far greater value than a system that produces endless materials and a physical power that is always on the warpath'.[59] The argument is far more complex than it appears on the surface. At one level, he was not reluctant to borrow from the West in view of the fact that it was an aid to perfectly understanding the human race as an entity; at another, being critical of mindless borrowing, since it led to intellectual servility, he also insisted on being aware of one's own socio-cultural traditions being spread out in codified texts and prevalent practices in their support. So, what he reinforced here was his philosophical belief in evolving a creative synthesis of ideas and practices which were complementary to one's understanding of universal humanism.

Questioning the imperialist drive for essentializing the national identities of those subjugating nations, he further argued that

> if the spiritual swallows up the material interests of man, the result cannot be called a synthesis of spirit and matter [because] the synthesis takes place only when they remain separate and yet unite. Only by admitting the individuality of men in matters in which they are separate can we arrive at their real unity in matters in which they are one.[60]

Here, the poet, by drawing attention to his mission, suggested that the unity of men despite being socio-culturally disparate was to be attained, since, as human beings, 'our sole object was to realize the Truth [which was essential] ... for liberating and revealing man's soul

---

[58] Das, 51.

[59] Das, 51–2.

[60] Tagore, 'The Unity of Education,' 246.

[and] ... the doctrine of man's revelation must be propagated through our education and practised through our action'.[61] This was a gigantic task which needed to be undertaken as early as possible before the damage became irreparable. How was it to be done? Tagore's answer was very simple. 'Only by honouring the mankind, ... we shall overcome the infirmity of the age [which will help us] build a new agree appreciative of those integral values on which universal man stands'.[62] By drawing out the limitations of the prevalent English education, Tagore now dealt with another distinctive feature of the system of education that Visva-Bharati devised. According to his well-thought-out views,

> the education given in out Government schools and colleges has unfortunately very little that is Indian, and most consists of alms begged from the West. So, the excuse is made on behalf of Indian educational institutions that, since they themselves subsist on alms, they cannot [afford] to be hospitable to guests.[63]

Implicit here are two points which are useful to conceptualize Tagore's thoughts on education. On the one hand, he raised the conventional nationalist point of view accusing the English education of being clearly 'partisan'. As argued above, it was a deliberate design of education that was imposed by the British following the adoption of the 1835 Macaulay's Minute that introduced English education to create out of the Indians a set of people who remained Indian in blood, but became British in taste, culture and expression by way of thorough training to that effect. There was also, on the other, a concern for being economically independent, which was essential to do things in accordance with what was required to be done for the sake of the Indians. This was a clamour for being sufficiently economically strong to effectively challenge the British authority seeking 'to coil-up Indians like a python'.[64] The indigenous voice was completely lost. In a very critical manner, the bard brought out his anguish at the adverse

---

[61] Tagore, 251.

[62] Tagore, 251.

[63] Tagore, 250.

[64] Tagore, 246.

consequences of such circumstances. As a result of Indians' intellectual servility and 'the voice of India' being muzzled,

> when the inquirers from the West come to India and listen at her door, they simply hear a feeble echo of their own western voice and it sounds like a parody! I too have noticed that modern Indians fresh from their study of Max Muller always sound like the European brass bands, irrespective of whether they are bragging about their ancient civilization or condemning and repudiating the West.[65]

This was a scathing critique of Indians' blind surrender to the Western mode of learning which, for obvious reasons, was heavily tilted in favour of what was appropriate for the continuity of the British Empire. So, Visva-Bharati was a design seeking to create a space in which learning in the Indian way was to be installed. Logically, it was a natural step for Tagore, who, being sensitive to India's rich civilizational heritage and, at the same time, appreciative of Western philosophical traditions, was keen to develop a common template for education in which knowledge from both these repositories of wisdom was recognized as important inputs for human gratification. In other words, given his belief that borrowing was not blind imitation, but a method of drawing on other's creativity, was a useful tool for intellectual enrichment and also a self-satisfying design for intellectual advancement out of mutual exchange of ideas and values despite their foreign origin. In a very poignant manner, he thus exhorted that

> great civilizations in the East as well in the West, have flourished in the past because they produced food for the spirit of man for all time; they had their life in the faith in the ideals, the faith which is creative. These great civilizations were [now] run to death by me of the type of our precocious school boys of modern times, smart and superficially critical, worshippers of self, shrewd bargainers in the market of profit and power, efficient in their handling of the ephemeral, who presumed to buy human souls with money and threw them into dust-bins when they had been sucked dry, and who, eventually, driven by suicidal forces of passion, set their neighbours' houses on fire and were themselves enveloped by the flame.[66]

[65] Tagore, 251.

[66] Das, *Rabindranath Tagore*, 94.

The idea is crystal clear. Tagore's primary concern was to develop a system of learning where neither xenophobia nor blind surrender to fundamentalist orthodoxy had a place; he, being a champion of mutual borrowing from both the East and the West leading to a creative blending of ideas, upheld a viewpoint which informed the processes that finally culminated in the establishment of Visva-Bharati and its allied schools in the early part of the 20th century. It was a venture seeking to generate enthusiasm among the children for appreciating the importance of being an integral part of a collective multitude. The task did not seem to be an easy one, the bard strongly felt, in view of the well-entrenched prejudicial beliefs that children were being regularly introduced to in the wake of their learning in the English education system. The outcome of their learning was bound to be tainted, since, according to the poet,

> the prevalent education has lacked idealism in its mere exercise of an intellect which has no depth of sentiment. The one desire produced in the heart of the students has been an ambition to win success in the world, not reach some inner standard of perfection, not to obtain self-emancipation.[67]

What is iterated here is the same idea based on Tagore's concern for creating a system of education that was sensitive to humanity, since he attributed the survival of human beings as they were to the strengthening of values and mindset in its support. In order to grasp the true nature of Visva-Bharati that evolved as a twin-campus university since its inauguration in 1921, it needs to be emphasized that it was an outcome of Tagore's unique conceptual belief drawing on both the Upanishadic ideals that he must have gotten from his father and his own understanding of the derivative Western socio-philosophical discourses. So, Visva-Bharati, in that sense, was not merely a centre for learning, which was usually the case in most of the universities, but a way of life which was to be conceptualized not in isolation but in conjunction with those complementary politico-ideological ideas and designs which were of great help in realizing what the poet preferred to christen as 'universal humanism'. This was

---

[67] Uma Dasgupta, ed., *The Oxford India Tagore: Selected Writings on Education and Nationalism* (New Delhi: Oxford University Press, 2009), 129.

an endeavour to bring together people irrespective of their natural differences. Visva-Bharati drew on this motto that Tagore explained by saying: 'our effort has been to include this ideal of unity in all the activities in our institution, some educational, some that comprise different kinds of artistic expression, some in the shape of service to our neighbours by way of helping the reconstruction of village life'.[68] It was needed to be undertaken for protecting humanity, which was being sacrificed in the wake of the consolidation of the machine civilization. Echoing the concern that Gandhi had expressed in his *The Hind Swaraj* (1909), the poet also condemned industrialization, which, despite having 'multiplied working capacity... has cut at the root of the inter-relation of town and village, and the town has become a drain on the village because it has ceased to make its return'. With the growing human greed, the machine-driven acts appeared to have been privileged, ignoring the adverse effect on mankind. Towns, and not villages, became prominent, leading to the emergence of a situation in which

> the artificial lights of the town are ablaze, - lights have no connection with sun, moon or star—but the light of the village has gone out. The dawn no longer comes with its obeisance, the evening with adoration. Not only have the waters of the village run dry, but also its heart. The festivals of life, which used to spring us as freely as the meadow of flowers, are withered to the dust.[69]

Attributing the human decadence to unbridled industrial growth that led human greed to structurally design human relations, Tagore also drew our attention to the fact that this was not so in the past, when human beings were linked with one another through care, compassion and empathy. 'In the past, at least in our country', argued the poet, 'there was not so wide a gulf between rich and poor, ... and wealth did not create barriers between man and man, but rather gave facilities for varied intercourse [which was possible because] ... the

---

[68] Rabindranath Tagore, 'To Teachers,' in Das, *The English Writings of Rabindranath Tagore*, Vol. 2, pp. 612–3.

[69] Rabindranath Tagore, 'Sriniketan,' in Ghosh, *The English Writings of Rabindranath Tagore*, Vol. 4, p. 401.

rich acknowledged their responsibilities to the poor'.[70] People being morally conscious and religiously dutiful, the interpersonal relations between neighbours were guided by empathy for one another. The situation was now reversed, since 'the *Anna* (food) that was once realized as spiritually great, having now degenerated to the *anna* of material self-aggrandisement, that which had originally been the upholder of the community has become its destroyer'.[71] Although it was debilitating insofar as human existence was concerned, it was a temporary state of affairs, Tagore was persuaded to believe, since the Upanishads conveyed that

> He, who is One, gives to the many races, according to the inmost need of each [which] ... the God had hidden in their nature. It is for man to discover it, and then only can divine gift become his wealth; it is within man's reach with his many-sided effort, the capacity of which is given along with the need.[72]

There are two important ideas that are pertinent to grasp Tagore's approach to education that was not merely confined to rote learning, as we have argued. His education was a package that contained concerns for human beings as axiomatic, especially for those who were at the lower rungs of society, which Visva-Bharati upheld, and the idea of serving the poor being as good as serving god was always privileged by the taught. It was made possible since, as Tagore elaborated, from the very beginning of their entry into the ashrama, the children were 'encouraged ... to be of service to the neighbouring villages';[73] while being engaged in rural reconstruction, the students not only came to appreciate nature but also human beings located in various strata of society, which allowed them to aspire for 'a higher freedom, a freedom from all racial and national prejudices'.[74] The aim was to create togetherness by discarding narrow-mindedness and partisan desires. With the establishment of Visva-Bharati, Tagore gave an institutionalized

[70] Tagore, 402.

[71] Tagore, 402.

[72] Tagore, 405.

[73] Tagore, 'The Educational Mission of the Visva-Bharati,' 627.

[74] Tagore, 627.

voice for one's engagement in rural reconstruction. Similar to Gandhi, he also believed that 'the villages are the cradles of life and if we cannot give it what is due to it, then we commit suicide. Modern civilization is doing it', warned the poet, 'by depriving the villages of life-stuff and draining away everything from the village to the pampered towns'.[75] By involving the students in developmental works in the villages, Tagore would fulfil two objectives: on the one hand, it would give the students first-hand knowledge about the socio-economic health of Indian villages; it would also create, on the other, a bonhomie between the villagers and the students by their being together for a cause. On the whole, this project was useful to accomplish the goal that Tagore aspired to achieve with the establishment of Visva-Bharati as a qualitatively different kind of centre of learning. For Tagore, Visva-Bharati was a design for uniform socio-economic development in areas around the university and not just a degree-giving conventional university. It was stated unambiguously when he elaborated his idea of 'a school' by saying that since he believed that education was empowering, he started night schools in the surrounding villages to teach the villagers, especially the Santals. Simultaneously, the students involved in the activities for rural reconstruction were also entrusted with the transmission of knowledge for 'up-to-date methods of cultivation and of fighting diseases [because he always believed that] … to impart merely academic information, but how to live a complete life is, according to [him] the purpose of education'.[76] There had emerged a clear division between city-bred *bhadraloks* (gentlemen) and village folk, drawn primarily on the contempt held by the former for the latter. What became a cause of concern was the fact that those who had, in the past, contributed to the villagers' well-being no longer lived in the villages, and

> their sense of values has undergone complete reorientation, [and, as a result] the village folk are no more able to benefit from what knowledge we have acquired or amassed; or rather, we are no more able to plough back our stored knowledge into the soil of their mind.[77]

[75] Tagore, Vol. 3, p. 645.

[76] Tagore, 644.

[77] Rabindranath Tagore, 'Sriniketan and the Villages: II,' in Dasgupta, *The Oxford India Tagore*, 132.

This was not a matter of coincidence but one that had evolved over generations, in view of the openly nurtured disdain by the city dwellers for those in villages, though they seemed to have overlooked the fact that it was because, underlined the bard, 'they deserted their villages that the villages have become a desert'.[78] Being terribly upset with this social hiatus between those living in urban and rural areas, Tagore endeavoured to create a platform where they could meet and learn from one another. It was not likely to happen so easily, since the roots of this division were not only well-entrenched but also carefully protected. This was the outcome of a mindset that drew on the idea that in view of the Europeans or white skins, being privy to knowledge which the Indians lacked, it was logically prudent to draw on what they taught. As the poet mentioned, 'given such contempt for their own village people, educated Indians prefer to learn about their country's history and society from the Europeans',[79] which was neither logical nor authentic, since those who were accepted as a true repository of knowledge had neither the capacity to understand Indian villages nor had had a first-hand experience with the village life. Still, the city brethren continued to cling to their fascination for Europeans, which, according to Tagore, was servility of our mind which needed to be discarded to avoid further damage to the collectivity that India represented. With the establishment of Visva-Bharati, Tagore appeared to have found an alternative that drew on his conceptual parameters for rejuvenating Indian villages. In particular, the Sriniketan campus of Visva-Bharati was founded with this mission in view, as its aims and objectives clearly stipulated that

> the object of Sriniketan is to bring back life in its completeness into the villages making them self-reliant and self-respectful, acquainted with the cultural tradition of our country, and competent to make an efficient use of the modern resources for the improvement of their physical, intellectual and economic condition.[80]

[78] Tagore, 132.

[79] Tagore, 133.

[80] Rabindranath Tagore, 'Sriniketan: The Institute of Rural Reconstruction,' Visva-Bharati Bulletin, no. 11 (December 1928), reproduced in Dasgupta, The Oxford India Tagore, 135.

Given the purpose for which Sriniketan was established, it was evident that Tagore was, in addition to being a formidable theoretician, also a committed activist. What was striking, as the Sriniketan experiment demonstrated, was how the poet translated his distinct view of rural development into practice. He was keen that the villages that Visva-Bharati adopted should also receive the latest scientific know-how for agricultural development; towards that goal, he also sent his son, Rathindranath Tagore, and his friend's son, Santosh Kumar Majumdar, to the United States for further training in agriculture, which they utilized once they returned to Visva-Bharati. The role of Leonard K. Elmhirst was, as discussed in detail in Chapter 3, was no less insignificant; it was Elmhirst who put into practice the poet's ideas of village welfare and village reconstruction in his Sriniketan project. Influenced by the poet, he, by being integrally connected with the activities based on Tagore's vision, helped build a platform in Sriniketan which gradually became 'a training ground, a home into which the homeless idealist can come and find new paths of self-expression ever held out to him, new ideals of freedom, of friendship in service, of attitude to the simple villager'.[81] With his engagement in rural development in the villages around Sriniketan, he claimed to have received 'the first real education [which was] practice-driven'.[82] Fundamental here is the point that it was Tagore's breadth of vision that inspired a bevy of stalwarts to make their way to Visva-Bharati and join him in his activist endeavours.

CONCLUDING OBSERVATIONS

Tagore stood out amidst the pantheon of thinkers, as he not only introduced a new template for conceptualizing human development but also devised practical schemes to implement some of his well-nurtured designs for change. What is most striking is the fact that

[81] Leonard K. Elmhirst to Ramananda Chatterjee, 25 December 1924, reproduced in Ajit K. Neogy, *Santiniketan and Sriniketan: The Twin Dreams of Rabindranath Tagore* (New Delhi: National Book Trust, 2011) (reprint), 271.

[82] Leonard K. Elmhirst to Gretchen Green, 6 April 1923, reproduced in Neogy, 271.

the poet provided a clear blueprint for all-round development which then did not seem to be the main nationalist priority. In view of his unalloyed faith in universal humanism, the poet set out his notion of education as complementary to his wider concerns. According to him, education, being critical to human development, needed to be linked with the prevalent socio-economic reality; otherwise, it ceased to be an effective design for fulfilling the goal that it was expected to fulfil. For Tagore, education, if conceptualized merely as a mechanical design, was sure to breed circumstances in which human beings became an inert object waiting to be guided for direction, which, in his perception, was a clear distortion of the objectives that it was slated to fulfil. In a nutshell, there are two critical points that emerge out of an analytical survey of the ideas that the bard articulated while elaborating his distinct approach to education. On the one hand, what provoked him to get involved in the quest for an alternative education was certainly his disappointment with the system of education that flourished with government patronage. In other words, the support of the alien ruler for 'the Macaulay's poison tree, the English education', created in Tagore a zeal for intervention in the field of education. It was therefore a contextual response as well. His conceptualization of education as linked with his wider concern for human emancipation bore, on the other hand, a testimony of his idea of education being a critical aid to humanizing human beings, a concern that was the outcome of the steady degradation of humanity in the wake of the consolidation of tendencies in its favour. Complemented by the growing fascination for the English education, the young minds appeared to have been alienated from the reality of life, and, in the process, they simply became a cog in the machine that the British rulers had devised for the Empire's well-being. The outcome was debilitating, if not devastating, insofar as the youths of India were concerned; not only did they lose their voice, but they also became partners, rather unknowingly, in the processes that generated views characterizing the continuity of the British rule as divinely ordained.

The establishment of Visva-Bharati in 1921, a continuity of the endeavour that Tagore had undertaken in 1901 when he founded the school Patha Bhavana, was a powerful step in pursuance of his wider sociopolitical concerns for humanity. Being a firm believer in the organic connection of education with the context, Tagore was vehemently opposed to English education, as it was not rooted in the Indian context, which was one of the reasons why this system failed to become a source of inspiration to the Indian youths. In his address to the students in London in 1920, he referred to the devastating outcome of such an incongruity when he said that

> the Western university is an organic part of European civilization and cannot be imported to India. ... the solid completeness of some of the new universities was like a hard-boiled egg from which no chicken could be hatched. To drive after a material completeness which did not belong to the essence of the university, was to squander money on mere money-bags.[83]

By being explicit in his condemnation of the British desire to export the system of education that flourished in Britain, since it lacked organic roots with the Indian socio-economic and cultural reality, Tagore created a space for alternative education on the basis of his arguments that exposed the inappropriateness of the English education which was completely hollow and therefore not adequate for discharging its true role. Reiterating the view, he further commented that 'many universities created by the British government have been artificial and not bearing the fruit'.[84] This was one of the reasons which persuaded Tagore to embark on the project which led to fruition with the establishment of Visva-Bharati, spread across the two contiguous areas of Santiniketan and Sriniketan, christened by Tagore. For the poet, the university was not just a device for transmission of knowledge within the confinement of a classroom, but it was also a design of a creative life of incessant search by those who were engaged in making human life better through their deeds. Tagore wanted Visva-Bharati to have

> great scholars to do research work and live their own studious lives, and to have their scholars come around them. These scholars and their apostles will create the university. The process of creation will be perpetual. They

---

[83] Tagore's address was reproduced in *Modern Review*, 1920, cited in Neogy, 265.

[84] Rabindranath Tagore's interview in *New York Evening Post*, 7 July 1921, cited in Neogy, 265.

must explore the realm of truth, and this studious life will creative force when the university will be built up.[85]

Projected as a centre for continuous knowledge creation and dissemination, Visva-Bharati was conceptualized as a platform generating enthusiasm for involvement in rural reconstruction. For the university to be true to its goal, it was expected to be a source of inspiration for generation after generation; in other words, to remain viable, the university needed to be continuously creative in its responses. Of the two campuses of Visva-Bharati, the activities that the Sriniketan campus had undertaken were illustrative of what a university should do to justify its existence. Characterizing Sriniketan as 'a research laboratory'[86] which helped build a bridge of sustained communication with the villagers, Elmhirst thus argued that it set in motion 'processes and the means out of which the society is slowly and painfully evolving its salvation'. Sriniketan was, in that respect, not merely an intermediary between the villagers and their search for socio-economic well-being, but was also 'a pathfinder through the maze of development [processes] and helping [the villagers] to arrive at a decision [regarding] the alternative courses open to them'.[87] Sriniketan was therefore a design of rural development that Tagore had conceptualized in collaboration with his like-minded colleagues, including Leonard K. Elmhirst. What is noticeable is the fact that his endeavour was not just confined to sharing with the villagers the new techniques seeking to augment production, but also included giving a human touch to the effort. In his words,

> it was not the kingdom of the Expert in the midst of the inept and ignorant which we wanted to establish [because] ... the villages are waiting for the living touch of creative faith, and not for the cold aloofness of science which

---

[85] Rabindranath Tagore, 'My Views on Education,' *Modern Review* (1921), cited in Neogy, 265.

[86] Leonard K. Elmhirst, 'The Application of Research to Rural Life,' *Modern Review* (April 1935): 506.

[87] Dikshit Sinha, *A Poet's Experiment in Rebuilding Samaj and Nation: Sriniketan's Rural Reconstruction* (Bolpur: Birupjatio Sahitya Sammiloni, 2019), 187.

uses efficient machinery for extracting statistic, the statistics that deal with fragments of dissected life.[88]

Basic to Tagore's concern was to treat villagers with respect and empathy, which was sadly missing with the increasing hiatus between cities and villages. Instead of a grand plan, he was persuaded to get involved in activities that were doable. In a note, he thus wrote that since his

> path ... lies in the domain of quiet, integral action and thought, my units must be small and I can but face human problems in relations to some basic village or cultural area [which led him to] stick to Santiniketan and Sriniketan [with the hope] that [his] efforts will touch the hearts of ... the neighbouring villagers, and help them in reasserting themselves in a new social order.[89]

A realistic to the core, Tagore appears to have been convinced that, in most likelihood, a grand plan remained confined to the level of conceptualization since the socio-economic milieu might not have been ready. This was a continuity of the argument that unless the groundwork was ready, it was difficult to execute a grand plan. In other words, what he hinted at here was the possibility of the plan being doomed to be a failure unless it was made realistic. Hence, Tagore's idea was, explained Leonard Elmhirst, 'to illustrate a few basic principles by winning the confidence of a few villages at first'.[90] Once the villagers found that, he further mentioned, 'they could stand on their own feet, once they had confidence in their power to progress, they were more able to say what they required most and when'.[91] Two ideas are prominent here: on the one hand, the poet was confident that villagers had the potential to be independent in their thinking once they were inspired to think and not conditioned by any

---

[88] Rabindranath Tagore's statement, cited in *Rabindranath Tagore: Pioneer in Education (Essays and Exchanges Between Rabindranath Tagore and LK Elmhirst)* (London: John Murray, 1961), 28.

[89] Rabindranath Tagore's statement on 21 December 1937, cited in *Rabindranath Tagore*, 38.

[90] *Rabindranath Tagore*, 41.

[91] *Rabindranath Tagore*, 41.

of the social barriers segregating them from the city brethren; on the other hand, what was also critical to Tagore was the construction of a society not fragmented by artificially raised social walls, which was possible with the reconceptualization and introduction of a system of education that was not exclusive in character but instead generated bonhomie among the people, irrespective of their respective socio-economic locations.

Tagore's Comprehension of Universal Humanism

A product of the Bengal Renaissance, Rabindranath Tagore represented a new intellectual trend in which ideas of nationalism, internationalism and humanism coalesced: politically, he was a nationalist, because he supported the effort challenging the British rule in India, though he did not always endorse the means that the revolutionary nationalists, and later Gandhi during the Non-Cooperation Movement of 1920–1922, had adopted; he was not xenophobic, because he openly declared his debt to the socio-cultural ideas that evolved in the West, particularly Great Britain, while defending his concern for political freedom, which was, however, according to him, not enough to secure freedom from the well-entrenched social prejudices segregating one section of the population from another. Since political freedom was partial in character, it was also not adequate for the attainment of human emancipation. In Tagore's opinion, a society remained a lifeless structure unless it was alert to the basic human values which were instinctive to it. In view of the rise of brutal colonialism complemented by the wild search of a market for its survival and expansion, the colonizers conveniently sacrificed core human values for their partisan gains. It was difficult to stop the juggernaut of colonialism that thrived in circumstances in which forcible occupation of territories neither faced steep challenges nor was opposed with adequate power and strength. A tragedy of history, this phase of human progress was the beginning of an era in which the exploitation of human beings by human beings did not, at all, seem to be an aberration. Instead, the conquerors were hailed as saviours, since they took on to themselves the task of 'civilizing the barbarians' in several parts of the globe. India was not an exception. Once it became a British colony, it was appreciated by many reformers in the early part of the 19th century, because colonialism was, to them, a design capable of radically altering the prevalent archaic social structure. An impediment to radical structural changes, the governing sociopolitical ideas were naturally complementary to what was then socially acceptable. Implicit here are two core conceptual points which are useful to understand what led Tagore to think as he did. First, Tagore's sociopolitical thoughts were contextual responses, since by the late 19th and early 20th centuries, the ideas supportive of national liberation had gained ground; soon, it was realized that the existent social structure, by being prejudicial to one section because of the accident of birth, was a deterrent. Hence, for Tagore, political liberation was but one step towards attaining the goal for national liberation. In other words, nationalism was worthwhile as a goal so long as it complemented human emancipation. Here, Tagore appeared to have upheld the Marxist notion of liberation of human beings from all kinds of shackles; human beings were to be absolutely free in order to become emancipated. The second aspect relates to his concern for internationalism, which is evident in his poetic expression in favour of inviting 'Aryans and non-Aryans in this India which represented a confluence of cultural influences from all over the world'.[1] In a similar vein, he was receptive to the ideas, despite their foreign origin, since they supported his plan for inclusive development. It was thus not merely coincidental that Leonard K. Elmhirst was invited by Tagore himself when he undertook the Sriniketan project. Furthermore, his appreciation of cooperative principles was largely based on his European experiences, because they helped him understand how togetherness had brought about radical socio-economic changes in the West. Not only was cooperation conducive to generating the urge of coming together for a cause, but it was also an effective means to fulfil common goals, as shown in chapter 3. Tagore elaborated his model in the 1904 tract, *Swadeshi Samaj*, and later in his *The Cooperative Principle* of 1928. There are a plenty of examples to show that Tagore endeavoured to derive whatever that was good from many sources, because he believed that the goal was prior to the means. Unlike many of his nationalist colleagues who did

---

[1] Rabindranath Tagore, 'Bharattritha.'

not always stand by him simply because he differed from them by being internationalist in his attitude and perspectives, Tagore's reconceptualization of the nationalist goals were neither xenophobic nor clearly deviant from the indigenous traditions and views shaping the agenda for social, economic and political changes under the aegis of the Indian National Congress. It is true that Tagore was never involved in the nationalist campaign as a street fighter, but his contribution in the shaping up of the nationalist agenda was of immense significance. The idea of nationalism that Tagore put across was neither xenophobic nor averse to borrowing from other civilizational resources, because at the core of his belief remained his unconditional faith in universal humanism. So emphatic was his belief that he hardly wavered in clinging to his ideological priorities, despite having displeased the Mahatma. In his reminiscences, Elmhirst thus mentioned that in opposition to Gandhi's attempt at mobilizing Indians for the nationalist goal, Tagore was reported to have stated that

> the whole world is suffering today from the cult of a selfish and short-sighted nationalism. India [as history has shown] offered hospitality to the invader of whatever nation, creed or colour. I have come to believe that, as Indians, we not only have much to learn from the West but that we also have something to contribute. We dare not therefore shut the West out. But we still have to learn among ourselves how, through education, to collaborate and achieve a common understanding because we are emotionally knit-together [since] ... we are all human beings.[2]

The last sentence of the above citation is most significant, for here Tagore explicitly stated his preferences for humanism. The difference between the colonizers and the colonized was certainly a source of irritation; nonetheless, it was not desirable to completely ignore the influences that came with the British rule. For Tagore, the political rivalry was an offshoot of a particular phase of human history that did not, of course mean that the communication that the Indians had with the British was to be severed, since we were all human beings. The idea that as human beings we had many commonalities with one another

---

[2] Leonard K. Elmhirst's 'Personal Reminiscences,' in his *Poet and Plowman* (Kolkata: Visva-Bharati, 2008), 6.

and we needed to build a bridge with them; it conformed to Tagore's conceptualization of universal humanism which he never sacrificed even when it was contrary to the mainstream nationalist approach to the Gandhi-led freedom struggle.

As argued above, the bard was a strong believer of universal humanism, which was always privileged over the narrow politico-ideological considerations that the mainstream nationalists upheld. The aim of this chapter is to develop this point with reference to Tagore's written texts. A perusal of the characters Nikhilesh in *Ghare Baire*, Ela in *Char Adhyay* and Paresh Babu in *Gora*, among others, unambiguously demonstrate that the poet was always alert to this concern while highlighting the weaknesses of the politico-ideological campaigns that appeared to have vitiated the nationalist vision by focusing only on political freedom. The chapter is thus an elaborate statement of how Tagore negotiated with many possibilities in a context when the nationalists were organized solely for political freedom. On the basis of a careful analysis of the issues that figured prominently in Tagore's idea of universal humanism, the chapter reinforces the argument that being a true humanist, the bard never allowed his vision to be clouded by a parochial nationalist inclination, as it stood in contradiction with his core belief.

UNFOLDING OF UNIVERSAL HUMANISM

It does not seem odd to argue that Gandhi was a macro-activist and remained so despite having dealt with many such issues. It is also true that before he became a pan-Indian nationalist leader, he successfully handled the micro-movements in Champaran (in Bihar), Kheda and Ahmedabad (both in Gujarat), where he was instrumental in mobilizing support for the cause that he stood for. Although, despite being micro-movements, these campaigns had national implications, and in that sense, they can also be characterized as efforts towards generating support for movements against British atrocities. Whatever interpretations one may offer, the fact remains that before he arrived on India's political scene as a pan-Indian leader, Gandhi was a Congress nationalist who evolved a scheme for political mobilization by bringing people in a locality together for a cause that cemented a bond cutting across social strata and religious denominations. With his success in galvanizing the masses during the 1920–1922 Non-Cooperation Movement, 1930–1932 Civil Disobedience Campaign and 1942 Open Rebellion, he established his reputation of being a macro-activist in the sense that support was garnered by referring to macro-issues, and these movements became pan-Indian movements with Gandhi reigning as the supreme leader. A macro-activist, Gandhi approached many micro-issues while being engaged in macro-activism. It was just the opposite as far as Tagore was concerned. The poet was involved in sorting out micro-issues which had macro-implications. In other words, by concentrating on how to alter the socio-economic circumstances of the villagers inhabiting the villages around Visva-Bharati, the bard's engagement in ameliorating the conditions of a tiny section of India's demography was confined to few villages. This was anything but macro in character, since his effort was consciously directed towards a very selectively chosen group of villagers who were in those villages which were adopted by Tagore to experiment with his distinct approach to rural reconstruction. Tagore's *Swadeshi Samaj* (1904) is an elaboration of the idea that he wanted to put forward. As he said, 'I cannot take the responsibility of India as a whole; but we could make a start with one or two villages. If we could free even one village from the shackles of helplessness and ignorance, an ideal for the whole of India would be established'.[3] This was a model of rural reconstruction which, despite being confined to a limited number of villages, would have ripple effects throughout the country, which reinforces the point that the poet's design had a wider impact since it was directional in character; in other words, to use the conceptual parlance, despite being confined to a micro-context, as it was about one or two villages, the bard's framework had had macro-implications, since the experiment had shown how it resulted in radical socio-economic changes at the grassroots. This was not an isolated thought. A perusal of his tract *Nationalism* (1916) also reveals that Tagore was not, at all, nationalist in the sense of being enamoured by the individual identity of nations;

[3] Rabindranath Tagore, 'City and Village,' *Universal Man*, ed. Rabindranath Tagore (Bombay: Asia Publishing House, 1962) (reprint), 322.

instead, he strongly argued for internationalism as perhaps the only way of human salvation. It was therefore not an exaggeration when he said that 'the idea of the Nation is one of the most powerful anesthetics that man has invented. Under the influence of its fumes the whole people can carry out its systematic programme of the most virulent self-seeking without being in the least aware of its moral perversion'.[4] Not merely an antidote to universalism, nationalism was clearly a threat to even the conceptualization of human togetherness, as it ran contrary to the very idea of nationalist separatism, which led Tagore to firmly say that 'the very idea of Nation has thriven long upon mutilated humanity. Man, the fairest creations of God, came out of the National manufactory in huge numbers as war-making and money-making puppets, ludicrously vain of their pitiful perfection of mechanism'.[5] What is reiterated here is the poet's well-entrenched views in favour of internationalism, which he clearly brought out by being extremely critical of the idea of nation, nationalism and national identity which could never be an aid to human prosperity, presumably because of the inherent limitations of the concept itself.

That he pursued his concern for universalism or macro-concerns is evident if one goes through what is figuratively characterized as the poet's talisman, which explains why he adopted the specific steps that he did. That Visva-Bharati was conceptualized on the basis of the Upanishadic ideal, *yatra vishwam bhavati eka needam*, where the whole becomes a nest, supports the contention that Tagore never shied away from expressing his preferences for universalism despite the hegemonic presence of views supporting nationalism. As he mentioned,

> wherever we go, we see man within his racial limits and not as part of one mankind. Let [Visva-Bharati] … be the one place in the world where we can mingle without differences in religion, language and race. Surely that must be the way forward to the new age.[6]

---

[4] Rabindranath Tagore, *Nationalism* (Madras: Macmillan, 1950), 25–6.

[5] Tagore, 26.

[6] Rabindranath Tagore, *Visva-Bharati Bulletin* (1923), 65, cited in Uma Dasgupta, ed., *Rabindranath Tagore: My Life in My Words* (New Delhi: Penguin, 2006), 199.

The idea is too vividly described to create any kind of confusion: as mankind was one, Tagore felt, the artificial wall separating one section from another was an impediment towards building the idea of togetherness irrespective of national/geographical boundaries. The poet further complemented his heartfelt desire to conceptually articulate his idea of universal humanism by making another Upanishadic dictum integrally connected with his theoretical articulation for the same. Visva-Bharati's motto, *Vasudhaiva Kutumbakam,* which means 'the world is one family', was the other conceptual pillar that his activism rested on. Critical of narrow nationalist leanings, Tagore thus argued:

> I have formed the nucleus of an International University in India as one of the best means of promoting mutual understanding between the East and West ... [by] regularly inviting students from the West to study the different systems of Indian philosophy, literature, art and music in their proper environment, encouraging them to carry on research in collaboration with scholars from across the word, [who are] already engaged in the task.[7]

It is clear now that in Tagore's perception, academic collaboration was an effective way of bridging the gulf between human beings located in different parts of the globe. The idea of exchange of scholars was a time-tested device and examples abound to prove the point. In order to carry forward the tradition that had evolved in ancient India for facilitating the movement of scholars from one place to another, Tagore's Visva-Bharati was a blueprint towards the attainment of that goal.

The above detailed discussion substantiates the point that Tagore devised a design to translate into reality his concern for universal humanism, since he believed that mankind was one and indivisible. In the wake of the unconditional support for nations to become hegemonic even at the cost of humanity, his firm commitment to internationalism was articulated with the foundation of Visva-Bharati as a centre of learning. Here, perhaps it is conceptually valid to argue that as Visva-Bharati was a baby step towards realizing his commitment to universal humanism, the poet's design was illustrative of his

---

[7] Rabindranath Tagore, 'An Eastern University,' reproduced in Sisir Kumar Das, ed., *The English Writings of Rabindranath Tagore*, Vol. 2 (New Delhi: Sahitya Akademi, 1996), 557.

micro-activism with wider implications, as he himself stated on many occasion. To further clarify the point, it was based on his belief that the example of Visva-Bharati was certain to inspire many others to imitate the steps which Tagore undertook as ideationally compatible with universal humanism. Conceptually speaking, it was a micro-step that had macro-implications, since many of his colleagues and detractors realized, especially in the light of the two world wars fought for nationalistic hegemony, how devastating the concern for nation could be for humanity. Here, Visva-Bharati, despite just being a micro-step that the poet had taken, set in motion processes for bringing about macro-changes involving people from all over the globe. One needs to add a caveat here, since the distinction between micro- and macro-activism is purely analytical, because in practice it cannot be so neatly captured, and also there is a difficulty in segregating the two types of activism into watertight compartments. As seen in history, Gandhi's calls for any of the pan-Indian movements had a character in accordance with the context in which they were organized, which means that they did not have a uniform macro-manifestation. Similarly, Tagore's faith in the earmarked Upanishadic ideals was a testimony of his urge for universal humanism, though it was articulated in the form of Visva-Bharati, a university located in a remote area of the then Bengal. It is therefore fair to argue that micro- and macro-concerns are dialectically interconnected and Tagore's endeavour was as much illustrative of his micro-concerns as they were of his macro-concerns. This is also applicable to Gandhi who, despite being a national leader, had no control over how the local movements were organized, though there was a well-defined, uniform agenda for all the activists across India whom Gandhi spearheaded. This reinforces the point that the distinction appears to have been blurred in practice when the micro- and macro-leanings of activism drew on each other.

INTELLECTUAL INPUTS

How did Tagore get drawn to the talisman which had its roots in the Upanishads? It was obvious that, being born in one of the established Brahmo families, he inherited a rich intellectual legacy that can be said to have significantly influenced the prevalent socio-cultural practices and also traditions. His was a family that always encouraged debates, discussions and critical dialogue on directional socio-economic and political issues. Being an open-minded person who was also well-grounded in the Vedic and Upanishadic texts, Tagore's father, Debendranath Tagore, was also free from the prejudices upholding social seclusion seeking to raise a wall of difference between human beings according to their caste, religious and ethnic identities. In other words, Tagore owed a great deal to his father who not only raised his voice against Hindu idolatry but also created a space for the free flow of ideas and thoughts, since he also believed that bereft of this no society progressed, if not survived. It is true that in his battle against Hindu orthodoxy, which was neither drawn on Vedic texts nor justified as divinely ordained but was injected primarily for satisfying vested interests, he was adequately supported by many of his like-minded colleagues who also felt inclined to pursue the goal of creating a discrimination-free society. At one level, this was an attempt to address the structural infirmities that had grown in Indian society, as they were protective of the selfish interests of a section of the population; at another level, it was also an effort to expose the inherent limitations of the socio-culturally justified schemes of division, which were deliberate designs to consciously segregate human beings around the axes of caste, religion and ethnicity.

As Tagore's own text reveals, it was possible for his father's generation of thinkers to persuasively argue against the sociopolitically prejudicial practices presumably because they also were mentored by many of their predecessors, who can be said to have pioneered enlightening ideas which brought about a radical, emotional revolution in the then Bengal. In his little booklet entitled *Charitrapuja* (1907), he specially mentioned the contribution of Vidyasagar, Raja Ram Mohan Roy and his father, Debendranath Tagore. As shown in Chapter 1, Tagore owed a great deal to these important social reformers of Bengal who remained prominent insofar as the history of social reform was concerned. Vidyasagar's role in legalizing widow remarriage[8] and

---

[8] In a petition to the Government of India on 4 October 1855, Vidyasagar, along with other petitioners, urged the legislators 'to remove all legal obstacles to the escape from a social evil of such magnitude which, though sanctioned by custom, is felt by

spreading women's education was formidable, and his account of the then Bengal's socio-economic circumstances continues to be of great use in articulating the context in which he raised his voice against social prejudices. Opposed to artificial social compartmentalization of people in terms of their socio-economic locations, the Sanskrit scholar helped build a persuasive critique of the contemporary inter-personal social relations which drew on the archaic and also prejudicial mindset. Vidyasagar, who was also keen to develop social amity, also believed that social schism was essentially contrived by partisan designs; hence, it was a deterrent to universal humanism. Tagore's father, Debendranath Tagore, followed the same path, since he also held the view that for uniform social progress, the artificial division in society around the axes of caste, religion and ethnicity needed to be eradicated. His trenchant critique of Hindu idolatry bore testimony to his politico-ideological views which he applied to reorient his religious identity of being a Hindu to a Brahmo. It was a source of strength to his son, Rabindranath Tagore, who held Debendranath in high esteem, since it was the latter who helped him understand the intricacies of human existence amidst various kinds of socially debilitating tendencies. According to Rabindranath, his father 'was the leader of a new religious movement, a strict monotheism based upon the teachings of Upanishads [which led to a complete] ostracization of Tagore family by others; it was a boon in disguise', claimed Tagore, since it 'saved [him] from another disaster, that of imitating our own past'.[9] Fundamental here is the point that given the social ostracism, Tagore was allowed to think out of the box or had had an opportunity to review and also intellectually assess the ideas that the Vedic texts, including the Upanishads, epitomized. In other words, since he did not carry any conceptual package, which would have been likely had

many Hindus to be a most injurious grievance, and to be contrary to a true inter-pretation of Hindoo law; it might shock the prejudices of those who conscientiously believe that the prohibition of the marriage of widows is sanctioned by the Sahastras, or who uphold it on fancied grounds of social advantage'. The part of the petition was reproduced in *Iswar Chandra Vidyasagar* by Benoy Ghose, Publication Division, Ministry of Information and Broadcasting, Government of India, New Delhi, 1971, 66–7.

[9] Rabindranath Tagore, 'The Religion of an Artist,' in *Boundless Sky*, ed. Rabindranath Tagore (Kolkata: Visva-Bharati, 2008) (reprint), 211.

he been introduced to some specific texts in accordance with what was traditionally prescribed, it was possible for him to start afresh in exploring what constituted the core of these texts. On the basis of the intellectual inputs that he received from his father and those around him, it was possible for Tagore to explore what appeared to him as worth exploring for realizing the crux of humanity. In view of his growing up in an environment free from restrictive instructions that were usual in most of the families, Tagore could easily pursue what he felt inclined to in accordance with his own socio-cultural priority. As he elaborated,

> I had been blessed with that sense of wonder which gives a child his right of entry into the treasure-house of mystery which is in the heart of existence. I neglected my studies because they rudely summoned me away from the world around me, which was my friend and companion, and when I was thirteen, I freed myself from the clutch of an educational system that tried to keep me imprisoned with the stone-walls of lessons.[10]

Implicit here is the idea that by not being blinded by derivative discourses, it was easier for Tagore to accept what he felt appropriate to quench his thirst for knowledge. He was allowed to explore the unknown because of the environment in which he was raised, and in creating such an environment at home, the contribution of his father was decisive. 'Through living channels of communication from all sides', claimed Tagore,

> he learnt a lot, … [and] it was a great thing for [him that his] consciousness was never dull about the facts of surrounding world. That the cloud was the cloud, that a flower was a flower, was enough, because they directly spoke to me, because I could not be indifferent to them.[11]

Here too, what is highlighted was the freedom that Tagore had enjoyed, largely due to his father being committed to giving him a free environment to enable him to think independent of any preconceived emotional/intellectual packages. The advantages that he accrued by being raised in a very different but enlightening environment were

[10] Tagore, 214.

[11] Tagore, 214.

useful for Tagore, who now had an opportunity to tread a path which would not have been possible had the home environment been different.

There are three important points which are also pertinent in conceptualizing Tagore's approach to humanity. First, it was his familial upbringing in an environment which was not burdened with derivative ideas of human behaviour which were largely prejudicial and thus not worth-imbibing. Second, having been baptized by an unconventional father, Tagore was introduced to equally unconventional ways of thinking, which made him 'greedy for freedom, not just the physical sort, but the psychological kind, which [created a zeal in him] to break the chains of school life'.[12] Finally, with access to the Brahmo philosophy that privileged humanity in contrast with the stereotypical understanding of Hinduism upholding mysticism and superstitious beliefs, justified as divinely ordained, it was also possible for Tagore to generate a voice of inquisitiveness seeking to judge whether the so-called axiomatic visions were truly so. As a result, there had emerged a powerful directional view that created a space of intellectually innovative dialogues and interactions between the believer and non-believers as well.

IMPORTANCE OF RAM MOHAN ROY

As Tagore admitted in his *Charitrapuja* (1907), it was Ram Mohan Roy who made a lasting impression on him, not only because of his zeal to stand against socially nurtured discriminatory practices but also because of his undaunted enthusiasm in fulfilling the goal that might not have been so easy to achieve given the constraints of the historical age in which he had functioned. Being socially deviant (in the eyes of the Hindu orthodox protagonists), he had the courage to challenge 'the customs, traditions and usages that caused and maintained divisions among sections of the people [impeding the rise of] a new social morality based on social equality and a recognition that the welfare

---

[12] Subrata Dasgupta, *Awakening: The Story of the Bengal Renaissance* (London: Random House, 2010), 436.

of man is the primary social objective'.[13] So, Ram Mohan brought a new wave of thinking that received its nourishment in an atmosphere in which many of his friends and colleagues joined hands with him. His primary concern was to treat human beings as human beings and with respect which was denied in view of the well-entrenched social prejudices; being a crusader against injustice, Roy was one of the first social reformers in India who raised his voice against the socially endorsed designs undermining humanity by devising means for permanently segregating the majority from the rest; this was anything but humane, argued Roy.

While assessing the contribution of Ram Mohan Roy as a social reformer, Tagore firmly argued for 'the brotherhood of interdependence of individuals as well as of nations in all spheres of thought and activity'.[14] According to Tagore, this was 'the principle of humanity' that Ram Mohan applied

> with his extraordinary depth of scholarship and natural gift of intuition … to social, literary and religious affairs, never acknowledging limitations of circumstance, never deviating from his purpose lured by distractions of temporal excitement. His attempt was to establish our peoples on the full consciousness of their own cultural personality, to make them comprehend the reality of all that was unique and indestructible in their civilization, and simultaneously, to make them approach other civilizations in the spirit of sympathetic cooperation.[15]

Reference to Ram Mohan's model of cross-cultural communication with awe and appreciation is illustrative of how Tagore admired the endeavour of this great Indian personality. By being uncompromising in what he held so dear, Ram Mohan had shown to the poet a path which helped him build his conceptual framework. This was elaborated upon by Tagore:

[13] Sachindra Lal Ghosh, *Raja Ram Mohan Roy: Pathmaker of Modern India* (New Delhi: National Council of Educational Research and Training, 1970), 89.

[14] Rabindranath Tagore, 'Ram Mohan Roy,' in Das, *The English Writings of Rabindranath Tagore*, Vol. III, p. 668.

[15] Tagore, 668.

Ram Mohan devoted himself to the task of rescuing from the debris of India's decadence the true products of civilization, and to make our people build on them, as the basis, the superstructure of international culture. Deeply versed in Sanskrit, he revived classical studies, and while he imbued the Bengalee literature and language with the rich atmosphere of our classical period, he opened its doors wide to the spirit of the age, offering access to new words from other languages and to new ideas. To every sphere of our national existence he brought the sagacity of a comprehensive vision, the spirit of self-manifestation of the unique in the light of the universal.[16]

Implicit here are three complementary points which Tagore made while explaining why Ram Mohan Roy was a pathfinder for him and also those who were also engaged in the same mission that the poet had aspired to fulfil. First, Ram Mohan Roy helped build the foundation of Indian civilization by (a) addressing its weaknesses and (b) generating interests in intercultural borrowings. In other words, by arguing that Indian civilization needed to be purged of its sources of social ailments, Roy sought to evolve a tempo for change which had been long overdue. It was not possible, he further argued, without being receptive to the ideas that contributed to the strengthening of civilizations elsewhere. This was a new argument in a context when the mainstream ethos was generally in favour of going back to the past. Second, Ram Mohan also contributed to those changes in Bengalee which, by being averse to borrowings, remained non-sensitive to those distinct social forces supportive of being less-orthodox in its vocabulary. For Roy, it was an attempt to take life out of the language which would hardly flourish if it became overtly boundary-conscious. Furthermore, in the context of colonialism, the excessive concern for one's purity might not be an appropriate measure to sustain Bengalee as a language, which is organically linked with those who spoke the same. Questioning those who castigated Roy for his strong arguments for taking words from other languages, Tagore appreciated his courage which was not only a source of inspiration for the youth but was also an eye-opener to the bard, because he was now persuaded to accept that borrowings were hardly debilitating for a language. Finally, Roy was admired by the bard for creating an access for the people in the

---

[16] Tagore, 668.

East to the repositories of knowledge located elsewhere. A universalist to the core, he was always in search of ideas that were conducive to universal betterment and well-being. There was a caveat too. It is true that Roy was supportive of drawing upon ideas which were part and parcel of universal knowledge, regardless of their place of origin. He was not xenophobic in his perception and attitude; he was truly a universalist who always endeavoured seriously to generate a model for ensuring the well-being of human beings irrespective of their locations. His vision was thus a combination of both indigenous values and ideas and those that emanated from the universal arena, which, according to him, led to the articulation of the unique spirit on which concern for universalism rested.

For Tagore, Roy provided him with the foundational notions and ideas on which he later built his model of universal humanism. Tagore claimed to have been benefitted in two major ways from what Roy suggested while making a strong case for not being xenophobic. On the one hand, it was Roy who introduced to Indians the ideas of the Enlightenment philosophy, which allowed a total reassessment of the prevalent interpersonal relationships based on the well-entrenched prejudicial values supportive of an equally archaic mindset. This was evident when Roy effectively challenged many of the age-old social practices, including Sati, that had hardly received a threat in the past. Roy's voice of protest against the widely accepted discriminatory social practices persuaded Tagore, on the other, to challenge those socially acceptable, but clearly deviant from being humanistic, in circumstances when they did not seem to have lost their sheen. By setting the ball in motion, the poet both created a new template for thinking and designed a new social manifesto that immediately received the attention of those who felt alike vis-à-vis social and economic practices fracturing humanity.

HUMANISM IN NOVELS

As it is not possible to expound the poet's idea of universal humanism by referring to his huge corpus of writings, here too, the argument shall be made by being selective in the sense that only some of his major literary pieces shall be scrutinized to defend the claim. On the surface, the methods may provoke criticism, which is addressed by drawing attention to the fact since the following discussion is theme-based, it is sufficient to identify a few of his written tracts that are critical to the argument being made here. In fact, it does not seem odd to suggest that by only concentrating on some of the main characters in some of his major novels, one can clearly show how Tagore dealt with the phenomenon of universal humanism. It is also significant here to mention that for the bard, human beings remained so since they evinced human sentiments that are articulated in various ways. Being committed to the core values of Enlightenment—love, care and empathy—the poet wasted no opportunity to elaborate on their importance in conceptualizing human beings as they were. This was articulated very unambiguously by Nandini in *Rakta Karabi* (1926), Damini in *Chaturanga* (1916), Ela in *Char Adhyay* (1933) and Gora in *Gora* (1909). There is a common thread in all these novels; it is a thread of love for others that cemented a conceptual bond between these characters. What is striking here is Tagore's endeavour to do away with the well-entrenched code of conduct that appeared to have emotionally crippled the Indians presumably because being colonized which was explicable since the political milieu did not appear to be favourably disposed to ideas and values on which the Indianness evolved by being true to India's socio-cultural roots. Nonetheless, the poet's argument that human values remained eternal despite attempts to gag them was neither exceptional nor made to highlight a unique point but was one that always figured in all his creative writings. Basic here is the contention that in Tagore's conceptual universe, the concern of universal humanism appears to have remained central to his written texts. With an example, the point will be clarified. For instance, Tagore was critical of colonialism and of the efforts that the nationalists undertook to raise their voice of protest during the 1905–1908 Swadeshi Movement, since they had no respect for the basic values of humanism either. Colonialism, being a design of sociopolitical segregation, was instinctively prejudicial to the colonized, which explains why the concern for basic human values remained peripheral in colonial India; similarly, the nationalists, especially those of the Sandip (in *Ghare Baire* of 1916) variety, by being indifferent to core human sentiments, had hardly succeeded in developing a powerful politico-ideological platform by involving the Bengalees irrespective of religion, which was one of the important reasons for Tagore to remain detached from the militant nationalism that India witnessed at the dawn of the 20th century.

Tagore's *Rakta Karabi* (1926) was an analytical statement to argue that love always cemented a bond among human beings. The cruel king in the novel surrendered to Nandini when the latter made him realize what he was losing by being entrapped in the quagmire of narrow human passions. Nandini was not just a character but one who epitomized Tagore's lifelong mission of championing concerns for humanism in which love for one another was a fundamental pillar. Ranjan's love for Nandini and vice versa was novel to the king, who prioritized the extraction of gold to become richer over other considerations. That he also had human feelings was evident when he came in touch with Nandini. Core here is the point that Tagore made to strongly argue that under no circumstances were empathy, care and concern likely to be submerged by narrow human passion for partisan aims and objectives.

Rakta Karabi is an articulation of how human greed for more at the cost of others contributed to the collapse of the system that evolved by denigrating the basic humanness of human beings—a product of circumstances in which values that were basic to human beings seemed to have completely lost their relevance as they hardly mattered when human greed appeared to have hailed without shame. It was a situation wherein men

> make use of men and leave out this elemental touch of kindliness, … when they crush and mutilate not merely victims but the humanity which is in themselves; … they use every variety of machinery to fortify themselves or their selfish ends against the dissolving power of beauty and love.[17]

The increasing importance of the ruthless pursuit of greed immediately caused devastation to human relations, though the poet, a born

---

[17] 'Red Oleanders (Rakta Karabi): An Interpretation,' in *The English Writings of Rabindranath Tagore*, ed. Nityapriya Ghosh, Vol. 4 (New Delhi: Sahitya Akademi, 2008) (reprint), 337.

optimist, did not seem to have been jittery, since it was, he was confident, a temporary phase in human history. It was very poignantly expressed when he stated that

> into a loveless world where men have ceased ever to be a evil, a world of "foreign investment" comes Nandini, the embodiment of that light that is beauty and love. She represents the highest truth in the human world, in the nature of man, a truth for which all down the ages, the great have lived, suffered and even died. She too is willing to suffer torture, a death, a mental crucification. In losing her lover, she loses her all to save all, the truth of love, for humanity.[18]

There are two interrelated aspects to the play. On the one hand, it is a story of how inhuman greed was responsible for the dwindling of human values and the simultaneous decadence of human society. In other words, lack of love, concern and sympathy for one another was an important factor of human decay. This is specific in nature, but there is a wider implication if such an indifferent mindset is allowed to flourish. The worldly endeavour for fulfilling one's partisan desires did not escape the poet's attention. Hence, he also castigated those who, by their indifference to the soil which made their life safer, appeared to have completely ignored its devastating consequences on human existence. It is thus argued that

> in mutilating the soil, that source of beauty that is also wealth, we mutilate ourselves. It was the same soil that these simple villagers had cherished, cultivated and loved, out of which they had grown and produced their needs of livelihood, food, clothes and implements. In it [the exploiters] were now digging their own damnation in service to the god of greed, of profit making, but no longer to the ideal of mutual cooperation and love.[19]

Here, the poet dealt with how the ruthless industrialization was at the root of dehumanizing human existence. It was inevitable, since human beings became prey to greed, which created in them the desire for wealth that became the only justified reason for whatever they undertook. This was one aspect. Linked with this was also the

---

[18] 'Red Oleanders (Rakta Karabi),' 339.

[19] 'Red Oleanders (Rakta Karabi),' 340.

well-entrenched view that this was inescapable, since 'they took for granted the perpetual domination of the strong, the continued oppression of the weak, and that, in the effort to pile up material wealth, they should, by their own fellows, be transformed from men into machineries, to the mutilation of their own humanity'.[20] The idea that the strong continued to oppress the weak evolved as axiomatic, and the urge for being wealthy by hook or crook was considered to be unavoidable. For Tagore, this was an aberration, as history demonstrated. The acceptance of what emerged as relevant in the context of colonialism was thus highly ephemeral, and with the ushering in of a new era, new ideas appeared, empowering the vision that was always integral to the existence of human beings as they were. What was thus visible was certainly the growing hegemony of the machine-bred civilization that was devoid of happiness as it belittled core human sentiments like love, care and sympathy. The argument was most succinctly stated by the poet:

> like the red oleander flower [Rakta Karabi] happiness too must be the fruit of love, of labour that is true, that is civil, that is honest, the fruit of human sympathy and consideration, and of human sacrifice in the cause of that great unity which is truth.[21]

Hence, in the end, it was the fine human sentiments that prevailed despite the adverse circumstances in which they appeared to be highly fragile and thus easy to ruthlessly suppress. Through Nandini's love for Ranjan and also her optimism in an otherwise very disparaging sociopolitical milieu, the poet conveyed that ultimately it was love, care and sympathy for one another which were critical for human existence. These were core sentiments that not only sustained but also consolidated the bond among human beings, despite intermittent and also apparently strong threats erasing their importance in doing so. It was articulated when the poet mentioned that even if 'the love-ties are ruthlessly molested by megalomaniac ambition, … Nandini's pervading influence will someday restore the human to the desolated world

[20] 'Red Oleanders (Rakta Karabi),' 340.

[21] 'Red Oleanders (Rakta Karabi),' 341.

of man'.[22] It was a source of great joy and also confidence to Tagore who, while expressing his feelings at the sight of Nandini's sacrifice for basic human sentiment, namely love, thus said that the joy of his faith in humanity 'inspired [him] to pour all my heart into painting against the background of black shadows—the nightmare of a devil's temptation—the portrait of Nandini as the bearer of the message of reality, the saviour through death'.[23] Even at the risk of repeating, two points need to be reiterated. First, *Rakta Karabi* was Tagore's persuasive comment on how the unconditional desire to amass wealth led to a situation in which human relations were easily corrupted, seemingly in a seamless manner. As an optimist and also humanist to the core, that Tagore was not to be persuaded does not require even a mention. Second, in line with the above argument, it was obvious that the poet would express his contrarian views, since his literary creativity rested on his unconditional faith in universal humanism; it was an exalted idea that he consistently nurtured in whatever he wrote to present his exclusive point of view.

Along with the above detailed analysis of how *Rakta Karabi* represented a seriously pursued endeavour that Tagore had already undertaken, the characters, Damini in *Chaturanga* and Ela in *Char Adhyay*, reiterated the point that the poet had already articulated through Nandini. In these two novels, relatively less complicated in their storyline, the poet focused primarily on the love that allowed Damini and Ela to make a supreme sacrifice for their love for Sribilash and Atin, respectively. Set in the nationalist context, these two female protagonists did not appear to have stated their feelings towards their beloved; it was not clearly articulated though there are reasons to believe that the poet hinted at their weaknesses which were reflected in their liking for those male protagonists. Willing to die for her love, it was not unusual for Damini to refuse to be cowed by any force while being candid in stating that she loved Sribilash and nobody else in the group. Even she knew her end was near; she thus expressed her love for him by stating: 'my longings are still with me. I go with the prayer

[22] 'Red Oleanders (Rakta Karabi),' 346–7.

[23] 'Red Oleanders (Rakta Karabi),' 347.

that I may find you again in my next life'.[24] The storyline does not seem to be very different in *Char Adhyay*; here, Ela, who was deeply in love with Atin, spoke in the same language when she knew that she was to be killed by the person whom she loved. Nonetheless, being a committed humanist, Tagore did not allow her to be revengeful, even when she felt completely clueless as to why this was happening. Even her possible death did not deter Ela from expressing what she passionately felt about Atin. She was explicit when she stated:

> I belong to you Ontu [Atin]; I shall continue to remain yours even after death since I love you from the core of my heart. I completely surrender to you and please protect me if anyone dares to touch me because this body is yours and hence, I cannot tolerate anyone, but you, touching me.[25]

This was again an example of how the love of Ela for Atin created in her the desire of complete surrender, regardless of what the other person thought. It may appear to be little idiotic since Ela who loved Atin despite knowing that his feelings for her did not seem to be unconditional as he privileged his commitment to the nation over others. Nonetheless, the author did not allow Ela to be swayed by these mundane considerations, which perhaps explains why she continued to remain devoted to Atin despite having had inputs that her love was not likely to be reciprocated.

These three novels dwell on specific human sentiments, namely love, care and empathy, which were never undermined by Tagore, presumably to make a strong case for his faith in universal humanism. Under no circumstances were human sentiments allowed to be sacrificed, because they remained critically linked with the existence of human beings as they were. Implicit here was also the warning that in view of the consolidation of forces seeking to belittle these sentiments, one needed to be careful. Or, in other words, in a situation when human beings began to nurture mean sentiments for their partisan

[24] Rabindranath Tagore, *Chaturanga (Quartet)*, translated in English in *Classic Rabindranath Tagore* (New Delhi: Penguin, 2011), 663.

[25] Rabindranath Tagore, *Char Adhyay* (Bangla) (Kolkata: Visva-Bharati, 1400) (Bangavda), 116.

gains, they were likely to be irrelevant; but that does not denote that they were completely finished. It was just like a sapling that grew into a big tree in course of time though, at the outset, it might not appear possible given the small and also tiny seed that led to what it became later. Although these novels were written in different phases of Tagore's literary career, they were woven together since there was one common human sentiment that ran through them. Nandini in *Rakta Karabi* represented a fresh wave amidst attempts at denigrating humanity, while Ela and Damini held views that drew their sustenance from their unconditional love for human beings. These women protagonists had also shown the strength of their character even when they were suffering, which was also an attempt to demonstrate how varied human sentiments were around the gender axis. Women were projected to have had the instinctive calibre to absorb shocks and hardships or distress, which their male counterparts lacked. Fundamental here are two ideas. On the one hand, Tagore clearly demarcated a definite space for human sentiments which always survived, presumably because they were integral to human civilization. On the other hand, he also added a note of optimism, because core human values, believed the poet, never lost out despite the increasing strength of the contrarian tendencies that were seemingly overpowering and hegemonic on the surface.

The novel *Gora* belongs to a different genre, since there were many issues, familial, national and also international, that got entangled while Tagore endeavoured to conceptualize human sentiments as perhaps the only means of supporting the rise and consolidation of humanity amidst a crisis. Gora, in the narrative, was the principal protagonist who, despite his foreign origin (which he discovered almost at the end of the novel), was drawn to Hindu orthodoxy, which however was not a deterrent for him to emerge as a staunch nationalist with concerns for humanity. The main protagonist, he was conceptualized as an orthodox Hindu who also had a nationalist bent of mind which drew on his concern for the hapless Indians because of their mental servility to the values and mores that informed the British Empire. Being critical of colonialism and unable to appreciate the servile Indian mindset, Gora 'seethed with indignation at the arrogance of the educated Bengalee who could invite a foreigner to join him in mocking at the plight of the masses'.[26] While accusing the Bengalees of being indifferent to India's rich cultural heritage, he endeavoured to generate enthusiasm for the nationalist cause by drawing the attention of the participants towards the ancient ideals which appeared to have made India a confident one as it was then. It was Tagore's voice, which was expressed when the poet articulated his feelings by saying that

> Gora's heart seemed to burst with anguish at the deep-seated, nationwide ignorance at the roots of his countrymen's submission to all sorts of humiliation and ill-treatment, for even when abused like animals, all of them would accept it as natural and appropriate [and] ... what galled him most was the educated class' indifference towards the nation's degradation and misery.[27]

That the Bengalee educated middle class was indifferent to the national heritage and was always appreciative of what they had derived from the British culture was articulated unambiguously in his novel, *Nastanirh* (*The Broken Nest*), published in 1901. Here one of the main protagonist, Bhupati, held the similar views in his regularly published political newspaper which contained scathing critiques of those who busked on the glory of being more English than the royal family of Britain. It was therefore surprising, as the novel shows, that there was a grand celebration of the victory of the liberal party in 1899 in middle-class Bengalee households, since it meant a radical change in British politics. This sentiment seems to have been prevalent through the 19th century, which Tagore captured well in *Gora*. Along with a loathing criticism of the attitude of the educated Bengalees, Gora also placed himself as one of the Indians who was proud of his unique socio-cultural roots that he had by virtue of being born as an Indian. To defend his point, he thus argued:

> I have glimpsed a vast, profound unity in the manifestation and multiple endeavours of *Bharatvarsha*, a unity that drives me wild with joy. Rejoicing at such unity, I have no hesitation in mingling with the most ignorant

[26] Rabindranath Tagore, *Gora*, translated in English in *Classic Rabindranath Tagore*, 319.

[27] Tagore, 319.

of *Bharatvarsha*'s inhabitants, taking my place beside them in the dust. Some understand this message of *Bharatvarsha*, others don't, but never mind—In am one with everyone in *Bharatvarsha*—they are all my own people—within all of them, I have no doubt, eternal *Bharatvarsha*'s concealed presence is constantly at work.[28]

What was sought to be articulated and shown was Gora's firm commitment to the people of India who hardly remained in the reckoning while devising plans and programmes for India's sociopolitical rejuvenation. It was made clear that so long as these sections remained peripheral in all respects, the vision that evolved would only to be highly vitiated. On the surface, it was a concern for nationalist rejuvenation; the underlying sense was far deeper in the sense that it was also a call challenging the well-entrenched social and economic prejudices separating the vast majority from the miniscule minority of the educated middle class. This was therefore a call that drew its inspiration from the concern for universal humanism. The idea that the care for the inhabitants of *Bharatvarsha* regardless of caste, class and community was tantamount to serving humanity. What Gora referred to here was unambiguously elaborated by Paresh Babu, one of the learned companions that he always looked up to. As Paresh Babu most agitatedly expressed, 'when I see with my own eyes that people in our country are treating other people with intolerable contempt, tearing us apart, how can I in such circumstances remain indifferent'.[29] For him, the nationalist endeavour for freedom made no sense unless it was accompanied by an effective attack on those artificial devices which resulted in socio-economic divisions in the country. That was anything but desirable, exhorted Paresh Babu, while suggesting that the concern for equality was not just our heart's call but needed to firmly established in our conceptual university, which meant that it was not just an emotional issue. 'Equality concerns knowledge, not emotions of the heart', thus said Paresh Babu, who defended his point by attributing the continuity of discriminatory practices to the lack of awareness of the adverse consequences of social division on the rise and consolidation of humane values in India. In other words,

[28] Tagore, 377.

[29] Tagore, 391.

due to the lack of awareness of equality being a device for building togetherness, discrimination was being practised as normal. As he said, 'despite the claim of being devoted to the exalted values of egalitarian philosophy, [the same educated class] happily accept the embargo on the lower caste's entry into the temples [which stands in contradiction with] what they endorse philosophically'.[30] Hence, he ended his argument by sarcastically asking: 'if our country does not permit even equality of worship, how does it matter whether such ideas exist in philosophy'?[31] This is the most poignant of all the statements in *Gora,* because here the poet exposed the limitations of the contemporary nationalist thinking which, instead of openly challenging the divisive social and economic practices, took refuge in the high-sounding philosophical discourses that remained vacuous unless definite steps were consciously taken to implement the ideas which were tuned to the attainment of universal humanism.

That Gora was a humanist to the core was evident in his expressed views, which were based on his understanding of the reality that he confronted in the metropolitan city of Calcutta. His colleagues shed tears at the agony and distress of those at the lower rungs of the Indian society, though these were mere verbal expressions and were miles away from fulfilling the objective by deeds. As one who always believed in practising what he believed in, Gora decided to undertake a journey into India's hinterland, which, he thought, was the only way to see the real *Bharatvarsha.* With his visit to the villages away from Calcutta, 'for the first time Gora saw what [his] country is like, outside the social worlds of the respectable bhadraloks, the educated and the Kolkata dwellers'.[32] The real India had dawned before him. This caught him by surprise when he saw

how fragmented, narrow-minded and feeble was this vast, concealed realm of rural *Bharatvarsha*—how utterly unaware of its own power, how completely ignorant and indifferent about its own interests! How extreme were the social indifferences between places only ... ten to fifteen miles

[30] Tagore, 391.

[31] Tagore, 391.

[32] Tagore, 400.

apart—how many self-created and imaginary obstacles constrained the land from advancing in the world's giant workspace—how much importance it attached to trivialities, how moribund it had grown, clinging to every prejudice and superstition—how somnolent was its mind, how faint its heart, how feeble its efforts![33]

With his introduction to the real India, Gora realized how important it was to effectively shake the foundation on which the so-called Indian civilization rested. The India that Gora confronted, contrary to the Upanishadic Ideals of *yatra vishwam bhavati eka needam* (where the world becomes a nest) and *Vasudhaiva Kutumbakam* (the world is one family), was a complete mismatch with how he visualized his idea of India. Keen to attain universal humanism, which knew no division around any of the artificial/deliberately chosen devices to fulfil partisan aims and objectives, Tagore, through Gora, expressed his own understanding of the reality which he was introduced to during his many trips to India's rural areas. According to him, India's political independence was necessary but not a sufficient condition for realizing the ultimate goal of human emancipation; there were obvious social and economic constraints that appeared to have clearly conditioned the human mind across the length and breadth of India. One needs to add a caveat here. Tagore was not opposed to the endeavours that the nationalists had undertaken to politically liberate India. With his intervention, he simply added a new dimension that did not appear to have received adequate attention during the nationalist struggle for freedom. Persuaded to hold the view that mere liberation from the British rule was not enough, because of the well-entrenched socio-economic schism resulting in permanent compartmentalization of people around the axes of caste, class and ethnicity, Tagore did not feel inclined to be part of the 1905–1908 Swadeshi Movement in Bengal, since it never took into account the view that without eradicating social divisions among human beings, political freedom was meaningless. Even during Gandhi's Non-Cooperation Movement (1920–1922), Tagore expressed his displeasure, because the boycott of schools, colleges and other institutions was likely to cause chaos in society, which was a deterrent to the wider concern of common well-being;

---

[33] Tagore, 400.

furthermore, the burning of foreign clothes was also a self-defeating design, since it caused an alienation between the rich and poor who were not in a position to buy expensive home-spun Indian clothes. In 'The Call for Truth', he elaborated why he deviated from what the Mahatma stood for in this regard. In response to Gandhi's 'command to burn foreign clothes',[34] Tagore openly opposed him because it was an imposition on the hapless mass, seeking to inject 'the terrible habit of obeying orders'.[35] Furthermore, he also felt that the clothes to be burnt

> are not mine, but belong to those who most sorely need them. If those who are going naked [had] ... given us the mandate to burn, it would, at least, have been a case self-immolation and the crime of incendiarism would not lie at our door. But how can we', asked the poet, 'expiate the sin of the forcible destruction of clothes which might have to women whose nakedness is actually keeping them prisoners, unable to stir out of the privacy of their homes?[36]

By forcing the poor to accept the nationalist dictation, the Gandhi-led mainstream nationalist campaign unfortunately helped create further estrangement of the poor from the struggle for freedom. As per Tagore, instead of bringing people together, being myopic in their vision, the nationalists failed to gauge the adverse consequences of such a strategy on the campaign itself. Historically speaking, one of the reasons for the Muslims to support the divisive campaign for a separate Muslim land was located in the Congress-misdirected attempt to pursue the nationalist goal by adopting a political template which appeared to have paid less attention to generating bonhomie among the people irrespective of their socio-economic locations.[37] There was, however, a silver lining which encouraged Gora to believe that there remained an inner strength which made India what it had been in the past. In one of the villages, Gora saw humanity in action when the local Hindu

---

[34] Rabindranath Tagore, 'The Call for Truth,' in Das, *The English Writings of Rabindranath Tagore*, Vol. 3, 423.

[35] Tagore, 423.

[36] Tagore, 423.

[37] I have pursued this argument in my *The Partition of Bengal and Assam, 1932–47: Contour of Freedom* (London and New York: Routledge, 2004).

barber took care of Pharu's wife and his son, Tamiz, once Pharu was incarcerated following his involvement in 'thrashing the police after being harassed by the indigo planters'.[38] It was an eye-opener for Gora, since he realized that for the Hindu barber too, the concern for humanity was prior to any other consideration; it was not agreeable to the barber to allow them to starve while Pharu was in jail for a right cause. Here, religion was not an impediment for the coming together of a Hindu barber and his Muslim brethren. In order to provide a contrast, Tagore referred to the selfishness of Madhab Chatujje, the local administrator, who, being obsessed with his religious and caste identity, not only stayed away from helping the family in distress but abused the Hindu barber for his help to them. Gora was clueless and ashamed at accepting his hospitality when he visited the village. Terribly anguished by Chatujje's attitude, Gora thought:

> [w]hat a great heresy we are committing in *Bharatvarsha*, making purity of appearances alone! It would save my caste purity to dine at the home of a man [Madhab Chatujje] who torments Muslims by creating all sorts of trouble, but I would lose my caste status in the home of a person who accepts such torment to protect a Muslim boy, and is even ready to suffer social condemnation for it.[39]

This was the most revealing comment, clearly explicating Tagore's conceptualization of universal humanism, the roots of which are to be located in human concerns for the core values on which humanity rests. That the Hindu barber came forward to take care of Pharu's wife and his son, Tamiz, ignoring the social denunciation, was testimony of how humanism was privileged in adverse circumstances. It was beyond Gora's comprehension that for protecting his caste purity, the acceptance of the wicked Chatujje's hospitality was preferable to that of the Hindu barber who was kind and morally upright. Here, we see Tagore raising his voice against the hypocritical and moralistic pretensions of caste Hindus and also demonstrating the need for the consolidation of universal humanism that overrode partisan interests.

[38] Tagore, *Gora*, 401.

[39] Tagore, 403.

IDEATIONAL ARTICULATION OF
UNIVERSAL HUMANISM

Tagore always remained a high priest of universal humanism, because he believed that unless human beings were attentive to their role as human beings, the future of humanity was bleak. An optimist to the core, the poet also supported the idea that the incessant attack on humanity was sure to devastatingly harm, if not completely uproot, the finer values on which it rested. Under no circumstances, tendencies inhibiting, to a great extent, the rise and consolidation of humanity were to be allowed, not for anything else but for the sake of the continuity of human beings as human beings. Humanity survived and grew in leaps and bounds out of 'the power of sympathy and the power of self-sacrifice'. Tagore was not uncertain about the future of humanity, because 'like the sun it can be clouded, but never extinguished'. Referring to the various colonial designs for constricting humanity in India, since in the eyes of the colonizers Indians were not required to be treated as human beings, he thus mentioned that with their mastery over science the rulers claimed that they 'have the eternal right to rule, as the explosive force of the earthquake once might have claimed, with enough evidence, its never-ending sway over the destiny of this earth. But they, in their turn, will be disappointed'.[40] There are two levels at which the argument is made: at a rather obvious level, the poet believed that 'for men to come near to one another and yet to continue to ignore the claims of humanity is a sure process of suicide',[41] which is a clear testimony of his unconditional faith in humanity; at the level of confidence-building, Tagore had carved out a definite space for humanity to prosper, and he was confident that 'the spirit of the age will be incarnated in a complete human truth and the meeting of men will be translated into the Unity of man'.[42] A careful analytical dissection of his argument makes us believe that for the bard, the idea of humanity did not seem to have died or been completely

---

[40] Rabindranath Tagore, 'The Voice of Humanity,' Das, *The English Writings of Rabindranath Tagore*, Vol. 3, p. 523.

[41] Tagore, 523.

[42] Tagore, 523.

disowned; it might only have lost the appeal that it had had in the past when the market-driven and ruthless commercialization of the globe was hardly at the centre stage of human activities. This was an era of decadence that was linked with the wild growth of values drawing on tendencies seeking to undermine humanity. This was more so in India, which did not seem to have adapted itself to the changed global environment. According to Tagore, it was possible for the British to easily subjugate India because

> we are not the kind of a market crowd, jostling and elbowing one another so vulgarly, quarrelling over privileges and titles, advertising our own worth in unashamed exaggeration. The whole thing is sheer imitation and mostly sham. It has no redeeming feature of courtesy of gratefulness.[43]

Here was the reason for India's failure to effectively counter the colonizers' evil design. To sharply make his point, Tagore drew on history:

> we, the Indians, had an inherent dignity of our own, which was not impaired by plain living or poverty. This was for us like a congenial armour which used to protect us against all the insults and trials of our material vicissitudes. But this natural protection has been wheedled away from us, driving us to take our stand behind bluster and bluff. Dignity has now become an outside thing which we must bolster up by outward show. As we no longer reckon inward satisfaction to be the fulness of wealth, we have to hunt for its paraphernalia in foreign shops, and never can gather together enough.[44]

There are two important points that were implicitly made by Tagore. On the one hand, he was a little disappointed that due to a peculiar unfolding of history the Indians lost their vitality, since they were clearly uprooted from their rich socio-cultural traditions. In other words, being forgetful of their socio-cultural rootedness, the Indians appeared to have become entrapped in a vicious circle from which they were unable to come out. The vacuum thus created among them explained, on the other hand, why the Indians joined the rat race of

---

[43] Rabindranath Tagore, 'The Fourfold Way of India,' in Das, *The English Writings of Rabindranath Tagore*, Vol. 3, p. 502.

[44] Tagore, 502–3.

imitating as perfectly as possible the imposed sociopolitical and cultural designs of human existence. The implications were disastrous, for it caused a chasm between the Indians and the rest of humanity. It was a trap in which the Indians had been caught by the clever foreign rulers. They appeared to have lost the pace of life which they had had in the past, which Tagore explained in a metaphorical way by saying that

> the stream of water in a river does carry sand, but so long as the stream can still flow it will push away the sand from its path; like that, if the mental attitude is right, we need not be afraid of mistakes. That is why the individual in the West has no unsurpassable barrier between himself and the rest of the humanity. He may have prejudices, but no irrational injunctions to keep him in internment away from the wide world of men.[45]

This comment of Tagore drew on years of introspection regarding India's socio-economic decadence, which might have clearly manifested during the British period, though it had its roots in the growing importance of an archaic and supremacist mindset. In view of sustained support, this mindset became prominent, and all those constrictive values supportive of social restrictions for one section of the people to benefit others were endorsed as axiomatic. This was most unambivalently articulated in his 'The Way of Unity' when he said that

> we have to realize this in India, and know that the religion, chiefly based upon a fixed code of custom, which we have allowed to fasten upon the entire region of our life, has been the one radical cause of separateness of our races, and has made the cracks from which comes out the poisonous gas of degeneracy. The problem of untouchability is merely one of the numerous symptoms of this fatal malady. By suppression these through external means we do not cure the disease. The thorny bushes of evil are overspreading out social soil, made barren by the obsession of a religion that insults reason. Uprooting a few of these will not help us in improving the soil, the impoverishment of which is the real origin of our futility.[46]

---

[45] Rabindranath Tagore to Gilbert Murray, 16 September 1934, reproduced in Das, *The English Writings of Rabindranath Tagore*, Vol. 3, p. 349.

[46] Rabindranath Tagore, 'The Way to Unity,' in Das, 463.

Tagore was opposed to any of the socio-economically justified designs of segregation which did not seem to be odd as he always believed in the unity of man. Untouchability was a social aberration that drew its sustenance from the human desire of a section of mankind for fulfilling partisan aims at the cost of the rest. This was unreasonable and socially retarding, for it caused an irreparable damage to humanity which, if devoid of vitality, was going to be permanently ruined and devastated. Hence, it needed to be strengthened and protected by way of creating a powerful social, economic and political design in which tendencies towards crippling humanity were effectively contained and challenged, since they, being deviant, were absolutely harmful. What was the means that we were required to adopt, asked Tagore. Here too, the poet expressed his preferences very unambiguously by underlining that

> it is for the sake of our humanity, for the full growth of our soul, that we must turn our mind towards the ideal of the spiritual unity of man. We must use our social strength, not to guard ourselves against the touch of others, considering it as contamination, but generously to extend hospitality to the world, taking all its risks however numerous and grave.[47]

What is reiterated here seems to be a continuity of the argument that Tagore was consistently pursuing in support of universal humanism that was one and indivisible. Unless we, as human beings, were tuned to this goal, we ceased to be human beings. It was not a difficult aim to fulfil, felt the poet, since core to this design was nothing but compassion for others, which was possible provided no wall of separation between human beings was erected. Here, Tagore made a wider point which directs our attention to both social infirmities and political division based on the application of coercive power by one section of the global population against another. To be precise, Tagore had in mind the obnoxious caste system which, by degrading one segment of the population as untouchables, created and also consolidated a social chasm supportive of the permanent pigeonholing of people in terms of their caste identity. Following India's colonization by the British, there emerged another schism, a schism between the foreign ruler and

---

[47] Tagore, 465.

the colonized subjects. Hence, the division had a further manifestation in the political arena. In a nutshell, India remained segmented due, first, to social segmentation on account of caste division and, second, owing to the political segmentation on being brought under the colonial governance.

Tagore's aim was to bridge the gulf between human beings, whether it was based on the age-old caste identities leading to social segmentation or on the politically contrived segmentation of the population in a colonized existence of human beings in terms of the ruler and the ruled. Here the bard drew on the teachings of one of his intellectual mentors, Ram Mohan Roy who drew on the Upanishadic ideals to draw inspiration for his mission of purging Hindu society of social orthodoxy. According to him, humanism was a casualty in India simply because the Indians lacked spiritual bond with one another. The spiritual bond was dependent on compassion, care and sympathy for each and every member of the community. Such a bonhomie was not possible 'within sectarian sanctuaries, nor ... could it be [developed] ... by men who have the professional right to preach it as a doctrine'.[48] This spiritual togetherness, argued Roy, could be realized once 'it is linked with the whole of humanity [leading to a] fundamental unity of human relationship, of human efforts and achievements'.[49] Primary to Roy's concern was an endeavour to develop a collectivity of minds that, being respectful to differences, was an important aid for generating oneness amidst diversity. It was not an easy task, especially in a situation where the old values defending a system of human relationship had survived over generations for protecting the partisan interests of a few. The caste system or religious divisions were nurtured deliberately to create the alienation of one section of the population by another. Had Roy not undertaken a thorough analysis of the ancient texts, including the Vedas and Upanishads, to prove that what was projected as sociopolitically justified had no basis whatsoever. It was a design

[48] Conversations between Roman Rolland and Rabindranath Tagore, Geneva, 28 August 1930, reproduced in Chinmoy Guha, ed., *Bridging East & West: Rabindranath Tagore and Roman Rolland Correspondence (1919–1940)* (New Delhi: Oxford University Press, 2018), 109.

[49] Conversations between Roman Rolland and Rabindranath Tagore, 109.

which had been constructed for the fulfilment of selfish interests. Being endowed with linguistic skills, Roy stood out amidst the pantheon of scholars who had the courage to question the well-established but archaic value systems, because 'his learning … trained his mind for the acceptance of truth'.[50] That it had provoked attacks on him is too obvious to be stated. Nonetheless, as Tagore mentioned, he developed

> the courage and capacity to discriminate between things that are essential and those that are non-essential in the culture which was his by inheritance. This helped him to realize that the truth can never be foreign, that money and material may exclusively belong to a country which produces them, but not knowledge or ideas of immortal forms of art.[51]

By distinguishing between the essential and non-essential in India's culture, Roy helped build a methodological design for evolving thoughts which were contextually relevant and culturally relevant. Instead of blindly imitating the Western philosophical discourses, which was the rule of the day as the colonized found it convenient then, he also put before us those conceptual inputs that the Indian authors had provided by articulating their ideas in the Vedas and the Upanishads; they needed to be unearthed, since these ideas, being born out of the then Indian socio-economic and political context, were likely to be meaningful in conceptualizing the indigenous reality. Being selective in his choice, since Roy felt that there were clearly certain aspects of our traditional knowledge system which were irrelevant in the context in which he defended his preferences, he took out

> from the storehouse of his country's past things that were living … to build a bridge between the past, present and future [since he believed in] the dialectical interconnection between different phases of history' [that also established] a link [not only] between the past and future [but also] between India and the world [as] knowledge knows no boundaries.[52]

Roy was admired for his critical role in demonstrating the immeasurable contribution of the texts that had evolved in India's ancient

---

[50] Tagore, 'The Way to Unity,' 465.

[51] Tagore, 465.

[52] Tagore, 465–6.

past, which appeared to have been conveniently forgotten in the then present. It was not an attempt to blindly go back to the past, as was interpreted by his detractors, but one that created a zeal among the Indians for detecting what was useful and what remained futile in out ancient knowledge. His effort was directed at generating in us the creative faculty which would be of assistance to undertake this task. According to Tagore, awareness of the past had also relevance to set out the task that was required to be undertaken to come out of this inertness. In his appreciation for the priceless contribution of Roy in conceptualizing the endeavour towards comprehending humanity, which was transcendental in character, the bard thus stated,

> in Ram Mohan's life we find a concrete illustration of what India seeks, the true indication of her goal. Thoroughly steeped in the best culture of his country, he was capable of finding himself at home in the larger world. His culture was not for rejection of those cultures which came from foreign sources, on the contrary, it had an uncommon power of sympathy which adjust itself to them with respectful receptiveness. His mind had natural reverence for *Saraswati*, the goddess of knowledge, - for the Truth, whose dwelling is in the hundred-petalled lotus-heart of humanity.[53]

This was an unqualified admiration for the first modern man of India, as Ram Mohan was characterized by the poet. In two critical ways, Roy helped us build meaningful theoretical/conceptual discourses which drew on both Western and indigenous intellectual inputs. First, for him, intellectual borrowing was not servility but an illustration of the claim that knowledge, regardless of its origin, always remained global. It also underlines the argument that only on the basis of creative blending of ideas one was able to contribute to the global well-being of the people despite being socio-culturally different. Second, once we understood that one needed to be open to welcome views, notwithstanding being incompatible with the widely accepted ones, the root cause of schism among human beings would evaporate. In other words, what is hinted here was the idea that one did not require to be either blind or indifferent to their origin in different socio-economic locations. The litmus test for the ideas to become relevant was whether

---

[53] Tagore, 466.

they were of use for human betterment, which Tagore claimed to have learnt from Roy.

In the poet's conceptualization, without Ram Mohan's powerful intervention, India would not have had an opportunity to realize her inner potentials. He was an independent-minded individual who was also not averse to borrowing ideas from the West in case they were useful to contribute to universal well-being. His was a package of enlightening ideas which was an offshoot of his relentless endeavour towards evolving a meaningful design for change and radical trans-formation of interpersonal relationships across the world; it was an endeavour towards accomplishing a mission which was not meant to be nationalistic but universalist in appeal and texture, since it evolved out of a creative blending of ideas with different socio-economic and politico-cultural roots. As the discussion shows, Tagore appears to have been heavily indebted to Roy in conceptualizing his approach to humanism and global amity. That it was so was evident when the poet castigated Gandhi in a rather unguarded manner when the latter criti-cized Roy for his 'backward politico-ideological thinking'. In a letter to his colleague, C. F. Andrews, the anguished Tagore thus wrote that

> I strongly protest against Mahatma Gandhi trying to cry down such great personalities of modern India as Ram Mohan Roy in his blind zeal for declaiming against modern education. It shows that he is getting enamoured of his own doctrines—a dangerous form of egotism.[54]

The situation was so bad that Tagore and Gandhi's common friend, the French poet Roman Rolland, had to intervene to stop both of them from ventilating their respective grievances in the public domain. As one who understood both of them, Rolland conveyed the view that India required both Tagore and Gandhi: while the former was concerned for universal humanism, the latter 'wants to adapt to the ephemeral requirements of people and time'.[55] So, there is no

---

[54] Tagore to C. F. Andrews, 10 May 1921, reproduced in Prasant Pal, *Rabijibani*, Vol. 8 (Kolkata: Ananda Publishers, 2003), 142.

[55] Roman Rolland to Kalidas Nag (who were closely linked with Tagore), 19 October 1925, cited in Guha, *Bridging East & West*, 79.

contradiction except that they held different methodological tools to realize their respective goals.

To conclude, the above discussion is an elaboration of the distinctive feature of Tagore's idea of humanity and how to remain committed to humanity amidst temptations to the contrary. As a foundational idea, Ram Mohan Roy's endeavours towards creatively blending the ideas of east with those of the West, appears to have supplied Tagore with the basic conceptual parameters that ultimately evolved as his out of his dialogical interaction with him and others supportive of what Roy stood for. On this foundation rested the poet's unique conceptualization of humanism with its global tentacles. Two arguments remained paramount in his ideas which informed his model of universal humanism. First, it was true that India lost to the West and became a colony in which the will of the colonizers took precedence over others in a relationship of hierarchy and segmentation between the colonizers and the colonized. Judged in a worldly way, the ideal that India endeavoured to attain, argued Tagore, 'led her best men to the isolation of a contemplative life, and the treasured she gained for mankind by penetrating into the mysteries of reality cost her dear in the sphere of worldly success'.[56] On the surface, it was a great loss for India, since it had to succumb to the Western intervention, presumably because it was not capable of combatting the attack engineered by the West, as it lacked adequate striking power. Nonetheless, for Tagore, it was not a source of disappointment, since with their contemplative thinking the Indians had also accomplished a goal by discerning that 'it was the supreme manifestation of that human aspiration which knows no limit, and which has, for its object nothing less than the realization of the infinite'.[57] This was a matter of great joy to the bard, who saw in this endeavour a providential design of helping human beings to realize their ultimate goal. It was made explicit when he said that the contemplative thinking created a vibe among

---

[56] Rabindranath Tagore, 'The Relation of the Individual to the Universe,' in Das, *The English Writings of Rabindranath Tagore*, Vol. 2, p. 285.

[57] Tagore, 285.

the poet-prophets ... to cross the limiting barriers of the individual, to become more than a man, to become one with the All ... [which was] not a mere play of the imagination, but it was the liberation of consciousness from all the mystifications and exaggerations of the self. These ancient seers felt in the serene depth of their mind that the same energy, which vibrates and passes into the endless forms of the world, manifests itself in our inner being as consciousness, and, there is no break in unity. They never acknowledged even death itself as creating a chasm in the field of reality. ... They also knew that appearance and disappearance are on the surface like waves on the sea, but life which is permanent know no decay or diminution.[58]

Profound here was Tagore's firm belief in the Upanishadic ideal of life, which, despite being ephemeral on the surface, continued to survive since the *atma* (soul) never died; with its all-pervading presence in humanity, there was no reason to be sad and disappointed at one's failure, because by being involved in one's assigned duty (*karma*), one was destined to follow a specific path of life which was the only way of realizing 'one's self in its true manifestation in the all-pervading God'.[59] This contemplative idea was useful to avoid being attached with the worldly existence of human beings, since what was visible was illusory. In other words, the idea that things did not disappear but continued to exist helped build an atmosphere in which human beings realized the utility of remaining 'unattached', since there was nothing permanent in life. According to Tagore, this selfless existence also helped generate a belief that

man's abiding happiness is not in getting anything but in giving himself up to what is greater than himself, to ideas which are larger than his individual life, the idea of his country, of humanity, of God. They make it easier for him to part with all that he has, not excepting his life. His existence is miserable and sordid till he finds some great idea which can truly claim his all, which can release him from all attachment to his belongingness. Buddha and Jesus, all our great prophets, represent such great ideas. They hold before us opportunities for surrendering our all. When they bring their divine alms-bowl we feel we cannot help giving, and we find that

---

[58] Tagore, 289.

[59] Tagore, 289.

in giving is our truest joy and liberation, for it is uniting ourselves to that extent with the infinite.[60]

The idea that Tagore offered here does not seem to be a new one, since it constituted one of the significant pillars of his thoughts on how to achieve universal humanism. In two interrelated ways, his model is a manifestation of his sustained urge to be in communion with the infinite. Persuaded by the Upanishadic ideal, the poet firmly believed, on the one hand, that oneness with the infinite was the only way to generate a consciousness that, being indifferent to the self, was capable of thinking of others, which meant the humanity as a whole. In other words, it was an urge to be submerged with humanity as one collectivity, regardless of differences on the surface, which helped create a concern for common well-being. Once this was established, which was, Tagore felt, not an aberration, as human history demonstrated, the Upanishadic ideal of a communion with the infinite did not seem to be a concoction of wild imagination but one that was realistically formulated. To substantiate his point, Tagore, on the other hand, drew on the remarkable contribution of the great saints like Buddha and Jesus who appeared on the scene to persuasively put across the point that only by giving did human beings contribute to the processes whereby they perennially existed, since humanity was imperishable. Here too, the same point is iterated, namely, by being connected with humanity, human beings neither disappeared nor faded away simply because they were part of a whole which was indestructible. Conforming to the core Upanishadic idea that the *atma* survived, Tagore here reinforced what he learnt by way of imbibing the very spirit on which he built his conceptual universe, which, by being receptive to multiple socio-cultural impulses, emerged as a unique one directed to fulfil an identical goal that the saints in the past aspired to achieve. The model that the poet constructed was thus both unique and also derivative: unique because it had characteristics which were linked with the typical Indian context in which it evolved, and derivative because it had features which were rooted in the Western ways of

---

[60] Tagore, 'The Realization of the Infinite,' in Das, *The English Writings of Rabindranath Tagore*, Vol. 2, p. 340.

conceptualizing human existence. At the end, it was a creative blending that was typical of Tagore's ideational aspirations based on his unique approach to human history as having blossomed with both indigenous and exogenous socio-cultural inputs.

TAGORE'S CIVILIZATIONAL CONCERNS

The narrative shall remain inconclusive if it does not deal with Tagore's concern for civilizational imperatives which remained critical in his conceptualization of universal humanism. There are two specific texts, 'The Religion of Man' (1930) and 'The Crisis in Civilization' (1941), that clearly explicate his unique views on humanism in particular and civilizational bond among those appreciative of humanism in general. These texts were based on lectures that he delivered, respectively, at Oxford in 1930 and in Calcutta in May 1941, three months before his demise. While the former is a well-argued, long statement of what constitutes humanity, what are the threats to its natural unfolding and what are the factors inhibiting its progress, the latter is a rather simple text that focuses on Tagore's disillusionment with the British Empire which, like any other colonial power, was ruthless and discriminatory in pursuing its exclusive interests. In other words, as his speech 'The Crisis in Civilization' demonstrates, he was completely disillusioned, since the British colonialism was not, at all, different from any other European colonial power when it came to fulfilling its partisan interests; it was clearly exploitative and had no sympathy for the subjects, since they were colonized. It was well argued in this speech, when he said that despite being an admirer of the British state for its role in injecting liberal values, he was completely disillusioned. As he said, though he held the British Raj in high esteem at the outset, he later realized that it was a wicked government that had emerged in the wake of colonialism. In his words, he did set the English on 'the throne of my heart',[61] presumably because the British rule drew on the Enlightenment values. 'The parting of the ways,' argued Tagore, came soon 'with a painful feeling of disillusion when [he] began increasingly

---

[61] Rabindranath Tagore, 'The Crisis in Civilization,' in Das, The English Writings of Rabindranath Tagore, Vol 3, p. 723.

to discover how easily those who accepted the highest truth of civilization disowned them with impunity whenever questions of national self-interests were involved'.[62] It was possible for the British rulers to establish their hegemony in India presumably because of their 'mastery over the machine', which helped them consolidate 'their sovereignty over their vast empire'.[63] Industrialization *per se* was not bad; what was most disappointing was the reluctance of the alien rulers to share the fruits of industrialization that were 'kept as a sealed book, to which due access has been denied to this hapless country'.[64] This was morally wrong, since had India been industrially developed, it would have joined those countries that reaped the fruits of industrialization. As a result, instead of marching ahead, India smothered under the dead weight of British administration, 'lay static in her utter helplessness'.[65] According to Tagore, this was 'a heinous crime on the part of the rulers ... [because] the best and noblest gifts of humanity cannot be the monopoly of a particular race or country'.[66] In two interrelated ways, India was subjected to immeasurable suffering: on the one hand, by keeping it away from being industrially developed, the rulers expressed their priority of not allowing India to prosper in unambiguous terms; on the other, by bulldozing India into uncritically accepting the colonizers' sociopolitical preferences, the alien administration did not allow any space for the Indians to really become a British citizen, which created a situation in which

> the demon of barbarity [gave] up all pretence and ... emerged with unconcealed fangs, ready to tear up humanity in an orgy of devastation. From one end of the world to the other, the poisonous fumes of hatred darken the atmosphere. The spirit of violence which perhaps lay dormant in the psychology of the West, has, at last, roused itself and desecrates the spirit of Man.[67]

[62] Tagore, 723.

[63] Tagore, 723.

[64] Tagore, 723.

[65] Tagore, 724.

[66] Tagore, 722

[67] Tagore, 726.

Disenchanted with the British Raj for being clearly selfish and sectarian in its attitude to the colonized Indians, Tagore attributed the arrogance of the rulers to their failure to truly comprehend the ideals of the philosophy of Enlightenment that remained foundational to the British civilization. On the basis of his understanding of how industrial civilization contributed to the decadence of human values, he pursued this scathing critique of the British rule that had prospered as a global power presumably because of its rise as a global hegemon in the wake of the industrial revolution. The language in which the poet expressed his displeasure did not seem to be radically different from that of Edward Carpenter, who was perhaps one of the first critics of unbridled industrialization causing terrible human misery, which he articulated in his *Civilization: Its Cause and Cure* of 1889. Gandhi's 1909 tract, *The Hind Swaraj,* had also the same concern, namely, ruthless industrialization that informed that the British colonialism was responsible for human decadence across the globe, for its very nature was exploitative and discriminatory.[68] Being humanists to the core, both Tagore and Gandhi were among the few thinkers who fiercely criticized indiscriminate industrialization, since it caused severe disruption in the natural progress of humanity. There was, however, a difference, perhaps a significant difference, in their approach. Insofar as the attack on industrialism was concerned, both the Mahatma and Gurudev left no stone unturned to express their disenchantment with British colonialism, since colonialism was an outcome of industrialization that constantly searched for new markets for its survival and expansion. The difference lay in the fact that while Gandhi offered a political solution to the difficulties confronting India in the wake of its colonization by an industrial power, Tagore, being a perennial optimist, found a way out in the buoyancy of relentless hope, which he saw as a human trademark. Hence, despite having witnessed 'the crumbling ruins of a proud civilization [as India had been in the past] strewn like a vast heap of futility', he never 'lost faith in Man'.[69] It was 'the opening of

---

[68] I have dealt with this issue in my *Social and Political Thought of Mahatma Gandhi* (London and New York, Routledge, 2006), 23–9.

[69] Tagore, 'The *Crisis in Civilization*,' 726.

a new chapter in Man's journey after the cataclysm is over and the atmosphere rendered clean with the spirit of service and sacrifice',[70] claimed Tagore. By pursuing this argument, he further noted that 'a day will come when the unvanquished Man will retrace his path of conquest, despite all barriers, to win back his lost human heritage'.[71] Persuasively argued here are two complementary points directing our attention to the critical features of Tagore's humanism. On the one hand, the ruthlessness that accompanied industrialization ended up taking humanity out of human beings; human worth was thus judged by what one was capable of producing by one's labour. It was a clear attack on the fundamental values which made human beings different from other living creatures. Conditioned by his uncritical faith in humanism, Tagore created, on the other hand, a definite space for humanism to flourish amidst sociopolitical circumstances which were not exactly in its favour. This can be interpreted at two levels. At a rather mundane and less complex level, being instinctively a humanist, the poet was convinced that there was nothing beyond humanity, which he consistently upheld in his creative writings and speeches. That he never diluted his concern for mankind till the fag end of his life is testimony of the view that for him, humanity was the ultimate truth. At a far more conceptual level, he unfolded a new dimension of nationalism that neither the nationalists nor their detractors had recognized, namely, the nationalist capture of power was of no consequence unless it was accompanied by the concern for humanism. In other words, being a relentless crusader for humanism, which led him to be fiercely critical of Gandhi's narrow nationalism, Tagore left an indelible imprint in human history despite being a lonely fighter for a cause that hardly had supporters in comparison with what the Mahatma had while pursuing his politico-ideological mission.

Notwithstanding its brevity, 'The *Crisis in Civilization*' is one of the powerful statements that Tagore articulated in favour of his very uniquely conceptualized model of universal humanism. The argument did not seem to be extraordinary, in the sense that both Carpenter

---

[70] Tagore, 726.

[71] Tagore, 726.

and Gandhi made similar arguments in the late 19th and early 20th centuries, respectively. Even the title of this 1941 lecture was more or less identical to that of Carpenter's text; while Carpenter focused primarily on the adverse impact of industrialization in Britain, which was manifested in the debasement of human relations in the wake of the uninhibited journey of industrialism, Tagore dealt with its devastating nature that unfolded with the consolidation of colonialism in India. Although colonialism was a manifestation of industrial civilization, Carpenter did not seem to have paid much attention to this aspect, presumably because his priority was to understand the inner dynamics of industrialism and how adversarial it was to the workers who struggled day in and day out to contribute to the industrial growth. Tagore, as mentioned above, had a different approach to the crisis of civilization, which he explained by (a) looking at the ruthlessness which accompanied the colonial rule in India and (b) assessing the nature of the nationalist counter-attack, which, according to the poet, was very restrictive due to its almost discarding of the humanist concern. Tagore's 'crisis of civilization' was thus a crisis of humanity, since both the colonial power and the nationalists did not pay adequate attention to the issue: the colonial power was not, for obvious reasons, expected to appreciate humanism, given the ideological priorities that it pursued for fulfilling sectarian interests, while the nationalists remained indifferent as they always held national independence as prior to human emancipation that, for the poet, was necessary for political freedom to flourish in totality.

Being not just 'a philosophical text' but one that contained his 'religious experience',[72] 'The Religion of Man' was Tagore's Hibbert lecture of 1930 which he delivered at the Manchester College in Oxford. He also admitted that not only was he inspired by his unique religious experiences he also devoted his energy, to a great extent, to conceptualize them which 'often remained unrevealed'[73] to him. What Tagore wanted to convey was (a) his constant search for the infinite, which provided him with a permanent source of inspiration, and (b) also

[72] Rabindranath Tagore's preface to *The Religion of Man*, in Das, *The English Writings of Rabindranath Tagore*, Vol. 3, p. 83.

[73] Rabindranath Tagore's preface to *The Religion of Man*, 83.

an elaboration of how he internalized the feelings that were difficult to articulate in words. Nonetheless, this text was Tagore's endeavour that had its manifestation in the argument supportive of humanism, since, in his perception, the realization of the infinite was contingent on service to human beings, given his firm belief that service to living creatures was tantamount to service to god.

That Tagore was drawn to the Infinite was partly explained by his birth in a family where spiritualism was practised as a means to associate with the supreme being, Brahma. Accordingly, his idea of religion was also remarkably different. As he mentioned, 'my religion is … neither that of an orthodox man piety nor that of a theologian. Its touch comes to me through the same unseen and trackless channel as the inspiration of my songs'.[74] It was an inspirational touch that always acted as a source of emotional gratification amidst crises. It was spiritual too, for the bard was introduced to these fine human sentiments through a providential touch which was like 'the morning light [that] … revealed an inner radiance of joy'.[75] Implied here are two important and also interrelated aspects of Tagore's spiritual communion with the Supreme Self. On the one hand, he felt that the feelings that he was able to fathom at a particular phase of his life did not come from the outside but were very much part of his being. As they were not exogenous, the poet also admitted, on the other hand, his inability to internalize the feelings, presumably because he was not endowed with the calmness that one was expected to have to realize these finer sentiments of life. As soon as these feelings became part of his existence, the poet appeared to have been elevated to a different stage of realization where he understood the real meaning of human life in conjunction with the Infinite. In a frank confession, he thus stated that

> once I became conscious of a stirring of soul within me, … [m]y world of experience in a moment seemed to become lighted, and facts that were detached and dim found a great unity of meaning. The feeling which had was like that which a man, groping through a fog without knowing his

[74] Tagore, 121.

[75] Tagore, 121.

destination, might feel when he suddenly discovers that he stands before his own house.[76]

This was an articulation of a foundational philosophical idea suggesting that the concern for sublimity was neither alien nor so easily realizable; instead, it was something that one had access to only when one was capable of raising one's consciousness above the mundane level. In other words, for this idea to flourish, what was essential was to have a sensitive and also compassionate mind, without which the idea would remain elusive. A careful reading of this emotional churning that Tagore experienced since his introduction to spiritualism at the early phase of his life presumably because of his distinct socio-cultural roots, reveals that ultimately it was about a level of consciousness which was not always privy to by just being born as a human being. It perhaps came to Tagore naturally because, as he admitted, '[f]rom my infancy I had a keen sensitiveness which kept my mind tingling with consciousness of the world around me, natural and human'.[77] The idea here is critical to conceptualize Tagore's mindset, which was ready to explore beauty in whatever he saw around him. It was not surprising that he saw 'miracles of beauty'[78] in the garden which gave different kinds of flowers in different seasons without shifting its location. The analogy is of tremendous significance, since it established the argument that Tagore found the world around him as a source of sustained joy and enjoyment. This is comprehensible at two levels. At a very worldly level, it does not seem odd if one argues that beauty is in the eyes of the beholder. Accordingly, one is persuaded to argue that it was Tagore's probing eyes which allowed him to enjoy the beauty of nature which easily escaped the attention of ordinary mortals. At a philosophical level, it was a clear articulation of a grand idea that was otherwise illusive, which, for Tagore, was immanent in him and thus gradually evolved as soon as he developed a mindset appreciative of the omnipresent Infinite. A priest of universal humanism, the poet was persuaded to believe that without extending love or being loved, one's

---

[76] Tagore, 122.

[77] Tagore, 124.

[78] Tagore, 124.

birth as a human was futile. This was evident when he adumbrated his views by saying that

> we are made conscious of the fact that a relationship evolves out of love, care and empathy, … and, from this experience of ours we have the right to say that the Supreme One, who relates all things, comprehends the universe is all love—the love that is the highest truth in human existence.[79]

There are two critical components to this claim of Tagore. On the one hand, as a humanist to the core, the poet was now convinced that love was a critical foundational value bringing human beings together regardless of differences in socio-economic and cultural terms. With love in place, the poet also subscribed to the view, on the other hand, that it was an effective medium through which human beings' solid bond with the Supreme Being was established. This was manifested in the feeling of being glad and joyous once one's enjoyment reached a pinnacle. It might not be easy to articulate these feelings in words, since they were all internalized emotions expressing themselves in a particular way; this was, in other words, not created but generated in human beings as a response to the bond that contributed to joy and pleasure. As Tagore most elegantly explained, the feeling of being glad and joyous was not like

> the ether waves that we receive light; the morning does not wait for some scientist for its introduction to us. [In a similar vein,] we touch the Infinite reality immediately within us only when we perceive the pure truth of love of goodness, not through the explanations of theologians, not through erudite discussion of ethical doctrines, … but through one's submerging with the Supreme One.[80]

Here too, Tagore upheld the critical role that the Infinite and also the inexplicable force played in creating a universe of love, joy and pleasure. As a result, the morning, not at all dependent on endeavour of any kind, unfolded naturally, just like the darkness which followed the sunlit day. Nature was thus bountiful and had a course of action which was guided by an invisible force; similarly, human society, in the sense

[79] Tagore, 124.

[80] Tagore, 127.

of being dependent on relationships around many axes, remained as it was because love was, according to Tagore, what sustained its continuity. The argument was made at two levels: at one level, the sustenance of human existence was attributed to human sentiments; at another, the role of the Supreme One was shown to be supportive of its continuity. It was stated by the poet in a very philosophical way when he said that

> [t]he man whose inner vision is bathed in an illumination of his consciousness at once realizes the spiritual unity reigning supreme over all differences. His mind no longer awkwardly stumbles over individual facts of separateness in the human world, accepting them as final. He realizes that peace is in the inner harmony which dwells in truth and not in any outer adjustments. He knows that beauty carries an eternal assurance of our spiritual relationship to reality, which waits for its perfection in the response of our love.[81]

Here is also a foundational idea directed at showing that mankind survived due principally to the appreciation of the importance of an interconnection between human beings and the Supreme One. What was required was a bent of mind appreciative of the fact that without being safeguarded by the Supreme Being, it was difficult, if not impossible, for mankind to exist as integral to the former. The idea that Tagore offered here was one of those Upanishadic ideals championing the view that mankind was one and inalienable. To him, the idea did not seem to be odd, given his upbringing in an atmosphere in which the Vedantic texts were perhaps the most persuasive sources of knowledge. Hence, the argument had philosophical roots that can be traced back to these tracts which Tagore upheld as the ones that provided him with a conceptual tool to fathom how, despite attacks on humanity, mankind survived. His uncritical faith in humanity, which reached the level of obsession at some point or the other, also helped him forcibly argue the view that the best natural creation in the universe was certainly the man, which he put forward by stating that '[l]et me asset by saying that this world, consisting of what we call animate and inanimate things, has found its culmination in man,

---

[81] Tagore, 128.

its best expression'.[82] How did he justify the contention? As one who never diluted his faith in humanity, he further argued that

> [m]an, as a creation, represents the Creator, and this is why of all creatures it has been possible for him to comprehend this world in his knowledge and in his feeling and in his imagination, to realize in his individual spirit a union with a Spirt that is everywhere.[83]

Two integrally connected points are made here. On the one hand, Tagore, being a humanist to the core, always put mankind as a force with tremendous buoyancy, which meant that it was potentially strong enough to sustain its continuity. It was possible for mankind to survive, Tagore argued, on the other hand, because mankind had the ingrained power to devise what was deemed to be appropriate not only for its continuity but also for generating ideas, values and mores for its growing strength, in contrast with other living creatures. Here, the poet was referring to the level of intelligence that mankind had to carve out a specific roadmap for its journey, avoiding what could have been a source of danger or irritation. In other words, Tagore, being appreciative of the endeavour of those who fought for mankind, drew our attention to the role that human beings discharged in different phases of human history for its sustenance despite adverse circumstances. It was very unambiguously articulated when the bard stated that 'the primitive barbarity of limitless suspicion and mutual jealousy fills the world's atmosphere today—the barbarity of the aggressive individualism of nations, pitiless in its greed, unashamed of its boastful brutality'.[84] As a perennial optimist, the poet, despite being disenchanted with the unfolding brutality at the behest of the colonial power in India, never lost faith in humanity, since he also believed that it had its inner strength which would take human beings out of danger. It manifested in two complementary ways: on the one hand, by transmitting socio-culturally propitious ideas and values,

[82] Tagore, 126.
[83] Tagore, 126.
[84] Tagore, 187.

humanity created a shield for defence which was neither transitory nor ephemeral but was ingrained; on the other hand, this shield did not come from outside, as Tagore noted, but evolved because of the instinctive human desire. The idea was justified by the poet because, in his conceptual universe,

> [f]reedom in the mere sense of independence has no content, and therefore n meaning. Perfect freedom lies in a perfect harmony of relationship, which we realize in this world not through our response to it in knowing, but in being. Objects of knowledge maintain an infinite distance from us who are the knowers. For knowledge is not union. Therefore, the further world of freedom awaits us there where we reach truth, not through feeling it by our senses or knowing it by reason, but through the union of perfect sympathy.[85]

Profound here is the idea that freedom did not simply mean shackles-free existence which could have been possible in the brutal colonial rule since it was based on a clear distinction between those who had complete freedom at the cost of those who suffered due to denial of freedom or unfreedom of that section which had no freedom in the colonial hierarchy of relationship. For Tagore, this was a society in which prejudices drawn on the artificial division of human beings enabled the ruler to create and consolidate the chasm, which the ruler utilized in his favour. Besides the brutality that the colonized were subjected to in India, the poet perhaps had in mind the devastating consequences of the colonial *divide-et-impera* (divide and rule) strategy that the British government deployed to its advantage by segregating the Hindus from their Muslim counterparts. The result was a permanent fissure between the two communities which had lived amicably before the onset of colonialism in India. Here comes the validity of Tagore's contention: sympathy, care and concern for human beings remained the driving forces for humanity which was another way saying that bereft of these concerns our existence as human beings was just a matter of knowledge but not exactly in the sense of a conscious being.

[85] Tagore, 157.

CONCLUDING OBSERVATIONS

Tagore's approach to humanism was historically conditioned and, philosophically, uniquely textured: the contemporary socio-economic and politico-ideological context constituted an important pillar of his distinctive approach to humanity, and philosophically, the Upanishadic ideals of *yatra vishwam bhavati eka needam* (where the world becomes a nest) and *Vasudhaiva Kutumbakam* (the world is one family) provided the intellectual resources on which the bard rested his peculiarly designed model of universal humanism. On the basis of a careful assessment of his views, one is persuaded to make three major arguments. First, the British colonialism was severely criticized by the poet, since it was deviant from the core Enlightenment values of concern, care and empathy for fellow human beings. Colonialism unleashed perhaps the most brutal form of governance in India, ignoring the fundamental ethos from which the British system of governance drew its nourishment. Not merely a villain of history, colonialism was also inhuman in nature, for it survived and flourished by being extremely brutal while fulfilling its partisan aims. In such a sociopolitical milieu, it was but natural that humanism would be the first casualty. Second, humanism completely evaporated as colonialism devised the most widely discussed divide-and-rule strategy, which, by instilling division around the axes caste, class and ethnicity, created an unbridgeable chasm between communities in India. One of the outcomes of this strategy was the partition of India and the birth of Pakistan following the British withdrawal in 1947. Here too, because of the contextual compulsion, humanism was conveniently sacrificed through the injection of hatred, bitterness and enmity by one section of human beings in another. As the contemporary historical evidence demonstrates, India's partition was a manifestation of how human beings were brutalized just for petty political gains. Finally, Tagore was pained since the growing alienation of human beings from one another also represented a brutal violation of the Upanishadic ideals, stated above, which had helped build bonhomie among human beings in the past. In view of being raised in an environment which was free from social prejudices, it was perhaps easier for the poet to appreciate and imbibe the spirit of global bonhomie that the Upanishads exhorted.

Although the Upanishads provided the poet with some of his fundamental assumptions regarding humanism, he was equally influenced
by other socio-cultural traits, which made him not rigid but receptive
to other ideas. As a result, his views on life became clearly 'unconventional', which Tagore articulated by saying that 'the unconventional
code of life for our family has been a confluence of three cultures: the
Hindu, Mohammedan and British'.[86] Following the onset of colonial
rule and his grandfather, Dwarkanath Tagore's acceptance of the
Victorian manners and values, the poet was introduced to a world in
which 'the modern citybred spirit of progress had just begun driving
its triumphal car over the luscious green life of our ancient village
community [amidst] the wailing cry of the past'.[87] This is a revealing
comment suggesting how Tagore was terrified at the devastating impact
of modern civilization on the natural unfolding of humanism, although
he also admitted that with his access to the Western Enlightenment
values he also considerably enriched himself. What he questioned
was the demonization of those foundational ideas and values by the
colonizers that had contributed to the rise of civilization in the East
since time immemorial. Nonetheless, being receptive to myriad socio-
cultural inputs, Tagore produced a unique blending of ideas supportive
of humanism in circumstances when prejudicial sociopolitical ideas
appeared to have held sway. Here, Tagore was not an exception, as
the above text demonstrates, since some of his leading predecessors,
Ram Mohan, Vidyasagar and his father, Debendranath Tagore, had had
their significant contributions in creating an ideational ambience in
which concern for humanity regardless of the socio-cultural differences
among human beings appears to have received adequate attention.

As argued above, one of the most powerful driving forces was
the Upanishadic ideals which allowed Tagore to understand that
human beings were unable to realize themselves fully without being
dependent on one another. Citing the Upanishads, he thus said that
'when we realize others in us and ourselves in others, then alone we
attain truth: we can hide ourselves no longer: then alone we express

[86] Tagore, 156.
[87] Tagore, 156.

ourselves'.[88] The idea that is philosophically conceptualized was articulated in clear terms when the bard mentioned that

> in civilization, man expresses himself; in barbarism, man is unexpressed. The truer the realization in one another, the clearer becomes the real nature of civilization. Wherever in the name of religion, duty, worldliness and patriotism man creates divisions in the human world, consciously or unconsciously the cause of disaster is strengthened. There man hurts the law of his own nature; that way lies suicide. To this history bears testimony throughout the ages.[89]

Tagore attributed the devastation of humanity to all kinds of divisions around religion, caste and nationalistic patriotism. As was shown in Chapter 2, being opposed to narrow nationalism, Tagore put forward a thorough analytical account highlighting the importance of togetherness regardless of chasms of any kind. By drawing attention to history, the poet also argued that despite having realized the disastrous consequences of being nationalistic, human beings made the same mistake repeatedly, which was a little perplexing to him. Nonetheless, being an optimist, he felt that one needed to work towards fulfilling the goal contributing to human well-being, and unless everybody shared this concern, the future of humanity would be anything but bright. While pursuing this argument, he further stated that, as history had shown, 'the distortion or disruption of human relations ... [caused] the destruction of civilization'.[90] According to him, social disharmony was responsible for degeneration in human relationships, which was manifested in the distance 'between the strong and the weak'. As a result,

> the flow of life in the social body has been obstructed by the division of society into masters and slaves, into those who enjoy and those who are deprived, leading to disease owing to bloated indulgence on the one hand and anemic emaciation on the other. In all civilized societies today, the

---

[88] Rabindranath Tagore, *Letters from Russia* (Calcutta: Visva-Bharati, 1984) (reprint), 147.

[89] Tagore, 147.

[90] Tagore, 147.

messenger of death finds entrée through this opening. In our country, the gate of his entrance seems wider than elsewhere.[91]

Profound here is the argument that Tagore offered to defend the contention that human beings who undermined humanity at the slightest pretext were responsible for creating a milieu in which universal humanism was conveniently sacrificed. It was more so in colonial India, where the British rulers deliberately chose a politico-ideological design seeking to fulfil their selfish interests by denying Indians of their basic rights as human beings. Opposed to the socio-economic hierarchy which dehumanized the globe to a significant extent, Tagore, being a public intellectual, raised his voice against discrimination of any kind. A staunch supporter of global human unity, he was also persuaded to believe that unless this was addressed effectively the globe was likely to become a place for battling out of one's partisan privileges at the cost of those who were unable to stand against those supportive of vested interests. This was a manifesto that he developed along with his colleagues who thought alike. Conceptually, his views had a lot of similarity with those of Tolstoy, who, being committed to Christian ethics, argued against the artificial chasm that the powerful nation states created for protecting their partisan interests which ran contrary to the core values of Christianity. Although Tagore and Tolstoy held compatible views, since both of them had privileged universal humanism over any of the other sociopolitical objectives, the former differed radically from the Mahatma, who appeared to have paid less attention to the issue of humanism which, in his perception, could have easily been tackled once India gained political freedom. The argument hinged on Gandhi's hope that as soon as Indians had political power it would be easier for them to adopt steps to avoid social and economic alienation among the countrymen. In clear terms, notwithstanding his strong opposition to the discrimination against the untouchables, the Mahatma, for instance, hardly organized a campaign to completely weed out caste hierarchy, though he was aware that so long as it remained his ideal of a Ram Rajya would remain a distant goal.

[91] Tagore, 147–8.

Tagore's concern for universal humanism was articulated very persuasively when he argued strongly for respect for diverse opinions, since disagreements and freedom of the mind were Siamese twins and thus inseparable. In order to make this point, he thus argued that

> there must be disagreement where minds are allowed to be free. It would not only be an uninteresting but a sterile world of mechanical regularity if all of our opinions were forcibly made alike. If you have a mission which included all humanity, you must, for the sake of that living humanity, acknowledge the existence of differences of opinion.[92]

The above point is a further elaboration of his conceptualization of universal humanism, which also involved appreciation of diverse opinions. This was most logical for him, since he had had access to Hindu, Muslim and British cultures (as argued above), having been raised in a family that allowed the free flow of ideas regardless of their origin. Reinforcing the point that humanity was diverse in socio-cultural connotations, it was most likely for Tagore to appreciate the cross-cultural communion through dialogical inter-connection which was unlikely to happen if multiple voices were muzzled for fulfilling partisan goals. Here, his argument, though supportive of the free exchange of ideas with different socio-cultural roots, had wider implications, for it also endorsed the view that given their diverse origins, human beings located in different socio-cultural circumstances were likely to hold views that were anything but compatible with those of their counterparts elsewhere. Furthermore, he also believed that 'freedom of mind is needed for the reception of truth, [and] terror hopelessly kills it',[93] which allowed Tagore to link his concern for humanity with the search for truth. In conceptual terms, underlying this endeavour was a perennial optimism that the poet always had evinced through his creative writings and critical essays. It was an idea that also had its origin in the complex unfolding of Tagore's mental universe which, as he himself underlined, was an offshoot of multiple socio-cultural roots. A real renaissance man, the bard imbibed those distinct traits that were both contextual and transcendental: contextual given their

[92] Tagore, 215–6.

[93] Tagore, 216.

roots in the prevalent socio-economic and cultural milieu which was also creatively blended, and transcendental because his insistence that global human progress was possible only by being sensitive to the inherent values of socio-cultural inputs irrespective of how and from where they had emerged continues to remain inspirational. It had to be a mindset that needed to be inculcated accordingly. Humanism in its undiluted sense was, as the poet consistently argued, clearly a design championing ethos and values in such a way as to develop and consolidate togetherness among human beings despite their being socio-culturally diverse. Tagore, a humanist to the core, shall perennially remain relevant to humanity not only for his uniquely textured socio-cultural views but also for his distinct socio-cultural design that remains pertinent even today in explicating the reasons for human decadence and also possible solutions to get out of it.

CONCLUSION

I

Rabindranath Tagore had a vision for universal humanism. Born and raised in colonial India, the scion of the wealthy Tagore family left his imprint in every walk of life. Although his global reputation is based on his identity as a creative poet who initiated various trends in literature, his contribution as a social thinker with well-defined politico-ideological views is of immense significance in many ways. Prominent among his endeavours was his relentless struggle for inclusive development. He was a nationalist, albeit in a markedly different sense; his nationalism, far from being circumscribed, in fact denoted an urge for political freedom, which was just a part of his wider concern for human emancipation. For Tagore, political freedom was not a panacea, because it was not adequate to bring about qualitative changes in our existence unless we were free from well-entrenched social, economic and political prejudices that created an unbridgeable gulf between 'we' and 'they'. This needed to be bridged. In other words, he firmly believed that mere political freedom, which his nationalist colleagues had always privileged, was not enough to eradicate the age-old socio-economic designs allowing the exploitation of one section of human beings by another. It was a clear deterrent towards attaining human emancipation, which was Tagore's primary, if not the only, aim.

There is no denying the fact that Tagore's ideas were, to a great extent, shaped by being nurtured in a Brahmo family; Brahmoism was a protestant campaign to purge the orthodox Hindu society of many socially justified sets of rules creating an unbreakable wall between the people. As the history of Brahmo Samaj, of which Tagore's father, Debendranath Tagore, was one of the pioneering leaders, shows, it was a campaign that gradually gained momentum particularly with the support of the educated Bengalees. Inspired by Ram Mohan Roy, one of the most effective social reformers in the 19th century, the poet was also persuaded to believe that unless the well-entrenched divisive designs segregating the so-called 'Other' from the rest of the society were discarded, India hardly had a future. The British rule was certainly bad, but worse was India's socio-economic reality which put a large section of its demography permanently in chains. In Tagore's creative writings, there are instances demonstrating that he was not, at all, comfortable with the alien rule; his giving up of his knighthood following the brutal British attack on the hapless Indians in Jallianwala Bagh in 1919 is illustrative here of his clearly anti-British attitude and sentiments. Nonetheless, he was not always enthusiastic when the Gandhi-led mainstream nationalist campaign undertook several steps, which, of course, invited loads of criticism. Tagore's arguments are persuasive. He was of the view that the foreign administration was meant to fulfil partisan aims and objectives and hence it was not desirable. While sharing this point of view, he went further by suggesting that liberation from the British rule would not be meaningful unless it was accompanied by the rescinding of all other sources of unfreedom. He was referring to the exploitation of the Indians by another section in myriad ways around the caste, class and religion axes. Unless and until the social distance and economic disparity disappeared, the removal of colonialism could never be a source of joy to the bard. The primary concern that Tagore had always displayed even by annoying those nationalist leaders who aspired for political freedom was the change of the mindset, appreciative of a design resulting in creating a milieu in which segregation of any kind was an anathema. This was probably not visible to his colleagues, whom he admired for their being engaged in a relentless battle against the British presumably because of their being obsessed with mere political freedom. Hence, he argued that

one need to dive deep … to discover the problem of India; it is so plainly evident on the surface. Our country is divided by numberless differences – physical, social, linguistic, religious; and this obvious fact must be taken into account in any course which is destined to lead us into our own place among the nations who are building up the history of man.[1]

The point is crystal clear, which Tagore expressed unequivocally. Two ideas deserve attention here: on the one hand, Tagore had hardly had a doubt that India had great potential to contribute significantly to the consolidation of universal humanism; on the other hand, this was unlikely to happen, argued Tagore, in view of the well-entrenched social, economic and cultural prejudices permanently compartmentalizing Indians on the basis of constructed designs for fulfilling selfish interests. Here, Tagore's arguments can be said to have drawn on his own experiences, first in his zamindari in East Bengal and later in Santiniketan, where he founded Visva-Bharati in 1921. An eye-opener to him, his interaction with the villagers allowed Tagore to conceptualize what needed to be done to accomplish the goal that he nurtured. The primary aim was to support the evolution of a society being drawn towards the mission of completely eradicating artificial segregations surrounding caste, class and religion. While inaugurating Visva-Bharati, Tagore thus declared: 'let our Ashram be one place in the world where we can mingle without differences in religion, language and race'.[2] This was the fundamental commitment that Tagore held dear to his heart. Seeking to build an institution based on his unflinching dedication to universal humanism, he devised Visva-Bharati as a hub of exchange of ideas and views from across the world. He elaborated on the objectives of this centre of learning by saying that

I have formed the nucleus of an International University in India, as one of the best means of promoting mutual understanding between the East and West. This Institution, according to the plan I had in mind, invites students from the West and the Far East to study the systems of Indian philosophy, literature, art and music in their proper environment, encouraging them to carry on research work in collaboration with the scholars engaged in this task.[3]

[1] Uma Dasgupta, ed., *Rabindranath Tagore: My Life in My Words* (New Delhi: Penguin, 2006), 337.

[2] Dasgupta, 199.

[3] Dasgupta, 202.

Santiniketan, which was mainly 'academic',[4] had evolved as a centre of learning *par excellence,* and Tagore appeared contented with its success, though it was not adequate to achieve the goal that he had assiduously nurtured for long, namely, inclusive development of the rural masses, which needed to be addressed, felt the poet, on a war footing. It was necessary, as the bard rightly perceived, to develop agriculture, on which most Indians were dependent for their livelihood, which he clearly stated:

> it has been my earnest desire for long that we in this country should deal with the problem of agriculture in a big way. I had sent some of young men abroad to study agriculture so that on their return him they might tackle this problem and serve their motherland. ... [In] my article entitled *Swadeshi Samaj* ... I had said that we have reconstruct our national life with the village as the centre.[5]

A practitioner to the core, he translated his ideas into reality when he laid the foundation for Sriniketan as a twin campus of Visva-Bharati in 1928. Tagore's argument had an uncanny similarity with that of Gandhi who, in his conceptualization of *gram swaraj* (village republic), had argued in a similar fashion: core to their arguments was the point that for India's balanced socio-economic growth, one was required to pay adequate attention to the village economy. Agriculture needed primary attention, because the majority of villagers were dependent on it for their livelihood, and augmented production was useful not only for them, for it enabled them to earn more, but also for the rest of the society; the extra amount that they earned was to be utilized for other purposes, namely, creating facilities for the villagers to take care of their other basic needs.

Economic development was certainly required, but it was not enough to attain 'happiness', argued Tagore. In other words, wealth creation was a means, perhaps an effective one, to lift villages out of poverty, though there was a danger, the bard noted, since 'wealth is a synonym for the production and collection of things and men can use

---

[4] Dasgupta, 209.

[5] Dasgupta, 212.

it ruthlessly [which] can crush life out of earth and flourish'.[6] Here, Tagore dealt with the issue at a philosophical level: for him, happiness was the ultimate goal, which perhaps remained distant if one focused on the augmentation of production as an exclusive goal. As the poet most graphically illustrated,

> we forget that [wealth generation] brings about a greater exhaustion of materials [which] ... gives to the few excessive opportunities for profit at the cost of the many. It is food which nourishes, not money; it is fullness of life which makes one happy, not fullness of purse.[7]

This is one aspect of the argument wherein he castigated the endeavour that focused on enhancing production without being sensitive to its pernicious impact on human civilization, since it was certain to create a chasm between the haves and the have-nots. So, what he emphasized was the rise of a mindset which, by being compassionate, would take care of the needs of those who remained socio-economically peripheral. It was not a difficult task; what it required was a sense of empathy for those who needed to be helped to enjoy the fruits of augmented production. To do otherwise was morally wrong, because, as he argued, 'civilization has grown in conjunction with man's intellect with the gifts of Nature. These two must always work in partnership. Whenever the acquisitions of the intellect are hoarded in some strong-rooms, the store goes on dwindling'.[8] Here, Tagore had in mind two important aspects of contemporary civilization. On the one hand, he was critical of the West for not sharing the technological know-how for increased agricultural production, in particular, and overall development through machine-driven production. There is another aspect that was perhaps an illustration of his 'self-introspection' on the insistence of Indians on 'living in the past laurels'. It was evident when he categorically stated: 'we cannot afford to live on the accumulation of a bygone age for long, in fact, we have already come to the end of

---

[6] Rabindranath Tagore, 'City and Village,' in *Towards Universal Man*, ed. Rabindranath Tagore (Calcutta: Asia Publishing House, 1962) (reprint), 316.

[7] Tagore, 316.

[8] Tagore, 308.

our resources'.[9] This was a warning, though as a born optimist he also drew attention to the civilizational truth that India epitomized. With its inner strength, revival was not far away since India was open to outside influences as a source of empowerment and energy. As he mentioned, India never encouraged the idea of being confined to itself, nor

> keep a sentry over its boundaries to prevent the encroachments of recreations and amusements, poetry, and literature, science and art [because it always upheld that] *Dharma* [not in the narrow sense of Semitic religion] is not for the satisfaction of our partial needs; the whole world exists for its fulfilment.[10]

This was a conceptual point that received, for obvious reasons, immediate criticisms from those who survived and also thrived on superstitious beliefs justified in the name of Hinduism. Nonetheless, it was a source of inspiration for those who joined hands with Tagore in his experiment for rejuvenating Indian villages. Believing that 'man's power is divine power [and] ... to repudiate it is blasphemy',[11] he was confident that his mission for revamping villages was bound to succeed, as it was based on human endeavour. Hence, he insisted that

> the latest manifestation of man's power must be brought into the heart of the villages. It is because we have omitted to do so that our water-courses and pools have run dry; malaria and disease, want and sin and crime stalk the land; a cowardly resignation overwhelms us.[12]

There are two points that deserve attention here: on the one hand, Tagore, being grounded to his roots and also receptive to the Western influences, provided an innovative design of indigenous development by involving the villagers and also those with identical socio-economic aims; by setting his priority in unequivocal terms, the poet stated, on the other hand, that 'since we have neglected the villages so far, we 'are required to devote our energy to the plans and programmes [directed]

---

[9] Tagore, 308.

[10] Rabindranath Tagore, *The Religion of Man* (Kolkata: Visva-Bharati, 2015) (reprint), 15.

[11] Dasgupta, *Rabindranath Tagore*, 213.

[12] Dasgupta, 213.

to ensure rural well-being'.[13] The design that Tagore developed yielded results with the inauguration of Sriniketan that emerged as complementary to Santiniketan, which also aimed at generating academic zeal for common weal.

As shown in the book, Tagore was not an accident of history but an outcome of the confluence of multiple cultural influences that emanated from both indigenous and exogenous sources. In view of being born in a family that allowed the free flow of ideas regardless of their origin, it was easier for the poet to gain access to global literature, especially English creative texts. With the introduction of English education, there had emerged a conscious interest in learning the English language, which was both a passport for jobs in colonial India as well as a medium to get acquainted with the literature in English. It was therefore a boon in disguise for the colonized, because it created an opportunity for them to find a stable source of livelihood and also allowed their intellectual enrichment, with the easy availability of both literary and philosophical texts, in the changed sociopolitical milieu. The poet thus admitted that 'circumstances almost compel us to learn English, and this lucky accident has given us the opportunity of access into the richest of all poetical literature of the world'.[14] For Tagore, despite its obvious adverse cultural consequences, the forcible imposition of English education did not seem to have been entirely bad, since it established a bridge between the Eastern and Western minds; in other words, the English education set in motion processes whereby the colonized were introduced to the values of Enlightenment, which also shaped Indians' nationalist aspirations in a particular fashion. Hence, it was both an empowering device and a source of future worries, as the firm grip of English resulted in the decline of indigenous learning and the pampering of English education. Furthermore, by being fiercely critical of colonialism, as it led to the exploitation of the Indians, Tagore had shown that, unlike that of some of his contemporary colleagues, his approach to colonialism was uniquely textured, which Amartya Sen captured by

[13] Tagore, 'City and Village,' 308.

[14] https://www.nobelprize.org/prizes/literature/1913/tagore/article/. Tagore was cited by Amartya Sen in his 'Tagore and his India,' *New York Times*, 28 August 2001.

saying that 'there seems to be much force in Rabindranath Tagore's argument for clearly distinguishing between the injustice of a serious asymmetry of power [due to colonial subjugation] and the importance nevertheless of appraising Western culture in an open-minded way'.[15] What is striking here is the claim that Tagore was neither partisan nor narrow-minded in welcoming ideas, because he believed that progress of human civilization was possible with a free flow of ideas cutting across social and cultural boundaries. Truly global in his perspective, the poet always held views championing the argument in favour of the free exchange of views and ideas despite their disparate roots. Only with the creation of such a milieu was the future of humanity certain to be free from possible decay. In his collection of poems entitled *Gitanjali*, he articulated his distinct views by exhorting that

Where the mind is without fear
and the head is held high;
Where knowledge is free;
Where the world has not been
broken up into fragments
by narrow domestic walls; ...
Where the clear stream of reason
has not lost its way into the
dreary desert sand of dead habit; ...
Into that heaven of freedom,
my Father, let my country awake.[16]

The above poem is illustrative of Tagore's idea of human existence in a world in which the artificial dissociation of human beings from one another was an anathema. Yet, it was difficult for human beings to naturally thrive so, largely due to the innumerable social and cultural restrictions. In his letter to Edward Thompson, he thus conveyed that 'my soul seems to be struggling to cut its path across all outside impositions that are barring the passage of the light which gives it life and

---

[15] Sen, 'Tagore and His India.'

[16] Rabindranath Tagore, Gitanjali, and Sisir Kumar Das, eds., *The English Writings of Rabindranath Tagore*, Vol. 1 (New Delhi: Sahitya Akademi, 1997) (reprint), 53.

inspires its song'.[17] At one level, it was an endorsement of the view that the poet was in chains presumably because of the myriad restrictions which appeared to have crippled his existence as a human being; at another, it was also an urge of a poet who failed to pursue the path that he wanted, again largely due to the constraints, some of which were contextual and some of which were embedded in his peculiar understanding of global humanity. Being aware that colonialism was a severely restrictive system, he hardly had the independence which he longed for, and he thus attributed his failure to conceptualize the Supreme One to his highly suffocating circumstances. Nonetheless, whatever he achieved in accordance with his socio-cultural and politico-ideological preferences was remarkable, presumably because he never allowed himself to be pigeonholed in a stereotypical, national-ist fashion. Truly global in his approach to humanism, Tagore relent-lessly fought for 'a new kind of man, neither Eastern nor Western, but a reconciler of the best of both'.[18] To argue that it was a mere reconcili-ation of the East with the West is conceptually little simplistic because it was an endeavour based on Tagore's life-long search for a design which gradually became integrally connected with his philosophical dispositions supportive of a creative blending of socio-cultural ideas and practices emanating from both the West and East. It was a unique contribution, since, for Tagore, colonialism, despite being a system of exploitation, generated in him a quest to conceptualize it as an important source of sociopolitical rejuvenation.

II

It is difficult to pigeon-hole Tagore presumably because he represented in him a peculiarly blended socio-cultural and politico-ideological inputs. Some of them were obviously contextual and some of them which he had internalized through having been born and raised in

---

[17] Rabindranath Tagore to Edward Thompson, 22 January 1922, reproduced in Uma Dasgupta, ed., *A Difficult Friendship: Letters of Edward Thompson and Rabindranath Tagore, 1913–1940* (New Delhi: Oxford University Press, 2003), 137.

[18] Edward Thompson to Rabindranath Tagore, 14 October 1934, reproduced in Dasgupta, 167.

a family that never put an embargo on the free flow of ideas. India's unique social, economic and cultural texture remained an important source of Tagore's conceptualization of the world around him and the pressing issues that he confronted. He was not one of those traditional intellectuals who discharged his responsibilities with mere commentaries on what he felt was critical to human existence. Contrarily, he devised means and ways to address some of the burdensome social and economic issues that, to him, were an impediment to social progress, which reinforces the point that he was an organic public intellectual who was integrally involved in those activities which were conducive to the creation of a society of his choice. Basic to the argument is the contention that Tagore was a breath of fresh air in the then Bengal which was passing through a cognitive revolution entailing 'a radical transformation in the way one thinks, perceives, reasons and conceptualizes'.[19] This was an era of significant social changes wherein new values replaced the old ones, which became redundant and were dismissed as archaic. There is no denying that the change of political guards with the onset of colonialism was certainly an important input in this regard. With colonialism in place, the socio-cultural ideas that informed Western civilization naturally came along with the foreign rulers. These ideas were opposed as undesirable interventions, since they ran contrary to some of the well-established but anachronistic ideas in approach and content; in other words, the established values and mores, being organically linked with the prevalent social, economic and political circumstances, stood in contradiction with these exogenous influences. The orthodox elements put up, for obvious reasons, a strong opposition. The British rulers seemed to have been a little uncertain once the conservatives raised their voice presumably to sustain their claim as the natural custodians of what was considered to be 'truly Indian'. Gradually, however, the opponents lost steam, and the Western ideas were championed, as they were claimed to have brought a new set of ideas upholding human dignity, global bonhomie and social tranquillity. There were institutional changes, including the replacement of the indigenous form of education by the Western

---

[19] Subrata Dasgupta, *The Bengal Renaissance: Identity and Creativity from Ram Mohan Roy to Rabindranath Tagore* (Ranikhet: Permanent Black, 2007), 5.

mode of learning; with the approval of the famous Macaulay's Minute on Education in 1835, the process of cultural/educational mingling between the East and the West gained momentum. It is true that the Education Minute of Macaulay brought about radical social change in India by creating a mindset that was receptive to Western ideas; it is also true that once this became legally mandatory, the prevalent system of education became futile. Whether it was socially appropriate or conducive is debatable. Nonetheless, there is no doubt that the advent of colonialism hastened the free flow of ideas that contributed to the burgeoning intellectual culture in Bengal. The *dramatis personae* of this rich philosophical landscape included Ram Mohan Roy, who played a historical role in the shaping of a voice of protest against superstitious mindsets. What is striking about Roy was his ability to creatively blend socio-religious inputs from both the East and the West. Being a Hindu Indian, he not only 'consumed Hindu and Christian precepts, but could engage successfully as a producer of doctrines or theses with both Indian and Western consumers',[20] which was manifested in the conceptual construction of 'a cross-cultural coin, Brahmoism'.[21] Tagore owed a great deal to Roy, who baptized his father, Debendranath Tagore, into the new religion of Brahmoism, which was also a protestant voice against idolatry and Hindu orthodox social practices. At one level, it was a social protest; at another, it was an urge to draw on the ancient texts which, so far neglected, were a rich repository of knowledge. It is thus argued that Tagore's cognitive self was an outcome of his interaction with the leading Brahmo ideologues, including his father, who stood out for being appreciative of the ideas that Vedantic texts, the Upanishads, in particular, had left for posterity. In short, Tagore was raised at a particular point of Bengal's history when interests were raised for the ancient texts along with those of Western tracts which were critical in generating axiomatic ideas and conceptualizations. This was an era of dialogue with the West without disparaging one's Indian roots. A careful analysis of Tagore's texts reveals that the poet, who had been inspired by the Upanishadic texts, also admitted to having been enriched by Western philosophical discourses.

[20] Dasgupta, 74.

[21] Dasgupta, 74.

There has to be a caveat here, since Macaulay's Minute set in motion processes whereby English education gained momentum in India. It also facilitated the flow of Western ideas on to Indian shores, which ultimately firmly established the Raj as not merely a system of governance but also a way of life in which Western ideas were also an important ingredient. Characterizing Macaulay's Minute as having planted 'a poisonous tree',[22] since it almost guillotined the indigenous system of education in India, there are scholars who are caustic in reviewing its role in Indian education. It is true that English education helped build the Raj in a systematic manner, which was one of the reasons why the British rule remained in vogue for almost 200 years. However, there is another aspect that needs to be mentioned as well. The Macaulay's minutes, by being negative to India's ancient texts, seemed to have generated an unprecedented zeal in unearthing the traditional wisdom they contained in themselves. Viewed thus, the Minute had obviously led a search for knowledge in Western philosophical texts and also provoked interests simultaneously in Indian texts. The Indian intellectual repository thus became enriched with inputs drawn on both Western and Eastern philosophical discourses, resulting in a peculiar admixture of ideas supportive of the so-called forward-looking liberal and rationalist approach to humanity with those that were identified as backward-looking and conservative. It is therefore explicable why a traditional Vidyasagar approached the British judiciary to legally adopt steps for widow remarriage, which he justified by referring to the Vedic texts. In other words, it would have been a Herculean task for him to accomplish the mission had the British government not agreed with him with regard to this decision which had serious social and political implications. Furthermore, it was easier for Vidyasagar to convince the British judiciary, since his arguments conformed to the fundamental values of the Enlightenment philosophy on which the Raj claimed to be rested. In view of his knowledge of typical Hindu texts, it was also possible for him to justify the contention that widow remarriage was neither unjustified nor contrary to the core ideas of the Vedas and Vedantic texts. The point being made here is about the

---

[22] Partha Chatterjee, 'The Fruits of Macaulay's Poison Tree,' in *The Present History of West Bengal*, ed. Partha Chatterjee (New Delhi: Oxford University Press, 1997), 91–110.

advantages of being grounded in both the philosophical discourses which was made possible with the adoption of the Macaulay's minutes. While the English education was an outcome of the minutes, the concern for going back to the indigenous philosophical roots, though came as a result of the protest against the deliberate weeding out of the ancient Indian texts, came naturally to the Indians as perhaps a means to establish that they also had a rich heritage to bank upon. Instances abound. The literary creations of Bankimchandra Chattopadhyay along with his critical essays, Vidyasagar's insistence on learning from Western philosophical texts, Debendranath Tagore's interests in the rationalist thinking of the West—all are illustrative of the initiatives that the leading thinkers of the era had undertaken. What is worth noting here is also the interest they evinced in also drawing on indigenous texts. It was therefore not strange that Bankim, Vidyasagar and Debendranath paid adequate attention to those Indian texts which they considered as axiomatic and which had proven to be a cultural reset. In his *Charitrapuja* (1907), Tagore, while drawing on the ideas of Ram Mohan, Vidyasagar and his father, developed a strong argument in favour of learning from the Vedantic texts. According to him, they played a critical role in reshaping the prevalent social map in circumstances wherein the Hindu orthodoxy was not only well-entrenched but also too terribly strong to be uprooted so easily. As shown in Chapter 6, Tagore was so impressed with Ram Mohan's contribution that he did not feel hesitant to even challenge Gandhi, who did not appear to have been as enamoured as Tagore was in his assessment of Roy. Nonetheless, the fact remains that Macaulay's so-called poison tree helped generate processes for radical social, economic and political transformation by building a bridge between the West and the East and also by creating adequate enthusiasm among the Indians to go back to their philosophical roots. Macaulay's Minute was thus historically the most important intervention explaining how Bengal's future was shaped with its adoption in a way that despite provoking opposition then, it became part of the story of a new genre of thinking in India.

Tagore stood apart as a thinker in the nationalist phase; he was a nationalist in the internationalist mould who was not swayed by nationalism in 'both of its meanings – as the aspiration of subjugated peoples for political self-determination, and as the pride of already free nationals in their nationality'.[23] Opposed to the idea of nationhood being the telos of politics, the poet questioned the viability of the campaign that Gandhi and his colleagues spearheaded in India to do away with the British rule. Contrary to the conventional approach to temporal human existence in which the nation was privileged, Tagore, in his *Swadeshi Samaj* (1904), argued strongly for a society-based bonhomie among human beings. Whether it was feasible is debatable, although it was a uniquely textured argument that upheld his innovative sociopolitical preferences on the basis of his careful understanding of the prevalent societal bond and also the ancient texts that informed its articulation. Not only did Tagore's approach stand in contradiction with the mainstream conceptualization, but it was also clearly 'original ... distanced no less from the colonialist historiography propagated by the Raj and the ideologues of imperialism than from the narrowly sectarian Hindu view of the past that had been influential in nationalist thought since its formulation by Bankimchandra Chattopadhyay in the 1870s'.[24] This was also the view of Isaiah Berlin, who felt that Tagore was nether 'left nor right, neither Westernizer nor traditionalist [but] a rare form of intervention',[25] which persuasively explains the complex socio-economic and political reality that had evolved in colonial India. As a creative thinker, Tagore always believed that the idea of nation was most vicious, since it created in the minds of the colonized a concern which was considered as perhaps the only means of one's salvation. By suggesting that the expressed commitment to the idea of nation was a form of mental servility which unknowingly became part of one's mindset, he dubbed nationalism as dangerous, for it would effectively cloud one's vision from seeing things in a proper perspective. Neither a hardcore

[23] Ananya Vajpayi, *Righteous Republic: The Political Foundations of Modern India* (Cambridge: Harvard University Press, 2012), 93.

[24] Ranajit Guha, *History at the Limit of World History* (New York: Columbia University Press, 2002), 75–6.

[25] Isaiah Berlin, 'Rabindranath Tagore and the Consciousness of Nationality,' in *The Sense of Reality: Studies in Ideas and Their History*, ed. Henry Hardy (London: Chatto and Windus, 1996), 260.

traditionalist nor a servile Westernizer, the poet was a realist who believed that neither clinging to the traditional values nor accepting uncritically the Western discourses was going to be of great use in persuasively conceptualizing the typical Indian socio-economic and political reality. An example will suffice here: Tagore believed that English education was neither a boon nor exactly a menace but a useful instrument in the colonial context. It was not a tricky situation for the poet, for he realized that the choice was not between two options but to make a decision that was most appropriate in a particular socio-economic and political context. He was aware that shutting the door on Western civilization was as idiotic as was being obsessed with one's past. Hence, the best option was to creatively blend the inputs that one received from the West with what one derived from being in the East. It was articulated in a very persuasive way when the poet exhorted that though

> I acclaim our newly awakened national self-respect in so far as it is impel-ling us to go forward, I also condemn it in so far as it is trying to keep us permanently tied to the past like a sacrificial goal tethered to a post. National self-respect is making us turn our face forward to the world and demand political authority, it is also making us turn our face backward to our country and demand that in all religious, social and even personal matters we do not move one step against the Master's will. This is what I call the revival of Hinduism. National self-respect is ordering us to perform the impossible task of keeping one of our eyes wide awake and the other closed in sleep.[26]

Here, the poet clearly articulated his philosophical predispositions. A practitioner to the core, Tagore held the view that a nation needed to be self-sufficient to establish its claim as an independent entity. He condemned 'romantic over-attachment to the past'[27] and also servile submission to the colonial rule; instead, one needed to be self-dependent on the basis of an intelligent borrowing from both the past and the present, since they contained useful inputs for a country to stand on its own. Tagore was thus of the view that one was required

---

[26] Rabindranath Tagore, 'The Master's will be Done,' in *Towards Universal Man*, ed. Rabindranath Tagore (Bombay: Asia Publishing House, 1962) (reprint), 186–7.

[27] Berlin, Rabindranath Tagore and the Consciousness of Nationality,' 265.

to creatively blend the available options to arrive at the appropriate means for realizing the predetermined options.

The above discussion directs our attention to a very interesting turn in our quest for a persuasive theoretical–conceptual mould for explaining the genre of thinking of which Tagore was a powerful exponent. In view of the features that the poet's distinct approach to human existence evinces, one is tempted to argue that his ideas can easily be clubbed in the category of cosmopolitan political thought, which is an innovative mixing of 'liberalism and other West-centric modes of thought with a series of plural and coeval engagements of thinkers and texts from all traditions, moving through and past the dichotomies that ground these encounters'.[28] Theoretically, cosmopolitanism was a far more persuasive way of comprehending the non-Western world than the widely held but highly suspect conceptualization of orientalism, for one major reason. As Said put before us, the obvious theoretical weakness of the idea of orientalism is largely due to the fact that

> it approaches a heterogenous, dynamic and complex human reality from uncritically essentialist standpoint [which] ... suggests both an enduring Oriental reality and an opposing but no less enduring western essence, which observes the Orient from afar and, so to speak, from above.[29]

Critical here is the idea that the so-called oriental reality cannot be persuasively conceptualized in any derivative format. Just like Benedict Anderson's model of nation being an imaginary community,[30] which was not applicable to all situations, since the imagination is contingent on the prevalent socio-economic circumstances, the orientalist predispositions in favour of a straightjacketed formula regarding political thoughts appear unhesitatingly overstretched.[31] Tagore certainly stands

---

[28] Farah Godrej, *Cosmopolitan Political Thought: Method, Practice and Discipline* (New York: Oxford University Press, 2011), 143.

[29] Edward W. Said, *Orientalism: Western Conceptions of the Orient* (New Delhi: Penguin, 1995) (reprint), 333.

[30] Benedict Anderson, *Imagined Communities: Reflections on the Origins and Spread of Nationalism* (London and New York: Verso, 1991). (reprint)

[31] I have pursued this argument in my work (Bidyut Chakrabarty, *Confluence of Thought: Mahatma Gandhi and Martin Luther King Jr* [New York: Oxford University Press, 2013], 190–3).

out because he realized that narrow nationalism, instead of contributing to the strengthening of a bond, caused fissures among human beings, more so in a demographically diverse country like India. Having been raised in a multicultural environment, the poet appears to have internalized the idea of being open to diversity, which he captured well in his creative writings and critical essays. It was therefore natural for Nikhilesh in *Ghare Baire* (1916) to be critical of Sandip's attitude of hatred towards Muslims during the 1905–1908 campaign for the revocation of the Partition of Bengal. Even at the fag end of the novel, when Nikhilesh went out to quell the communal tension in the estate, he expressed his disappointment with the nationalist politicians for their failure to accept Muslims as integral to India. The idea was echoed in *Gora* (1910) when the main protagonist, Gora, was clueless in view of the well-entrenched animosity in rural Bengal against Muslims. It was thus not difficult for him to comprehend why the Muslim Pharu's wife was starving and her son, Tamiz, had nobody to look after him when his father was taken to jail for having attacked the British manager of an indigo factory. Aghast with this behaviour of the villagers *vis-à-vis* one who had pursued the nationalist cause, *Gora* realized that this communal hatred was far more deep-rooted than he had assumed. Tagore pursued an identical concern in his creative essays, as we have shown in the book. Two essays deserve mention here: the 1930 Hibbert lecture, which was later published with the title *The Religion of Man*, and his last speech entitled '*Crisis in Civilization*' (1941). In the former, Tagore's argument hinges on his concern for universal humanism, because religion did not mean to him mere loyalty to a religious denomination but respect to humanity regardless of one's religious or diverse socio-cultural identities. Furthermore, according to him, freedom was realized when sources of unfreedom were completely weeded out. Philosophically persuasive and conceptually meaningful, the idea of fraternity brings people together despite their being socio-culturally disparate. Tagore's argument was pitched at two levels. At a very mundane level, he was arguing for creating a template for togetherness among human beings across the globe; this was an idea that many of his predecessors had upheld, especially with the onset of industrial civilization that not only created a hierarchy of relationship between the owner and the owned but also consolidated a supremacist mindset drawing its sustenance from the well-entrenched divisive mentality. At another level, Tagore's argument was also an endeavour for reviving sociability among human beings, which, in the past, had helped develop a strong bond regardless of whether one was rich or poor. Tagore's 1941 lecture, 'Crisis in Civilization', was illustrative of the poet's frustration at the growing animosity among human beings at the national as well as the international level. As shown in the book, the poet was terribly upset when World War II broke out, because it was potentially dangerous for humanity as a whole. According to him, crises in civilization were to be attributed to the lack of concern of the rich nations towards those nations in which people suffered terribly due to poverty. Having previously been impressed by 'the evidence of liberal humanity in the character of the English',[32] the bard however soon changed his opinion, since 'the generosity [of the English] was vitiated by the imperialist pride'.[33] Describing his disenchantment with the British rule in a very poignant manner, the poet thus mentioned that

> then came the parting of the ways accompanied with a painful feeling of disillusion when [he] began increasingly to discover how easily those who accepted the highest truths of civilization disowned them with impunity whenever questions of national self-interest were involved.[34]

Basic here was Tagore's disillusionment with the unfolding of the British rule in India as the most torturous form of governance. This was a perversion on the part of the rulers who drew on the Enlightenment values for their sustenance; they conveniently ignored those exalting values once they stood in contradiction with the fulfilment of their narrow/partisan socio-economic gains. In other words, Tagore felt that nationalism was jingoism, which was reflected in Britain being deviant from the core philosophical dispensations of the Enlightenment

---

[32] Rabindranath Tagore, 'Crisis in Civilization,' in The English Writings of Rabindranath Tagore, ed. Sisir Kumar Das, Vol. 3 (New Delhi: Sahitya Akademi, 1996), 722.

[33] Tagore, 722.

[34] Tagore, 723.

discourse. Being caustic in his remarks, the poet had also shown that he was consistent insofar as his ideological commitment to universal humanism was concerned, which became a casualty with the rise of a chauvinistic nationalist venture at the behest of the colonial powers. The crisis in civilization was thus an outcome of the selfish desire of the self-seeking nations to realize their partisan aims despite the fact that it was in no way conducive to humanity as a whole.

These examples are illustrative of Tagore being sensitive to the complex demographic characteristics of the then Bengal. Hence, a ready-made nationalist model, however sophisticated it be, was unlikely to be of use in conceptualizing equally uniquely textured responses from the grassroots. Fundamental here is the point that sociopolitical preferences can neither be exactly derivative nor based on ideas with their roots in a different socio-economic milieu. This is one aspect of the argument suggesting that one's ideational leanings cannot be divorced from the prevalent context in which they are shaped. Tagore's unique responses to politico-ideological issues bear testimony to this contention. This is persuasive to the extent that they had evolved out of a dialectical inter-connection with the existent socio-economic reality; it is meaningful since it also helps us build a conceptual model questioning the inclination towards imposing the 'one-size-fits-in-all' formula regardless of circumstances.

III

In conceptualizing his unique philosophical discourse, Tagore was indebted to Gandhi and his other nationalist colleagues, not because they helped him build his model but because they provoked him to think differently. Of all the dialogical interactions, prominent was the one that put the poet and the Mahatma in regular interactions. The purpose here is not to dwell on this aspect again to make the same point. Instead, the aim here is to highlight some of the principal features of the dialogue that brought the two great minds of the 20th century on to one platform, since both of them were keen to contribute to India's well-being. Despite their having held different conceptual parameters with regard to India's nationalist struggle, there was a running thread that linked the poet and the Mahatma, since their goal was to evolve a society which was not fractured or divided but remained committed to the core values of humanity. Tagore did not seem to have been enamoured by the politico-ideological goal that the Mahatma aspired to realize, since mere political freedom was not enough to attain humanism in its genuine sense. In other words, the withdrawal of the British from India was not a panacea so long as India's society remained divided in terms of caste, class and ethnicity. Hence, Tagore had reasons to question Gandhi's politico-ideological preferences. Nonetheless, they continued their friendship by being supportive to each other in conceptualizing their unique sociopolitical ideas in their ways. This was most clearly suggested by a Tagore biographer who stated that

> these two great minds … have for each other esteem and admiration, but they are fatally separated from each other like the sage and apostle, like Saint Paul and Plato. On the one hand, the genius of faith and charity, which can be the seed of a new humanity. On the other, that of intelligence, free, vast, serene, which embraces the whole existence.[35]

Tagore and Gandhi thus represented two sides of the same coin, in the sense that both of them together pursued a goal for human betterment, though they had different methodological paths. It was a rare occasion in human history, and also, according to Roman Rolland, 'unique happiness for India to have possessed at the same time two great men, each expressing the facet of the highest truth'.[36] The differences of opinion between them were far more substantial than what appeared on the surface. As shown in Chapter 2, the poet and the Mahatma differed radically from each other, despite the fact they had great respect for each other, presumably because of the convergence of politico-ideological interests that they had in common.

There is also a conceptual point that deserves mention here. One of the points of differences between Tagore and Gandhi was related to

[35] Krishna Kripalani, *Rabindranath Tagore* (Santiniketan: Visva-Bharati, 1962), 305.

[36] Roman Rolland's assessment of Gandhi and Tagore, February 1939, cited in Chinmoy Guha, ed. and trans., *Bridging East & West: Rabindranath Tagore and Roman Rolland Correspondence (1919–1940)* (New Delhi: Oxford University Press, 2018), xlvii.

how they viewed Western civilization and colonialism, in particular. As argued above, the Mahatma was vehemently criticized by Tagore for being very critical of Ram Mohan Roy who, according to Gandhi, did not allow independent thinking by being blind to the Western philosophical discourses. By criticizing Roy for his intellectual servility, Gandhi raised his voice against those nationalist thinkers who 'saw India through the Western prism, borrowed from it too hastily, and ended up undermining the integrity of the very civilization they professed to safeguard'.[37] Furthermore, Gandhi defended his critique of Roy by saying that Ram Mohan's role in engendering momentum for social change was highly limited, since he was 'an ardent advocate of reform rather than growth or internally generated change'.[38] The argument has substance, since, as evidence demonstrates, Roy's endeavour was uncritically supported by the British rulers, who adopted specific legal steps to facilitate his campaign for social change. The Sati custom was abolished once a law was accepted to permanently abolish this cruel practice. Whether Gandhi's assessment of Roy was appropriate is debatable, though the interpretation that he offered established the point that in order to be a permanent feature of a society, social change needed to be generated from within and with internal resources; the outside support was to act as a facilitator but needed to be supplemented by internal initiatives and involvement. In Tagore's perception, the considerations that Gandhi had did not seem to be critical, since he felt that the contextual constraints were an impediment then, which justified Ram Mohan's apparently excessive dependence on the British help. Gandhi was not persuaded, though he appreciated the role that Roy had discharged at a time when the incipient nationalist campaign had had no significant impact in the country.

A careful study of the points of differences between these two great minds were based on fundamental conceptual contrasts. Tagore was aghast when he saw that 'man for some purpose of his own imposes upon his society pruning of mind, a niggardliness of culture, a

---

[37] Bhikhu Parekh, *Debating India: Essays on Indian Political Discourse* (New Delhi: Oxford University Press, 2015), 88.

[38] Parekh, 89.

puritanism which is a spiritual penury, it makes me sad'.[39] Hence, at one level, his critique of Gandhi drew on his own conceptualization of what human beings should avoid doing as it was an impediment towards realizing the ultimate goal for humanity. At another level, it reflected the politico-ideological schisms that put Tagore and Gandhi in two mutually exclusive compartments. It did not seem odd when the former made a caustic remark with the onset of the Non-Cooperation Movement (1920–1922) that

> the word non-cooperation still chokes me. I cannot get over the shame that it carries. It will always proclaim the fact that our cooperation came to us by a road of ignominy that it missed its true route and did not enter into the heart of our country through the great triumphal arch of love.[40]

As shown earlier in the book, Tagore and Gandhi were engaged in a battle of words, seeking to justify their respective points of view.[41] Since we have already dealt with this aspect, it will serve no useful purpose if the same discussion is pursued here. However, for the sake of a fair understanding of what caused the dissension between the poet and the Mahatma, it is incumbent to dwell on why they differed in the nationalist context. Tagore's speech to the students of Santiniketan and Sriniketan on 20 September 1932 provides useful inputs to articulate the differences in clear terms and in a clear perspective. Seeking to completely eradicate social prejudices and economic discrimination, Tagore set out his conceptual universe on the basis of the core values of humanity, striving to cement a perpetual bond among human beings despite their being socio-culturally diverse. He believed that

> [n]o civilized society can thrive upon victims whose humanity has been permanently mutilated, whose minds have been compelled to dwell in the

[39] Rabindranath Tagore to C. F. Andrews, 14 July 1921, reproduced in Uma Dasgupta, ed., *Friendships of "Largeness and Freedom": Andrews, Tagore and Gandhi: An Epistolary Account* (New Delhi: Oxford University Press, 2018), 293.

[40] Rabindranath Tagore to C. F. Andrews, 7 January 1921, reproduced in Dasgupta, 269.

[41] It has been very beautifully captured by Sabyasachi Bhattacharya in his *The Mahatma and the Poet: Letter and Debates Between Gandhi and Tagore, 1915–1941* (New Delhi: National Book Trust, 1997).

dark. Those who we keep down inevitably drag us down and obstruct our movement in the path of progress. The indignity with which we burden them grows into an intolerable burden of the whole country; we insult our own humanity by insulting Man where he is helpless or where he is not of our own kin.[42]

Based on his uncritical faith in universal humanism, Tagore was convinced that unless humanity was free from artificial divisions around caste, class and ethnicity, human emancipation would remain an elusive goal. This was a historical truth in the sense that despite strong opposition, these tendencies were allowed to continue, which perhaps indicated that human society was not well equipped to completely eradicate the sources of discriminatory designs and practices. For Tagore, one needed to pay attention to this; otherwise, the call of human amity was likely to be defeated, since it was vacuous. As one who always believed in togetherness, he was thus determined not to get swayed by the narrow political objectives that the mainstream Indian nationalists aspired to fulfil. Being inspired by the Upanishadic ideals of the world being a nest and the world being a family, the poet was convinced that it was not merely a conceptual aim but was a realistic aim to pursue. It was easier said than done, since, as history had shown, the vested interests, with their tentacles spread out, had always stood against the forces that sought to crush them. By drawing attention to the activities of Vidyasagar, Ram Mohan and his father, Debendranath Tagore, Tagore was, however, convinced that it was not impossible, and presumably because of the role that these great men had played despite adverse circumstances, he appeared to have been inspired to undertake the same steps for realizing his ideal of universal humanism. The endeavour that led to the development of Santiniketan and Sriniketan was tuned to the fulfilment of his conceptual dream of creating a socio-economic environment free from discrimination of any kind.

On the basis of his unique philosophical dispensations, he separated from the nationalist activities of the Mahatma and those who were

---

[42] Rabindranath Tagore's address to the staff and students of Santiniketan and Sriniketan, 20 September 1932, reproduced in Das, *The English Writings of Rabindranath Tagore*, 326.

involved in the mainstream nationalist movement. According to him, political freedom was not, at all, sufficient for attaining human emancipation in the sense of being completely free from the prejudicial socioeconomic customs practised by a section of human beings for fulfilling their partisan interests at the cost of others. He was disappointed with the Mahatma, who seemed to have ignored, in its entirety, the concern for universal humanism with his emphasis on political freedom as prior to anything else. While Tagore who remained steadfastly committed to the goal of human emancipation, Gandhi did not seem to have paid much attention to this aspect presumably because his campaign was primarily governed by the will to wrest political power from the British. Being fiercely critical of Gandhi's political ideology championing freedom from the British rule, Tagore did not keep his anguish under the carpet; he ventilated it by saying that

> Mahatmaji has repeatedly pointed out the danger of the social divisions in our country that are permanent insults to humanity, but our attention has not been drawn to the importance of its rectification with the same force as it has been to the importance of the Khaddar. The social inequities upon which all our enemies find their principal support have our time-honoured loyalty making it difficult for us to uproot them.[43]

The differences were made explicit: according to Tagore, the struggle that the Mahatma had launched had a narrow aim, since it was not enough to effectively combat the supremacist mindset that always overpowered the contrarian forces. In other words, the poet was not hopeful, since mere political freedom was futile in a country which was horizontally and also vertically divided and in which denial of freedom to those at the lower rungs of society was a rule rather than an aberration. By being committed to universal emancipation, Tagore had a wider concern, which was not, at all, shared by the Mahatma, presumably because their politico-ideological priorities were radically different; while the Mahatma felt that political freedom was a stepping stone towards eradicating the sources of social disharmony, the poet, by championing his cause for human emancipation, demonstrated how

---

[43] Rabindranath Tagore's address to the staff and students of Santiniketan and Sriniketan, 20 September 1932, reproduced in Das, 327.

his politico-ideological priorities were completely different from those of the Mahatma. It was made explicit when the poet issued an appeal to the countrymen insisting on their participation in doing away with the prejudicial system of untouchability segregating a large contingent of Indians from their brethren. The appeal was articulated by the poet himself to exhort the Indians that

> they must not delay a movement effectively to prove that they are in earnest to eradicate from their neighbourhood untouchability in all its ramifications. The movement should be universal and immediate, its expressions clear and indubitable. All manner of humiliation and disabilities from which any class in India suffers should be removed by heroic efforts and self-sacrifice. Whoever of us fails in this time of grave crisis to try his utmost to avert the calamity facing India would be held responsible for one of saddest tragedies that could happen to us and to the world.[44]

Couched in a persuasive mould, the appeal that Tagore made in September 1932 provides us with significant inputs as regards his politico-ideological predilections. He was at pains to witness human beings being brutalized on the basis of the accident of birth. So long as this social design supportive of violent mutilation of the so-called untouchables was made sacrosanct, no social reform campaign was likely to succeed. Here, Tagore was hinting at his disenchantment with the Mahatma, who appeared to have played safe by not disturbing the well-established socio-economic design that drew its sustenance from the well-entrenched caste divisions. Gandhi had his explanation which the poet did not appear to have accepted since going for mere political freedom was a conscious effort, he felt, on the part of the mainstream nationalists, including the Mahatma, towards diluting the campaign for human emancipation.

A clear understanding of the Tagore–Gandhi debates is useful in interrelated ways. On the one hand, since these two great men viewed the nationalist campaign in two completely different perspectives, their interaction helps us comprehend the principal arguments that they offered to substantiate their respective politico-ideological preferences:

[44] Rabindranath Tagore's address to the staff and students of Santiniketan and Sriniketan, 20 September 1932, reproduced in Das, 328.

Tagore fought for human emancipation, which ran counter to Gandhi's concern for the political liberation of India. The debates are thus, on the other hand, not merely indicative but also illustrative of how they evolved their respective ideological visions in conjunction with their emotional/sentimental tilts. At one level, the differences between them do not seem to be substantial, since both of them had engaged in activities contributing to inclusive human welfare. Hence, one does not need to pay much attention to this. At another level, it was merely the ideational differences that had their manifestations in the politico-ideological priorities that they respectively held. Hence, it was a difference based on fundamental conceptual assumptions: for Tagore, the goal of human emancipation was the only one that could never be diluted, though the Mahatma was persuaded to believe that it could be easier for the Indians to realize Tagore's objective in a politically free India; hence, in the latter's perception, the nationalist mobilization for political freedom was anything but wrong.

IV

Tagore was not merely a novelist or a playwright but one who also wrote several thought-provoking essays on those social themes which, he felt, were critical in conceptualizing the contemporary nationalist scene in India. Before this aspect is dealt with, there are two points that need attention. On the one hand, being an organic intellectual, Tagore focused on those social issues which, according to him, required a detailed analytical discussion, perhaps for a better analysis of why the country remained backward and politico-ideologically less assertive. The explanation lies in the age-old internalized separations in view of schisms around many axes. He was aware that unless these divisions were weeded out, India's rise as a self-dependent collective unit was likely to remain unrealized. This conceptualization of Indian society is interlinked with, on the other hand, another important feature of Tagore's writings. To be precise, there was a seamless movement between what he articulated in his novels, plays and short stories and that in his critical essays. In other words, the ideas that he championed in his creative writings were pursued with the same zeal in his criti-cal essays. His collection of essays in *Kalantor* (1937) is, for instance, illustrative here. Most of the essays, despite being brief, are sharply argued.

The aim here is to briefly discuss how this seamless transmission took place in Tagore's creative writings and those critical essays in which he elaborated on some of the important social themes with his comments. There are two major themes that run through the texts that Tagore left for posterity. As seen in Chapter 2, the poet was vehemently opposed to revolutionary nationalism that figured prominently in the context of the 1905–1908 nationalist campaign challenging the Partition of Bengal. It is also an important point that Tagore did not appreciate the Gandhian mode of non-cooperation with the British government by indulging in the boycott of schools and colleges, besides the forcible imposition of the burning of foreign clothes. The novel *Ghare Baire* (1916) is a testimony of how Tagore elaborated on his argument in defence of his model of economic self-sufficiency, which he articulated in his 1904 text entitled *Swadeshi Samaj*. By dwelling on the complex unfolding of nationalism, the bard also dealt with issues of gender, Hindu–Muslim communal amity and animosity and the selfishness of the nationalist leaders, among others. By being committed to the well-being of those living in his zamindari estate regardless of religion and caste schisms, Nikhilesh of *Ghare Baire* epitomized the distinctive socio-economic and politico-ideological priorities that Tagore upheld. An identical point was pursued in *Gora* (1910), where Gora, the principal protagonist, realized why it was not possible for the Indians to collectively oppose the alien rule. One of the reasons was the failure of the upper-caste Hindus to rise above their prejudicial attitude against the untouchables and Muslims. Gora was unable to fathom why Pharu Sardar, a Muslim, was not hailed for the courage that he had shown while opposing the British indigo planter. The reason was located in Pharu being a Muslim; it was a reason that appeared to have restrained the Hindus from joining the campaign for Pharu. His family suffered. Tagore very graphically described all these just to explain how the well-entrenched communal distance between the Hindus and Muslims caused a permanent alienation between them. In a very poignant manner, he thus wrote in his essay 'Hindu-Mussalman' that 'while religion, as history shows, builds a bridge between communities elsewhere, in India, it is religion that put communities in watertight compartments leading to create unbridgeable gulf and never-ending enmity among them'.[45] That it was the main cause of separation between Hindus and Muslims does not require any elaboration, argued the poet. Similarly, the social distance resulting in a permanent fissure between the Hindus and their Muslim counterparts was also a source of worry to the bard, because this had estranged the Muslims from the Hindus in such a way as not to bring them together ever. By referring to the nationalist policy of boycott of foreign goods that adversely affected the poor Muslims, both in the context of the 1905–1908 campaign for rescinding the Bengal Partition and later the 1920–1922 Non-Cooperation Movement, the mainstream nationalist forces caused an irreparable damage to the collectivity that the Congress sought to develop for the nationalist cause. As Tagore wrote, the result of 'the forcible imposition of the boycott resulted in pushing the Muslims to the periphery, especially in Bengal, since it was simply beyond their financial capacity to buy hone-spun or Khadi clothes'.[46] Similarly, his caustic remarks on untouchability, which was a social sin, also help us understand his approach to caste divisions. Insisting that manual work was as socially respectable as the intellectual deeds undertaken by the upper castes, Tagore reiterated the point that John Ruskin raised in his *Unto The Last* (1860) by suggesting that division of labour was a means to accomplish a task as efficiently as possible and not a criterion for socially segregating one section of the population from another. Hence, he forcefully argued in his essay 'Shudra Dharma' that 'unless and until the principle of dignity of labour shape our attitude to those involved in activities that require manual labour,

---

[45] Rabindranath Tagore, 'Hindu-Mussalman,' in *Kalantor*, ed. Rabindranath Tagore (Kolkata: Visva-Bharati, 2008) (reprint), 324.

[46] Tagore, 327.

our country shall continue to reel under social hatred'.[47] One of the most powerful expositions of this sentiment, as shown in Chapters 3 and 4, was Tagore's dance–drama *Chandalika*, in which a Sudra girl, Prakriti, articulated his critical views questioning the continuity of caste prejudices which were both inhuman and socially retarding. In a similar vein, Tagore was also categorical in arguing for gender parity, the lack of which was also responsible for social decadence in India. Many of his female protagonists held the views challenging the well-established prejudicial attitudes against women. The female voices were plenty: Binodini in *Chokher Bali* (1903), Kumud in *Jogajog* (1929), Sucharita in *Gora* (1916), Ela in *Char Adhyay* (1934) and Damini in *Chaturanga* (1916). Key to Tagore's approach to gender equity was his urge for equality regardless of class, caste and gender. These characters spoke in one voice, though their styles of expressing their opposition to the well-established system of gender disparity differed from one another. For instance, Sucharita in *Gora* participated in debates on gender equality, while Damini in *Chaturanga* and Ela in *Char Adhyay* articulated their conceptualization of being independent despite the well-entrenched social restrictions when they expressed their love and preferred mode of sexuality without being hesitant.

There is one final point in this section. Tagore had a scientific bent of mind, which he had demonstrated clearly. One of the widely quoted examples of the differences of opinion between Tagore and Gandhi pertains to the 1934 Bihar earthquake. As shown in Chapters 1 and 2, the Bihar earthquake brought out the differences between them in public. Gandhi was reported to have attributed the earthquake to the sin being committed by allowing the practice of untouchability to continue. Per Gandhi, 'visitations like droughts, floods, earthquakes and the like, though they seem to have only physical origins, are, for me, somehow connected with man's morals. Therefore, I instinctively felt

---

[47] Rabindranath Tagore, 'Shudradharma,' in *Kalantor*, ed. Rabindranath Tagore (Kolkata: Visva-Bharati, 2008) (reprint), 282.

that this earthquake was the visitation for the sin of untouchability'.[48] Given his appreciation for the rational/scientific mode of thinking, it was obvious that Tagore did not endorse Gandhi's characterization of the earthquake as god's caprice. Being very curt, Tagore expressed his contrary point of view by saying that 'it has caused my painful surprise to find Mahatma Gandhi accusing those who blindly follow their own social custom of untouchability of having brought down God's vengeance upon certain part of Bihar, evidently specially selected for His desolating displeasure'.[49] A rationalist to the core, it was expected of Tagore to react in response to Gandhi's claim of the earthquake being a manifestation of god's wrath. For Gandhi, there was a possibility that he wanted to create a feeling of being scared due to God's anger which was likely to restrain them from being prejudicial to the untouchables. It could have been a strategy that the Mahatma had adopted for realizing his sociopolitical goal in those circumstances wherein untouchability was being openly practised unhesitatingly by upper-caste Hindus. This means that he was persuaded to believe that this was likely to work in view of people being fearful of the unknown.

V

Tagore was a voice of protest, which was articulated in many forms, in a context when the Gandhi-led mainstream nationalist campaign appeared to have caught the imagination of the masses. This was a politico-ideological voice, since it was an endeavour to chart out a specific course of action for Indians at large. Gandhi was engaged in politically mobilizing those who endorsed his ideological concern for political freedom as the first step to weeding out all kinds of social prejudices and economic constraints causing an unbridgeable gulf between the haves and the have-nots. As argued in the book, Tagore, not being in agreement with Gandhi in this regard, never diluted his

---

[48] Krishna Dutta and Andrew Robinson, eds., *Selected Letters of Rabindranath Tagore* (Cambridge: Cambridge University Press, 1997), Appendix 2: the Bihar earthquake, 538.

[49] Dutta and Robinson, 537.

concern for human emancipation. Hence, he believed that until and unless the sources of unfreedom were completely eradicated, the political freedom that Gandhi championed would neither remain self-fulfilling nor be a concrete step towards building a society that was free from social prejudices and inequalities. Hence, the ideological rift between them was based on differences that ran very deep. Nonetheless, they came together often as allies and friends, thanks to their shared commitment to social change.

The fact that Tagore used his fictional writings as a vehicle for his politico-ideological views comes out most starkly in his critical essays. There seems to be a seamless, dynamic transition from these political texts to his novels, dance–dramas and short stories. Through its delineation of the complexities and nuances that surrounded the poet as a political thinker, *Sociopolitical Thought of Rabindranath Tagore* provides a contextually grounded and uniquely textured template for conceptualizing the distinctive thoughts nurtured by the bard. Instead of being a run-of-the-mill text, the effort reveals how, out of a dialectical interconnection with his socio-cultural milieu, Tagore not only created a new genre of thinking but also helped build a conceptual framework seeking to comprehend an ideational revolution in the nationalist context when the competing politico-ideological forces did not seem to be insignificant. As the history of India's freedom struggle shows, with the arrival Gandhi on India's political scene in the first quarter of the 20th century, the nationalist interventions had undergone a sea change. Gandhi was certainly one of the main priests who not only shaped the voice of opposition against the British rule but also devised new socio-economic and politico-ideological parameters for sustaining the campaign that he spearheaded. That Tagore's perception was much wider than that of the Mahatma is amply illustrated by his creative writings, and what is also worth noting is that the poet was consistent in expressing his ideational priorities in clear terms. Unlike many of his nationalist colleagues, he was an activist–theoretician who left no stone unturned to translate his ideas into practice, even in adverse circumstances; his activist persona was most clearly revealed with the foundation of the school Patha Bhavana in 1901, and Visva-Bharati in 1921, which was not just an institute offering an alternative form of education but was also a well-formatted design capable of bringing about radical socio-economic changes in India, both during colonialism and in its aftermath.

A firm believer in universal humanism, Tagore stayed away from the hurly-burly of nationalist politics, presumably because it was, to him, 'a scene of intrigues and maneuvers with politicians of all hues haggling over the terms of a constitutional settlement and squabbling about the rival claims of sectarian and regional interests sponsored by themselves'.[50] As he was disappointed with those who joined Gandhi's campaign for political freedom, his disapprobation did not seem odd. What caused severe disenchantment to him was 'the rising barbarity … ready to tear up humanity in an orgy of devastation [leading to] the desecration of the spirit of Man'.[51] Even in the midst of the increasing strength of contrarian ideational forces, Tagore never diluted his concern for humanity, which was evident when he unambiguously stated: 'I shall not commit the grievous sin of losing faith in Man'.[52] It was indeed a powerful exposition of his faith in humanity. To be precise, amidst the growing hegemony of the attitudes supportive of narrow/partisan gains, the poet remained committed to the politico-ideological preferences that he deemed appropriate for realizing his humanist mission. In other words, despite sharing the nationalist condemnation of the colonizers, Tagore never allowed this restrictive vision to cloud his concern for human emancipation. It was evident in his open opposition to some of the politico-ideological agendas that the Mahatma put across to him. He never associated himself with any of the brigades active in the nationalist movement, presumably because he held the view that the Gandhi-led anti-British counteroffensive was not adequate for

---

[50] Ranajit Guha, 'Epilogue: The Poverty of Historiography—A Poet's Reproach,' in *History at the Limit of World History*, ed. Ranajit Guha (New York: Columbia University Press, 2002), 94.

[51] Tagore, *'Crisis in Civilization,'* 726.

[52] Tagore, 726.

realizing universal humanism, his lifelong mission. On the surface, Tagore's approach to nationalism appeared to have been an escapist attitude, presumably because of his fascination for the philosophical discourses on which the Western civilization rested. However, a careful reading of his arguments for specific ideational leanings reveals that the poet, instead of being swayed by immediate political gain, as Gandhi was, fought for the ultimate goal of humanity—the laying out and also consolidation of socio-economic foundations for a society which was equity-driven and politico-ideologically tuned to universal humanism. Tagore thus stands out as an organic intellectual who acted as a pathfinder for the nationalists while being involved in activities resulting ultimately in the attainment of human emancipation.

BIBLIOGRAPHY

It is customary for an author to add a bibliography in the book that he/she writes. There is, of course, a valid purpose. In two ways, a bibliography is integral to a book. On the one hand, it contains a list of books and other texts that form the background to the arguments that are offered in the book in favour of a contention, which means that they are, to some extent, foundational ideas behind the textual elaboration of a theme. There is, on the other hand, the idea that the list of books and other texts also help others who propose to deal with the theme in question or related themes. In a nutshell, a bibliography has a very useful purpose, and without its inclusion, the book shall remain incomplete.

One should also add another note of caution. It is difficult to prepare an exhaustive bibliography because of the paucity of space and also of the specific priorities that an author has while adding or deleting books or other texts to/from this list. To be precise, since the author has the final say in this regard, a bibliography is bound to be author-driven. It is not wrong but indeed most logical for the author, while making his/her argument, to choose a specific set of texts to pursue the point of his/her tilt.

With the above prefacing remarks, let me dwell on the specific feature of the bibliography that follows. It is true that literature on Tagore is in abundance; it is also true that there is no dearth of studies insofar as his literary contributions are concerned. Primarily, the studies that are available now are analytical accounts of the texts that usually go with him as a poet of global repute. For instance, his 1910 publication *Gitanjali* (Song Offering), perhaps the most widely circulated of Tagore's creative texts, is always referred to whenever there is a discussion on the poet's contribution as a literary genius. Here, our focus is different. The aim here is to dwell on Tagore's social and political thoughts. The book also argues that in order to meaningfully understand the poet's distinctive contribution as a thinker with clear socio-economic views and politico-ideological priorities, one needs to take into account his literary creations in tandem with the creative essays that he wrote to defend his well-argued points.

Research on any aspect of Tagore's own creative writings is made simpler with the easy availability of *Rabindra Rachanabali* (Collected Works of Rabindranath Tagore), published by Visva-Bharati and also the Government of West Bengal. There are very good collections of Tagore's writings which are useful sources for research on any aspect of his creative persona. Needless to say, the book heavily draws upon these sources to analytically comprehend the distinct nature of Tagore's social and political thoughts. The set of four collections of the bard's English Writings which are most useful sources of research on the poet's sociopolitical ideas. While Sisir Kumar Das edited the first three volumes of *The English Writings of Rabindranath Tagore* (Sahitya Akademi, New Delhi, 1994 and 1996), Nityapriya Ghosh put in the public domain the fourth volume of *The English Writings of Rabindranath Tagore* (Sahitya Akademi, New Delhi, 2007). For the English translation of a selective set of novels, I have depended on *Classic Rabindranath Tagore* (Penguin, New Delhi, 2011). Further, *Rabi Jibani* (nine volumes, published by Ananda, Kolkata, 2007–2016) by Prasanta Pal is also an important source to assess Rabindranath Tagore's contribution as a thinker. Besides these texts, there are many collections of letters exchanged between Tagore and his colleagues, which also help build the story. Prominent among them are: Krishna Dutta and Andrew Robinson (ed.), *Selected Letters of Rabindranath Tagore*, (Cambridge University Press, Cambridge, 1997); Uma Dasgupta (ed.), *A difficult friendship: letters of Edward Thompson and Rabindranath Tagore, 1913–1940*, (Oxford University Press, New Delhi, 2003); Uma Dasgupta (ed.), *Friendships of 'largeness and freedom'*:

Andrews, Tagore and Gandhi: an epistolary account, 1912–1940, (Oxford University Press, New Delhi, 2018). Apart from these collections of letters, there are useful texts which contain thematically chosen texts from among Tagore's own writings. Of these, three are very useful: (a) Rabindranath Tagore, *Towards Universal Man*, (Asia Publishing House, Bombay, 1961); (b) Uma Dasgupta (ed.), *Selected Writings on Education and Nationalism*, Oxford University Press, New Delhi, 2009; and (c) Uma Dasgupta (ed.) *Rabindranath Tagore: My Life in My Words* (Penguin, New Delhi, 2006).

In view of the publication of Tagore's written texts by Visva-Bharati, which are reasonably priced, one can easily procure them for one's own collection. This means that the texts in which Tagore had articulated his ideas are now easily available. In other words, with the easy availability of the written tracts that Tagore left for posterity, researchers do not have to run around to get hold of the original texts. This is a great support to those seeking to fathom the complexities of Tagore's politico-ideological preferences. Visva-Bharati has taken the lead in this regard.

There is a note of caution, however. Being a very thought-provoking poet, Tagore continues to generate interest among researchers, which means that (a) his ideas are relevant and thus they are required to be extensively studied, on the one hand; and (b) there is also the need, on the other hand, to objectively dissect his distinctive thoughts to lay out an alternative mode of thinking that was clearly different from the mainstream nationalist viewpoints, of which the Mahatma was the chief priest. The difference between them was substantial, since Tagore felt that human emancipation was prior to political liberation, because the latter remained peripheral so long as the former was not attained. Although he did not appreciate the Marxist notion of violent revolution, he appears to have been persuaded by Karl Marx, at least in this respect, because of his convincing arguments for human emancipation as perhaps the only mode of making one's existence free from sources of unfreedom. Nonetheless, there is no denying that Tagore's arguments for human emancipation created a new genre of thinking in the nationalist phase of Indian history. By seeking to unearth this aspect of Tagore's creative conceptualizations, the book is a step, perhaps a meaningful one, to dwell on the idea of India that the Mahatma and the poet had conceptualized differently.

BIBLIOGRAPHY

Anderson, Benedict. *Imagined Communities: Reflections on the Origin and Spread of Nationalism*. London and New York, NY: Verso, 1991.

Bera, Sadananda, and Narayan Chandra Sau. *Rabindranath O Rajniti: Eekhan O Thakhan* (in Bangla). Kolkata: Kallol, 2013.

Berlin, Isaiah. *The Sense of Reality: Studies in Ideas and Their History*. New York, NY: Farrar, Straus and Giroux, 1996.

Bhabha, Homi K. *The Location of Culture*. London and New York, NY: Routledge, 1994.

Bhattacharya, Sabyasachi. *The Mahatma and the Poet: Letter and Debates Between Gandhi and Tagore, 1915–1941*. New Delhi: National Book Trust, 1997.

———. 'Antinomies of Nationalism and Rabindranath Tagore.' *Economic and Political Weekly* 51, no. 6 (February 2016): 39–45.

Chakrabarty, Dipesh. 'Friendships in the Shadow of Empire: Tagore's Reception in Chicago, circa, 1913–1932.' *Modern Asian Studies* 48, no. 5 (2014): 1161–1187.

Chatterjee, Partha. *The Nation and Its Fragments: Colonial and Postcolonial Histories*. New Delhi: Oxford University Press, 1994.

———. 'The Fruits of Macaulay's Poison Tree.' In *The Present History of West Bengal*, edited by Partha Chatterjee, 18–25. New Delhi: Oxford University Press, 1997.

Chatterjee, Kalyan. 'Gora: Tagore's Paradoxical Self.' *Indian Literature* 49, no. 3 (May–June 2005): 185–195.

Chaudhuri, Rosinka. 'The Flute, Gerontion, and Subalternist Misreadings of Tagore.' *Social Text,* 78 22, no. 1 (2004): 103–122.

Chaudhuri, Rasinka. 'Hemchandra's Bharat Sangeet (1870) and the Politics of Poetry: A Pre-history of Hindu Nationalism in Bengal?' *Indian Economic and Social History Review* 42, no. 2 (2005): 213–247.

Chaudhuri, Sukanta. (ed.). *The Cambridge Companion to Rabindranath Tagore*. Cambridge: Cambridge University Press, 2020.

Collins, Michael. *Empire, Nationalism and the Post-colonial World: Rabindranath Tagore's Writings on History, Politics and Society*. Oxford: Routledge, 2013.

Dasgupta, Uma. *Rabindranath Tagore: A Biography*. New Delhi: Oxford University Press, 2004.

Dasgupta, Subrata. *The Bengal Renaissance: Identity and Creativity—From Ram Mohan Roy to Rabindranath Tagore*. Ranikhet: Permanent Black, 2007.

Dutta, Pradip Kumar. *Rabindranath Tagore's 'The Home and the World': A Critical Companion*. London: Anthem Press, 2004.

Dutta, Krishna, and Andrew Robinson. *Rabindranath Tagore: The Myriad-minded Man*. New York, NY: St. Martin's Press, 1995.

Elmhirst, Leonard K. *Rabindranath Tagore: Pioneers in Education*. London: John Murray, 1960.

———. *Poet and Plowman*. Kolkata: Visva-Bharati, 2008. (reprint)

Ghose, Benoy. *Iswar Chandra Vidyasagar*. New Delhi: Publication Division, Ministry of Information and Broadcasting, Government of India, 1971.

Ghosh, Sachindralal. *Raja Ram Mohan Roy: Pathmaker of Modern India*. New Delhi: National Council of Educational Research and Training, 1970.

Godrej, Farah. *Cosmopolitan Political Thought: Method, Practice, Discipline*. New York, NY: Oxford University Press, 2011.

Guha, Ranajit. *History at the Limit of World History*. New York, NY: Columbia University Press, 2002.

Guha, Chinmoy (ed.). *Bridging East & West: Rabindranath Tagore and Roman Rolland Correspondence (1919–1940)*. New Delhi: Oxford University Press, 2018.

Hay, Stephen H. *Asian Ideas of East and West: Tagore and His Critics in Japan*. Cambridge: Harvard University Press, 1970.

Jones, Kenneth W. *Socio-religious Reform Movements in British India*. Cambridge: Cambridge University Press, 1994.

Kaviraj, Sudipta. 'Tagore and Transformation in the Ideals of Love.' In *Love in South Asia: A Cultural History*, edited by Francesca Orsini. Cambridge: Cambridge University Press, 2006.

Khilnani, Sunil. *The Idea of India*. London: Hamish Hamilton, 1997.

Kopf, David. *The Brahmo Samaj and the Shaping of the Modern Indian Mind*. New Delhi: Archives Publishers Pvt. Ltd., 1988.

Kripalani, Krishna. *Rabindranath Tagore: A Biography*. New Delhi: UBS Publications, 2008. (reprint)

Kumarappa, J. C. *Gandhian Economic Thought*. Bombay: Vora and C, 1951.

Mahalanobis, Prasanta Chandra. *Prasange Rabindranath* (in Bangla). Kolkata: Mahalanobis Trust, 1985.

Mahalanobis, Prasanta. *Rabindranath* (in Bangla). Kolkata: Ananda, 2002.

Mehta, Uday Singh. *Liberalism and Empire: India in British Liberal Thought*. New Delhi: Oxford University Press, 1999.

Metcalf, Thomas R. *Ideologies of the Raj*. Cambridge: Cambridge University Press, 1998.

Mukherjee, Kedar Nath. *Political Philosophy of Rabindranath Tagore*. New Delhi: S. Chand & Company Ltd, 1982.

Mukherjee, Subrata. *The Political Ideas of Rabindranath Tagore: Reflections of a Public Intellectual*. New Delhi: Rupa, 2020.

Mukhopadhyay, Amartya. *Politics, Society and Colonialism: An Alternative Understanding of Tagore's Responses*. Delhi: Foundation Books, 2010.

Nandy, Ashis. *The Illegitimacy of Nationalism: Rabindranath Tagore and the Politics of Self*. New Delhi: Oxford University Press, 1994.

Nandy, Ashis. 'Nationalism: Genuine and Spurious: Mourning Two Early Post-nationalist Strains.' *Economic and Political Weekly* 41, no. 38 (2006): 3500–3504.

Naoroji, Dadabhai. *Poverty and Un-British Rule in India*. London: S. Sonnenschein, 1901.

Nehru, Jawaharlal. *An Autobiography*. London: John Lane the Bodley Head, 1941.

———. *The Discovery of India*. Delhi: Oxford University Press, 1989. (reprint)

Neogy, Ajit K. *Santiniketan and Sriniketan*. New Delhi: National Book Trust, 2015. (reprint)

O'Hanlon, Rosalind. *Caste, Conflict and Ideology: Mahatma Jotirao Phule and Low Caste Protest in Nineteenth-century Western India*. Cambridge: Cambridge University Press, 1985.

Omvedt, Gail. *Cultural Revolt in a Colonial Society: The Non-Brahmin Movement in Western India, 1873–1930*. Bombay: Scientific Socialist Educational Trust, 1976.

———. *Dalits and the Democratic Revolution: Dr Ambedkar and Dalit Movement in Colonial India*. New Delhi: SAGE Publications, 1994.

Parekh, Bhikhu. *Debating India: Essays on Indian Political Discourse*. New Delhi: Oxford University Press, Oxford University Press, 2015.

Petit, Philip. *Republicanism: A Theory of Freedom and Government*. Oxford: Oxford University Press, 1999.

Philips, Anne. *The Politics of Presence*. Oxford: Clarendon Press, 1995.

Poddar, Arabinda. *Tagore: The Political Personality*. Kolkata: Indiana, 2004.

Ray, Bhrati. 'New Woman in Rabindranath Tagore's Short Stories: An Interrogation of Laboratory.' *Asiatic* 4, no. 2 (December 2010): 68–80.

Roy, Satyendranath. *Rabindranather Samajchinta* (in Bangla). Kolkata: Granthalaya, 1985.

Rudolph, Lloyd, and S. H. Rudolph. *The Realm of the Public Sphere: Identity and Policy*. New Delhi: Oxford University Press, 2008.

Sen, Amartya. 'Tagore and His India.' *New York Review of Books* 44, no. 12 (1997): 55–63.

———. *Development as Freedom*. New Delhi: Oxford University Press, 1999.

———. *The Argumentative India: Writings on Indian History, Culture and Identity*. New York: Picador, 2005.

———. *Identity and Violence: The Illusion of Destiny*. London: Allen Lane, 2006.

———. *The Idea of Justice*. New York, NY: Allen Lane, 2009.

Sen, Sachin. *The Political Thought of Tagore*. Calcutta: General Printers and Publishers Ltd., 1947.

Sen, Ashok. *Rajnitir Pathakrame Rabindranth* (in Bangla). Kolkata: Visva-Bharati Granthan Bhivag, 2004.

Sengupta, Kalyan. *The Philosophy of Rabindranath Tagore.* Burlington: Ashgate, 2005.

Seth, Sanjay. 'Rewriting Histories of Nationalism: The Politics of "Moderate Nationalism" in India, 1870–1905.' *American Historical Review* 104, no. 1 (February 1999): 95–116.

Sinha, Dixit. *A Poet's Experiment in Rebuilding Samaj and Nation: Sriniketan's Rural Reconstruction Work, 1922–1960.* Bolpur, West Bengal: Birupjatio Sahitya Sammiloni, 2019.

Stokes, Eric. *The English Utilitarians and India.* Cambridge: Cambridge University Press, 1959.

Thompson, Edward. *Rabindranath Tagore: Poet and Dramatist.* London: Macmillan, 1926.

Thompson, E. P. *Introduction to Rabindranath Tagore's Nationalism.* New Delhi: Rupa & Co, 1992.

———. *'Alien Homage: Edward Thompson and Rabindranath Tagore.* New York, NY: Oxford University Press, 1993.

Vajpayi, Ananya. *Righteous Republic: The Political Foundation of Modern India.* Cambridge: Harvard University Press, 2012.

ABOUT THE AUTHOR

Bidyut Chakrabarty is Vice-Chancellor, Visva-Bharati, West Bengal. He was a Professor in the Department of Political Science in the University of Delhi till November 2018. He completed his PhD from the London School of Economics (LSE), and has been associated with teaching and research for more than three decades. He has taught in several prestigious educational institutions, such as the LSE; Indian Institute of Management (IIM) Calcutta, Kolkata; Monash University, Australia; National University of Singapore; and the University of Hamburg, Germany. Professor Chakrabarty has also authored several textbooks and academic books. Among his publications are *Public Administration: From Government to Governance* (2017), *Winning the Mandate: The Indian Experience* (SAGE, 2016), *Communism in India: Events, Processes and Ideologies* (2014), *Indian Politics and Society since Independence: Events, Processes and Ideology* (2008) and *The Governance Discourse: A Reader* (2008).

INDEX

Rabindranath Tagore in Japan

Courtesy: Rabindra-Bhavana, Visva-Bharati, Santiniketan

Rabindranath Tagore, C. F. Andrews and Mahatma Gandhi

Courtesy: Rabindra-Bhavana, Visva-Bharati, Santiniketan

Rabindranath Tagore with Mahatma Gandhi

Courtesy: Rabindra-Bhavana, Visva-Bharati, Santiniketan

Rabindranath Tagore with Jawaharlal Nehru

Courtesy: Rabindra-Bhavana, Visva-Bharati, Santiniketan

Felicitation ceremony of Netaji Subhas Chandra Bose at Amrakunja. Sitting beside him are Rabindranath Tagore and Kshitimohan Sen

Courtesy: Rabindra-Bhavana, Visva-Bharati, Santiniketan

Rabindranath Tagore attending a class of the Frech Indologist Sylvain Levi in Amrakunja

Courtesy: Rabindra-Bhavana, Visva-Bharati, Santiniketan

Rabindranath Tagore and Albert Einstein

Courtesy: Rabindra-Bhavana, Visva-Bharati, Santiniketan

Rabindranath Tagore with Sigmund Freud

Courtesy: Rabindra-Bhavana, Visva-Bharati, Santiniketan

Rabindranath Tagore and the students of his Santiniketan School after a 'Sahityaa Sabha' or literary meet

Courtesy: Rabindra-Bhavana, Visva-Bharati, Santiniketan

Rabindranath Tagore and Helen Keller

Courtesy: Rabindra-Bhavana, Visva-Bharati, Santiniketan

Rabindranath Tagore with C.F. Andrews at Shalbithi

Courtesy: Rabindra-Bhavana, Visva-Bharati, Santiniketan